OXFORD MONOGRAPHS IN
INTERNATIONAL LAW

General Editor: PROFESSOR VAUGHAN LOWE,
*Chichele Professor of Public International Law in
the University of Oxford and Fellow of All Souls College, Oxford*

Jurisdiction in International Law

OXFORD MONOGRAPHS IN
INTERNATIONAL LAW

The aim of this series is to publish important and original pieces of research on all aspects of international law. Topics that are given particular prominence are those which, while of interest to the academic lawyer, also have important bearing on issues which touch upon the actual conduct of international relations. Nonetheless, the series is wide in scope and includes monographs on the history and philosophical foundations of international law.

RECENT TITLES IN THE SERIES

Jurisdiction in International Law
Cedric Ryngaert

**The Fair and Equitable Treatment Standard in International
Foreign Investment Law**
Ioana Tudor

Targeted Killing in International Law
Nils Melzer

Defining Terrorism in International Law
Ben Saul

Diplomatic Protection
Chittharanjan F. Amerasinghe

Human Rights and Non-Discrimination in the 'War on Terror'
Daniel Moeckli

The Decolonization of International Law
Matthew Craven

Investment Treaty Arbitration and Public Law
Gus van Harten

**International Organizations and their Exercise
of Sovereign Powers**
Dan Sarooshi

Peremptory Norms in International Law
Alexander Orakhelashvili

Jurisdiction in
International Law

CEDRIC RYNGAERT

Lecturer in international law
Catholic University of Leuven
University of Utrecht

OXFORD
UNIVERSITY PRESS

OXFORD

UNIVERSITY PRESS

Great Clarendon Street, Oxford OX2 6DP

Oxford University Press is a department of the University of Oxford.
It furthers the University's objective of excellence in research, scholarship,
and education by publishing worldwide in

Oxford New York

Auckland Cape Town Dar es Salaam Hong Kong Karachi
Kuala Lumpur Madrid Melbourne Mexico City Nairobi
New Delhi Shanghai Taipei Toronto

With offices in

Argentina Austria Brazil Chile Czech Republic France Greece
Guatemala Hungary Italy Japan Poland Portugal Singapore
South Korea Switzerland Thailand Turkey Ukraine Vietnam

Oxford is a registered trade mark of Oxford University Press
in the UK and in certain other countries

Published in the United States
by Oxford University Press Inc., New York

British Library Cataloguing in Publication Data

Data available

Library of Congress Cataloging in Publication Data
Ryngaert, Cedric.
Jurisdiction in international law / Cedric Ryngaert.
p. cm.—(Oxford monographs in international law)
Includes bibliographical references.
ISBN 978–0–19–954471–4 (acid-free paper)   1. Jurisdiction
(International law)   I. Title
KZ4017.R96 2008
347'.012—dc22   2008028203

Typeset by Newgen Imaging Systems (P) Ltd., Chennai, India
Printed in Great Britain
on acid-free paper by
Biddles Ltd., King's Lynn

ISBN 978–0–19–954471–4

1 3 5 7 9 10 8 6 4 2

Acknowledgements

This book is based on the general part of a Ph.D. thesis ('Jurisdiction in International Law: United States and European Perspectives') which the author successfully defended at the Faculty of Law of Leuven University in 2007. I attempted to make the work current to 1 January 2008.

The author would like to acknowledge the great assistance given by a number of professors, colleagues, friends, and institutions. I of course take responsibility for any possible mistakes.

Special mention should obviously be made of my supervisor Professor Jan Wouters, who offered me the opportunity to write my Ph.D. thesis at the Institute for International Law of the Law Faculty of Leuven University. It was Professor Wouters who proposed, in late 2001, to study divergent approaches to international law from a transatlantic perspective. I acknowledge the confidence he had in me and the many academic opportunities which he gave me, both in research and teaching. He has always challenged me to give my own informed opinion on controversial academic questions. Thanks Jan.

I would also like to thank the Fund for Scientific Research Flanders (FWO), which generously funded my Ph.D. research at Leuven University (2002–2006), my research study at the European Law Research Center at Harvard Law School (2005), and other study trips abroad.

Thirdly, I would like to extend my thanks to my colleagues at the Leuven Institute for International Law, who have always been a great source of support for my research: Roemer, Sten, Maarten, Bruno, Tom, Dominic, Bart, Frederik, Dries, Leen, Heidi and Viviane. I also appreciate their commitment to society and their desire to bring about more justice in this world through scientific research and teaching.

Doubtless, I would not have been able to write this book without the support of friends and family. In particular, I would like to thank my parents and Lilian, who have always supported me.

Finally, I acknowledge everyone who was my companion on the road to self-fulfilment, of which this book was only a minor part.

Cedric Ryngaert
Utrecht,
April 2008

Contents—Summary

List of Abbreviations   xiii
Table of Cases   xix

1. Introduction   1
2. Public International Law Approaches to Jurisdiction   21
3. The Territoriality Principle   42
4. The Principles of Extraterritorial Criminal Jurisdiction   85
5. A Reasonable Exercise of Jurisdiction   134
6. A New Theory of Jurisdiction in International Law   185

Index   239

Contents—Outline

List of Abbreviations   xiii
Table of Cases   xix

1. Introduction   1

1.1 Scope and Method of This Study   1
1.2 Structure of the Study   4
1.3 Jurisdiction as a Concern of International Law   5
1.4 The Concept of Jurisdiction in Transnational Private Litigation   10
    (a) Adjudicative and subject matter jurisdiction   11
    (b) The interplay of private and public international law   14
    (c) Distinguishing private and public international law rules   18
1.5 Concluding Remarks   20

2. Public International Law Approaches to Jurisdiction   21

2.1 The *Lotus* Case   22
2.2 Customary International Law   26
    (a) Persisting influence of *Lotus*   26
    (b) The priority of territorial jurisdiction under customary
        international law   27
    (c) Legitimate interests, foreign harm, power, and reasonableness   31
    (d) Relevant international law principles   35
    (e) Method of ascertaining customary international law   36
    (f) Giving effect to international jurisdictional rules in the
        domestic legal order   38

3. The Territoriality Principle   42

3.1 Historical Growth of the Territoriality Principle in
     Continental Europe   43
    (a) Ancient times: personality prevailing over territoriality   44
    (b) Rome   44
    (c) Medieval Italy   45
    (d) Rise of territoriality in the seventeenth century   47
    (e) Extraterritoriality under unequal treaties   54
    (f) The 'continental European' view   55
3.2 The Territoriality Principle in England   55
3.3 The Territoriality Principle in the United States   59
    (a) Territoriality as a restraining principle derived from
        international law   59

(b) Territoriality as a restraining principle derived from congressional
intent: the presumption against extraterritoriality   63

3.4 Territorial Jurisdiction Over Cross-border Offences   75
3.5 Territorial Jurisdiction Over Transnational Antitrust Violations   76
3.6 Territorial Jurisdiction Over Transnational
     Securities Transactions   77
3.7 Territoriality and Orders for Discovery Abroad   79
3.8 Concluding Observations   83

4. **The Principles of Extraterritorial Criminal Jurisdiction**   85

4.1 Continental Europe v The Common Law Countries   85
4.2 Active Personality Principle   88
4.3 Passive Personality Principle   92
4.4 Protective Principle   96
4.5 Universality Principle   100
     (a) Vicarious jurisdiction   102
     (b) *Aut dedere aut judicare*   104
     (c) Universal jurisdiction: justifications   106
     (d) The historical trail of universal jurisdiction   108
     (e) Universal jurisdiction over 'core crimes' against
         international law   110
     (f) Lawfulness of universal jurisdiction over core crimes against
         international law   115
     (g) Universal jurisdiction *in absentia*   119
     (h) Universal tort jurisdiction   126
4.6 Concurrent Jurisdiction and Normative Competency Conflicts   127

5. **A Reasonable Exercise of Jurisdiction**   134

5.1 Comity as a Discretionary Principle of Jurisdictional Restraint   136
5.2 'Reasonable Jurisdiction' under International Law   142
     (a) Principle of non-intervention   144
     (b) Genuine connection   145
     (c) Equity   146
     (d) Proportionality   148
     (e) Abuse of rights   150
     (f) Responsibility or duty to protect   152
5.3 The Jurisdictional Rule of Reason of § 403 of the Restatement
     (Third) of US Foreign Relations Law (1987)   153
     (a) Antitrust origins of the rule of reason   153
     (b) § 403 of the Restatement   154
     (c) Balancing sovereign and private interests   156
     (d) Multiple reasonableness   160
     (e) Relationship of the jurisdictional rule of reason with the
         presumption against extraterritoriality   161

5.4 The Problematic Character of the Jurisdictional Rule of
    Reason as an International Law Norm or Principle   163
    (a) The international law claim of § 403   164
    (b) US practice   166
    (c) European practice   167
5.5 The Jurisdictional Rule of Reason as a Norm of International Law   178
    (a) Customary international law   178
    (b) General principles of law   180
    (c) The unfinished quest for reasonableness   182

6. A New Theory of Jurisdiction in International Law   **185**

6.1 Inevitability   187
6.2 The Discontents of Extraterritoriality   188
6.3 The Reciprocity Maxim and its Limits   190
6.4 Substantivism   193
    (a) The substantivist approach   194
    (b) Substantivism in practice   196
    (c) The limits of substantivism   199
6.5 Devising a Jurisdictional Framework: Using Transnational
    Regulatory and Judicial Networks   203
6.6 Subsidiarity   211
    (a) The *Schutzzweck*-based rule of reason   211
    (b) A transversal application of the subsidiarity principle   214
    (c) From nexus to international interests   225
6.7 A Transatlantic Gap over Jurisdiction   227
    (a) Shedding common law restrictions on the exercise of
        economic jurisdiction in the United States   228
    (b) Shedding common law restrictions on the exercise of
        antitrust jurisdiction in Europe   230
    (c) US exceptionalism and strict economic regulation   231
    (d) The transatlantic gap over international criminal justice   233
6.8 Final Concluding Remarks   236

Index   239

List of Abbreviations

AFDI	Annuaire français de droit international
AJIL	American Journal of International Law
Ala L Rev	Alabama Law Review
Alb L Rev	Albany Law Review
Am J Comp L	American Journal of Comparative Law
Am U J Int'l L & Pol'y	American University Journal of International Law and Policy
Am U L Rev	American University Law Review
Ann IDI	Annuaire de l'Institut de Droit International
Antitrust LJ	Antitrust Law Journal
ASIL Proc	Proceedings of the Annual Conference of the American Society of International Law
Aust'l J Int'l Aff	Australian Journal for International Affairs
Aust'l LJ	Australian Law Journal
AWD	Aussenwirtschaftsdienst der Betriebsberater
BC Int'l & Comp L Rev	Boston College International and Comparative Law Review
BC Third World LJ	Boston College Third World Law Journal
Berkeley J Int'l L	Berkeley Journal of International Law
Brigham Young U L Rev	Brigham Young University Law Review
Brookl J Int' L	Brooklyn Journal of International Law
BU Int'l LJ	Boston University International Law Journal
BU L Rev	Boston University Law Review
Butterworths J Int'l Banking & Fin L	Butterworths Journal of International Banking and Financial Law
BYIL	British Yearbook of International Law
Cal L Rev	California Law Review
Cal West Int'l LJ	California Western International Law Journal
Can Bus LJ	Canadian Business Law Journal
Can-US LJ	Canada—United States Law Journal
Cardozo J Int'l & Comp L	Cardozo Journal of International and Comparative Law
Cardozo L Rev	Cardozo Law Review
Case Western Res J Int'l L	Case Western Reserve Journal of International Law
Cath U L Rev	Catholic University Law Review
Chi J Int'l L	Chicago Journal of International Law
CFI	European Court of First Instance
CLR	Criminal Law Review
Colum Bus L Rev	Columbia Business Law Review
Colum Hum Rts L Rev	Columbia Human Rights Law Review
Colum J Eur L	Columbia Journal of European Law

Colum JL & Soc Probs	Columbia Journal of Law and Social Problems
Colum J Transnat'l L	Columbia Journal of Transnational Law
Colum L Rev	Columbia Law Review
CMLR	Common Market Law Review
Conn J Int L	Connecticut Journal of International Law
Cornell J Int'l L	Cornell Journal of International Law
Cornell LQ	Cornell Law Quarterly
Cornell L Rev	Cornell Law Review
Del J Corp L	Delaware Journal of Corporate Law
Denver J Int'l L & Pol'y	Denver Journal of International Law and Policy
DePaul L Rev	DePaul Law Review
Dick J Int'l L	Dickinson Journal of International Law
Dick L Rev	Dickinson Law Review
DoJ	US Department of Justice
Duke J Comp & Int'l L	Duke Journal of International and Comparative Law
Duke LJ	Duke Law Journal
EC	European Community
ECJ	European Court of Justice
ECR	European Court Reports
ECFR	European Company and Financial Law Review
ECLR	European Competition Law Review
EIPLR	European Intellectual Property Law Review
EJIL	European Journal of International Law
EL Rev	European Law Review
Emory Int'l L Rev	Emory International Law Review
Emory J Int'l Disp Res	Emory Journal of International Dispute Resolution
Emory LJ	Emory Law Journal
EPIL	Encyclopedia of Public International Law
EuZW	Europäische Zeitschrift für Wirtschaftsrecht
Fla J Int'l L	Florida Journal of International Law
Fletcher F World Aff	Fletcher Forum of World Affairs
Fordham Int'l LJ	Fordham International Law Journal
Fordham J Corp & Fin L	Fordham Journal of Corporate and Financial Law
Fordham L Rev	Fordham Law Review
FTC	Federal Trade Commission
Ga J Int'l & Comp L	Georgia Journal of International and Comparative Law
Ga L Rev	Georgia Law Review
Geo LJ	Georgetown Law Journal
Geo Mason L Rev	George Mason Law Review
Geo Wash J Int'l L & Econ	George Washington Journal of International Law and Economics
Golden Gate U L Rev	Golden Gate University Law Review
GYIL	German Yearbook of International Law
Hamline L Rev	Hamline Law Review
Harv Int'l LJ	Harvard International Law Journal

Harv L Rev	Harvard Law Review
Harvard Hum Rts J	Harvard Human Rights Journal
Hastings Int'l & Comp L Rev	Hastings International and Comparative Law Review
Hofstra L Rev	Hofstra Law Review
Houston J Int'l L	Houston Journal of International Law
Hum Rts Q	Human Rights Quarterly
ICJ	International Court of Justice
ILR	International Law Reports
ILSA J Int'l & Comp L	International Law Students Association Journal of International and Comparative Law
Ind Int'l & Comp L Rev	Indiana International & Comparative Law Review
Ind J Global Legal Stud	Indiana Journal of Global Legal Studies
Indian J Int'l L	Indian Journal of International Law
ICLQ	International and Comparative Law Quarterly
IFLR	International Financial Law Review
Int Bus Law	International Business Lawyer
Int Law	International Lawyer
Inter-Am L Rev	Inter-American Law Review
Int'l L Forum	International Law Forum
Int'l Tax & Bus Law	International Tax and Business Law
Iowa L Rev	Iowa Law Review
IPRax	Praxis des Internationalen Privat- und Verfahrensrechts
J Air L & Com	Journal of Air Law and Commerce
JC & UL	Journal of College and University Law
J Corp L	Journal of Corporate Law
JDI	Journal du droit international (Clunet)
J Crim L & Criminology	Journal of Criminal Law and Criminology
JICJ	Journal of International Criminal Justice
J Int'l . & Econ	Journal of International Law and Economics
J Mar L & Com	Journal of Maritime Law and Commerce
J Marshall L Rev	John Marshall Law Review
J Pub L	Journal of Public Law
J Small & Emerging Bus L	Journal of Small and Emerging Business Law
J Transn'l L & Pol'y	Journal of Transnational Law & Policy
J World Trade L	Journal of World Trade Law
JWT	Journal of World Trade
Law & Contemp Probs	Law and Contemporary Problems
Law & Pol'y Int'l Bus	Law and Policy in International Business
LQR	Law Quarterly Review
LJIL	Leiden Journal of International Law
Lloyd's Mar & Com LQ	Lloyd's Maritime and Commercial Law Quarterly
Louis L Rev	Louisiana Law Review
Loy Consumer L Rev	Loyola Consumer Law Review

Loy LA Int'l & Comp. LJ	Loyola of Los Angeles International and Comparative Law Journal
Loy U Chi LJ	Loyola University of Chicago Law Review
Manitoba LJ	Manitoba Law Journal
McGill LJ	McGill Law Journal
Md J Int'l L & Trade	Maryland Journal of International Law and Trade
Me L Rev	Maine Law Review
Mich L Rev	Michigan Law Review
Mil L Rev	Military Law Review
Minn L Rev	Minnesota Law Review
Modern L Rev	Modern Law Review
NCJ Int'l L & Comm Reg	North Carolina Journal of International Law and Commercial Regulation
NCL Rev	North Carolina Law Review
Neth Q Hum Rts	Netherlands Quarterly of Human Rights
New Eng L Rev	New England Law Review
NILR	Netherlands International Law Review
NJW	Neue juristische Wochenschrift
Notre Dame L Rev	Notre Dame Law Review
NTER	Nederlands Tijdschrift voor Europees Recht
Nw J Int'l L & Bus	Northwestern Journal of International Law and Business
Nw U L Rev	Northwestern University Law Review
NYIL	Netherlands Yearbook of International Law
NY Law Sch J Int'l & Comp L	New York Law School Journal of International and Comparative Law
NYLJ	New York Law Journal
NYU J Int'l L & Pol	New York University Journal of International Law and Politics
NYU L Rev	New York University Law Review
Ohio St LJ	Ohio State Law Journal
Or L Rev	Oregon Law Review
Pac Rim L & Pol'y J	Pacific Rim Law and Policy Journal
Pal Yb Int'l L	Palestine Yearbook of International Law
Pepp L Rev	Pepperdine Law Review
RabelsZ	Rabels Zeitschrift für ausländisches und internationales Privatrecht
RBDI	Revue belge de droit international
RCADI	Recueil des Cours de l'Académie de droit international
RCDIP	Revue critique de droit international privé
RDAI	Revue de droit des affaires internationales
Regent J Int'l L	Regent Journal of International Law
Rev dr pén	Revue de droit pénal
Rev dr int sc dipl pol	Revue de droit international, de sciences diplomatiques et politiques

Rev int dr écon	Revue internationale de droit économique
Rev sc crim dr pén comp	Revue de science criminelle et de droit pénal comparé
Rev suisse dr int concurr	Revue suisse du droit international de la concurrence
Rev tr dr eur	Revue trimestrielle de droit europeén
RGDIP	Revue générale de droit international public
RIW	Recht der internationalen Wirtschaft
RTDE	Revue trimestrielle de droit européen
San Diego L Rev	San Diego Law Review
S Cal L Rev	Southern California Law Review
Seattle J for Soc Just	Seattle Journal for Social Justice
Seattle U L Rev	Seattle University Law Review
SEW	Sociaal-Economische Wetgeving. Tijdschrift voor Europees en Economisch Recht
S Ill U LJ	Southern Illinois University Law Journal
Sing J Int'l & Comp L	Singapore Journal of International and Comparative Law
SMU L Rev	Southern Methodist University Law Review
Spanish Yb Int'l L	Spanish Yearbook of International Law
Stan J Int L	Stanford Journal of International Law
Stan L Rev	Stanford Law Review
St John's J Legal Comment	St. John's Journal of Legal Comment
St Louis U LJ	St. Louis University Law Journal
St Thomas L Rev	St. Thomas Law Review
Suffolk Trans'l LJ	Suffolk Transnational Law Journal
Sup Ct Rev	Supreme Court Review
Syracuse J Int'l L. & Comm	Syracuse Journal of International Law and Commerce
Temple Int'l & Comp LJ	Temple International and Comparative Law Journal
Temp L Rev	Temple Law Review
Tex L Rev	Texas Law Review
Tex Int'l LJ	Texas International Law Journal
Tilburg For L Rev	Tilburg Foreign Law Review
Transnat'l Law	The Transnational Lawyer
Transnat'l L & Contemp Probs	Transnational Law and Contemporary Problems
Tul J Int'l & Comp L	Tulane Journal of International and Comparative Law
Tulsa J Comp & Int'l L	Tulsa Journal of Comparative and International Law
Tulsa L Rev	Tulsa Law Review
U Chi Legal F	University of Chicago Legal Forum
U Chi L Rev	University of Chicago Law Review
U Chi L Sch Roundtable	University of Chicago Law School Roundtable
U Cin L Rev	University of Cincinnati Law Review
UCLA J Int'l L & For Aff	University of California Los Angeles Journal of International Law and Foreign Affairs

U Miami L Rev	University of Miami Law Review
U Pa L Rev	University of Pennsylvania Law Review
U Pa J Int'l Econ L	University of Pennsylvania Journal of International Economic Law
U Pitt L Rev	University of Pittsburgh Law Review
U Rich L Rev	University of Richmond Law Review
U SF L Rev	University of San Francisco Law Review
Utah L Rev	Utah Law Review
Vand J Transnat'l L	Vanderbilt Journal of Transnational Law
Va J Int'l L	Virginia Journal of International Law
Wash L Rev	Washington Law Review
Wash U LQ	Washington University Law Quarterly
Wash Univ Glob L Rev	Washington University Global Studies Law Review
Wayne L Rev	Wayne Law Review
W Comp	World Competition
Whittier L Rev	Whittier Law Review
W Va LQ	West Virginia Law Quarterly
Wm & Mary L Rev	William and Mary Law Review
Wisc Int'l LJ	Wisconsin international law journal
WuW	Wirtschaft und Wettbewerb
Yale J Int'l L	Yale Journal of International Law
Yale J Reg	Yale Journal on Regulation
Yale LJ	Yale Law Journal
Yb Eur L	Yearbook of European Law
Yb Int'l Human L	Yearbook of International Humanitarian Law
ZaöRV	Zeitschrift für Ausländisches Offentliches Recht und Völkerrecht
ZEuS	Zeitschrift für Europarechtliche Studien

Table of Cases

PERMANENT COURT OF INTERNATIONAL JUSTICE (PCIJ)

PCIJ, Advisory Opinion *Nationality Decrees in Tunis and Morocco*, PCIJ Reports,
Series B, No. 4 (1923) 22
PCIJ, *SS Lotus* (France v. Turkey), PCIJ Reports,
Series A, No. 10 (1927) 9, 22–31, 75, 92–3, 116, 134
PCIJ, *Legal Status of Eastern Greenland* (Denmark v. Norway), PCIJ Reports,
Series A/B, No.53 (1933) 29
PCIJ, *Meuse Case* (Belgium v. Netherlands), PCIJ Reports, Series A/B, No. 70 (1937) 147

INTERNATIONAL COURT OF JUSTICE (ICJ)

ICJ, *Nottebohm* (Liechtenstein v. Guatemala), ICJ Rep 4 (1955) 36, 146
ICJ, *North Sea Continental Shelf Cases* (Germany v. Denmark;
Germany v. Netherlands), ICJ Rep 3 (1969) 38, 147
ICJ, *Barcelona Traction, Light and Power Co. Ltd.* (Belgium v. Spain),
ICJ Rep 4 (1970) 26, 32, 91, 143, 146
ICJ, *Case Concerning the Continental Shelf* (Tunisia v. Libya), ICJ Rep 18 (1982) 147
ICJ, *Application of the Convention on the Prevention and Punishment of the Crime
of Genocide* (Bosnia and Herzegovina v. Serbia and Montenegro),
ICJ Rep 235 (1993) 113
ICJ, *Application of the Convention on the Prevention and Punishment of the Crime of Genocide*
(Bosnia and Herzegovina v. Yugoslavia), ICJ Rep 594 (1996) 113
ICJ, *Case Concerning the Gabcikovo-Nagymaros Project* (Hungary v. Slovakia),
ICJ Rep 7 (1997) 150
ICJ, *Arrest Warrant* (Democratic Republic of Congo v. Belgium),
ICJ Rep 3 (2002) 8, 26–7, 30, 94, 101, 104–5, 114, 116, 119–23

PERMANENT COURT OF ARBITRATION

Perm. Ct. Arb., *Island of Palmas* (U.S. v. Netherlands), 2 RIAA 829 (1928) 28, 60

INTERNATIONAL CRIMINAL TRIBUNAL FOR THE FORMER
YUGOSLAVIA (ICTY)

Case No. IT-94-T, *Prosecutor v. Tadic*, Trial Chamber, 10 August 1995 113
Case No. IT-94–1, *Prosecutor v. Tadic*, Appeals Chamber, Decision on the Defense
Motion for Interlocutory Appeal of the Jurisdiction, 2 October 1995 111
Case No. IT-95–17/1-T, *Prosecutor v. Furundzija*, 10 December 1998 112
Case No. IT-95–14-AR, *Prosecutor v. Blaskic*, 29 October 1997 113

INTERNATIONAL CRIMINAL TRIBUNAL FOR RWANDA (ICTR)

Case No. ICTR-90–40-T, *Ntuyahaga*, 18 March 1999 113

EUROPEAN COURT OF HUMAN RIGHTS (ECHR)

ECHR, Bankovic and others v. Belgium and 16 other Contracting States,
Application No. 52207/99, 12 December 2001 128
European Court of Justice (ECJ) and European Court of First Instance (CFI)
ECJ, Case 48/69, *ICI* v. *Commission*, [1972] ECR 619 .... 174, 230–1
ECJ, Case 60/81, *IBM* v. *Commission*, [1981] ECR 2639 172–3
ECJ, Joined Cases 89, 104, 114, 116, 117 & 125 to 129/85, *A. Ahlstrom Osakeyhtio* v.
Commission ('Wood Pulp') [1988] ECR 5193 .... 39, 77, 172–4, 207, 230
CFI, Case T-115/94, *Opel Austria GmbH* v. *Council* [1997] ECR II-39.................... .151
CFI, Case T-102/96, *Gencor Ltd* v. *Commission* [1999] ECR II-753 .... 77, 174–5, 207, 230

US SUPREME COURT CASES

Murray v The Schooner Charming Betsy, 6 US (2 Cranch) 64 (1804) 15, 58, 66
Rose v Himely, 8 US (4 Cranch) 241 (1808)....................................... 60
Schooner Exchange v McFaddon, 11 US (7 Cranch) 116 (1812) 60–1
United States v Palmer, 16 US (3 Wheat) 610 (1818)............................... 65
The Appolon, 22 US (9 Wheat) 362 (1824) 61
The Antelope, 23 US (10 Wheat) 66 (1825) 14, 61, 196
Ogden v Saunders, 25 US (12 Wheat) 212 (1827) 139
Whitney v Robertson, 124 US 190 (1888) 65
Hilton v Guyot, 159 US 113 (1895).. 137
The Paquete Habana, 175 US 677 (1900) 41
American Banana v United Fruit Co, 213 US 347 (1909) 62, 72
United States v Nord Deutscher Lloyd, 223 US 512 (1912)......................... 61
Western Union Telegraph Co v Brown, 234 US 542 (1914) 62
Mutual Life Ins Co v Liebing, 259 US 209 (1922) 62
United States v Bowman, 260 US 94 (1922) 72–3
New York Central RR v Chisholm, 268 US 29 (1925)............................. 63
Erie v Tompkins, 304 US 64 (1938).. 41
International Shoe Co v Washington, 326 US 310 (1945) 12, 13, 126
Vermilya-Brown v Connell, 335 US 377 (1948).................................. 70
Foley Bros Inc v Filardo, 336 US 281 (1949) 58, 62, 64, 67
Lauritzen v Larsen, 345 US 571 (1953)... 33
McCulloch v Sociedad Nacional de Marineros de Honduras, 372 US 10, 21 (1963).... 34, 66
M/S Bremen v Zapata Off-Shore Company, 407 US 1 (1972)......................... 153
United States v Kimbell Foods Inc, 440 US 715 (1979)............................ 65
World-Wide Volkswagen Corp v Woodson, 444 US 286 (1980)....................... 13
Helicopteros Nacionales de Colombia v Hall, 466 US 408 (1984) 13
Burger King v Rudzewicz, 471 US 462, 473 (1985) 13
*Société Nationale Industrielle Aerospatiale v United States District Court for the
Southern District of Iowa*, 482 US 522 (1986)................................. 61
Asahi Metal Indus Co v Superior Court, 480 US 102 (1987)........................ 12
United States v Verdugo-Urquidez, 494 US 259 (1990) 8
Burnham v Superior Court, 495 US 604 (1990) 12
EEOC v Arabian Am Oil Co (Aramco), 499 US 244 (1991) 58, 62–4, 69, 226
FTC v Ticor Title Ins Co, 112 S Ct 2169 (1992)................................. 71
United States v Alvarez-Machain, 112 S Ct 2188 (1992) 23
Sale v Haitian Ctrs Council Inc, 509 US 155 (1993).......................... 64, 73
Hartford Fire Insurance Co v California, 509 US 764 (1993)............14, 16, 63, 66, 72, 137,
160, 166, 207, 231

Steel Co v Citizens for Better Environment, 523 US 83 (1998) 5
F Hoffman-La Roche Ltd et al v Empagran SA et al, 124 S
  Ct 2359 (2004) 145, 166, 207, 209, 226
Sosa v Alvarez-Machain, 124 S Ct 2739 (2004) 209

US FEDERAL APPEALS COURT CASES

United States v Aluminium Corp of America, 148 F 2d 416 (2d Cir 1945) 15, 62, 76, 153, 196
Gillars v United States, 182 F 2d 962 (DC Cir 1950) 73
Tag v Rogers, 267 F 2d 664 (DC Cir 1959) 65
Boryk v de Havilland Aircraft Co, 341 F 2d 666 (2d Cir 1965) 12
United States v Pizzarusso, 388 F.2d 8 (2d Cir. 1968) 99
Schoenbaum v Firstbrook, 405 F 2d 200 (2d Cir 1968) 202, 232
United States v King, 552 F 2d 833 (9th Cir 1976) 60
Timberlane Lumber Co v Bank of America, NT & SA, 549 F 2d 597
  (9th Cir 1976) 153, 175–6, 207
Mannington Mills, Inc v Congoleum Corp, 595 F 2d 1287 (3d Cir1979) 153, 176, 207
Filartiga v Pena-Irala, 630 F 2d 876 (2d Cir 1980) 235
United States v Baker, 609 F 2d 134 (5th Cir 1980) 73
FTC v Compagnie de Saint-Gobain-Pont-à-Mousson, 636 F 2d 1300 (DC Cir 1980) 65
United States v Khalje, 658 F 2d 90 (2d Cir 1981) 99
United States v Bank of Nova Scotia I, 619 F 2d 1384 (11th Cir 1982) 80
United States v Marino-Garcia, 679 F 2d 1373 (11th Cir 1982). 105
United States v Pinto-Mejia, 720 F 2d 248 (2d Cir 1983) 65
Cleary v United States Lines, 728 F 2d 607 (3d Cir 1984) 68
Chua Han Mow v United States, 730 F 2d 1309 (9th Cir 1984) 60, 73
Tel-Oren v Libyan Arab Republic, 726 F 2d 774 (DC Cir 1984) 96
Laker Airways Ltd v Sabena, Belgian World Airlines, 731 F 2d 909
  (DC Cir 1984) 62, 91, 128–9, 208
United States v Allen, 760 F 2d 447 (2d Cir 1985). 65
In re Anschuetz & Co, 754 F 2d 602 (5th Cir 1985). 80–1
Pfeiffer v Wm Wrigley Jr Co, 755 F 2d 554 (7th Cir 1985) 68
DeYoseo v Bell Helicopter Textron Inc, 785 F 2d 1282 (5th Cir 1986). 68
United States v Quemener, 789 F 2d 145 (2d Cir 1986). 65
Boureslan v Aramco, 857 F 2d 1014 (5th Cir 1988) 179
United States v Felix-Gutierrez, 940 F 2d 1200 (9th Cir 1991) 60, 73, 179
United States v Yunis, 924 F 2d 1086 (DC Cir 1991). 105, 234
United States v Javino, 960 F 2d 1137 (2d Cir 1992) 179
Kollias v D & G Marine Maintenance, 29 F 3d 67 (2d Cir 1994) 63–4, 73
United States v Vasquez-Velasco, 15 F 3d 833 (9th Cir 1994) 73–4, 179
Gushi Bros v Bank of Guam, 28 F 3d 1535 (9th Cir 1994) 64
Neely v Club Med Management Services Inc, 63 F 3d 166 (3d Cir 1995). 179
United States v Juda, 46 F 3d 961 (9th Cir 1995) 179
United States v Vanness, 85 F 3d 661 (DC Cir 1996). 5
United States v Lin, 101 F 3d 760 (DC Cir 1996) 105
In the Matter of an Application to Enforce Admin Subpoenas Duces Tecum of the
  SEC v Knowles, 87 F 3d 413 (10th Cir 1996) 13
United States v Nippon Paper Indus Co, 109 F 3d 1 (1st Cir 1997). 154, 163
United States v Wang Kun Lue, 134 F 3d 79 (2d Cir 1997) 105
United States v Rezaq, 134 F 3d 1121 (DC Cir 1998) 105
United States v Plummer, 221 F 3d 1298 (11th Cir 2000) 73

United States v Ramzi Ahmed Yousef and others, 327 F 3d 56 (2d Cir 2003) 96, 234
United Phosphorus Ltd v Angus Chemical Co, 322 F 3d 942 (7th Cir 2003) 5, 14
Flores v S Peru Copper Corp, 343 F 3d 140 (2d Cir 2003) 107
Alvarez-Machain v United States, 331 F 3d 604 (9th Cir 2003) 23

US FEDERAL DISTRICT COURT CASES

Guiness v Miller, 291 F 769 (SDNY 1923) 15, 196
The Over the Top, 5 F 2d 838 (D Conn. 1925). 65
United States v Rodriguez, 182 F Supp 479 (SD Cal 1960) 99
United States v Keller, 451 F Supp 631 (DPR 1978). 99
United States v Newball, 524 F Supp 715 (EDNY 1981) 99
SEC v Banca della Svizzera Italiana, 92 FRD 111 (1981) 81, 202
Adidas Canada v SS Seatrain Bennington, F Supp 1984 WL 423 (SDNY 1984) 80
Graco Inc v Kremlin Inc, 101 FRD 503 (ND Ill 1984) 80
United States v Zehe, 601 F Supp 196, 200 (D Mass 1985) 73
de Atucha v Commodity Exchange Inc, 608 F Supp 510 (DCNY 1985) 63
Hudson v Hermann Pfauter GmbH & Co, 117 FRD 33 (NDNY 1987). 62
United States v Evans et al, 667 F Supp. 974 (SDNY 1987) 96, 100
United States v Yunis, 681 F Supp 896 (DDC 1988) 105
Baptist Churches v Meese, 712 F Supp 756 (ND Cal 1989) 65
United States v Chen De Yian, 905 F Supp 160 (SDNY 1995). 105
United States v Rezaq, 899 F Supp 697 (DDC 1995) 105, 234
United States v Ni Fa Yi, 951 F Supp 42 (SDNY 1997). 105
United States v Bin Laden, 92 F Supp 2d 189 (SDNY 2000). 73

ENGLISH CASES

Robinson v Bland, 1 W Bl 234, 256, 96 Eng Rep 120, 141, 2 Burr 1077,
   97 Eng Rep 717 (KB 1760) 138
Regina v Keyn, LR 2 Ex D 63, 13 Cox CC 403 (1876). 55, 230
HM Advocate v Hall, (1881) 4 Couper 438 56
MacLeod v Attorney-General for New South Wales, [1891] AC 455. 55
The Queen v Jameson, [1896] 2 QB 425. 56
R v Page, [1954] 1 QB 171 56
Cox v Army Council, [1963] AC 48 56
Treacy v DPP, [1971] AC 537 57
Lawson v Fox, [1974] AC 803 57
Air India v Wiggins, [1980] 1 WLR 815 57
British Airways Board v Laker Airways Ltd, [1984] 3 WLR 410; [1985] AC 58. 208
R v Jameson, [1986] 2 QB 425 57
Liangsiriprasert v US Government, [1991] 1 AC 225 58
Regina v Bartle and the Commissioner of Police for the Metropolis &
   Others Ex Parte Pinochet, 2 All ER 97 (HL 1999) 121
R v Bow Street Metropolitan Stipendiary Magistrate, ex p Pinochet Ugarte (No. 3),
   [2000] 1 AC 147. 234
Jones v Saudi Arabia, [2006] UKHL 26 39
Al-Skeini v Secretary of State, [2007] UKHL 26 58

GERMAN CASES

BGH, *Dost*, 20 October 1976, *BGHSt* 27, S. 30 f. 102
BKartA, WuW/E 1943, 1953 (*Morris/Rothmans*) (1982) 40, 164, 177
Philip Morris Inc. v. Bundeskartellamt, [1984] E.C.C. 393 (Kammergericht) (F.R.G.),
    KG WuW/E OLG 3051 .... 137, 177

FRENCH CASES

Société Fruehauf Corp. v. Massardy, 1968 D.S. Jur. 147, 1965, (1966) 5 ILM 476
    (Ct. Appel Paris 1965) 100, 130

DUTCH CASES

Hoge Raad, *Bouterse*, (2001) 32 NYIL 287 40
Gerechtshof 's-Gravenhage, LJN: AZ9366, 09–751005-04, 29 January 2007.............. 40

BELGIAN CASES

Investigating Judge Brussels, ordonnance of November 6, 1998, *Pinochet*, (1999)
    Journal des Tribunaux 308... 39, 112, 117

SPANISH CASES

National Criminal Court, *Pinochet*, Rulings of 4 and 5 November 1998, available
    at http://www.derechos.org/nizkor/arg/espana/juri.html......................... 217
Supreme Court of Spain, *Peruvian Genocide*, 42 ILM 1200 (2003) 217
Constitutional Court Spain (Second Chamber), Guatemala Genocide case,
    judgment No. STC 237/2005, available at http://www.tribunalconstitucional.es/
    stc2005/stc2005–237.htm... 217–8

1

Introduction

1.1 Scope and Method of This Study

In his 1964 Hague Lecture on the international law of jurisdiction, the late Professor Mann stated that, '[a]lthough there exists abundant material on specific aspects of jurisdiction, not a single monograph seems to have been devoted to the doctrine as a whole'.[1] This statement still holds true as we write. Impressive monographs have been written about the international law of antitrust jurisdiction,[2] securities jurisdiction,[3] export controls,[4] and universal jurisdiction.[5] An over-arching study of the theory of jurisdiction is, however, lacking, although Mann and Akehurst have made a commendable effort at connecting the threads of jurisdiction.[6] To be true, some authors have published on 'extraterritorial' jurisdiction in general, yet typically they only addressed extraterritorial jurisdiction in the field of economic law (antitrust and export controls in particular).[7]

The compartmentalization of the law of jurisdiction stems from the very nature of the concept of jurisdiction. As an abstract concept, it is in need of

---

[1] FA Mann, 'The Doctrine of Jurisdiction in International Law', (1964-I) 111 RCADI 1, 23.

[2] eg RA Epstein and MS Greve, eds, *Competition Laws in Conflict: Antitrust Jurisdiction in the Global Economy* (2004); R Deville, *Die Konkretisierung des Abwägungsgebots im internationalen Kartellrecht* (1990); E Nerep, *Extraterritorial Control of Competition Under International Law with Special Regard to U.S. Antitrust Law* (1983); JB Townsend, *Extraterritorial Antitrust: the Sherman Antitrust Act Versus U.S. Business Abroad* (1980); JB Griffin, *Perspectives on the Extraterritorial Application of U.S. Antitrust and Other Laws* (1979); KM Meessen, *Völkerrechtliche Grundsätze des internationalen Kartellrechts* (1975); F Hermanns, *Völkerrechtliche Grenzen für die Anwendung kartellrechtlicher Verbotsnormen* (1969); E Rehbinder, *Extraterritoriale Wirkungen des deutschen Kartellrechts* (1965).

[3] eg G Schuster, *Die internationale Anwendung des Börsenrechts* (1996); I Tunstall, *International Securities Regulation* (2005).

[4] eg ALC de Mestral and T Gruchalla-Wesierski, *Extraterritorial Application of Export Control Legislation: Canada and the U.S.A.* (1990).

[5] eg M Inazumi, *Universal Jurisdiction in Modern International Law: Expansion of National Jurisdiction for Prosecuting Serious Crimes under International Law* (2005); L Reydams, *Universal Jurisdiction: International and Municipal Legal Perspectives* (2003); A Peyro Lopis, *La compétence universelle en matière de crimes contre l'humanité* (2003).

[6] Mann (n 1 above) 1; FA Mann, 'The Doctrine of Jurisdiction Revisited after Twenty Years', (1984-III) 186 RCADI 9; M Akehurst, 'Jurisdiction in International Law', (1972–73) 46 BYIL 145.

[7] eg CJ Olmstead (ed), *Extraterritorial Laws and Responses Thereto* (1984); KM Meessen (ed), *Extraterritorial Jurisdiction in Theory and Practice* (1996).

application and elaboration in particular areas of substantive law. A clear grasp of the underlying substantive regulations is often required, so that substantive law specialists rather than general international lawyers have ventured into the vast field of international jurisdiction.[8] The nitty-gritty of highly technical analyses of the scope *ratione loci* of particular substantive regulations has, not surprisingly, not always been helpful in clarifying the theory of jurisdiction under public international law.

This study does not pretend to represent the ultimate monograph on the law of jurisdiction. It does not, and cannot, examine all substantive branches of the law which have been given extraterritorial application, or in which jurisdictional problems have arisen. It makes a selection of those branches of the law in which jurisdictional assertions have been most controversial, in particular from a transatlantic point of view. Starting from the field of criminal law, in which the theory of jurisdiction finds its roots, it will also touch such fields as antitrust law, securities law, discovery, the law of export controls, and international humanitarian and human rights law.[9] It will eventually be endeavoured to discern and propose common principles of jurisdiction.

This study does not aim to develop the ideal level of international regulation in different legal fields. It will not discuss the merits of either multilateral regulation by international institutions or unilateral (jurisdiction-based) regulation. It will assume that unilateral jurisdictional assertions by States will in almost all legal areas persist, since all-encompassing international regulation by international supervisors and dispute-settlement and enforcement mechanisms, will, for sovereignty-related reasons, prove elusive for the time being. In areas where more centralized international mechanisms exist, such as in the field of international humanitarian law (the International Criminal Court (ICC) and ad hoc international criminal tribunals), the specific procedural features and the shortcomings of such mechanisms will ensure that national jurisdictional assertions will continue to exist alongside them.[10] In the field of international criminal law for instance, the international criminal tribunals only have limited jurisdiction. Even if they have broad jurisdiction, such jurisdiction may be subsidiary to State jurisdiction. The ICC, for instance, may only exercise its jurisdiction if a State is genuinely unable or unwilling to investigate or prosecute the crimes over which the ICC has

---

[8] Cf A Bianchi, 'Extraterritoriality and Export Controls: Some Remarks on the Alleged Antinomy Between European and U.S. Approaches', (1992) 35 GYIL 366, 374 n 32 (stating that '[t]he remarkable amount of litigation antitrust cases have caused has favored the development of principles and techniques the application of which seems to be the object of a somewhat autonomous scientific debate').

[9] Areas of the law which will not be studied, but where important issues of extraterritoriality have nevertheless arisen, include bankruptcy law, trademark law, environmental law, tax law, employment law, and cyberspace law. In this dissertation's general theory of jurisdiction, reference may however be made to these areas.

[10] Also B Van Schaack, 'Justice Without Borders—Universal Civil Jurisdiction', (2005) ASIL Proc 120, 121 ('Supranational mechanisms will never supplant domestic proceedings, so domestic courts will continue to play a central role in enforcing international law').

jurisdiction (complementarity principle).[11] In the field of antitrust and securities law, centralized enforcement still has a long way to go, given the relative absence of applicable substantive international economic law and the strong sovereign interests involved. However, the general trend may be towards more international cooperation. As is common in international institutional law, this will occur in the first place through negative integration, ie through mutual recognition of each others' jurisdictional and regulatory assertions. In due course, positive integration, involving harmonization of substantive law and establishment of centralized enforcers, may follow.

Having said what this study does not pretend to do (not presenting the ultimate overview of the law jurisdiction, nor analysing the benefits or feasibility of regulation by international institutions), it may be useful to state what it does pretend, in all modesty, to do. For one, as will probably be clear by now, it only studies the law of jurisdiction *ratione loci*, and not the law of jurisdiction *ratione temporis, personae* or *materiae*, although, if useful for the analysis, such issues will be touched upon (eg foreign sovereign immunities, norms amenable to (universal) jurisdiction). For another, two threads run throughout this study. The first is the thread of jurisdictional reasonableness. This study indeed aims at developing a theory of (unilateral) jurisdiction which, informed by an overarching principle of jurisdictional 'reasonableness', takes into account the sovereign interests of States other than the forum State (ie the State exercising its jurisdiction), yet which at the same time ensures that the interests of the forum State *and* of the international community are sufficiently heeded. A reasonable exercise of jurisdiction may alleviate the 'extraterritorial' impact of jurisdictional assertions. It may render unilateral jurisdiction in fact 'multilateral', inter alia, through low-level contacts between regulators and courts, and thus obviate the need, if any, for an international institutional solution to regulatory problems.

The second thread is the comparative US-EU perspective. Granted, other States (or groups of States) may also have applied, and apply, their laws to foreign situations (notably other Western countries such as Canada, New Zealand, Australia...). However, almost all assertions of jurisdiction over foreign situations, in both the field of economic law and the field of human rights law, have originated in either the United States or in the European Union. In addition, the international conflict which the expansion of the reach of national law has given rise to, has, to a great extent, been a *transatlantic* conflict between the world's two most powerful economic and political blocks. This justifies a limitation of the scope of this study to the jurisdictional practice of the United States and Europe. Occasionally, if useful for this study, reference will be made at the jurisdictional practice of other States. This limitation will be further rationalized in the subsection on the method used to ascertain customary international law.

---

[11] Article 17 of the Statute of the International Criminal Court.

This study is a study in international law. In order to determine what the international law in a particular area is at a given time—and apply it—international lawyers, rely, in accordance with Article 38 of the Statute of the International Court of Justice, on international conventions, international custom, 'the general principles of law recognized by civilized nations', judicial decisions, and 'the teachings of the most highly qualified publicists of the various nations'. This study will follow the international law method. Given the near total absence of useful treaty law in the field of jurisdiction,[12] the study will mainly be geared to identifying customary international law norms on the law of jurisdiction. To that effect, and in keeping with the nature of customary international law, it will primarily analyse State practice, as could be gleaned from States' adoption of certain laws, their application by courts and regulatory agencies, and protests by States against the application of other States' laws adversely affecting them. Because State jurisdictional practice has historically been influenced in no small measure by doctrinal writings, legal doctrine on the law of jurisdiction will also be given a prominent place, although *actual* State practice will be the main point of reference of the study. The lengthy footnotes will illustrate that the relevant material is abundant, if not overwhelming. Yet this study aspires to distil from this wealth of sources *common principles*, which may be of use for States and legal practitioners looking for a solution to jurisdictional problems. It may be noted, finally, that the primary sources will be examined in their original version and language (English, French, German, Dutch, and Spanish). Translations will not be used, although, in footnotes, reference will be made at them (if available) for the reader's convenience.

1.2 Structure of the Study

Having set out this study's scope and method, it is appropriate now to present its structure. The starting point of a study of the law of jurisdiction is, inevitably, the *Lotus* case (Chapter 2). This case, decided by the Permanent Court of International Justice (PCIJ) in 1927, is to date still the only case in which the World Court has addressed the question of jurisdiction head-on. In *Lotus*, the PCIJ took a rather liberal view of a State's rights to exercise jurisdiction, these rights only being limited by 'prohibitive rules'. It will be argued that this approach may be obsolete as we write, since, under customary international law, States have considered the territoriality principle to be the basic principle of international jurisdictional order (Chapters 2 and 3). Principles of extraterritorial jurisdiction have nonetheless been developed (Chapter 4).

---

[12] Only in the field of international *criminal* jurisdiction have treaties been concluded, although none of these treaties dealt exclusively with the law of jurisdiction. Their jurisdictional provisions are often vague and in need of clarification by State practice.

Even when the classical principles of jurisdiction could subsume a jurisdictional assertion, reasonableness is not assured. The international system of jurisdiction is one of *concurrent* jurisdiction. As more than one State could have jurisdiction over one and the same situation, there is a clear risk of international conflict. In order to solve conflicts, and to mitigate exorbitant assertions of jurisdiction, in Chapter 5, a jurisdictional rule of reason, which draws on conflict of laws principles, and is set forth in the US Restatement of Foreign Relations Law, is proposed. This rule requires that a State weigh the interests of different States and private actors, and that it only assert jurisdiction when its interests outweigh other States' interests and private actors' interests. In this chapter, it will be examined whether this rule in fact represents international law, or whether it is a mere principle of (non-binding) comity. It will be argued that there is insufficient evidence that the rule of reason indeed is a rule of international law.

This study supports jurisdictional reasonableness as a *de lege ferenda* concept. Yet it proposes to put the interests of the international community rather than sovereign or private interests centre-stage. In Chapter 6, this study's own rule of reason will be elaborated upon. It is a rule that not only requires that States restrain their jurisdiction, but also one that may require them to actually exercise their jurisdiction when such would be in the interest of the international community. It is a rule the practical application of which is given shape through low-level contacts between regulators, prosecutors, judges, and non-State actors.

1.3 Jurisdiction as a Concern of International Law

How to define 'jurisdiction under international law'? While international lawyers often employ the term 'jurisdiction', and most of them have an inkling of what it means, defining jurisdiction is hardly self-evident.[13] What is certain is that jurisdiction somehow relates to sovereignty. In a world composed of equally sovereign States, any State is entitled to give shape to its sovereignty or *imperium* by adopting laws,[14] to '*juris-dicere*', to state what the law is relating to persons, activities, or legal interests.[15] Jurisdiction becomes a concern of international law

---

[13] eg BJ George, 'Extraterritorial Application of Penal Legislation', (1966) 64 Mich L Rev 609, 621 (stating that '[o]ne of the most difficult words in the legal lexicon to delineate is the term "jurisdiction"'). Also *United States v Vanness*, 85 F 3d 661, 663, n 2 (DC Cir1996); *Steel Co v Citizens for Better Environment*, 523 US 83, 118 S Ct 1003, 140 L Ed 2d 210 (1998); *United Phosphorus, Ltd v Angus Chemical Co*, 322 F 3d 942, 948 (7th Cir 2003) ('Jurisdiction is a word of many, too many, meanings').

[14] HE Yntema, 'The Comity Doctrine', (1966) 65 Mich L Rev 9, 19 (referring to 'the principle definitively established by Justinian, that the first attribute of the *imperium* is the power of legislation').

[15] JH Beale, 'The Jurisdiction of a Sovereign State', (1923) 36 Harv L Rev 241 (1923) (defining jurisdiction as 'the power of a sovereign to affect the rights of persons, whether by legislation, by executive decree, or by the judgment of a court'); CL Blakesley, 'United States Jurisdiction over Extraterritorial Crime', (1982) 73 J Crim L & Criminology 1109 (defining jurisdiction as

when a State, in its eagerness to promote its sovereign interests abroad, adopts laws that govern matters of not purely domestic concern.[16]

The public international law of jurisdiction guarantees that foreign nations' concerns are also accounted for, and that sovereignty-based assertions of jurisdiction by one State do not unduly encroach upon the sovereignty of other States. The law of jurisdiction is doubtless one of the most essential as well as controversial fields of international law, in that it determines how far, *ratione loci*, a State's laws might reach.[17] As it ensures that States, especially powerful States, do not assert jurisdiction over affairs which are the domain of other States, it is closely related to the customary international law principles of non-intervention and sovereign equality of States.[18] Guaranteeing a peaceful coexistence between States through erecting jurisdictional barriers which States are not supposed to cross, the law of jurisdiction is one of the building blocks of the classical, billiard-ball view of international law as a 'negative' law of State coexistence.

The international law of jurisdiction is sometimes referred to as the law of 'extraterritorial' jurisdiction, especially in the field of economic law.[19] The use of the term 'extraterritoriality' derives from the previous observation that jurisdiction becomes a concern of international law where a State regulates matters which are

the authority to affect legal interests). This is also what *jurisdictio* originally meant in the Roman period: 'the power of a magistrate to *ius dicere*, that is, to determine the law and, in accordance with it, to settle disputes concerning persons and property within his forum (sphere of authority)'. J Plescia, 'Conflict of Laws in the Roman Empire', (1992) 38 Labeo 30, 32.

[16] Mann (n 1 above) 9 (defining jurisdiction as 'a State's right under international law to regulate conduct in matters not exclusively of domestic concern').

[17] ibid 15 (stating that '[j]urisdiction . . . is concerned with what has been described as one of the fundamental functions of public international law, *viz.* the function of regulating and delimiting the respective competences of States . . .'). Also AF Lowenfeld, 'International Litigation and the Quest for Reasonableness', (1994-I) 245 RCADI 9, 29 ('I believe that while we will not here address the cosmic issues of war and peace, of nuclear weapons and terrorist assaults, we will deal with legitimate and serious concerns of private persons and of States, and surely of lawyers, embraced within what Story calls the comity of nations').

[18] RL Muse, 'A Public International Law Critique of the Extraterritorial Jurisdiction of the Helms-Burton Act (Cuban Liberty and Democratic Solidarity (Libertad) Act of 1996)', (1996–97) 30 Geo Wash J Int'l L & Econ 207, 241–2 ('Because each nation possesses exclusive authority within its territory—but no authority within the territory of another—each nation is co-equal in rights and status with other nations, regardless of disparities in economic or military power'). Also Bianchi (above n 8) 385 (submitting that 'principles of jurisdiction need to be studied in connection with other principles such as the prohibition of economic coercion and intervention, the consideration of which could be useful to set up standards of legitimacy for extraterritorial measures').

[19] eg R Higgins, *Problems and Process: International Law and How We Use It* (1994) 74 (arguing that '"extraterritorial jurisdiction" has come to have a discrete meaning of its own, over and above nationality, protective, and passive-personality jurisdiction', namely the ability 'to exercise jurisdiction over persons abroad (even non-nationals) for acts occurring abroad, which were intended to have, and indeed have, significant harmful [economic] effects within the territory asserting jurisdiction'); B Stern, 'Can the United States Set Rules for the World? A French View', (1997/4) 31 JWT 5, 13–14; B Stern, 'How to Regulate Globalization?' in M Byers, ed, *The Role of Law in International Politics* (2000) 255.

not exclusively of domestic concern.[20] The term 'extraterritoriality' is confusing, however. 'Extraterritorial jurisdiction' ought to imply that a State exercises its jurisdiction without any territorial link ('*extra*-territorial'), although the expression is typically used in a context of States asserting jurisdiction on the basis of some, admittedly non-exclusive, territorial link.[21] The term 'extraterritorial jurisdiction' is only accurate if it refers to assertions of jurisdiction over persons, property, or activities which have no territorial nexus whatsoever with the regulating State, ie assertions based on the personality, protective, or universality principle of jurisdiction.[22]

---

[20] A Bianchi, 'Reply to Professor Maier', in Meessen (above n 7), 74, 76 (stating that 'extraterritoriality' refers to situations where 'a state may regulate matters not exclusively of domestic concern or, in other words, matters which present more or less significant links with other legal orders'); B Stern, 'L'extraterritorialité revisitée: Où il est question des affaires *Alvarez-Machain, Pâte de bois* et de quelques autres…', (1992) 38 AFDI 239, 242 (submitting that a rule is applied extraterritorially 'si tout ou partie du processus d'application se déroule en dehors du territoire de l'Etat qui l'a émise'); P Demaret, 'L'extraterritorialité des lois et les relations transatlantiques: une question de droit ou de diplomatie?', (1985) 21 RTDE 1–2 (referring to extraterritoriality 'lorsqu'une autorité législative, gouvernementale, judiciaire ou administrative d'un Etat adresse à un sujet de droit un ordre de faire ou de ne pas faire à exécuter en tout ou en partie sur le territoire d'un autre Etat'); AT Guzman, 'Is International Antitrust Possible?', (1998) 73 NYU L Rev 1501, 1506 (stating that '"[e]xtraterritoriality" refers to a country's ability to govern activity in foreign countries').

[21] Extraterritoriality is often invoked to typify assertions of jurisdiction over violations of antitrust and securities laws abroad, which nevertheless impact on the regulating State. The very impact of the foreign conduct on the regulating State may be considered as a territorial effect. Jurisdiction on the basis of such an effect may be justified under the objective territorial principle. Eg E Colmant, '14 juillet 1972, une date pour le droit de la concurrence: neuf arrêts règlent trois grandes questions. Affaire des matières colorantes: suite et fin', (1973) Revue du marché commun 15, 21 ('[C]ertains, dont l'Avocat général [in the *Dyestuffs* case], ont parlé d'application extraterritoriale du droit communautaire. Il ne faut pas se laisser abuser par ce terme: la Commission est compétente à l'égard d'entreprises localisées ou n'étant pas localisées dans le Marché commun, dès lors que des actes de celles-ci ont des effets dans le territoire où la Commission a reçu mission de sauvegarder un régime de libre concurrence, c'est-à-dire celui de la Communauté économique européenne…Bien que qualifiée d'extraterritoriale, elle n'a rien d'extraordinaire et se retrouve généralement dans tous les ordres juridiques nationaux').

[22] Most international law handbooks either avoid the use of the word 'extraterritorial jurisdiction' or limit its scope to jurisdiction based on the nationality or personality principle, the protective principle or the universality principle. Bossuyt and Wouters, for instance, distinguish between territorial and extraterritorial jurisdiction, the latter denoting jurisdiction based on the aforementioned non-territorial principles of international jurisdiction (M Bossuyt and J Wouters, *Grondlijnen van internationaal recht* (2005) 286). Müller and Wildhaber for their part do not conceptually distinguish extraterritorial jurisdiction, stating that '[z]u den anerkannten Anknüpfungspunkte gehören neben dem Territorialitätsprinzip das aktive und passive Personalitätsprinzip, das Weltrechtsprinzip und das Auswirkungsprinzip' (JP Müller and L Wildhaber, *Praxis des Völkerrechts* (3rd edn 2001) 386). Similarly, Dixon and McCorquodale identify territoriality, personality, protective principle, the 'effects' doctrine, and universality as grounds for assertion of jurisdiction by national courts (M Dixon and R McCorquodale, *Cases and Materials on International Law* (2nd edn 1991) 318–52). Brownlie concurs as to criminal jurisdiction, but deals separately with 'extra-territorial enforcement measures'. (I Brownlie, *Principles of Public International Law* (1998) 301–24). Shaw for his part talks plainly of 'extraterritorial jurisdiction' (MN Shaw, *International Law* (1997) 452–90). According to Quoc Dinh, the powers of the State can be divided into 'compétences exercées par l'Etat sur son territoire' and 'compétences exercées par l'Etat hors de son territoire'. The extraterritorial application of national legislation is not dealt with in the latter section—as if the State would in that case not exercise any powers outside its territory—but in a third one, 'concurrence et

And even such jurisdiction is not wholly 'extra-territorial', as it is asserted by a State, or its courts, within a given territory.[23]

While 'extraterritorial' may nonetheless be useful as shorthand for 'not *exclusively* territorial', the term might best be avoided, because it is tainted by the pejorative connotation it has acquired over the years. As Lowenfeld has pointed out, those who term particular assertions of jurisdiction 'extraterritorial' indeed often believe them to be illegitimate or outrageous,[24] although they may in fact be more territorial than other, non-controversial jurisdictional assertions (such as assertions based on the active personality principle). This study therefore prefers, as far as possible, not to use the term 'extraterritorial jurisdiction'. At times, however, 'extraterritorial jurisdiction' will be used, for the sake of brevity, to denote jurisdiction over situations arising abroad, typically causing adverse economic effects within the State asserting jurisdiction.

The term 'extraterritorial jurisdiction' is often used to condemn the long arm of US law. Rock Grundman's contention that the United States' three biggest export products are rock music, blue jeans, and United States law,[25] inevitably springs to mind in this respect. Vexation stemming from the perceived hegemonical imposition of US law on other States could also be gleaned from the answer the author received when he asked an international students' audience the question who could claim jurisdiction over a criminal act initiated in Belgium

conciliation des compétences étatiques' (N Quoc Dinh, *Droit International Public* (6th edn 1999) 1455. By the same token, Dupuy only attributes territorial and personal jurisdiction to the State, although he deals with extraterritorial jurisdiction in a third section, 'concurrence de compétences exercées par deux Etats' (PM Dupuy, *Droit International Public* (5th edn 2000) 731).

[23] In their separate opinion in the 2002 *Arrest Warrant* case, a case concerning immunity from prosecution under Belgium's universal jurisdiction law brought by the Congo before the International Court of Justice, Judges Higgins, Kooijmans and Buergenthal, therefore believed it to be more accurate to use the term 'territorial jurisdiction for extraterritorial events'. ICJ, Joint Separate Opinion of Judges Higgins, Kooijmans and Buergenthal, *Arrest Warrant*, para 42.

[24] Lowenfeld (above n 17) 43–4 ('The search for a satisfactory definition of extraterritorial jurisdiction...is doomed to failure: "extraterritorial jurisdiction", like "bureaucratic", is a term that could never be rescued from its unattractive reputation'). Also J-M Bischoff and R Kovar, 'L'application du droit communautaire de la concurrence aux entreprises établies à l'extérieur de la Communauté', (1975) 102 JDI 675, 676 ('[P]lutôt que de parler d'application extra territoriale du droit communautaire de la concurrence, il semble préférable de poser le problème en termes d'application de ce droit à des entreprises établies à l'extérieur des Communautés. Par sa neutralité, cette formulation évite de préjuger la conformité ou la non-conformité de cette application au regard du droit international').

[25] V Rock Grundman, 'The New Imperialism: The Extraterritorial Application of United States Law', (1980) 14 Int Law 257, also quoted by Justice Brennan in his dissenting opinion in *United States v Verdugo-Urquidez*, 494 US 259, 280–1 (1990) ('Particularly in the past decade, our Government has sought, successfully, to hold foreign nationals criminally liable under federal laws for conduct committed entirely beyond the territorial limits of the United States that nevertheless has effects in this country. Foreign nationals must now take care not to violate our drug laws, our antitrust laws, our securities laws, and a host of other federal criminal sanctions. The enormous expansion of federal criminal jurisdiction outside our Nation's boundaries has led one commentator to suggest that our country's three largest exports are now "rock music, blue jeans, and United States law"').

and consummated in France: 'the United States'. The United States are perceived to champion a geographically almost unlimited application of their own 'exceptional' legislation, a perception which is stoked by US unilateralism in world politics. The European Union and its Member States, by contrast, may be perceived, especially by Europeans themselves, as multilateralists who have due regard for foreign nations' concerns when extending their territorial sphere of jurisdiction. The working thesis of this study will indeed be that the United States applies its own laws more assertively to foreign situations than European States and the European Union (Community) do. Yet far from seeing States' jurisdictional practice through biased glasses, this study will ascertain whether perception is indeed reality. It will emerge throughout this study that, by and large, the jurisdictional reality is not at odds with the perception. However, it will also emerge that in quite a few fields of the law, notably in antitrust law and international humanitarian law, the reach of European laws may be equally broad, or at times even broader than the reach of US laws.

In this study, the term 'jurisdiction' will be used interchangeably with prescriptive jurisdiction. Prescriptive jurisdiction refers to the:

jurisdiction to prescribe, ie, to make its law applicable to the activities, relations, or status of persons, or the interests of persons in things, whether by legislation, by executive act or order, by administrative rule or regulation, or by determination by a court.[26]

Put differently, questions of prescriptive jurisdiction relate to the geographical reach of a State's laws. Questions of adjudicative and enforcement jurisdiction will only be tangentially discussed, if needed to clarify prescriptive jurisdiction.

Enforcement jurisdiction refers to a State's jurisdiction 'to enforce or compel compliance or to punish noncompliance with its laws or regulations, whether through the courts or by use of executive, administrative, police, or other nonjudicial action'.[27] While States are entitled to prescribe laws that govern situations which may be located wholly or partly abroad under rules of prescriptive jurisdiction, it is generally accepted that they are not entitled to *enforce* their laws outside their territory, 'except by virtue of a permissive rule derived from international custom or from a convention'.[28] In order to enforce laws or decisions governing transnational or foreign situations, States are therefore required to resort to territorial measures. A conviction to imprisonment, for instance, could only be enforced if the convict is voluntarily present in the territory, or if his presence

---

[26] § 401(a) Restatement (Third) of US Foreign Relations Law.
[27] ibid § 401(c).
[28] PCIJ, *SS Lotus*, PCIJ Reports, Series A, No 10, 18–19 (1927). At times, States *have* exercised their enforcement jurisdiction abroad, without the consent of the territorial State, for instance by arresting persons outside their territory (eg, the kidnapping of Adolf Eichmann in Argentina by Israeli secret agents), but such actions have usually met with considerable protest by other States. A general permissive rule of extraterritorial enforcement jurisdiction may possibly be the rule which entitles the parties in an international armed conflict to wage war in the other party's or parties' territory.

is brought about by means of extradition. Monetary judgments could only be enforced by seizing territorially located assets, or by international cooperation with the State where the defendant's assets are located.

Adjudicative jurisdiction refers to a State's jurisdiction 'to adjudicate, ie to subject persons or things to the process of its courts or administrative tribunals, whether in civil or in criminal proceedings, whether or not the state is a party to the proceedings'.[29] Adjudicative jurisdiction thus refers to the jurisdiction of the courts rather than to the reach of a State's laws. States may have legitimate prescriptive jurisdiction over a situation under international law, but may lack adjudicative jurisdiction over the situation, for instance, because the defendant has no contacts with the State, or because the parties to a private contract have chosen another adjudicative forum. In section 1.4, the interplay between prescriptive jurisdiction and adjudicative jurisdiction will be illustrated in the context of transnational regulatory jurisdiction.

It may already be noted here that, somewhat counterintuitively, *the courts* may also exercise prescriptive jurisdiction under international law.[30] Admittedly, under the separation of powers theory, the judiciary is not authorized to enact rules but only to settle disputes on the basis of rules enacted by the political branches. Nonetheless, it may occur that the reach of a particular statute is not clear. In that situation, the courts might themselves determine the reach of the statute, in light of the international law principles of jurisdiction. In so doing, they exercise prescriptive jurisdiction. In common law countries, especially in the United States, courts are ordinarily loath to directly ground their exercise of prescriptive jurisdiction on international law. Instead, presuming that Congress does not intend to apply statutes extraterritorially, they only exercise jurisdiction when Congress indeed had the intent to apply the statute to foreign situations. Theoretically, prescriptive jurisdiction then remains with the political branches, although in practice, US courts have at times conjured up congressional intent where there was clearly none, eg in the field of securities law.[31]

1.4 The Concept of Jurisdiction in Transnational Private Litigation

In criminal law litigation, courts may encounter difficulties in determining the reach of the applicable criminal law, or, put differently, in determining their prescriptive jurisdiction under international law, but at least they do not have to factor in complicated conflict of laws issues, and problems of adjudicative (ie judicial

---

[29] § 401 (b) Restatement (Third) of US Foreign Relations Law.

[30] Mann (above n 1), 'The Doctrine of Jurisdiction in International Law', (1964-I) 111 RCADI 1, 13.

[31] Subsection 3.3.b.

or personal) jurisdiction. In private litigation, by contrast, courts do face all these issues. It is not surprising that the lines between prescriptive jurisdiction, conflict of laws, and personal jurisdiction, which all stem from the transnational character of private litigation, have become blurred. A conceptual reconstruction of the exercise of jurisdiction over extraterritorial and transnational situations by courts is not an easy undertaking then. In such situations, jurisdiction becomes a multi-layered legal concept involving both public and private international law elements.[32]

In this section, an attempt will be undertaken at sketching the subtle interplay of jurisdiction and conflict of laws in transnational litigation concerning regulatory law. This section is important in that regulatory law has been among the fields of law where assertions of jurisdiction have been most controversial, and that, accordingly, a clear grasp of the jurisdictional issues at stakes is desirable.

Regulatory law may be defined here as public 'market' law aimed at protecting a public economic order, that could, in certain legal systems such as the American system, also be privately enforced, eg antitrust law or securities law.[33] It is precisely in these fields of the law that most assertions of 'extraterritorial' jurisdiction have arisen, and especially in (US) private litigation, where actors do not exercise the same degree of jurisdictional caution that regulatory agencies do. As a preliminary matter, it is appropriate to offer in this introductory chapter necessary terminological and conceptual clarification, if the reader is not to get lost in a dense forest of unfamiliar legal concepts. It will become clear in this section that the law of jurisdiction bridges the private/public international law divide. In Chapter 5, it will be shown how solutions borrowed from private international law could serve to restrain the reach of a State's laws under public international law ('the rule of reason'). That rule of reason will in turn be applied to the different fields of the law studied, also those which fall outside the realm of regulatory law (universal jurisdiction over core crimes against international law, secondary boycotts).

(a) Adjudicative and subject matter jurisdiction

It is first important to further define adjudicative jurisdiction, termed personal or *in personam* jurisdiction in the United States and judicial jurisdiction in Europe. Adjudicative jurisdiction refers to the power of courts to claim jurisdiction over persons. The rules of adjudicative jurisdiction are designed to meet the foreign defendant's legitimate expectations of being hauled before a court. As they are

---

[32] Rules of public international law in theory connect a set of facts with a particular *legislator*, and rules of private international law connects these facts with a particular *legal system*. Mann (above n 6) 28.
[33] eg on the nature of antitrust law as a mixture of penal, administrative, and civil law: B Goldman, 'Les champs d'application territoriale des lois sur la concurrence', (1969-III) 128 RCADI 631, 641–5. Also Bischoff and Kovar (above n 24) ('En tant que droit du marché, le droit de la concurrence tend à la protection de l'ordre public économique').

mainly concerned with the interests of the party to the dispute and not with the interests of the party's home State, they may be considered as private international law rules. Overbroad rules of personal jurisdiction can, however, produce ripple effects on the conduct of foreign relations. Especially if they combine with the application of forum law instead of foreign law, a foreign sovereign may feel offended when on the basis of his own conflict-of-laws rules *his* law would have been applied. In that respect, the rules of adjudicative jurisdiction may also be a concern of public international law rules ensuring a smooth functioning of inter-State relations. It comes as no surprise that the Restatement (Third) of *Foreign Relations* Law urges US courts to exercise their adjudicative jurisdiction in a reasonable manner.[34]

Historically, US courts had personal jurisdiction over a defendant if they could deliver a writ to him. A writ could be delivered as soon as the defendant was present within US territory. His presence was considered to spark 'a corollary obligation to submit to jurisdiction upon proper notification'.[35] The requirement of territorial presence was later relaxed by US courts. Nowadays, 'minimum contacts' with the US suffice for a finding of personal jurisdiction over a defendant.[36] 'Minimum contacts' are liberally construed by US courts. The mere presence of a subsidiary of a foreign corporation in the United States may, for instance, provide the necessary minimum US contacts of the parent corporation.[37] Also, transient presence of a defendant may suffice for a finding of so-called 'tag' jurisdiction by US courts.[38] The minimum contacts doctrine was originally designed to address interstate activities, but it could easily apply to activities between different nations. It is codified in § 35(1) of the Restatement of Conflict of Laws (Second).[39]

The US minimum contacts standard goes much further than the standard for judicial jurisdiction used by continental European courts, which is mainly based on the place of domicile or residence of the defendant.[40] This has at times given rise to conflicts over the reach of US judicial jurisdiction. The US Supreme Court therefore stated in 1987 that 'great care and reserve should be exercised when extending our notions of personal jurisdiction into the international field'.[41] In

---

[34] § 421 of the Restatement (Third) of US Foreign Relations Law.

[35] B Pearce, 'The Comity Doctrine as a Barrier to Judicial Jurisdiction: A U.S.-E.U. Comparison', (1994) 30 Stan J Int'l L 525, 531.

[36] *International Shoe Co v Washington*, 326 US 310, 316 (1945).

[37] *Boryk v de Havilland Aircraft Co*, 341 F 2d 666 (2d Cir 1965).

[38] *Burnham v Superior Court*, 495 US 604 (1990).

[39] § 35(1) of the Restatement (Second) ('A state has power to exercise judicial jurisdiction over an individual who does business in the state with respect to causes of action arising from the business done in the state').

[40] Council Regulation (EC) 44/2001, [2001] OJ L 12/1. Defendants can ordinarily only be sued in their place of domicile, although a number of special rules of judicial jurisdiction relating to a particular subject matter (tort, property, contract...) allow plaintiffs to sue defendants in other fora as well. English and Irish courts, however, have historically recognized that judicial jurisdiction could be premised on the mere presence of a defendant. Pearce (above n 35) 536.

[41] eg *Asahi Metal Indus. Co v Superior Court*, 480 US 102, 115 (1987).

spite of this warning, the controversy over personal jurisdiction by US courts has generally been less heated than the controversy over the reach of US laws. Conflicts over the exercise of personal jurisdiction have, much more than conflicts over the exercise of prescriptive jurisdiction, been eased by the application of the international comity principle,[42] which involves a balancing of US and foreign interests,[43] and by the application of the constitutional principle of due process informed by 'traditional notions of fair play and substantial justice'.[44]

In the United States, the specific category of subject matter jurisdiction exists alongside the category of personal jurisdiction. Both personal and subject matter jurisdiction should be present before a US court can actually entertain a claim. Where personal jurisdiction refers to the court's jurisdiction over a person does subject matter jurisdiction refer to jurisdiction over the subject matter of a dispute. Subject matter jurisdiction relates to the existence of a cause of action for a controversy under US law, or simply put, to the question of whether a statute applies to a particular conduct.[45] Not all controversies can indeed be brought before US courts, even if personal jurisdiction over the parties can be readily secured. A claim is only actionable in US courts if US law provides for jurisdiction over its subject matter. For instance, if the Alien Tort Statute[46] had not provided for a cause of action in US district courts for violations of the law of nations, these courts would never be in a capacity to legitimately establish their subject matter jurisdiction over such violations, even if the parties to the dispute had sufficient minimal contacts with the US for purposes of personal jurisdiction.

In US practice, problems of subject matter jurisdiction usually arise not over *whether* US courts have subject matter jurisdiction over a case, but over *which*

---

[42] Pearce (above n 35) 536.

[43] eg *World-Wide Volkswagen Corp v Woodson*, 444 US 286 (1980) (calling on lower courts to weigh the interests of 'several States' in 'judicial resolution of the dispute and the advancement of substantive policies').

[44] *International Shoe Co v Washington*, 326 US 310, 315 (1945) (ruling that 'due process requires only that in order to subject a defendant to a judgment *in personam*, if he be not present within the territory of the forum, he have certain minimum contacts with it such that the maintenance of the suit does not offend traditional notions of fair play and substantial justice'); *Helicopteros Nacionales de Colombia v Hall*, 466 US 408, 415–16 (1984) (demanding that 'the defendant's contacts with the forum [be] continuous and systematic, or that the suit [arise] out of or is related to those contacts'); *In the Matter of an Application to Enforce Admin. Subpoenas Duces Tecum of the SEC v Knowles*, 87 F 3d 413, 417 (10th Cir 1996) ('Even a single purposeful contact may be sufficient to meet the minimum contacts standard when the underlying proceeding is directly related to that contact'); *WorldWide Volkswagen Corp v Woodson*, 444 US 286, 297 (1980) (requiring 'that the defendant's conduct and connection with the forum state are such that he should reasonably anticipate being haled into court there'); *Burger King v Rudzewicz*, 471 US 462, 473 (1985) ('Where a forum seeks to assert specific jurisdiction over an out-of-state defendant who has not consented to suit there, this "fair warning" requirement is satisfied if the defendant has "purposefully directed" his activities at residents of the forum, and the litigation results from alleged injuries that "arise out of or relate to" those activities') (citation omitted).

[45] eg PR Wood, *International Loans, Bonds and Securities Regulation* (1995) 363, nr 20–4.

[46] 28 USC § 1350 (1988).

US courts—federal or state courts—can entertain the case. Under US constitutional law, federal courts have only limited subject matter jurisdiction, while state courts enjoy plenary subject matter jurisdiction.[47] For the purposes of this study, the requirement of US subject matter jurisdiction may appear of lesser importance, in that the analysis is limited to disputes arising under statutes conferring specific federal question jurisdiction, such as the antitrust and securities laws, and the Alien Tort Statute.

(b) The interplay of private and public international law

US district courts have undisputed subject matter jurisdiction over complaints alleging antitrust and securities laws violations if they are not frivolous. The main question then is whether the plaintiff has a cause of action under US law, or whether instead foreign laws should apply to the dispute.[48] US courts may regard this as a question of subject matter jurisdiction as well,[49] although it is rather a question of conflict of laws (a question which also arises in European courts that have established their judicial jurisdiction). If a court has adjudicative and subject matter jurisdiction, this does not imply that it may apply forum law. Under the rules governing conflict of laws, a court may well be required to apply *foreign* law.

In regulatory, public law matters (which are nevertheless privately enforced), such as securities and antitrust matters, the courts do, however, not face the choice of applying forum law or foreign law. As courts do not apply the public laws of another nation,[50] they either apply domestic regulatory law, or they dismiss the

---

[47] Article III of the US Constitution. Statutory authorization for federal subject matter jurisdiction for federal courts can be found in 28 USC §§ 1331 and 1332(a)(2) and (3). These provisions set forth that federal courts have federal question jurisdiction, and diversity and alienage jurisdiction.

[48] *Compare Hartford Fire Insurance Co v California*, 509 US 764, 813 (1993) (Scalia J, dissenting) ('The second question—the extraterritorial reach of the Sherman Act—has nothing to do with the jurisdiction of the courts. It is a question of substantive law turning on whether, in enacting the Sherman Act, Congress asserted regulatory power over the challenged conduct'). The distinction between subject matter jurisdiction and the territorial scope of US (antitrust) laws as an additional element of the claim is not entirely academic. In the United States, issues relating to subject matter jurisdiction can be resolved early in the litigation by deciding whether plaintiffs have a federal claim under Federal Rule of Civil Procedure 12(b)(1) (which provides for a motion to dismiss for lack of subject matter jurisdiction). In contrast, if the determination of the territorial scope of US laws is treated as an additional element of the claim, the analysis goes to the merits (motion for summary judgment on the merits in the absence of a genuine issue of material fact) and could delay resolution of the case, thereby producing an effect on foreign markets while the case is pending. Courts have therefore often considered the effects test to be a matter of subject matter jurisdiction. The 7th Circuit recently ruled that, as a matter of policy, 'treating the matter [the Federal Trade Antitrust Improvements Act] as one of subject matter jurisdiction reduces the potential for offending the economic policies of other nations' (*United Phosphorus, Ltd v Angus Chemical Co*, 322 F 3d 942, 952 (7th Cir 2003)).

[49] Comment c to § 401 of the Restatement (Third) of US Foreign Relations Law.

[50] *Holman v Johnson* (1775) 98 ER 1120 (KB) ('No country ever takes notice of the revenue laws of another country'); *The Antelope*, 23 US (10 Wheat) 66, 123 (1825) (Marshall, CJ), ('The

case.[51] Unlike with respect to non-regulatory tort matters, courts of the forum are unlikely to enforce foreign securities and antitrust laws in private suits involving claims for damages, because securities and antitrust laws reflect, much more than classical tort laws, the particular political economy and sovereignty of a State.[52] In regulatory matters, rules on the conflict of laws have no decisive role to play. As a violation of the forum's economic regulations not only jeopardizes private but also public interests,[53] the court will shun traditional conflict of laws rules, and consistently apply forum law.

A court may, however, not apply forum law at will, lest it overstep the jurisdictional limits set by international law.[54] A determination of the applicable law then yields to a determination of the precise scope of forum law,[55] or again, choice of law dissolves into prescriptive jurisdiction under international law. An inquiry into whether or not forum law applies to regulatory cases is no longer a choice-of-law analysis, but rather an inquiry under public international law, which 'does not tell us what law is to be applied in a given case', but 'requires a choice between two systems each of which may claim to be closely connected with the issue at hand'.[56] In US terms, where US antitrust and securities laws

---

Courts of no country execute the penal laws of another'); *Guiness v Miller*, 291 F 769, 770 (SDNY 1923) ('[N]o court can enforce any law but that of its own sovereign.'); *United States v Aluminium Corp of America*, 148 F 2d 416, 443 (2d Cir 1945) ('[A]s a court of the United States, we cannot look beyond our own law.'). Dodge attributes the unwillingness to apply foreign law not only to the public law taboo, as epitomized by *The Antelope*, but also to the absence of a federal question in case US federal law does not apply—which deprives the federal courts of jurisdiction. WS Dodge, 'Extraterritoriality and Conflict-of-Laws Theory: An Argument for Judicial Unilateralism', (1998) 39 Harv Int'l L J 101, 109, n 40. Contra this received wisdom Lowenfeld (above n 17) 30. See for statutes that nonetheless provide for the application of another State's antitrust laws by the forum: article 137 of the Swiss Private International Law Code; article 99, § 2, 2° of the Belgian Private International Law Code.

[51] Also HL Buxbaum, 'Conflict of Economic Laws: From Sovereignty to Substance', (2002) 42 Va J Int'l L 931, 935 (pointing out that the extraterritorial application of US regulatory law does not raise choice-of-law questions in the strict sense of that term, although at the same time noting that 'traditional choice-of-law jurisprudence is often used to analyze the extraterritorial reach of regulatory laws').

[52] Also J Kaffanke, 'Nationales Wirtschaftsrecht und internationaler Sachverhalt', (1989) 27 Archiv des Völkerrechts 129. Cf MM Siems, 'The Rules on Conflict of Laws in the European Takeover Directive', (2004) European Company and Financial Law Review 458, 463 (pointing out that in economic law, 'the rules on conflict of laws do not follow the neutral principle of the closest connection, because their scope often depends on their content, namely the protection of the capital market and of the investors').

[53] eg HG Maier, 'Extraterritorial Jurisdiction at a Crossroads: An Intersection Between Public and Private International Law', (1982) 76 AJIL 280, 289 ('A government always has a direct interest in the outcome of a regulatory case, even when the governmental viewpoint is represented by a citizen-prosecutor seeking private recovery').

[54] Although norms of public international law may not always be directly applicable in the domestic legal order, they could, however, still be indirectly applied through the presumption of consistency of domestic law with international norms (Bianchi (above n 20) 81), an interpretive technique which is widely used in the United States, where it is known as the *Charming Betsy* canon of statutory construction (*The Charming Betsy*, 6 US (2 Cranch) 132, 143 (1804)).

[55] Cf GA Bermann, *Transnational Litigation* (2003) 80; Buxbaum (above n 51) 935.

[56] Mann (above n 6) 31.

confer exclusive and full subject matter jurisdiction on federal courts over antitrust and securities violations *in abstracto*, a determination of subject matter jurisdiction *in concreto* is subject to a determination of the laws' scope of application.[57]

The interesting thing now is that, especially in the United States, choice of law considerations are not entirely abandoned in the analysis, as courts may use the factors underlying choice of law analysis so as determine the precise scope of US law and the reasonableness of assertions of prescriptive jurisdiction under section 403 of the Restatement (Third) of US Foreign Relations Law, a section which will be discussed separately in Chapter 5. This may appear counterintuitive. While both public international law and conflict of laws delimit the competence of States and were historically not treated separately,[58] conflict of laws is now in essence *municipal* and thus *subjective* law. Is public international law, which is more objective in that its standards stem from the contemporary practice of States,[59] not supposed to limit the freedom of States in adopting conflict of laws rules in order to protect the interests of other States?[60]

The explanation for the resurfacing of choice of law factors in the analysis of the scope of regulatory law is that these factors are aimed at identifying the most significant relationship of a legal situation with a particular sovereign.[61] They may mitigate the excesses of jurisdiction stemming from the unqualified exercise

[57] Cf Buxbaum (above n 51) 941 ('The method of resolving [conflicts of legislative jurisdiction] is to fold a consideration of competing jurisdictional claims into the analysis of statutory scope: despite the existence of a jurisdictional basis [. . .], the regulatory interests of another country may be held sufficient to preclude application of U.S. law to that conduct'). Cf *Hartford Fire Insurance Co v California*, 509 US 764, 796 n 22 (1993) (majority stating, rebuffing Justice Scalia, that the Sherman Act is a 'prime exampl[e] of the simultaneous exercise of prescriptive jurisdiction [ie jurisdiction relating to the territorial scope of U.S. law] and grant of subject matter jurisdiction').

[58] Mann (above n 6) 17 and 24.

[59] Bianchi (above n 20) 80.

[60] Mann (above n 6) 19. Contra G. Fitzmaurice, 'The General Principles of International Law', (1957-II) 92 RCADI 1, 218–22 (submitting that 'apparently, public international law does not effect any delimitation of spheres of competence in the civil sphere, and seems to leave the matter entirely to private international law', and somewhat naïvely believing that States will apply their conflict of laws rules reasonably, without being required to do so under public international law, because such would be in their own national interests). One may wonder why, if 'honesty is the best policy', or 'sincerity is worth any artifice', the international community actually developed binding rules of criminal jurisdiction, as if in the field of criminal law, an organically developed world order proved more elusive than in the field of civil law. In the mould of Fitzmaurice also C Scott, 'Translating Torture into Transnational Tort: Conceptual Divides in the Debate on Corporate Accountability for Human Rights Harms', in C Scott, ed, *Torture as Tort* (2001) 52 (arguing that general public international law does not constrain private international law, and that each State chooses what rules to adopt). As the jurisdictional norms of both private and public international law are based on the nexus of a particular situation with (the law of) a particular sovereign, norms of private international law 'may sometimes in fact reflect an *opinio iuris* of international law', without it being necessary to systematically inquire the conformity of these norms with public international law. KM Meessen, 'Drafting Rules on Extraterritorial Jurisdiction', in Meessen (above n 7) 225, 227.

[61] § 6 of the Restatement (Second) of Conflict of Laws.

of jurisdiction on the basis of the classical public international law principles.[62] Although it is precisely public international law that is theoretically supposed to restrain private international law, the indeterminacy of the public international law rules of jurisdiction, the territorial principle in particular, makes these rules so malleable that they may justify nearly every jurisdictional assertion. Unlike public international law rules, which merely require a *strong* nexus of the regulating State with a situation, conflict of laws rules are ordinarily geared to identifying the State with the *strongest* nexus to the situation.[63] Rules of private international law are therefore particularly appropriate to solve normative competency conflicts.[64] In contrast, traditional rules of public international law, which allow several States to exercise their jurisdiction over one and the same situation, will cast aside only the most outrageous assertions.[65]

The choice of law rules resorted to so as to assess the reach of a State's regulatory laws are not only geared to mediating conflicts between sovereign nations. In fact, their traditional goal is to ensure predictability and legal certainty for private actors. Confusion and tension may arise here, because regulatory law is essentially public law, which is also enforced by private actors. The scope of application of regulatory law has typically been cast in public international law terms,[66] regulators being in the first place concerned not to overstep the international law limits that delimit their jurisdictional sphere from other regulators' spheres. If the reasonableness of a State's jurisdictional assertion may not only be a function of respect for the interests

---

[62] Also Lowenfeld (above n 17) 45 (submitting that 'the issues of jurisdiction to prescribe can and should be addressed by reference to contacts, interests, and expectations [ie the factors set forth in section 403 of the Restatement]—that is to say meaningful contacts, genuine interests, and justified expectations—rather than with reference to the traditional vocabulary of public international law, focused on the over-used concept of sovereignty').

[63] Schuster (above n 3) 59.

[64] Comment c to § 101 of the Restatement (Third) of US Foreign Relations Law clarifies the interplay of public and private international law as follows: 'In some circumstances, issues of private international law may also implicate issues of public international law, and many matters of private international law have substantial international significance and therefore may be considered foreign relations law... The concepts, doctrines, and considerations that inform private international law also guide the development of some areas of public international law, notably the principles limiting the jurisdiction of states to prescribe, adjudicate and enforce law [citing, inter alia, §§ 402–3]... Increasingly, public international law impinges on private international activity, for example, the law of jurisdiction and judgments...'

[65] Cf DJ Gerber, 'The Extraterritorial Application of the German Antitrust Laws', (1983) 77 AJIL 756 (arguing that the (public international law) jurisdictional principles are insufficiently developed to account for the needs of the forum States and the interests of other States). The structure of the jurisdictional sections of the influential Restatement (Third) of US Foreign Relations Law (1987) may serve to illustrate this. § 402 of the Restatement sets out the classical public international law principles on which jurisdiction may be premised: the territoriality, nationality and protective principles. Aware of the potentially broad sweep of § 402, § 403 subjects any exercise of jurisdiction on the basis of the § 402, by setting forth a set of conflict of laws-based factors to determine whether the exercise of jurisdiction is reasonable. The section 403 factors may protect the interests of private actors—by conferring predictability and legal certainty on their international transactions—as well as the interests of States.

[66] Cf HL Buxbaum, 'The Private Attorney General in a Global Age: Public Interests in Private Antitrust Litigation', (2001) 26 Yale J Int'l L 219, 220.

of sovereign nations, but also of predictability and legal certainty for private actors, the latter 'assumes more significance as a regulatory goal in itself'.[67] Thus, in the field of regulatory law, rules of prescriptive jurisdiction merge with choice of law rules, and, accordingly, do not only arbitrate sovereign interests, but also the claims and interests of private actors.[68] Needless to say, public interests and private interests will not always be neatly aligned in the absence of a robust mediation system conferring genuine predictability on the balancing process operated under § 403. This may explain the prevailing inconsistency in court decisions.[69]

(c) Distinguishing private and public international law rules

The mixture of public and private international law rules in the assessment of the reach of a State's regulatory laws captures the peculiar US approach to prescriptive jurisdiction. Europeans do not seem to inject private international law considerations into the analysis of prescriptive jurisdiction. The absence of such considerations may be explained by the fact that regulatory law is hardly privately enforced in Europe. However, as will be discussed, not only do US courts deciding private cases take choice of law into account, but so do US regulators. While it may be argued that US regulators piggybacked on the courts' approach—in the field of antitrust law there is some evidence thereof—it appears that there is something more at stake.

In regulatory cases, European States may put a higher premium on sovereignty-informed considerations than on considerations informed by predictability for private economic actors, because public international law purportedly does not oblige States to take private interests into account. Notably Professor Meessen has forcefully argued in favour of distinguishing public and private international law rules.[70] His main argument against the role of private international law in determining the reach of a State's laws indeed appears to be that 'on the level of relations between sovereign states, domestic rules of conflict of laws cannot, of course, be relied upon at all', as '[t]he perspective of conflict of laws lies within a state' and 'is directed to domestic interests, both public and private'.[71] In Meessen's view, in conflict of laws, '[f]oreign interests are relevant only insofar as they form part of the state's foreign policy, for instance, if they reflect considerations of reciprocity'.[72]

---

[67] Buxbaum (above n 51) 944.

[68] Buxbaum (above n 66) 262 (pointing out that 'the traditional separation between public and private becomes unproductive').

[69] In international contract disputes, the public interests have been subordinated to private interests, which may explain the more consistent application of conflict-of-laws rules. ibid 221.

[70] He has nonetheless admitted that 'in deciding practical cases, rules of each system will often have to be applied cumulatively'. KM Meessen, 'Antitrust Jurisdiction under Customary International Law', (1984) 78 AJIL 783, 789–90.

[71] ibid 790.   [72] ibid.

Meessen arguably takes an unduly narrow approach to the role of conflicts of law in deciding transnational regulatory cases. He may mistakenly believe that '[t]he perspective of [public] international law stands above the sovereign states'.[73] In the noumenal world, there may indeed be a layer of international law that is disinterested as it is precisely created by mutual consent of sovereign States. However, rules of customary international law, especially in the field of jurisdiction, are often vague, and need elaboration by domestic courts in order to be operationalized in a phenomenal world, in specific cases. In essence, classical public international law rules make up a set of extremely malleable principles that allow States to 'pull for the home crowd' at their discretion. Only domestic courts' development of a second layer of norms applicable to transnational situations might genuinely mitigate a State's jurisdictional assertions. These norms derive from the concept of comity. Comity has been adopted as an ill-defined principle of *public* international law, but, as will be shown in Chapter 5, at 5.1, is historically the concept underpinning the whole system of *private* international law, a system that tries to link a private legal transaction or situation to the law of a particular sovereign in order to confer predictability on legal transactions.

Predictability not only serves private actors, but also sovereign actors. States will usually be reluctant to apply their laws to private transnational situations that other States also have an interest in regulating. Private international law, although domestic law, is thus not necessarily a complex of norms that is pro-forum biased and does not adequately heed foreign interests. Obviously, in certain cases the forum State's interests may be considered as controlling even in the face of equally strong foreign States' interests. Yet as a general matter, rules of private international law attempt to tie a situation to a particular sovereign in a much more intricate and neutral way than catch-all rules of public international law do.

Meessen admits that public international law only provides modest answers, answers that 'may often be supplemented by richer ones of conflict of laws'.[74] One is therefore at a loss why he takes so much issue with the apparent lack of distinction between public and private international law. Classical public international law rules are indeed the poor relation in the field of prescriptive jurisdiction. Arguably, Meessen hopes that courts take a more public international law approach through looking for international consensus on the application of specific conflict of laws rules.[75] Conflict of laws rules may thus come to reflect public international law rules, and the fields of private and public international law may ultimately be (re-)united.

This brings us to the question whether the 'concepts, doctrines, and considerations that inform private international law' that make up the rule of reason set

---

[73] ibid.   [74] ibid.
[75] ibid. ('Rules of conflict of laws may be part of state practice and thereby contribute to the formation of customary international law'.)

forth in § 403 of the Restatement (Third) of US Foreign Relations Law are so widely shared within the international community as to constitute State practice and qualify as norms of *public* international law. The Restatement itself believes they are, and that the rule of reason is a rule of customary international law, which should accordingly be applied by any State—not only the United States—when exercising jurisdiction.[76] Most authors, however, believe that the rule of reason is *not* international law. In Chapter 5, the international law nature of the rule of reason will be discussed in greater detail.

1.5 Concluding Remarks

In this first introductory chapter, the scope and method of this study have been presented. It has been set out that this study aims at developing a rule-based framework of jurisdiction under international law, from a transatlantic perspective. In addition, as a preliminary matter, different concepts of jurisdiction—prescriptive or legislative, enforcement, adjudicative, judicial or personal, subject matter—have been clarified. It has been shown that, while this study is mainly concerned with issues of *prescriptive* jurisdiction under public international law, such issues become inexorably entangled in a web of private international law concepts of jurisdiction and choice of law, because, especially in the field of economic law, States typically apply their laws to private parties, and private parties may have a role to play in enforcing economic laws. Disentanglement requires recourse to one basic principle: reasonableness, the common thread throughout this study.

Under the classical law of jurisdiction under public international law, choice-of-law concepts of reasonableness did not play a prominent role, however, possibly because the law of jurisdiction was seen as primarily governing the ambit of the criminal law. In the next chapter, the traditional public international law approaches to jurisdiction will be discussed. Later on, this study will return to reasonableness, and advocate it as a solution for the curse of concurrent jurisdiction. Concurrent jurisdiction is indeed the inevitable result of the classical public international law approaches: especially in the economic field the effects of certain practices may fan out globally nowadays, thereby possibly providing connections that are sufficient for more than one State to exercise their jurisdiction.

---

[76] In an apparent rebuff of Professor Meessen's critique of the operation of private international law, comment a to § 403 states that '[t]he principle [of reasonableness/comity] applies regardless of the status of relations between the state exercising jurisdiction and another state whose interests may be affected. While the term "comity" is sometimes understood to include a requirement of reciprocity, the rule of this section is not conditional on a finding that the state affected by a regulation would exercise or limit its jurisdiction in the same circumstances to the same extent.'

2

Public International Law Approaches to Jurisdiction

Under public international law, two approaches could logically be taken to the question of jurisdiction. Either one allows States to exercise jurisdiction as they see fit, unless there is a prohibitive rule to the contrary, or one prohibits States from exercising jurisdiction as they see fit, unless there is a permissive rule to the contrary. The first approach was taken by the Permanent Court of International Justice (PCIJ) in the 1927 *Lotus* case (section 2.1). The second approach, which purportedly reflects customary international law, has been taken by most States and the majority of the doctrine. Under this approach, States are *not* authorized to exercise their jurisdiction, unless they could rely on such permissive principles as the territoriality, personality, protective, and universality principles (section 2.2). It is unclear which doctrine has the upper hand. Not surprisingly, for purposes of shifting the burden of proof to the other party, States which assert their jurisdiction tend to rely on *Lotus*, whereas States which oppose another State's jurisdictional assertions tend to rely on the permissive principles approach.

In practice, a consensus opinion has crystallized. This opinion seems mainly informed by the restrictive approach, in that it requires States to justify their jurisdictional assertion in terms of a permissive international law rule. Indeed, leaving States almost unfettered jurisdictional discretion may run counter to the very regulating purpose of the international law of jurisdiction: delimiting States' spheres of action and thus reducing conflicts between States.[1] However, because a strict categorization of permissive principles may fail to do justice to legitimate State interests threatened by unfriendly foreign action (a categorization which requires that States wait for a norm of customary international law authorizing

---

[1] eg JE Ferry, 'Towards Completing the Charm: The Woodpulp Judgment', (1989) EIPLR 19, 21 (stating, in the context of the law of jurisdiction, that 'the objective of international law' is to 'help to reduce conflicts between states'); J-M Bischoff and R Kovar, 'L'application du droit communautaire de la concurrence aux entreprises établies à l'extérieur de la Communauté', (1975) 102 JDI 675, 712 (stating that '[i]l appartient au droit international de s'efforcer de résoudre les conflits susceptibles de naître d'une...pluralité de compétences'); HL Buxbaum, 'Transnational Regulatory Litigation', (2006) 46 Va J Int'l L 251, 304 (stating that the very purpose of international law 'is to safeguard the international community against overreaching by individual nations').

a new jurisdictional assertion to crystallize),[2] this opinion has construed the permissive principles rather broadly: States are generally considered to be authorized to exercise jurisdiction if they could advance a legitimate interest based on personal or territorial connections of the matter to be regulated. The indeterminacy of 'connections' and 'interests' has made States' room for action actually very broad, and has led to an internationally sanctioned system of possibly harmful concurring jurisdiction. In Chapters 5 and 6, a way out of the conundrum of concurring jurisdiction engendered by the broadly construed permissive principles approach will be sought.

2.1 The *Lotus* Case

In 1923, the PCIJ held, in passing, in the case of the *Nationality Decrees in Tunis and Morocco* that 'jurisdiction which in principle, belongs solely to the State, is limited by rules of international law'.[3] Four years later, in the *Lotus* case, a case directly concerning the question of jurisdiction, the Court elaborated on this reference in an opinion which still constitutes the basic framework of reference for questions of jurisdiction under international law. Since *Lotus*, the PCIJ and the International Court of Justice (ICJ) have not directly addressed the doctrine of (extraterritorial) jurisdiction. This is not to say that this doctrine has not been developing, on the contrary. Yet the development has come about solely in national legal practice, without supervisory guidance by an international court or regulator.[4]

In 1926, the PCIJ was requested to settle a dispute between Turkey and France with regard to a collision on the high seas.[5] On 2 August 1926, the French mail steamer *Lotus* had collided with the Turkish collier *Boz-Kourt*, as a result of which eight Turkish sailors had perished. When the French steamer arrived in Constantinople the next day, Turkish authorities started investigations in

---

[2] W Meng, 'Neuere Entwicklungen im Streit um die Jurisdiktionshoheit der Staaten im Bereich der Wettbewerbsbeschränkungen', (1981) 41 ZaörRV 469, 471 (criticizing the permissive principles approach on the ground that under this approach, a State would violate international law 'der einen neu aftauchenden Sachverhalt rechtlich regelt, ohne dass hierzu bereits eine entsprechende völkerrechtliche Ermächtigungsnorm bestände. Schätzt man das Trägheitsmoment bei der Bildung von Völkerrechtsatzen realistisch ein, so bestehen bereits unter pragmatischem Gesichtspunkt entscheidende Einwände gegen diese Theorie').

[3] PCIJ, Advisory Opinion *Nationality Decrees in Tunis and Morocco*, PCIJ Reports, Series B, No 4, 23–4 (1923).

[4] FA Mann, 'The Doctrine of Jurisdiction Revisited after Twenty Years', (1984-III) 186 RCADI 9, 53 (pointing out that 'the material of international origin which has a bearing upon the doctrine of jurisdiction is extremely meager. The material of national origin is enormous'); CL Blakesley, 'Extraterritorial Jurisdiction', in MC Bassiouni, ed, *International Criminal Law II: Procedural and Enforcement Mechanisms* (2nd edn 1999) 37 (stating that the international law on jurisdiction is much less developed than the domestic law on jurisdiction).

[5] PCIJ, *SS Lotus* (France v Turkey), PCIJ Reports, Series A, No 10, p 19 (1927).

the case. Two days later, Lieutenant Demons, the officer of the watch of the *Lotus*, a French national, was placed under arrest. On 15 September 1926, a Turkish criminal court sentenced him to 80 days' imprisonment and a fine of twenty-two pounds. During the proceedings, France lobbied heavily, and contended that, by bringing Demons to justice, Turkey acted in conflict with the principles of international law.[6] On 12 October 1926, France and Turkey signed a special agreement in which they submitted the question of jurisdiction which had arisen in the *Lotus* case to the PCIJ. In 1927, in a controversial verdict, decided by the president's casting vote, the PCIJ ruled that Turkey was indeed entitled to institute criminal proceedings against the French officer. Even though the case could barely be considered as representative for jurisdictional conflicts, *Lotus* soon became the main standard of reference for such conflicts in all legal areas. It will also be treated as such in this study (although with quite a few reservations). It is therefore useful to discuss the Court's holdings in greater detail.

In *Lotus*, the PCIJ made the important distinction between enforcement and prescriptive jurisdiction. Whereas States would be precluded from enforcing their laws in another State's territory absent a permissive rule to the contrary, international law would pose no limits on a State's jurisdiction to prescribe its rules for persons and events outside its borders absent a prohibitive rule to the contrary. The Court held as to enforcement jurisdiction:

[T]he first and foremost restriction imposed by international law upon a State is that—failing the existence of a permissive rule to the contrary—it may not exercise its power in any form in the territory of another State. In this sense jurisdiction is certainly territorial; it cannot be exercised by a State outside its territory except by virtue of a permissive rule derived from international custom or from a convention.[7]

A State cannot use coercive power to enforce its rules outside its territory. Stating the contrary would mean shattering the sacrosanct principle of sovereign equality of nations. A State cannot use military force to compel another State to abide by its laws. Likewise, a State cannot resort to legal implementation measures such as penalties, fines, seizures, investigations, or demands for information to give extraterritorial effect to its rules.[8]

---

[6] ibid 18.
[7] ibid 18–19.
[8] Also *Alvarez-Machain v United States*, 331 F 3d 604 (9th Cir 2003). The United States had argued that the abduction of the plaintiff in Mexico was lawful pursuant to its authority to apply US criminal law extraterritorially under the Controlled Substances Act, 21 USC § 878(a)(3). The Ninth Circuit disagreed, noting that Congress did not authorize the unilateral, extraterritorial enforcement of this provision in foreign countries by US agents. According to the Ninth Circuit, '[e]xtraterritorial application, in other words, does not automatically give rise to extraterritorial enforcement authority. Cf *United States v Alvarez-Machain*, 112 S Ct 2188 (1992); B Stern, 'L'extraterritorialité revisitée: Où il est question des affaires *Alvarez-Machain*, *Pâte de bois* et de quelques autres...', (1992) 38 AFDI 268–88.

In contrast, the Court held that international law would *permit* jurisdiction to *prescribe* rules extraterritorially:

It does not, however, follow that international law prohibits a State from exercising jurisdiction in its own territory, in respect of any case which relates to acts which have taken place abroad, and in which it cannot rely on some permissive rule of international law. Such a view would only be tenable if international law contained a general prohibition to States to extend the application of their laws and the jurisdiction of their courts to persons, property and acts outside their territory, and if, as an exception to this general prohibition, it allowed States to do so in certain specific cases. But this is certainly not the case under international law as it stands at present. Far from laying down a general prohibition to the effect that States may not extend the application of their laws and the jurisdiction of their courts to persons, property and acts outside their territory, it leaves them in this respect a wide measure of discretion which is only limited in certain cases by prohibitive rules; as regards other cases, every State remains free to adopt the principles which it regards as best and most suitable.[9]

Thus, under *Lotus*, States could set rules for persons, property and acts outside their territory in the absence of a prohibitive rule, provided that they enforce these rules territorially (in keeping with the ban on extraterritorial enforcement jurisdiction). Indeed, the Court held that 'the territoriality of criminal law [. . .] is not an absolute principle of international law and by no means coincides with territorial sovereignty'.[10] Territorial sovereignty would relate to enforcement jurisdiction, but not to prescriptive jurisdiction. States would be free to exercise their jurisdiction extraterritorially absent a prohibitive rule to the contrary. Such a rule might emerge through abstract declarations of *opinio juris* made before the claim to extraterritorial jurisdiction is made, and by protesting the claim once it is made.[11]

On the face of it, it may require some imagination to separate extraterritorial prescriptive or legislative jurisdiction from its logical complement enforcement jurisdiction. Surely, a State that enacts rules governing conduct outside its territory (prescriptive jurisdiction) also wants to have them implemented there, under the threat of sanctions (enforcement jurisdiction)? This is no doubt true. However, a State can use indirect territorial means to induce the conduct it desires. As Jennings observed, '[. . .] the excessive devotion to legalism has often blinded us to the fact that the exercise of straight jurisdiction over a person present in the territory may—albeit indirectly—be in fact the most effective way of exercising the State's power extraterritorially'.[12] If a person outside the territory

---

[9] *Lotus* (above n 5) 18–19.   [10] ibid 20.

[11] AV Lowe, 'Blocking Extraterritorial Jurisdiction: the British Protection of Trading Interests Act, 1980', (1981) 75 AJIL 257, 263.

[12] R Jennings, *Extraterritorial Application of Trade Legislation* (1964) 311, cited in B Stern, 'Can the United States Set Rules for the World? A French View', (1997:4) 31 JWT 14. Illustrating that States may prescribe unreasonable laws while enforcing them reasonably, and vice versa, O'Keefe even argues that '[j]urisdiction to prescribe and jurisdiction to enforce are logically independent of each other'. He admits nonetheless that the act of prescription and the act of enforcement are, in

does not abide by the norm prescribed extraterritorially, he could be sued in the territory of the enacting State. If he does not pay the fine, his assets in the territory could be seized. Similarly, he could be precluded from entering the territory or registering with a government agency. Thus, territorial enforcement jurisdiction could compel persons to comply with norms prescribed extraterritorially. When a person has no assets in the territory of the prescribing State and does not entertain contacts with that State, extraterritorial jurisdiction will ordinarily prove ineffective.

In claiming jurisdictional freedom for States, *Lotus* reaffirmed the voluntary nature of international law. Reflecting on the nature of international law, the Court recalled that '[t]he rules of law binding upon States...emanate from their own free will', and that '[r]estrictions upon the independence of States cannot therefore be presumed'.[13] It paid no, or at least only marginal attention, to the sovereignty or independence of *another* State that might possibly be encroached upon by the assertions of the regulating State. While this may appear lamentable, one should nonetheless concede that the PCIJ in fact anticipated the increasing irrelevance of physical borders in a time of exploding transnational mobility of persons and activities.[14] In the modern era, genuine sovereign equality of States may not imply that States always refrain from exercising extraterritorial jurisdiction, but, rather on the contrary, that 'the people whom that sovereignty protects' ought not to be placed 'at the mercy of the internal acts and politics' of another sovereign.[15] Consequently, '[a] consensual legal system could not, in logic or practice, contain a rule prohibiting a sovereign state from prescribing rules against activities outside its borders that have harmful effects within the state's territory', ie from exercising (effects-based) jurisdiction.[16]

The flipside of the *Lotus* decision is an inflation of possible assertions of concurrent jurisdiction by different States.[17] Moreover, if States could, at the level of exercising jurisdiction, do as they please as long as no prohibitive rule to the contrary has crystallized, the very regulating role of international law may be negated.[18]

---

practice, intertwined. R O'Keefe, 'Universal Jurisdiction: Clarifying the Basic Concept', (2004) 2 JICJ 735, 741.

[13] *Lotus* (above n 5) 18–19.

[14] FA Mann, 'The Doctrine of Jurisdiction in International Law', (1964-I) 111 RCADI 1, 36 (pointing out that the rejection of a strict test of territoriality 'would not be inconsistent with the requirements of modern life').

[15] HG Maier, 'Jurisdictional Rules in Customary International Law', in KM Meessen, ed, *Extraterritorial Jurisdiction in Theory and Practice* (1996) 64, 66.

[16] ibid.

[17] Cf M Inazumi, *Universal Jurisdiction in Modern International Law: Expansion of National Jurisdiction for Prosecuting Serious Crimes under International Law* (2005) 138 (also drawing a link with the terrorism conventions of the 1970s, which seem to depart from the pre-eminence or even exclusivity of the principle of territoriality).

[18] WW Cook, 'The Application of the Criminal Law of a Country to Acts Committed by Foreigners Outside the Jurisdiction', (1934) 40 W Va LQ 303, 326 (arguing that 'if states really were fully "sovereign",... there would be no such thing as "international law"'); MR Garcia-Mora, 'Criminal Jurisdiction Over Foreigners for Treason and Offenses Against the Safety of the State

Aware of this danger, in the 1970 *Barcelona Traction* case before the ICJ (which did not directly revolve around issues of jurisdiction), Judge Fitzmaurice therefore implicitly amended, albeit cautiously, the *Lotus* decision, emphasizing jurisdictional limits and restraint under international law, without, however, indicating the existence of particular international norms.[19] In the field of criminal law, a number of jurisdictional principles have been derived from joint State practice and convictions. They arguably constitute customary international law. Their underlying structure appears as a scathing indictment of the *Lotus* theory of jurisdiction unbound. The basic norm is not the *Lotus*-like jurisdictional merry-go-round with States doing whatever they like, but the prohibition of extending a State's jurisdiction beyond its physical borders. Other jurisdictional principles merely function as exceptions to the territoriality principle (see Chapters 3 and 4).

2.2 Customary International Law

(a) Persisting influence of *Lotus*

The *Lotus* judgment has been vehemently criticized in the doctrine. It is nowadays often considered as obsolete,[20] and even as never having been a precedent at all.[21] Nevertheless, States continue to rely on it, as it is the only judgment of

Committed Upon Foreign Territory', (1958) U Pitt L Rev 567, 568 (terming the postulate of absolute sovereignty 'the denial of a community of interests existing in the World Society and the belief that States live in isolation concerned only with interests of their own', and that 'its continuous adherence is highly incompatible with the existence of a World Society fundamentally grounded on the conception of the interdependence of States').

[19] ICJ, Case concerning *Barcelona Traction, Light and Power Co Ltd* (Belgium v Spain), ICJ Reports 105 (1970) ('It is true that under present conditions international law does not impose hard and fast rules on States delimiting spheres of national jurisdiction in such matters—namely bankruptcy jurisdiction (and there are of course others—for instance in the field of shipping, "anti-trust" legislation, etc.)—but leaves to States a wide discretion in the matter. It does, however, (a) postulate the existence of limits—though in any given case it may be for the tribunal to indicate what these are for the purposes of that case; and (b) involve for every State an obligation to exercise moderation and restraint as to the extent of the jurisdiction assumed by the courts in cases having a foreign element, and to avoid undue encroachment on a jurisdiction more properly appertaining to, or more appropriately exercisable by, another State'). Also Chapter 5.

[20] eg Mann (above n 14) 35 (stating that *Lotus* countenances 'a most unfortunate and retrograde theory' which 'cannot claim to be good law'); ICJ, *Arrest Warrant* (Democratic Republic of Congo v Belgium), ICJ Rep 3 (2002), diss op van den Wyngaert, § 51 ('It has often been argued, not without reason, that the *"Lotus"* test is too liberal and that, given the growing complexity of contemporary international intercourse, a more restrictive approach should be adopted today').

[21] eg R Higgins, *Problems and Process. International Law and How We Use It* (1994) 77 ('... I do feel that one cannot read too much into a mere dictum of the Permanent Court. This is, for me, another example of the futility of deciding law by reference to an unclear dictum of a court made long years ago in the face of utterly different factual circumstances. We have better ways of determining contemporary international law'); Lowe (above n 11) 263 (believing that is it 'likely that the Court in the *Lotus* case only intended the presumption to apply in cases such as that then before it, where there is a clear connection with the forum'); Mann (above n 14) 35 (noting that 'there is no certainty that [the Court] was contemplating the doctrine of jurisdiction in general or any of

an international court directly relating to the problem of jurisdiction. In 1984, Kuijper stated that 'insufficient research has been done so far to decide with any degree of certainty whether or not the *Lotus* decision has been set aside by subsequent developments in international customary law'.[22] This statement probably still holds true as of today. Jurisdictional assertions based on the universality principle, which rose to prominence in the 1990s, are often implicitly premised on the permissive scheme of *Lotus*. Assertions of economic jurisdiction, for their part, are often only nominally premised on the principle of territoriality, with protesting States in practice bearing the burden of establishing that the territorial effects of a business-restrictive practice are insufficient to justify jurisdiction.

(b) The priority of territorial jurisdiction under customary international law

It is widely submitted that, whilst *Lotus* permits extraterritorial prescriptive jurisdiction as a principle, arguably even as an a priori theoretical construction,[23] customary international law based on *actual* State practice turns *Lotus* upside down. Under the customary international law of jurisdiction, as historically developed, extraterritorial prescriptive jurisdiction is arguably prohibited in the absence of a permissive rule.[24] Although both the *Lotus* approach and the customary international law approach could yield the same outcome in a particular case,[25] the fact that the *Lotus* approach places the burden of proof on the State assailing the

---

its ramifications outside the field of criminal law'). Also J Verhoeven, 'Remarques critiques sur les lois [belges] du 16 juin 1993 et du 10 février 1999', in J Wouters and H Panken, *De Genocidewet in internationaal perspectief* (2002) 188 ('Il est vrai qu'elle deviendrait singulièrement détestable si elle devait permettre à tous les Etats de se doter d'une compétence universelle…ce qui est bien autre chose que leur pouvoir de punir les infractions commises par ou sur un navire qui ne bat pas leur pavillon, seul en cause dans l'affaire soumise à la Cour permanente').

[22] PJ Kuijper, 'The European Community and the U.S. Pipeline Embargo: Comments on Comments', (1984) GYIL 72, 93.

[23] A Bianchi, 'Reply to Professor Maier', in KM Meessen, ed, *Extraterritorial Jurisdiction in Theory and Practice* (1996), 74, 89.

[24] Bradley terms this 'the conventional view'. CA Bradley, 'Universal Jurisdiction and U.S. Law', (2001) U Chi Legal F 323. Also ICJ, *Arrest Warrant* (above n 20), sep op Guillaume, § 4 ('Under the law as classically formulated, a State normally has jurisdiction over an offence committed abroad only if the offender, or at the very least the victim, has the nationality of that State or if the crime threatens its internal or external security. Ordinarily, States are without jurisdiction over crimes committed abroad as between foreigners').

[25] If, as a principle, international law allows States to exercise extraterritorial jurisdiction, the State that claims jurisdiction need not cite a rule of international law authorizing it to exercise jurisdiction. *Lotus*, (above n 5) 18–19. This consideration merely implies that the burden of proof shifts to the objecting or complaining State. It is not a blank cheque for States to apply their rules extraterritorially, as indeed, once a prohibitive rule is identified upon submission of the objecting State, the jurisdiction of the prescribing State is restricted. Harvard Research on International Law, 'Draft Convention on Jurisdiction with Respect to Crime', (1935) 29 AJIL 439, 468 ('The two points of view presented in the case of the *S.S. Lotus* may be regarded as essentially nothing more than two avenues of approach to a single principle, significant only as the choice between them may determine which contestant should take the initiative in proving the law in the case before the court').

jurisdictional assertion of another State doubtless has the effect of widening the scope for extraterritorial jurisdiction.

The 1935 *Harvard Research on International Law* in particular has been instrumental in the permissive principles approach becoming the main framework of reference for assessing the legality of jurisdictional assertions.[26] Its Draft Convention on Jurisdiction with Respect to Crime has, however, never been translated into a treaty, given the sensitivity of limitations on a State's jurisdiction.[27] The proper scope *ratione loci* of a State's laws thus remains a matter of customary international law, with the concomitant problems of ascertaining what that law actually is at a given moment in time.[28]

The permissive principles approach, as inductively derived from the practice of States, usually links sovereignty with territoriality ('territorial sovereignty'). It views territorial jurisdiction as the fundamental rule of the international jurisdictional order.[29] In the 1928 *Island of Palmas* arbitral case for instance, arbiter Max Huber held:

Sovereignty in the relations between States signifies independence. Independence in regard to a portion of the globe is the right to exercise therein, to the exclusion of any other State, the function of a State. This development [...] of international law [has] established this principle of the exclusive competence of the State in regard to its own territory in such a way as to make it the point of departure in settling most questions that concern international relations.[30]

[26] Harvard Research (above n 25) 444 (pointing out that 'the international law of jurisdiction must rest primarily upon a foundation built of materials from the cases, codes and statutes of national law').

[27] Cf GR Watson, 'The Passive Personality Principle', (1993) 28 Tex Int'l LJ 1, 40–1 (noting that 'a multilateral convention on jurisdiction would probably be riddled with reservations').

[28] ibid 39 (noting, discussing United States practice, that 'the public, Congress, and even many parts of the Executive Branch may never know whether the United States government repeatedly objects to or acquiesces in other governments' use of [extraterritorial] jurisdiction', as '[t]he relevant material may consist of confidential diplomatic notes or classified internal memoranda').

[29] However, see *Lotus* (above n 5) at 20 (holding that 'in all systems of law the principle of the territorial character of criminal law is fundamental', and that 'the exclusively territorial character of law relating to this domain constitutes a principle which, except as otherwise provided, would, *ipso facto*, prevent States from extending the criminal jurisdiction of their courts beyond their frontiers'); Mann (above n 4) 20 (stating that 'in assessing the extent of jurisdiction the starting point must necessarily be [the territoriality of sovereignty] such as it was developed over the centuries').

[30] Perm Ct Arb, *Island of Palmas* (US v Netherlands), 2 RIAA 829 (1928). It has been argued that the Permanent Court seemed to limit territorial sovereignty to 'the function of a State', and would thus limit the exclusivity of territorial jurisdiction to the field of public law. The regulation of the relations between private persons through private law would not be a function of a State, and would be subject to the concurring competency of all States. Stern (above n 8) 254; M Akehurst, 'Jurisdiction in International Law', (1972–73) 46 BYIL 145, 190–1. This reasoning should, however, be rejected. It is unlikely that the Permanent Court referred to the dichotomy public–private law, when referring to 'the function of a State'. '[T]he function of a State' may be just another word for 'the power to set rules', be they of a private or public law nature. Kelsenian legal theory for instance equates law with the State. The State has no other function or even *raison d'être* than setting rules of conduct according to a pyramidal structure the top of which is formed by the Constitution, or Kelsen's hypothetical *Grundnorm* H Kelsen, *Reine Rechtslehre: Einleitung in die Rechtswissenschaftliche Problematik* (1934). Similarly, the nineteenth century legal theoretician

The primacy of territorial jurisdiction is usually premised on the principle of sovereign equality of States and the principle of non-intervention (or non-interference),[31] which render unlawful 'such legislation as would have the effect of regulating the conduct of foreigners in foreign countries'.[32] Other grounds of jurisdiction than the territoriality principle ('extraterritorial jurisdiction') are not logically deduced from that principle. Instead, they function as exceptions to the cornerstones of international law—territoriality, sovereign equality and non-intervention[33]—'based upon ideas of social expediency'.[34]

It is interesting to point out here that both the expansive view taken by *Lotus* (based on prohibitive rules) and the restrictive view of the permissive rules approach are both underpinned by the principle of sovereignty. Jurisdiction is indeed, as the Permanent Court of International Justice held in the *Legal Status of Eastern Greenland* case, 'one of the most obvious forms of the exercise of sovereign power'.[35] The former view, however, takes the perspective of the prescribing State, emphasizing its absolute sovereign right of unilaterally exercising jurisdiction,[36] whereas the latter view takes the perspective of the State feeling the adverse effects of the jurisdictional assertions of the prescribing State, a view emphasizing notions of reciprocity that are necessary for any viable concept of sovereignty.[37]

John Austin considered law to be a set of sovereign commands that had to be obeyed by all citizens. He made no distinction between their dealings with each other and their dealings with the State: J Austin and R Campbell, *Lectures on Jurisprudence or the Philosophy of Positive Law* (1874). It may be objected that private actors could regulate themselves and that States are entitled to regulate private conduct on a subsidiary basis, even when performed outside their territory. Several States could then regulate private conduct on a unilateral basis, wherever it occurs. Pursuant to this argument, legislation of State X could apply to citizen A who resides and conducts all his activities in State Y which refrains, for one reason or the other, to apply its laws to citizen A. The absurd result of this approach is that it allows State X to know better what is good for State Y's citizens than the latters' democratically elected government. Doubtless, the Permanent Court of Arbitration cannot be said to have permitted such truly extraterritorial jurisdiction over private activities.

[31] Mann has argued that there exists merely a terminological difference between sovereignty, territoriality, and the principle of non-intervention. Mann (above n 4) 20. Compare I Brownlie, *Principles of Public International Law* (4th edn 1990) 310 ('Extra-territorial acts can only lawfully be the object of jurisdiction if...(ii)...the principle of non-intervention in the domestic or territorial jurisdiction of other states [is] observed'). The question obviously arises what the actual content of the principle of non-intervention is. Also subsection 5.2.a.

[32] FA Mann (above n 14) 47.

[33] Cf H Ascensio, 'Are Spanish Courts Backing Down on Universality? The Supreme Tribunal's Decision in *Guatemalan Generals*', (2003) 1 JICJ 690, 699 (who severely limits the scope of the principle of non-intervention as a general prohibitive rule in matters of extraterritorial prescriptive jurisdiction: 'Considering the customary process which led to the establishment of the principle, "intervention" is usually understood as a concrete, material act, infringing the exclusive jurisdiction of a state over its own territory. A normative act may constitute a kind of immaterial intervention only if it necessarily implies a material implementation in a foreign country, without the agreement of the territorial authorities, or a strong pressure over that country with considerable negative consequences').

[34] Cook (above n 18) 328.

[35] PCIJ, *Legal Status of Eastern Greenland* (Denmark v Norway), PCIJ Reports, Series A/B, No 53, 48 (1933).

[36] Cf Inazumi (above n 17), 133.

[37] eg Mann (above n 4), 20 ('[J]urisdiction involves both the right to exercise it within the limits of the State's sovereignty and the duty to recognize the same right of other States').

It may finally be noted that it is sometimes submitted that the PCIJ in *Lotus* did not mean to impose the burden of proof upon those objecting to assertions of jurisdiction,[38] or if it meant to, it was either plain wrong or its decision is by now obsolete.[39] States may indeed not have given themselves unlimited discretion in the matter of extraterritorial jurisdiction.[40] Espousing a historical reading of the *Lotus* case, ICJ Judge Guillaume even argued in his separate opinion in the *Arrest Warrant* case that '[t]he adoption of the United Nations Charter proclaiming the sovereign equality of States, and the appearance on the international scene of new States, born of decolonization, have strengthened the territorial principle'.[41] By the same token, three other ICJ judges considered, in their separate opinion in *Arrest Warrant*, *Lotus* to 'represent . . . the high water mark of *laissez-faire* in international relations, and an era that has been significantly overtaken by other tendencies'.[42] Probably, *Lotus* should be construed as principally authorizing jurisdiction on the basis of the *objective territorial principle*— which the Court repeatedly referred to (*in casu* jurisdiction based on the effects caused on a Turkish vessel which is to be assimilated to Turkish territory)[43]—or at least in cases with a strong nexus with the State, and *not* as a general matter.[44]

---

[38] AV Lowe, 'Jurisdiction', in MD Evans, ed, *International Law* (2003) 329, 335; Lowe (above n 11) 263 (rejecting the idea that the *Lotus* court would have accepted 'the view that there is a presumption in favour of the legality of claims to legislative jurisdiction').

[39] Inazumi (above n 17) 134 ('[N]owadays, States are expected to indicate the evidence for the legality of their act'); Bianchi (above n 23) 89 ('The *Lotus* case is too anachronistic and specific to be a starting point for analysis').

[40] RY Jennings, 'Extraterritorial Jurisdiction and the United States Antitrust Laws', (1957) 33 BYIL 146, 150 ('Are we to conclude then that extraterritorial jurisdiction is a matter left within the discretion of each sovereign State; that it is not governed by international law? The practice of States leans against such a conclusion. For the fact is that States do not give themselves unlimited discretion in the matter').

[41] ICJ, *Arrest Warrant* (above n 20), sep op Guillaume, § 15. Contra ibid, sep op Ranjeva, § 9 ('Sans aucun doute, on peut analyser l'évolution des idées et des conditions politiques dans le monde contemporain comme favorable à une atténuation de la conception territorialiste de la compétence et à l'émergence d'une approche plus fonctionnaliste dans le sens d'un service au profit des fins supérieures communes.' Judge Ranjeva subsequently noted, however, that '[l]e caractère territorial de la base du titre de compétence reste encore une des valeurs sûres, le noyau dur du droit international positif contemporain').

[42] ibid joint sep op Higgins, Kooijmans and Buergenthal, § 51 (arguing that the 'vertical notion of the authority of action [of States as agents for the international community] is significantly different from the horizontal system of international law envisaged in the *"Lotus"* case').

[43] *Lotus* (above n 5) 23. It may be noted that international conventions on the law of the sea overruled the *Lotus* holding: Article 11 of the 1958 Convention on the High Seas and Article 97(1) of the UN Convention on the Law of the Sea ('In the event of a collision or any other incident of navigation concerning a ship on the high seas, involving the penal or disciplinary responsibility of the master or of any other person in the service of the ship, no penal or disciplinary proceedings may be instituted against such person except before the judicial or administrative authorities either of the flag State or of the State of which such person is a national'). In *Lotus*, jurisdiction could also be premised on the passive personality principle, given the Turkish nationality of the victims, although—since the accident happened on the high seas—it may not be regarded as authority for passive personality jurisdiction within the territory of another State. Higgins (above n 21) 66.

[44] Also AV Lowe (above n 11) 258–9 ('If [the Court] intended more than this, it was probably wrong'). Also, although not specifically discussing *Lotus*, and taking a rather broad view:

As we shall see in this study, States—in particular the United States and the European Union and its Member States—have never primarily substantiated their claims of economic jurisdiction in *Lotus* terms. Instead, they relied upon the classical principles of jurisdiction, although such required stretching them at times.[45]

(c) Legitimate interests, foreign harm, power, and reasonableness

The permissive principles of jurisdiction are entwined in that they all put forward a link between the situation they govern and the competence of the State. This link is not necessarily the territory. It can as well be one of the two other constituent elements of the definition of a State, namely its population or its sovereign authority.[46] More generally, it may be submitted that a State may not exercise its jurisdiction when it has no legitimate interest in or when it is not affected by an activity.[47] Ramsey has termed this the 'none of your business' rule.[48] This may arguably be traced to the thirteenth century Italian jurist Bartolus.[49]

If a State does not have a link with, or an interest in, a subject matter, it could not exercise its jurisdiction over that matter, even if foreign protest against a jurisdictional assertion remains absent. However, even if a link or interest could be discerned, and a State could rely on an accepted permissive principle, the legality of the exercise of jurisdiction under international law might depend on the harm

KM Meessen, *Völkerrechtliche Grundsätze des internationalen Kartellrechts* (1975), 101 and 171; KM Meessen, 'Zusammenschlusskontrolle in auslandsbezogenen Sachverhalten', (1979) ZHR 143 (holding that, in the face of the multiplicity of economic and antitrust conceptions, a general international jurisdictional rule could not be developed, and that international law merely requires there to be a significant nexus).

[45] eg Lowe (above n 11) 263, citing (1973) Digest of United States Practice in International Law, 197–8.

[46] eg B Stern, 'L'extraterritorialité revisitée: Où il est question des affaires *Alvarez-Machain, Pâte de bois* et de quelques autres...', (1992) 38 AFDI 251; Brownlie (above n 31) 310 (arguing that the threshold principle to be observed if extraterritorial acts are lawfully to be the object of jurisdiction is 'that there should be a substantial and bona fide connection between the subject matter and the source of the jurisdiction').

[47] eg M Morris, 'High Crimes and Misconceptions: the ICC and non-Party States', (2001) 64 Law & Contemp Probs 13, 64 (stating 'the customary international law of criminal jurisdiction is based on a perceptible, if somewhat ill-defined, set of principles regarding the legitimate prosecutorial interests of states').

[48] MD Ramsey, 'Escaping 'International Comity', (1998) 83 Iowa L Rev 893, 920. Also Jennings (above n 40) 152 ('It is reasonable to say...that international law will permit a State to exercise extraterritorial jurisdiction provided that State's legitimate interests (legitimate that is to say the interests accepted in the common practice of States) are involved...'); AT Guzman, 'Choice of Law: New Foundations', (2002) 90 Geo LJ 883, 894 ('When an activity has no effect on any person within a jurisdiction, that jurisdiction has no reason to regulate the activity', thereby distinguishing between an interest in permitting and an interest in regulating an activity).

[49] D Oehler, *Internationales Strafrecht* (2nd edn 1983) 69 (stating that with Bartolus's principle '*statuta sunt jus proprium civitatis*', 'die Lehre, dass die Einzelnorm des Strafanwendungsrechts immer einen Anknüpfungs-, besser einen Beziehungspunkt benötige, erkannt und ausgedrückt [wird]', a doctrine which guards against political instrumentalization of the law).

that such exercise causes to other sovereigns.[50] As Beale held as early as 1923, the legal wrongfulness for a sovereign to exercise his will derives from his infringing upon the rights of other sovereigns.[51] Similarly, in 1972, Akehurst stated that '[t]he acid test of the limits of jurisdiction in international law is the presence or absence of diplomatic protests'[52] stemming from the harm purportedly caused to them by a particular jurisdictional assertion.

The harm test will in practice be the salient test to mediate jurisdictional conflicts.[53] Indeed, as States do not generally legislate or exercise jurisdiction when they have no interest in doing so, or when a situation does not somehow have a link with an element of their statehood,[54] assertions of jurisdiction are presumptively valid under public international law,[55] at least if one construes the classical ground of jurisdiction in a broad manner.[56] Accordingly, 'a theoretical

---

[50] Cf ICJ, *Barcelona Traction* (above n 19) 105, sep op Fitzmaurice (stating that under international law, every State should 'exercise moderation and restraint as to the extent of its jurisdiction' so as 'to avoid undue encroachment on a jurisdiction more properly appertaining to' another State); Jennings (above n 40) 153 (arguing that against the international law authorization to apply one's antitrust laws extraterritorially 'must be set also the legitimate and reasonable interests of the State whose territory is primarily concerned, for the extraterritorial exercise of jurisdiction must not be permitted to extend to the point where the local law is supplanted: where in fact it becomes an interference by one State in the affairs of another'); Brownlie (above n 31) 310 ('Extra-territorial acts can only lawfully be the object of jurisdiction if... (iii)... a principle based on elements of accommodation, mutuality, and proportionality [is] applied. Thus nationals resident abroad should not be constrained to violate the law of the place of residence'); Inazumi (above n 17) 134 ('[A]n act of State is generally presumed to be legal until it is proven that it undermines the rights of other States... It should also be remembered that merely because a jurisdiction is legal does necessarily mean that a State has the absolute right to exercise it'); Bianchi (above n 23) 78 (stating that '[p]henomena of extraterritorial jurisdiction... vary a great deal in intensity, depending on the potential of collision with other states' commands and on how intrusive into other legal orders the attempt to exercise authority turns out to be').

[51] JH Beale, 'The Jurisdiction of a Sovereign State', (1923) 36 Harv L Rev 241.

[52] Akehurst (above n 30) 176.

[53] Cf Ramsey (above n 48) 922.

[54] As any 'extraterritorial' jurisdictional assertion is aimed at defending the interests of the State as a territorially defined entity, this assertion may be said to always have a territorial nexus. Cf HG Maier, 'Jurisdictional Rules in Customary International Law', in KM Meessen, ed, *Extraterritorial Jurisdiction in Theory and Practice* (1996), 64, 65 ('Although the presumed limitation of governmental authority to a nation's territorial boundaries flows from the historic concept of the modern nation state, the proposition that a state may on occasion exercise authority over events beyond its borders also flows, paradoxically, *from the principle that the interests of the people that make up the state's population are territorially defined*') (emphasis added).

[55] Inazumi (n 17) 170; ES Podgor, '"Defensive Territoriality": a New Paradigm for the Prosecution of Extraterritorial Business Crimes', (2002) 31 Ga J Int'l & Comp L 1, 13–14 (finding that 'the reality is that few prosecutions of extraterritorial criminal conduct will be turned aside as falling outside the boundaries of international law. The bases of jurisdiction leave ample room for courts to find support for permitting the prosecution to proceed with cases premised on extraterritorial acts').

[56] Construed strictly, they may, as Bianchi pointed out, 'fall short of doing justice in many cases', given the fact that the 'internationalization of commercial and financial markets has enormously complicated factual matrices'. Bianchi (above n 23) 85. Indeed, as argued below in the context of inter alia antitrust, a strict reading of territoriality may give corporations free rein to prey on foreign markets.

preoccupation with the lawfulness *in abstracto* of these broad jurisdictional principles' may eclipse what Bianchi terms 'a realistic approach to the complexities of actual cases'.[57] Pursuant to the harm test then, it could be examined whether the exercise of jurisdiction in actual cases is reasonable, viz. whether it does not amount to an abuse of rights or to arbitrariness. Legal certainty in jurisdictional matters is then not derived from the classical extraterritoriality doctrine,[58] but from a case-by-case reasonableness analysis.

Harm is not an objective category. One particular sovereign may feel harmed by assertions of 'extraterritorial' jurisdiction, while another sovereign may not feel harmed. This renders extraterritoriality, as Bianchi put it, 'also a matter of degree'.[59] In practice, the harm caused by an assertion of extraterritorial jurisdiction is a measure of the foreign protest levelled at the assertion. This protest may be regarded 'as evidence of the fact that external effects of extraterritorial jurisdiction are being borne by the wrong parties'.[60] They may cause the State asserting its jurisdiction to take into account the harmful effects on parties to which it is not democratically accountable, and possibly forgo its assertions, now and in similar future cases. It may be noted that a State ordinarily protests as soon as another State makes undesirable assertions of prescriptive jurisdiction. The former State will not wait until the enforcement of these assertions because it will believe that the latter will sooner or later go on to effectively enforce its laws.[61]

Protests will, however, not always prove effective. Only if the affected State can credibly bring pressure to bear on the wrongdoer will he be likely to back down. International practice indicates that States scale back their jurisdictional assertions purportedly harming the interests of other States if the latter States bring pressure to bear on the former States, more in particular by launching a credible threat of retaliation against these States.[62] Not all foreign governmental

---

[57] ibid 83. Also A Bianchi, 'Extraterritoriality and Export Controls: Some Remarks on the Alleged Antinomy between European and U.S. Approaches', (1992) 35 GYIL 366, 429. Also, in the context of criminal jurisdiction: J Martin, *Strafbarkeit grenzüberschreitender Umweltbeeinträchtigungen. Zugleich ein Beitrag zur Gefährdungsdogmatik und zum Umweltvölkerrecht* (1989) 137 ('Die Prinzipien des internationalen Strafrechts lassen sich...gewissermassen als Regelbeispiele dafür verstehen, wann die Ausdehnung der Strafgewalt völkerrechtlich gestattet ist. Selbst wenn eine Staat formal unter ein solches Prinzip des internationalen Strafrechts einzuordnen ist, kann es aber sein, das die Anknüpfung im konkreten Fall nicht ausreicht').

[58] Cf X, Note, 'Predictability and Comity: Toward Common Principles of Extraterritorial Jurisdiction', (1985) 98 Harv L Rev 1310, 1319 (holding that '[e]xtraterritoriality doctrine lacks both the coherence imparted by guiding principles and the certainty provided by clear rules').

[59] Bianchi (above n 23) 79.

[60] G Schuster, 'Extraterritoriality of Securities Laws: An Economic Analysis of Jurisdictional Conflicts', (1994) 26 Law & Pol'y Int'l Bus 165, 183. In fact, these protests are not so much directed against the exercise of legislative jurisdiction but rather against the likelihood of enforcement. Mann (above n 14) 14 (stating that 'it is not difficult to visualize circumstances in which the exercise of legislative jurisdiction so plainly implies the likelihood of enforcement that foreign States are entitled to challenge its presence on the statute book').

[61] Bianchi (above n 57) 427.

[62] eg the rationale of restricting jurisdiction in *Lauritzen v Larsen*, 345 US 571, 582 (1953) (US Supreme Court stating that it 'cannot be unmindful of the necessity for mutual forbearance if

protests will indeed convince the 'aggressive' State to forsake its jurisdictional assertions. Only if the foreign State can cause similar or greater reciprocal harm to the aggressive State will the latter probably defer. As far as future cases are concerned, the aggressive State will defer if its expected losses through possible retaliatory action outweigh its expected gains through extraterritorial jurisdiction.[63] Deference will obviously depend on the foreign State's political and economic power.

The efficiency of assertions of extraterritorial jurisdiction is a function of relative power. Put differently, 'jurisdiction is grounded on the capacity to coerce (a "power" theory of jurisdiction)'.[64] Powerful States will be able to impose their legislation on weaker States, while weaker States will almost never be able to impose their legislation on more powerful States. While this may be construed as a general norm of international realist thought, the question arises whether it is also a rule of customary international law. Weaker States might in practice defer to the assertions of stronger States, but they will usually do this only grudgingly, not necessarily because they are convinced that it is the right thing to do from a normative point of view. If conduct is evidenced by State practice, but if it is not buttressed by *opinio juris*, ie by the conviction that the conduct has legal validity, the conduct (*Sein*) may not be considered to be a norm of international law (*Sollen*).

If deference to foreign governmental protests were considered to be a norm of international law, one may conflate an external legal norm with an internal realist norm. States do not defer to foreign governmental protests because they are required to do so by some legal norm 'out there' which they comply with in spite of their perception that not complying with it will advance their interests (external legal norm). On the contrary, States defer to such protests precisely because they have no other choice than deferring: foreign retaliation may directly cause them political or economic harm (internal realist norm). Accordingly, it appears that the restraints on the exercise of extraterritorial jurisdiction are not necessarily governed by law, but rather spontaneously by the intricate workings of the balance of power. This obviously hampers the construction of a legal framework of jurisdictional restraint.

The presence or absence of foreign protest is ill-suited as the defining factor to assess the legality of jurisdictional assertions because its argumentative strength is a function of relative power. Attempts have therefore been made at rendering the factors to be used in restraining jurisdiction more objective, with foreign protest being just one factor to be taken into account. Such attempts may face difficulties in obtaining a foothold in the real world of international relations, where various

---

retaliations are to be avoided'), and in *McCulloch v Sociedad Nacional de Marineros de Honduras*, 372 US 10, 21 (1963) (US Supreme Court stating that upholding jurisdiction in that particular case would 'invite retaliatory action from other nations as well as Honduras').

[63] Schuster (above n 60) 189.   [64] X (above n 58) 1319.

underlying threats and promises of States ordinarily determine the desired reach of a particular State's law. The danger is real that, even if States and their courts are required to exercise jurisdiction reasonably in light of a number of 'objective' although malleable factors, power-based jurisdiction will just masquerade as 'reasonable jurisdiction'.

To date, the most commendable attempt to develop a jurisdictional rule of reason has been the American Law Institute's adoption of § 403 of the Restatement (Third) of US Foreign Relations Law in 1987. This rule draws on the traditional international comity principle, but also on conflict of laws principles that protect private rather than sovereign interests. It operates as an overarching rule of jurisdictional restraint. Although the rule of reason considers the classical principles of criminal jurisdiction under public international law to be first-level principles of reasonableness,[65] it sets forth a more intricate reasonableness analysis, since the said principles, given their open-ended nature, may be ill-suited to guarantee reasonableness by themselves. Comity, the rule of reason, and jurisdictional interest-balancing will be discussed below in Chapter 5. In the next two chapters, the basic international law principles of jurisdiction ('first-level principles of reasonableness') will be examined: the territoriality principle (Chapter 3), and the personality, protective, and universality principles (Chapter 4).

(d) Relevant international law principles

The law of jurisdiction may be guided by a number of international law principles. These principles will be elaborated upon in Chapter 5 at section 5.2, where an international law basis for the rule of reason is sought. They will be briefly introduced here.

It has been pointed out that the classical principles of jurisdiction are all based on a link of the State invoking the principle with the situation over which jurisdiction is exercised. Put differently, a State should have a *genuine connection* with the relevant situation. This principle of genuine connection was put forward by the ICJ in the *Nottebohm* case, a case of diplomatic protection.[66] Jurisdiction based on the permissive principles could on the basis of 'genuine connection' be considered as prima facie 'reasonable'. The question then arises whether there is no need for a 'most genuine connection', since competing jurisdictional claims may all be based on a genuine connection. The principle of non-intervention may come to the rescue here: it may require that States only exercise jurisdiction when they do not intervene in the internal affairs of other States.

The principle of non-intervention is, however, an ill-defined principle. It requires States to take the legitimate interests of other States into account when

---

[65] § 402 of the Restatement (Third) of US Foreign Relations Law.
[66] ICJ, *Nottebohm* (Liechtenstein v Guatemala), ICJ Rep 4 (1955). For elaboration: See Chapter 5, section 5.2.b.

they exercise jurisdiction.[67] But how they should do so remains an enigma. A dominant line of argument in the doctrine has it that States should balance their contacts with a relevant situation and their interests in regulating it with other States' contacts and interests. The rule of reason, as set in forth in the US Restatement, is in fact based on this weighing of contacts and interests. It may be supported by a number of interrelated international law principles and concepts. The principle of proportionality, for one, may demand that States' jurisdictional assertions be proportionate to the regulatory aim which they pursue: is the encroachment on other States' sovereignty proportionate to the advantage that the asserting State secures for itself?[68] The related principle of abuse of rights similarly requires that States do not exercise their jurisdictional rights in a way that disproportionately harms other States' regulatory interests and goals.[69] In the final analysis, the exercise of jurisdiction should be equitable, ie it should be *substantively just*.[70]

Regrettably, in a jurisdictional context, reasonableness, and the principles that support it, have been construed in a *negative* manner. In the traditional conception of international law as a law of coexistence, the principle of reasonableness is mainly seen as a principle of restraint, namely as a principle *prohibiting* States from encroaching on other States' sovereignty. However, in a more modern conception of international law as a law of cooperation, jurisdictional reasonableness may be seen as a *positive* responsibility. Rather than being under a duty to *refrain* from exercising jurisdiction, States may in certain circumstances be under a duty to positively *assert* jurisdiction. This idea of sovereignty as responsibility will further be explored in Chapter 6.[71]

(e) Method of ascertaining customary international law

As this study looks at jurisdiction from an international law perspective, and the law of jurisdiction is, in the absence of treaty law, primarily customary international law, it is useful at this point to set out the method of ascertaining customary international law that will be used.

It has been argued that a jurisdictional assertion is presumptively valid if a State has an interest in regulation (the 'none-of-your-business rule'). This is an approach situated in between the *Lotus* approach and a strict permissive principles approach. Under *Lotus*, all jurisdictional assertions are prima facie lawful (unless there is a specific prohibitive rule to the contrary), while under the permissive principles approach, jurisdictional assertions are prima facie unlawful (unless they could be justified under a specific ground of jurisdiction). The approach advocated in this study sees merit in both. It starts from the permissive principles approach, and

---

[67] For elaboration: Chapter 5, section 5.2.a.
[68] See discussion in Chapter 5, section 5.2.d.
[69] See discussion in Chapter 5, section 5.2.e.
[70] See discussion in Chapter 5, section 5.2.c.
[71] See discussion in Chapter 5, section 5.2.f.

observes that, underlying this approach, is a desire by the international community to authorize States to exercise their jurisdiction if they can advance a nexus with or if they entertain an interest in regulating a particular situation (territory, personality, security...). As States will ordinarily not exercise their jurisdiction if they have no regulatory nexus or interest whatsoever, the bulk of their assertions will be presumptively valid: re-enter *Lotus*. This presumption of lawfulness of a unilateral assertion of jurisdiction could, however, be refuted if other States signal their objections in a timely manner. If the majority, or at least a significant portion of States that are, or could be, directly concerned by the assertion, indeed signal their objections through 'public and continuing protest',[72] a norm of customary international law prohibiting an assertion of that specific kind will come into being. Protest could also consist of verbal or written acts.[73] Especially in respect of the law of jurisdiction, it is unclear how a State could signal its disagreement other than by means of lodging a formal, non-physical, protest.

If a jurisdictional assertion is presumptively valid, States will have to signal their disapproval expressly or impliedly. If they remain silent, they may be assumed to consent. As Wolfke has indeed pointed out in his study on custom in international law, 'there is no ground for exclusion of abstention as a sort of practice leading to the formation of international custom'.[74] Meijers has similarly argued that 'participation which brings forth a rule of custom, can consist of positive acts but also could consist of the evident tolerance by a more passive state of the same acts'.[75] At any rate, States should, in the present state of international law, not be authorized to hide behind a veil of ignorance: if a particular jurisdictional assertion may have an impact on their territory, nationals, interests... they should voice their concerns swiftly; they should not be allowed to dispute the legality of an assertion long after its alleged adverse consequences have occurred.[76] Abstention often is, and should ordinarily be, seen as 'a result of positive decision or action'.[77]

It is not necessary, for a norm of universal customary international law to come into being, that all States have actively participated in its formation, nor even that they deliberately acquiesced in it.[78] It may suffice that the States that are specially

---

[72] H Meijers, 'On International Customary International Law in the Netherlands', in IF Dekker and HG Post, eds, *On the Foundations and Sources of International Law* (2003) 88.

[73] ibid 84 ('Oral and written discourses are acts, too'). Contra K Wolfke, 'Some Persistent Controversies Regarding Customary International Law', (1993) 24 NYIL 1, 3.

[74] K Wolfke, *Custom in Present International Law* (2nd edn 1993) 61.

[75] Meijers (above n 72) 86 and 88.

[76] Also Wolfke (above n 73) 8–9 ('The argument sometimes raised that the omission of any protest may be due to a reason other than the tacit acceptance of the practice is unconvincing. Whatever the reason for such an omission, nowadays a State does this at its own risk') (footnote omitted).

[77] Wolfke (above n 74) 61.

[78] International Law Association (ILA), Committee on Formation of Customary (General) International Law, Final Report, Statement of Principles Applicable to the Formation of General Customary International Law, Report of the 69th Conference (2000) 734, Rule 14 (ii).

affected by such a norm have done so.[79] Even if only a limited number of States are specially affected, the State practice requirement for a norm of customary general international law to come into being may be met. If a customary international law norm regarding the exercise of jurisdiction could be identified on the basis of the limited number of States that are specially affected, eg in the transatlantic area, newly-independent States and 'those new to a particular activity' will be bound by the norm as a norm of *general* customary law, even if these States which do not agree with the norm are bound by existing rules of customary law.[80] The rule has crystallized, and only to the extent that States have persistently and openly dissented from the rule, will they not be bound by it.[81] Legal certainty and stability demand nothing less, since customary international law, especially regarding such a basic category of international law as delimiting spheres of State jurisdiction, sets, more than treaty law, the basic 'rules of the game'.[82]

It may eventually be noted that the lawfulness of a jurisdictional assertion in one field of the law has no bearing on the lawfulness of a jurisdictional assertion in another field of the law: the scope of every field of the law, and even of every provision of every field of the law, has ordinarily to be assessed separately, given the widely diverging interests protected by different substantive legal rules and provisions (and the law of jurisdiction thus not being a monolith). If legal fields are sufficiently similar, however, reasoning on the basis of analogy for lawfulness purposes may be appropriate. The lawfulness of jurisdictional assertions in the field of antitrust law, for instance, could be based on the acquired lawfulness of certain assertions in the field of criminal law, while the lawfulness of universal *tort* jurisdiction over gross human rights violations could be based on the acquired lawfulness of universal *criminal* jurisdiction over the same violations.

(f) Giving effect to international jurisdictional rules in the domestic legal order

If a customary norm of jurisdiction has been ascertained, it is not a given that it will also be applied by State courts when they assess the reach of a domestic

---

[79] ICJ, *North Sea Continental Shelf Cases* (Germany v Denmark; Germany v Netherlands), ICJ Rep 3, 42, para 73 (1969).

[80] ILA (above n 78) 735, commentary (b) to Rule 14.   [81] ibid 738, Rule 15.

[82] While this is the generally accepted rule, it may appear as unfair. For one, the rules governing State succession to treaties sometimes allow newly-independent States to start with a clean slate in respect of *treaty* obligations (Vienna Convention on Succession of States in Respect of Treaties, 22 August 1978, 1946 UNTS 3). For another, one cannot expect that States track the development of customary international law in relation to activities which they do not have an interest in at present; developing countries already lack resources to monitor the development of customary law relating to activities which they do have an interest in. eg AE Roberts, 'Traditional and Modern Approaches to Customary International Law: A Reconciliation', (2001) 95 AJIL 757, 767 (criticizing the 'democratic deficit' of traditional custom). It may be noted, obviously, that, if the jurisdictional rule has a merely regional character, States belonging to another region could argue that no customary rule authorizing the jurisdictional assertion has crystallized as a matter of general international law.

legal provision. Ideally, the norm is applied, irrespective of a State's system of giving effect to (customary) international obligations in its internal law (monism, monism nuanced by the requirement of direct effect, or dualism). As Kuijper indeed pointed out, '[t]he rules relating to jurisdiction of states are so basic to the very existence of the state system itself, that the courts should not in any way encourage an excess of jurisdiction'.[83] Not all legal systems, however, are willing to give effect to customary international law to its full extent.

When the customary norm is a norm which purportedly *authorizes* the exercise of a pre-existing State jurisdiction, most legal systems may be willing to give effect to it. The European Court of Justice, for instance, has, in the *Wood Pulp* case, relied on the territoriality principle under customary law so as to justify the application of EC antitrust law to foreign-based cartel agreements implemented in the European Community.[84] Similarly, when there is purportedly no customary rule authorizing the exercise of jurisdiction, domestic courts may rely on the absence of such a rule to dismiss jurisdiction. In *Jones v Saudi Arabia*, for instance, the UK House of Lords predicated its rejection of universal tort jurisdiction over torture offences on the absence of permissive customary international law.[85] It appears that in these instances, international jurisdictional norms are given effect by the courts primarily because they vindicate home-grown restrictive or expansive views of jurisdiction (see also section 3.2), and only secondarily because they guarantee the peaceful coexistence of States.

International law rules that limit or expand *pre-existing* State jurisdiction, in contrast, face an uphill struggle in being given effect in the domestic legal order. Judges will ordinarily not be willing to expand their statutory jurisdiction on the ground that there is a customary international law norm authorizing them to do so.[86] For reasons of democratic legitimacy, judges will understandably refuse to act upon permissive jurisdictional rules of customary international law. It is indeed up to the legislature to decide whether or not to give effect to an authorization to exercise jurisdiction under customary international law.

---

[83] PJ Kuijper, 'From Dyestuffs to Kosovo Wine: from Avoidance to Acceptance by the European Community Courts of Customary International Law as Limit to Community Action', in Dekker and Post (above n 72) 169.

[84] ECJ, Joined Cases 89, 104, 114, 116, 117 and 125 to 129/85, *A Ahlstrom Osakeyhtio v Commission* [1988] ECR 5193, § 18.

[85] *Jones v Saudi Arabia*, [2006] UKHL 26, § 34 (citation omitted) ('The court asserted what was in effect a universal tort jurisdiction in cases of official torture for which there was no adequate foundation in any international convention, state practice or scholarly consensus...').

[86] Contra Investigating Magistrate Brussels, *Pinochet*, November 6, 1998, (1999) Revue (belge) de droit pénal 278 (investigating judge holding that universal jurisdiction, even *in absentia*, obtained over crimes against humanity under international law, even though Belgian law at the time did not provide for universal jurisdiction over such crimes, on the ground that 'in international humanitarian law, the risk does not so much seem to reside in national authorities reaching beyond their jurisdiction but rather in their looking for pretexts to justify their having no jurisdiction, thereby leaving the door open for impunity for the gravest crimes (which is surely contrary to the *raison d'être* of rules of international law' (own translation).

Somewhat counter-intuitively, courts may also be reluctant to give effect to *obligatory* international jurisdictional norms. Admittedly, States are ordinarily willing to give effect to (mostly treaty-based) international rules obliging States to *exercise* their jurisdiction (eg to exercise universal criminal jurisdiction over certain terrorist offences when they do not extradite the perpetrator).[87] But States will far less readily give effect to the (mostly customary law-based) international rules that require a State to *limit* its pre-existing domestic jurisdiction. In the field of international antitrust jurisdiction, the German *Bundeskartellamt* has given effect to the customary principle of non-intervention so as to restrict the exercise of statute-based German jurisdiction over foreign-based mergers in the *Morris/Rothmans* case.[88] Yet not all legal systems are willing to go as far as setting aside an incompatible statutory norm in favour of a customary international law norm. Article 94 of the Dutch Constitution, for instance, prohibits Dutch courts from doing so. On the basis of this constitutional provision, a Dutch court refused to review article 3 of the Dutch Criminal Law in Wartime Act (*Wet Oorlogsstrafrecht*), a provision which grants universal criminal jurisdiction over war crimes (also committed in non-international armed conflicts) to Dutch courts, in light of customary international law rules possibly prohibiting the exercise of universal jurisdiction over certain war crimes.[89]

It may be noted that the customary law on jurisdiction is essentially limiting in nature. Customary norms may well be incompatible with broad statute-based assertions of domestic jurisdiction, and may thus not be given effect in the domestic legal order. Where different interpretations of a statute are possible, however, courts may opt for the interpretation that is most in line with customary international law.[90] This method of 'consistent interpretation' undercuts sovereignty-related objections to applying customary international law in the face of incompatible domestic law. Yet where no interpretation in line with customary international law is reasonably possible, courts will need to set contrary domestic law aside if the customary law is to be given effect. Citing constitutional concerns,

---

[87] eg article 12*bis* of the Preliminary Title of the Belgian Code of Criminal Procedure (awarding obligatory jurisdiction to Belgian courts if international law obliges Belgium to establish its jurisdiction).

[88] BKartA, WuW/E 1943, 1953 (*Morris/Rothmans*).

[89] LJN: AZ9366, Gerechtshof 's-Gravenhage, 09–751005-04, 29 January 2007, para 5.4.2. For an appraisal: C Ryngaert, 'Universal Jurisdiction over Genocide and Wartime Torture: an Appraisal of the Afghan and Rwandan Cases (2007)', (2007:2) Hague Justice Journal 13. In the field of jurisdiction, this impossibility of reviewing statutory law in light of incompatible customary international law was affirmed by the Dutch Supreme Court (*Hoge Raad*) in the *Bouterse* judgment, reprinted in (2001) 32 NYIL 287. Citing constitutional concerns, the Court refused to ascertain whether a norm of customary international law authorized the exercise of universal jurisdiction over torture as early as 1982.

[90] On consistent interpretation: G Betlem and A Nollkaemper, 'Giving Effect to Public International Law and European Community law Before Domestic Courts: a Comparative Analysis of the Practice of Consistent Interpretation', (2003) 14 EJIL 569.

as in the Netherlands, they may refuse to do so, but in that case the State will be held responsible for the violation of international law.[91]

In view of US jurisdictional assertiveness, it may be appropriate to briefly discuss the role of limiting customary norms in the US legal order. In the United States, it is rather generally accepted that customary international law is the law of the land, and that US courts could apply customary norms.[92] A vocal minority, however, has argued that, after the US Supreme Court's decision in *Erie v Tompkins* (1938),[93] US federal courts no longer have the power to apply norms of customary international law, as such norms form part of general federal common law, which federal courts can no longer 'discover'.[94] At any rate, customary international law norms on jurisdiction play an extremely narrow role in circumscribing the reach of US law. Ordinarily, as will be argued below in section 3.3(b), the reach *ratione loci* of a US statute is based on an analysis of legislative intent, with the legislator being presumed not to have legislated extraterritorially. In some cases, courts seem to have relied, in appraising the reach of a statute, upon vague permissive customary norms so as to justify a jurisdictional outcome that was desirable from a policy perspective (subsection 3.3(b)5).

---

[91] A court is an organ of the State under Article 4 of the ILC's Draft Articles on State Responsibility. Court decisions may entail the international responsibility of that State.

[92] *The Paquete Habana*, 175 US 677, 700 (1900) ('International law is part of our law, and must be ascertained and administered by the courts of justice of appropriate jurisdiction, as often as questions of right depending upon it are duly presented for their determination').

[93] 304 US 64 (1938).

[94] Notably CA Bradley and JL Goldsmith, 'Customary International Law as Federal Common Law: a Critique of the Modern Position', (1997) 110 Harv L Rev 815; CA Bradley, 'Universal Jurisdiction and U.S. Law', (2001) U Chi Legal F 323, 329–30.

3

The Territoriality Principle

The territoriality principle is the most basic principle of jurisdiction in international law. Under the territoriality principle, jurisdiction obtains over acts that have been committed within the territory. Historically, however, personality rather than territoriality was the basic principle of jurisdictional order. Only in the seventeenth century did territoriality rise to prominence (section 3.1). Although territoriality is nowadays the primary basis of jurisdiction, common law countries in particular have, for reasons related to their peculiar system of domestic judicial organization, laid great emphasis on it (sections 3.2 and 3.3). In the United States, for instance, the Congress is presumed not to legislate extraterritorially. This presumption could only be rebutted by a clear congressional statement to the contrary.

Application of the territoriality principle is not as self-evident as it seems. Indeed, the question arises what territorial connections are decisive in case a legal situation has a nexus with several States. What State could then assert jurisdiction? In the criminal law, most countries espouse the constitutive elements approach, pursuant to which jurisdiction obtains as soon as an essential element of an offence takes place within the territory (section 3.4). Yet could this approach also be relied upon in the field of economic law?

In section 3.5, it will be shown how the constitutive elements approach has indeed been applied in antitrust law after the Second World War. Since 1945, US courts have premised jurisdiction over antitrust violations on the adverse territorial effects in the United States, even if the anticompetitive agreement was not made abroad. This 'effects doctrine' was later applied in Europe as well, notably for purposes of international merger control. In cartel matters, only the territorial implementation doctrine has been sanctioned by the highest European court, but the differences with the effects doctrine are in practice very small.

In the United States, the constitutive elements test has also been relied upon to clamp down on transnational securities fraud (section 3.6). Under the effects prong of the test, US securities laws may apply as soon as US investors fall victim to fraud. Under the conduct prong, US laws may apply as soon as part of the fraudulent conduct could be tied to the United States. Because the territorial link need not be very strong, US assertions of securities jurisdiction are actually straying rather far from the original criminal law constitutive elements test.

Again in the United States, orders for the disclosure of documents (discovery) located abroad, under the threat of a subpoena, have also been based on the territoriality principle, on the ground that the underlying judicial proceedings take place in the United States, and US officers do not go abroad to seize documents. Quite understandably, this interpretation of the territoriality principle has given rise to some tension, especially in transatlantic relations (section 3.7).

It will become clear in this chapter that the territoriality principle may sometimes create more problems than it solves. Whilst being the basic principle of jurisdictional order, it is open to diverging interpretations, and it could justify assertions that might be based on very tenuous territorial links. Different States may point to territorial conduct or effects of one and the same situation, and on that basis exercise jurisdiction over that situation. In order to defuse normative competency conflicts, other arbitrating principles may be called for. They will be discussed in Chapter 5 (the rule of reason).

3.1 Historical Growth of the Territoriality Principle in Continental Europe

In continental Europe, the territoriality principle, while being the basic principle of jurisdiction, is not endowed with the almost sancrosanct status which it has in common law countries (sections 3.2 and 3.3). As will be seen in Chapter 4, the geographical reach of continental European codes is fairly wide; the exercise of personality and universal jurisdiction is generally accepted. The lesser importance of territoriality harks back to ancient times, when personality, and not territoriality, was the basic principle of jurisdiction. While territoriality became more important later, with the rise of the sovereign nation State with undisputed borders, some forces, which were ironically fed by the very power of the sovereign State, complicated the rise of territoriality, notably the development of the inquisitorial system of criminal prosecution in the Middle Ages. Unlike the common law accusatorial system, the continental European inquisitorial system was geared toward uncovering the entire truth, and contained less due process guarantees for the defendant. The desire of seeing substantive justice done then almost naturally cast aside jurisdictional constraints such as territoriality.[1] In England, as will be discussed in section 3.2, due process rather than substantive justice was the guiding principle of the criminal law. The principle of territoriality was supposed to ensure due process, because it was feared that the interests of the defendant would suffer if he were not tried in the place where he committed his offence.

---

[1] D Oehler, *Internationales Strafrecht* (2nd edn 1983) 64.

(a) Ancient times: personality prevailing over territoriality

In the ancient world, composed of communities rather than territories, allegiances based on religion, race, or nationality prevailed over those based on territoriality.[2] Notions of territorial, as opposed to tribal, sovereignty and jurisdictional rules based on these notions were unknown. In ancient times, the emphasis placed on nationality usually translated into the exclusion of aliens from a community's law, and into their subjection to their own personal laws.[3] Only in ancient Palestine, resident aliens were subject to Jewish law (aliens of passage remained subject to their own laws). In ancient Egypt, foreign colonies such as the Jews, the Phoenicians, and the Greeks lived under their own laws. In Babylonia, disputes between foreigners were excluded from the application of sacred Babylonian law and were dealt with by special courts.[4] Greece, which did not provide for legal redress for aliens in its early period, similarly placed resident aliens under the jurisdiction of special magistrates (*polemarchs*) who often applied foreign law in private suits.[5]

(b) Rome

Even in the Roman time, a high-water mark of legal culture, did 'personal sovereignty' often seem to prevail over territorial sovereignty.[6] Aliens (*peregrini*) were typically allowed to resort to their own laws. When in Rome, they were not subject to the *jus civile*—which only applied to Roman citizens—but to the *jus gentium* (a sort of Roman Empire common law that had developed out of the law of the Roman *gentes* (clans) and later of the Italian tribes, but which was sufficiently romanized), or in case the *jus gentium* did not provide a solution, to the *jus peregrinum* (or *jus originalis*).[7] These latter laws were, however, not applied 'when the interest of State or public morality was endangered'.[8] The existence of this public order exception, which later became a mainstay of continental European conflict of laws doctrine, testifies to the importance of territorial sovereignty in

---

[2] S Kassan, 'Extraterritorial Jurisdiction in the Ancient World', (1935) 29 AJIL 237, 240.

[3] J Plescia, 'Conflict of Laws in the Roman Empire', (1992) 38 Labeo 30, 32.

[4] For an overview: Kassan (above n 2) 240 *et seq.*

[5] C Phillipson, *The International Law and Custom of Ancient Greece and Rome* (vol I, 1911) 171. In criminal suits, however, Greek law ordinarily prevailed, although foreigners were typically punished more severely than Greek citizens. ibid 172.

[6] ibid 295 ('In comparison with the legislative policy of modern nations, Rome undoubtedly concerned herself little with the task of effecting a reconciliation between personal law and territorial law, between personal sovereignty and territorial sovereignty, by determining the limits of their respective applicability'). Also FA Mann, 'The Doctrine of Jurisdiction in International Law', (1964-I) 111 RCADI 1, 24.

[7] Since the second century BC, a special magistrate, the *praetor peregrinus,* dispensed justice in conflicts involving aliens. The *praetor peregrinus* had jurisdiction over cases between non-citizens and over the diversity of citizenship cases. Plescia (above n 3) 45–6.

[8] Phillipson (above n 5) 299.

early European law.[9] In Rome, conflicts of laws were actually rare because the *jus gentium* was one body of law applicable to all foreigners.[10] After Emperor Caracalla granted Roman citizenship to all freeborn peoples of the Empire in 202 AD,[11] and especially after the centralization of the Roman Empire in the late Roman period, conflict of laws even fell into oblivion.[12]

As far as the competence of the courts (judicial jurisdiction) in the Roman Empire is concerned, Matthaeus, probably the most influential commentator of Roman criminal law texts, stated in his *De criminibus* (1622) that '[r]egarding a competent court, a primary rule of law is that the accuser follows the court of the accused'.[13] This rule applied to both civil and criminal law cases. Relying on the Justinian Commentary C.3.15.1, Matthaeus pointed out that in practice '[t]he court [was] chosen not only where the accused offended but also where he [had] domicile and wherever he [was] found',[14] although Accursius (1182–ca 1260), one of the earliest authorities on C.3.15.1, only included the latter forum for *vagabundi*, persons with no fixed abode.[15] A system granting criminal jurisdiction to the *forum delicti commissi* (the territorial State), the national State, and the custodial State (ie the State having custody of the offender present on its territory) also prevailed later, as will be seen in Chapter 4, in France and especially Germany. Its influence reaches until the present time.[16]

(c) Medieval Italy

Only after the fall of the Roman Empire,[17] and especially from the high Middle Ages on, when kingdoms and empires with more certain boundaries were built,

---

[9] The importance of the territoriality principle could already be gleaned from the first treaty between Rome and Carthage (509–08 B.C.), in which it was stated that salesmen had to comply with territorial regulations: 'Those who land for traffic shall not conclude any bargain except in the presence of a herald or town-clerk. That whatever is sold in their presence, the price is to be secured to the seller on the credit of the State, that is in the case of such sales as are effected in Libya or Sardinia' (given by Polybius, cited ibid 298).

[10] ibid 274.   [11] Plescia (above n 3) 34.

[12] Phillipson (above n 5) 300–1.

[13] A Matthaeus, *De criminibus*, translated by ML Hewett and BC Stoop as *On Crimes* (1994) 472, l xlvii, c 5, No 3.

[14] ibid.

[15] Cited ibid 473 ('The accuser ought to follow the court of the accused. But the court of the accused is not wherever he is found but where he has domicile or where he committed the offence'). Contra Matthaeus, ibid ('We base our assertion on the said C.3.15.1 which simply and without qualification states that accused persons can be accused where they are found').

[16] As far as genuine extraterritorial jurisdiction is concerned, understood as Roman jurisdiction exercised outside the borders of the Roman Empire, it could be submitted that, because of the sheer size of the Roman Empire, which at its height encompassed all ancient Western civilizations, and whereby commercial intercourse with outside territories was accordingly very limited, issues of extraterritorial application of Roman laws to situations outside the Roman Empire did not arise.

[17] Initially, when the German tribes overran the Roman Empire, they adopted the same nationality-based system as the Romans. Romans living in Gaul continued to live under Roman law, while Germans living in Gaul lived under their tribal laws. Plescia (above n 3), 'Conflict of Laws in the

scholarly attention turned to sovereignty problems surrounding the extraterritorial application of laws.[18] Nonetheless, in mediaeval conflict of laws doctrine, as coined by *glossatores* analysing Roman law, it was still generally accepted that laws, notably personal statutes concerning capacity, followed the person, wherever he might be found—although it was admitted that some statutes could only receive territorial application. Indeed, under the 'statutist doctrine', developed in Italy in the twelfth century, three sorts of laws were distinguished for purposes of territorial *c.q.* extraterritorial application. Real statutes, such as laws concerning property, ought to be applied on a territorial basis only. Personal statutes, such as laws concerning capacity or marriage, could be applied extraterritorially, in the sense that they follow the person wherever he or she goes. Mixed statutes, such as statutes concerning contracts, would be subject to a mixed territorial/extraterritorial regime.[19]

Bartolus of Sassoferrato (1314–1357), the great medieval jurist, was not a statutist. The sole principle of his conflict of laws doctrine was that a State's law only governs the State's subjects and not another State's subjects present in the State's territory.[20] Bartolus nevertheless set forth numerous exceptions to this principle, so that in terms of its practical results, his doctrine resembles the statutist doctrine. One of these exceptions, relating to the reach of criminal law, is of particular relevance for us, because almost all laws discussed in this study are of a penal or quasi-penal (regulatory) nature. Bartolus opined that a State's criminal law applied to any person within that State's territory, even if that person was an alien. This was progressive, because quite a few writers defended the thesis that an alien could only be penalized for acts done within the territory with penalties provided for in the *jus commune*, ie the law common to the Italian States, or even that he could only be penalized for acts which also constituted a crime under the *jus commune*.[21] Yet in keeping with the basic personalist principle of his doctrine, Bartolus allowed foreigners to frequently invoke their ignorance as to the penal nature of a particular act, at least if that act was not a *jus commune* crime.[22] Ignorance could typically result in milder sanctions.

Roman Empire', (1992) 38 Labeo 30; Montesquieu, *De l'esprit des lois* (edn 1869), p 466, l 28, c 2 (entitled 'Que les lois barbares furent toutes personnelles') ('C'est un caractère particulier de ces lois des barbares, qu'elles ne furent point attachées à un certain territoire: le Franc étoit jugé par la loi des Francs, l'Allemand par la loi des Allemands, le Bourguignon par loi des Bourguignons, le Romain par la loi romaine; et, bien loin qu'on songeât dans ces temps-là à rendre uniforme les lois des peuples conquérants, on ne pensa pas même à se fair législateur du peuple vaincu').

[18]   Phillipson (above n 5) 284 ('It is of course, after the fall of the Roman Empire, and the subsequent establishment of a number of European autonomous and independent States, characterized by different local customs, actuated by different needs, and, in consequence, originating different legislations, that the more rapid development of private international law became possible').

[19]   eg HE Yntema, 'The Comity Doctrine', (1966) 65 Mich L Rev 1, 9–16.

[20]   W Onclin, 'La doctrine de Bartole sur les conflits de lois et son influence en Belgique', in Università degli Studi di Perugia, *Bartolo da Sassoferrato. Studi e Documenti per il VI Centenario* (1962), vol II, 375, 377.

[21]   ibid 380–1 (although an exception was provided for in case a State's laws served public utility).

[22]   ibid 381.

It is only a small step from partially exempting aliens from the full reach of the territorial State's criminal laws to allowing the extraterritorial reach of the laws of the State of nationality of the offender. In one of the first theories of *extraterritorial* jurisdiction, Bartolus indeed stated, also in keeping with the personalist principle, that a State's law could bind its nationals abroad if the legislator had the explicit intent to do so. This principle was picked up by the seventeenth century Dutch jurist Paul Voet,[23] and would later, especially in the Anglo-Saxon world, morph into the presumption against extraterritoriality, pursuant to which a State's law is not given extraterritorial application unless the legislator had the clear intent to do so.[24] In Bartolus's time, this principle was as progressive as the principle that aliens ought to be subject to territorial jurisdiction. Other writers indeed opined that States could always apply their penal laws to an act committed by their own citizens abroad if such an act also constituted a crime under the *jus commune*.[25]

(d) Rise of territoriality in the seventeenth century

As early as the thirteenth century, canonical law emphasized that the reach of the law was limited to the territory of the State which enacted that law.[26] Yet it was only from the seventeenth century on, a century that witnessed the rise of the modern and fully sovereign nation State in the aftermath of the Westphalian Peace (1648), that the pre-eminence of the principle of territoriality in public international law became gradually entrenched in Europe. The importance of origin, nationality, or religion declined, and the theory that a person who moved to another territory did not carry his personal laws with him, but became subject to the laws of that territory, gained ascendancy.[27]

1. France

In the field of criminal law, it was primarily in France that the entrenchment of territoriality was facilitated by the reinforcement of royal power and the centralization of the State in the sixteenth century.[28] It was not surprising that in that

---

[23] P Voet, *De statutis eorumque concursus*, lib sing (1715), s 4, c 2, No 10 ('Sic itidem potestas statuentium sese extendit extra territorium ad hune effectum, ut poena subdito imponatur, de gestis extra territorium, siquidem id expressum sit statuto, ut teneantur si simpliciter loquatur').

[24] In particular section 3.3.b (the presumption against extraterritoriality in the United States). However also Reichsgerichtshof, 18 April 1921, Fontes Juris Gentium, Series A, section II, Volume I, at 69 (setting forth a presumption against extraterritoriality: 'a German law is a priori to be considered as enacted only for German territory').

[25] These authors argued that a particular State's law did not introduce a new criminalization because the crime already existed under the *jus commune*. Onclin (above n 20) 382.

[26] ibid 378 (Bonifatius VIII, *Ut Animarum*). Where the pontifical authority seemingly put this as an absolute principle of jurisdiction, Bartolus, as set out in the previous paragraph, slightly amended it, allowing States to exercise extraterritorial jurisdiction on the basis of the active personality principle in case the legislator had made clear his intent to do so. ibid 383.

[27] Kassan (above n 2) 237–8.

[28] Oehler (above n 1) 158.

century a *French* political philosopher, Jean Bodin, laid the theoretical ground-work for the sovereignty of the State.[29] A legal scholar, Pierre Ayrault, set out the jurisdictional consequences of the concept of sovereignty. Ayrault argued that a foreigner, when entering the territory of a State, voluntarily submitted to the jurisdiction of that State.[30] In 1670 then, the *grande Ordonnance criminelle* (1670) granted jurisdiction to the *forum delicti commissi*, ie the place where the crime was committed. Although the *grande Ordonnance* was directed at the internal competency of French prosecutors and courts, it may have facilitated the rise of territoriality as a principle of international jurisdiction ('*in foro interno, in foro externo*').[31]

In practice, however, the principle of territoriality was not rigorously applied in France. Ayrault himself for instance approved of active personality jurisdiction, arguing that the offender was more familiar with his home State's law than with the territorial State's law.[32] Because of the role of the inquisitorial system of criminal justice in France, the reach of French law became almost unlimited. Until the late eighteenth century, French courts routinely established jurisdiction on the basis of the active and passive personality principles, and on the basis of the mere presence of a foreign offender in France (even if the offence or offender had no other nexus with France).[33]

Only with the French Revolution did territoriality become firmly established as the basic, and initially almost exclusive, principle of jurisdiction. In the revolutionary *Décret* of 3/7.9 1792, it was even ordered that all foreigners imprisoned for crimes committed outside France be released.[34] The revolutionary preference for the territoriality principle drew heavily on French enlightened philosophy. Montesquieu, for instance, stated that '[l]es lois politiques demandent que tout homme soit soumis aux tribunaux criminels et civils du pays où il est, et à l'animadversion du souverain',[35] and that '[u]ne société particulière ne fait point de lois pour une autre société'.[36] He dismissed the extraterritorial application of laws because one society could not possibly make laws for another, given the cultural, historical, religious, and climatic differences between societies.[37]

---

[29] Also J Bodin, *On Sovereignty: Four Chapters from the Six Books on the Commonwealth,* translated and edited by JH Franklin (1992) 1 ('Sovereignty is the absolute and perpetual power of a commonwealth').

[30] P Ayrault, *L'Ordre, formalité et instruction judiciaire* (1642), article 4, nr 5, p 44 ('Car bien qu'il se contracte quelque espece d'obligation & submission tacite, és pays & terres où l'on délinque : & il semble que franchement & volontairement nous nous rendions sujets aux lois de la Patrie, dont nous corrompons le repos . . . ').

[31] Also HFA Donnedieu de Vabres, *Les principes modernes du droit pénal international* (1928) 14.

[32] Ayrault (above n 30) article 4, nrs 9 *et seq*, pp 47 *et seq*.

[33] Oehler (above n 1) 83 (arguing that 'die Strafgewalt gegen Ende des ancien régime fast uferlos war').

[34] ibid 113.   [35] Montesquieu (above n 17), p 451, l 26, ch 21.

[36] ibid p 448, l 26, ch 16.

[37] eg ibid 257, l 18, ch 8 ('Les lois ont un très grand rapport avec la façon dont les divers peuples se procurent la subsistance. Il faut un code de lois plus étendu pour un peuple qui s'attache au commerce et à la mer, que pour un peuple qui se contente de cultiver ses terres. Il en faut un

Rousseau for his part wrote in his *Contrat Social* that foreigners, when committing a crime within the territory, violated the social contract which the subjects of a given territory have agreed upon, because by entering the territory, the foreigner became part of the society that made the social contract.[38] This implies conversely that the home State of the offender has no interest in punishment because *its* social contract has not been violated. In Rousseau's conception, the social contract only serves to protect the interests of the territorially circumscribed people who 'signed' that contract. In Italy, a similar view was held by the great criminal jurist Beccaria, who argued that '[u]n crime ne doit être puni que dans le pays où il a été commis, parce que c'est là seulement, et non ailleurs, que les hommes sont forcés de réparer par l'exemple de la peine, les funestes effets qu'a pu produire l'exemple du crime'.[39]

The territoriality principle was inserted as the basic principle of jurisdiction into Article 3 of the French *Code Civil* in 1804. Nationalist pressure and a desire to prevent impunity from arising (ie, to see substantive justice done) later resulted, however, in a quasi-return to *ancien régime*-style jurisdictional provisions, with ample room for the exercise of active and passive personality jurisdiction, protective jurisdiction, and even vicarious jurisdiction (Chapter 4).

2. Germany

In Germany, until the seventeenth century, the *locus delicti* existed alongside the offender's place of residence, and the place where the offender was caught, as a basis for jurisdiction, without any one basis enjoying primacy. While territoriality was generally recognized as a valid basis, personality still enjoyed widespread support. Because the States of the German Empire mistrusted each other, the accused often had the right to be tried by his home State, especially when the Emperor had conferred that privilege on the State.[40] Nationality-based jurisdiction was also justified on the ground that penal sanctions tended to be

---

plus grand pour celui-ci que pour un peuple qui vit de ses troupeaux. Il en faut un plus grand pour ce dernier, que pour un peuple qui vit de la chasse'). Drawing on this insight, Montesquieu lambasted further on in his book the Spaniards for judging the Inca king Athualpa under Spanish law, instead of under Inca or international law, for offences committed within the king's own territory. ibid p 452, l 26, c 22 ('Les principes que nous venons d'établir furent cruellement violés par les Espagnols. L'inca Athualpa ne pouvoit être jugé que par le droit des gens: ils le jugèrent par des lois politiques et civiles. Ils l'accusèrent d'avoir fait mourir quelques'uns de ses sujets, d'avoir eu plusieurs femmes, etc. Et le comble de la stupidité fut qu'ils ne le condamnerait pas par les lois politiques et civiles de son pays, mais par les lois politiques et civiles du leur').

[38] JJ Rousseau, *Le contrat social ou principes du droit politique* (edn 1850), l 2, ch 5 ('Or, comme il s'est reconnu tel, *tout au moins par son séjour*, [tout malfaiteur]...doit être retranché [de l'Etat] par l'exil comme infracteur du pacte [*ie*, le traité social], ou par la mort comme ennemi public...') (emphasis added).

[39] C Beccaria, R Bellamy, eds, R Davies and others (transl), *On crimes and punishments and other writings* (edn 1995), para XXI, pp 152 *et seq*.

[40] eg Württemberg, Brabant (Goldene Bulle), the latter even taking (and being allowed to take) military reprisals when the Bulle was violated by foreign States. Oehler (above n 1) 86–9.

pecuniary in nature and had to be enforced where the accused had his assets, which was usually where he had his residence.[41] The place where the offender was caught was not a general ground of jurisdiction, but it was often used to try persons whose presence was deemed harmful to the State's interests and who could not be extradited.[42] As will be seen in Chapter 4, territoriality, personality, and the latter ground of jurisdiction, the principle of vicarious jurisdiction or *Stellvertretende Rechtsprinzip*, still exist, as of today, alongside each other in the German *Strafgesetzbuch*.

During the formation of more centralized German States in the late eighteenth century, the *forum delicti commissi* eventually rose to importance, to the detriment of the other principles,[43] under the influence of such rationalist philosophers as Samuel Pufendorf and Christian Wolff. Both held that persons voluntarily submitted to a State's jurisdiction when they entered its territory, and that accordingly, another State would not be authorized to exercise jurisdiction over acts done by them in foreign territory.[44] Pufendorf stated that sovereign States were not interested in what happened outside their borders.[45] He thus took a very

---

[41] ibid 86.   [42] ibid 90, 92.

[43] Donnedieu de Vabres (above n 31) 16.

[44] S Pufendorf, *De jure Naturae et gentium libri 8* (1688), English translation by CH Oldfather and WA Oldfather, in JB Scott (ed), *The Classics of International Law* (1934), p 403, l 3, c 6, § 2 ('A stranger who, in the guise of a friend, enters a state whose policy has been the friendly reception of foreigners, even without giving any expression of his fealty, is understood to have expressed tacitly, by his act of entering the country, his willingness to conduct himself by the laws of that state, in accordance with his station, so soon as he has found out that such a general law was promulgated for all who desire to sojourn within the limits of that state. And, on the same ground, he has tacitly stipulated from the state for a temporary defence of his person and the securing of justice'); C Wolff, *Jus Gentium Methodo Scientifica Pertractatum* (1764), translated by JH Drake, in JB Scott, ed, *The Classics of International Law* (1934) § 151 ('He who has offended against a nation or committed some crime against it cannot on that account be punished by another nation to which he has come. For since the evil is not such of itself that it ought to be punished, and by nature the right belongs to a man to punish one who has injured him; by nature also the right belongs to no nation to punish him who has not injured it. Therefore, although the right to punish is a part of the civil power, and consequently belongs to the nation against which any one has offended or committed some crime, nevertheless one nation cannot on this account punish him who has offended against another nation or committed some crime against it. And so it is plain that he who has offended against one nation or committed some crime against it, cannot be punished by another national to which he has come. Evil deeds are punished in a state because either some member of the state, or the corporation itself, has been injured. But he who for the purpose of escaping a penalty comes as an exile to another state, has not on that account injured any member of the state or any private citizen, nor the corporation itself. Therefore both reasons fail, as to why any one can be punished by a certain state, consequently a wrongful act committed in one state does not affect another state, nor from that thing itself does any right arise against an exile').

[45] S Pufendorf, *De jure Naturae et gentium libri 8*, l 8, c 6, § 16 ('Thus even when a man in a formal war has exceeded in his slaughter and rapine the limits set by natural law, he would not commonly be held a murderer or thief, or be punished, were he by chance brought before a third nation which was at peace; And this not only because it is not our concern what offences a man has committed elsewhere, but also because it appears that nations have a tacit agreement not to take upon themselves decisions growing out of the wars of others').

restrictive, territorial view of the law of jurisdiction.[46] Wolff concurred, yet he recognized the role of the active personality principle, limited to the situation where both perpetrator and victim were nationals of the regulating State—with the perpetrator returning to his home State—and subjected its operation to the *ne bis in idem* rule.[47] Other principles of jurisdiction were rejected. Cocceji, a criminal lawyer, similarly emphasized the *locus delicti*. He argued that the State having custody of the offender was required to extradite the offender to the territorial State, and that, if this were impossible, it should apply the *le x loci delicti*.[48]

Rationalist influence could be gleaned from the Bavarian Penal Code of 1751, the first German penal code. The Bavarian Code emphasized territoriality,[49] and although it upheld jurisdiction based on residence and presence, it stipulated that the *lex loci delicti* would always apply.[50] A similar emphasis on territoriality could be found in the Prussian *Allgemeines Landrecht* of 1794,[51] in the Prussian *Criminalordnung* of 1805,[52] and in Austrian law.[53] The final breakthrough of the territoriality principle in Germany came about in the Prussian Penal Code of

---

[46] Pufendorf may be said to have laid the groundwork for the billiard-ball view of international law. Oehler (above n 1) 103 ('Bei Pufendorf...zeigt [es] sich die Wirkung des bindungslosen Nebeneinanders der Vielzahl von souveränen Staaten viel tiefgreifender als bei *Grotius*').

[47] Wolff (above n 44) § 325 ('Since foreigners living in alien territory or staying there remain citizens, or subjects of their own nation, the obligation by which they are bound to their own nation is not terminated, nor are citizens or subjects deprived of the right which they enjoy with the same, for the reason that they live for some time in alien territory or stay there on account of some business, and consequently if a citizen injures a fellow citizen in alien territory and the offender returns to his own people, he can be punished there according to the laws of the place and compelled to repair the loss.... Take such an example as the one of punishing him who has killed a fellow citizen in an alien territory and has taken to flight in order that he might not be punished there. If he should return to his native country, it cannot be doubted that he can be punished on account of the murder committed. But the situation is quite different if one freed from the ordinary penalty in the place of the offence returns to his native country; for one cannot be punished twice on account of the same offence, and every nation is bound to recognize the jurisdiction of another nation in its own territory, consequently to acquiesce in the decision which the other, following its own law, has reached. For since a nation is not conceivable without civil sovereignty, if one nation should be unwilling to recognize the jurisdiction of another nation in its own territory, this would be just the same as it should be unwilling to consider it as a nation, a thing which assuredly is directly opposed to the respect which one nation owes another').

[48] H de Cocceji, *Exercitationum curiosarum*, vol 1, Longoviae (1722) Disputatio LIV, *De fundata in territorio et plurium locorum concurrente potestate* (1684) tit 4, nr 9, cited in Oehler (above n 1) 10.

[49] 2. Teil, 1. Cap, § 10.   [50] ibid § 21 and § 37.

[51] 2. Teil, 20. Titel, §§ 12 f. Extraterritorial jurisdiction was possible, but the *lex loci delicti* was applied. id, §§ 14–15.

[52] The *Criminalordnung* provides for active personality jurisdiction, but subjects its exercise to the requirement of double criminality. §§ 97–8.

[53] Oehler (above n 1) 108–9. *The Theresiana* (1768) recognized the three cited grounds of jurisdiction, but ordered that the *lex loci delicti* invariably be applied, a requirement which was abandoned in the *Josephinische Strafgesetz* (1787), § 12. Territorial jurisdiction was emphasized in § 31 of the Penal Code of 1803 and in §§ 37 and 234 of the Penal Code of 1852. Because Austria did not extradite its own nationals, impunity concerns underlay the insertion of the active personality principle into the Penal Codes of 1803 (§ 30) and 1852 (§ 36, § 235). Offences against the constitutional order and offences of counterfeiting were amenable to protective jurisdiction pursuant to § 32 of the Penal Code of 1803 and § 38 of the Penal Code of 1852. Vicarious jurisdiction applied

1851, the jurisdictional provisions of which were inserted, after German unifica-tion, in the *Reichsstrafgesetzbuch* of 1871.[54] Under French influence, these codes provided for only limited exceptions to the territoriality principle: they only authorized protective jurisdiction and subjected active personality jurisdiction to double criminality and the principle of *ne bis in idem.* As will be discussed in Chapter 4, territoriality came later under nationalist pressure in Germany, to the point that personality seemed to supplant territoriality as the basic principle. Although there are quite a few exceptions to territoriality nowadays, it remains nevertheless a cornerstone of German jurisdictional order.

3. Holland

Seventeenth century Holland boasted among the greatest international lawyers ever, whose influence is still palpable today. Unlike contemporaneous theorists in Germany and France, the Dutch thinkers had little influence on the Dutch law of jurisdiction proper, however. Hugo Grotius (Hugo de Groot), the 'father' of mod-ern public international law, was a staunch defender of territoriality. He argued that any State is entitled, and even obliged, especially as far as crimes harming other States are concerned, to exercise jurisdiction over violations occurring within its territory.[55] As a consequence, any State would be entitled to request the extradition of perpetrators who committed (serious) offences within the territory but had sought refuge abroad.[56] If the custodial State were to refuse to hand over the offender, it ought to establish its own (extraterritorial) jurisdiction over him (*aut dedere aut judicare*),[57] yet it had to apply the *lex loci delicti* (unless the act was prohibited by the law of nature or of nations).[58] Importantly however, Grotius abandoned territoriality where he advocated the exercise of universal jurisdiction

when extradition was impossible by virtue of § 34 of the Penal Code of 1803 and § 40 of the Penal Code of 1852.

[54] §§ 3 *et seq* of these codes.

[55] H Grotius, *De jure belli ac pacis*, translated by AC Campbell as *The Rights of War and Peace* (edn 1901) lib 2, c 21, No 3 ('But since established governments were formed, it has been a settled rule, to leave the offences of individuals, which affect their own community, to those states them-selves, or to their rulers, to punish or pardon them at their discretion. But they have not the same plenary authority, or discretion, respecting offences, which affect society at large, and which other independent states or their rulers have a right to punish, in the same manner, as in every country popular actions are allowed for certain misdemeanours. Much less is any state at liberty to pass over in any of his subjects crimes affecting other independent states or sovereigns. On which account any sovereign state or prince has a right to require another power to punish any of its subjects offending in the above named respect: a right essential to the dignity and security of all governments').

[56] ibid No 4 ('[I]t is necessary that the power, in whose kingdom an offender resides, should upon the complaint of the aggrieved party, either punish him itself, or deliver him up to the discre-tion of that party').

[57] ibid ('Yet all these instances [of demands to deliver up offenders in Antiquity] are to be under-stood not as strictly binding a people or Sovereign Prince to the actual surrender of offenders, but allowing them the alternative of either punishing or delivering them up'). Also ibid No 5.

[58] ibid No 6 ('If the act, of which refugees and suppliants are accused, is not prohibited by the law of nature or of nations, the matter must be decided by the civil law of the country, from which they come. This was received practice in ancient times,...').

by *any* State over violations of the natural law and the *jus gentium*.[59] Grotius's natural law views on universal jurisdiction over heinous crimes were to re-emerge after the Second World War, when they crystallized as positive conventional and customary international law.[60]

A natural law approach to jurisdiction was also taken by a contemporary of Grotius, Antonius Matthaeus. For Matthaeus, the spectre of impunity was a central concern. Because substantive justice ought somehow to be done to violators of the common good, he supported not only territorial jurisdiction but also extra-territorial jurisdiction based on residence and on the place of arrest.[61] Yet because an offence harms the territorial State in the first place, he argued that the *lex loci delicti* ought to be applied in any event.[62] While the *lex loci delicti* rule had no lasting influence on continental European criminal law, Matthaeus's concerns over *impunity* surely had. Combined with Kantian ideals of absolute justice unre-stricted by territorial borders, they caused continental European States to pro-vide for broad possibilities of extraterritorial jurisdiction. Together with Grotius's ideas, they provided the theoretical groundwork for the agenda of the late twen-tieth century civil society movement calling for an end to impunity for gross human rights violations.

Also in the field of the extraterritorial application of civil law did seventeenth century Dutch jurists prove very influential. These jurists reopened a debate which had disappeared since Italian jurists coined the statutist doctrine in the twelfth century. Considering the statutists to be unable to 'explain how one state had authority to legislate a rule with effect in another state',[63] the Dutch jurists developed another theory, against the background of the rise of independent States in Europe, and more directly, of the political organization of Holland as a polity of largely autonomous city States. This theory, the territoriality or comity theory, as developed notably by Paulus Voet and Ulrik Huber, cast conflict of

[59] Ibid l 2, c 20, No 40 ('It is proper also to observe that kings and those who are possessed of sovereign power have a right to exact punishment not only for injuries affecting immediately them-selves or their own subjects, but for gross violations of the law of nature and of nations, done to other states and subjects').

[60] Cf Chapter 4, section 4.5 on universal jurisdiction.

[61] Matthaeus (above n 13), p 472, l xlvii, c 5, no 5 ('For what is more to be regretted today than that so many murders go unpunished, now that the territories and jurisdictions of the Roman prov-inces have been chopped into such minute parts, and murderers easily flee and reach the boundar-ies of foreign lands. I know that the very cutting up of the jurisdiction is used as an excuse, because he who committed an offence on foreign soil cannot be deemed to have offended against us. And I think the reasoning behind this must be approved, namely that an offence, perpetrated on foreign soil, was perpetrated against the statutes and law belonging to that country. But since, when mur-der has been committed, Divine Law and the *Jus Gentium* is also violated, it is right and proper that each and every judge into whose hands the accused falls be the guardian and defender of Divine Law and the common weal. It does not matter whether it is Tros or Turnus who is killed, and it is no less a crime to murder men in India than in the middle of Spain. And so here, I most heartily approve of the edicts of those who, grasping basic principles, thought that they should investigate crimes committed outside the provinces').

[62] ibid c 4, No 24.

[63] JR Paul, 'Comity in International Law', (1991) 32 Harv Int'l LJ 1, 13–14.

laws theory for the first time in sovereignty terms.[64] The first maxim of Huber's *De Conflictu Legum* (1684) in particular conveys the power of territoriality: 'The laws of every sovereign authority have force within the boundaries of its state and bind all subject to it, but not beyond.'[65] On grounds of international comity, States could apply foreign law within their borders (and foreign States could thus apply their laws extraterritorially), but they were under no obligation to do so. Interestingly, in French doctrine, as developed by Bertrand d'Argentré in the same seventeenth century, the extraterritorial application of personal laws was not considered as a discretionary act, but as 'une nécessité de droit, une exigence de la justice'.[66] Huber's view was later echoed in Story's US conflict of laws theory (1834) (although Story also emphasized the importance of the nationality principle).[67] In Chapter 5, this study will return to Huber's comity principle, and argue that, in an amended form as the principle of jurisdictional reasonableness, the principle is especially useful to mediate present-day conflicts over economic jurisdiction between States.

(e) Extraterritoriality under unequal treaties

As could be gleaned from German and French practice, the rise of territoriality in modern Europe did not prevent European States from continuing to exercise personality-based jurisdiction. They not only did so by hauling their own nationals before their territorial courts, but also by setting up *extraterritorial* courts in foreign nations, notably in non-European States. European States often concluded treaties with non-Christian States to subject their own nationals exclusively to special consular jurisdiction, because they feared the barbarous character of territorial jurisdiction by non-Christian, often Muslim, States. This practice, however, is not exactly a return to the ancient practice of foreign communities living under their own law. Indeed, in ancient times, the foreigner sought 'to be equally treated with the native of the State and to be subject to his law',[68] whereas in the modern era, the foreigner, represented by his government, precisely sought *not* to be equally treated with the native of the State. To that end, Western States employed unequal treaties to cajole non-Christian States into granting jurisdictional favors to the former States' nationals. Bearing in mind that the principles of

---

[64] P Voet, *De Statutis eorumque Concursu* (1661) (holding that no statute according to the civil law, whether *in rem* or *in personam*, directly or indirectly, extends beyond the territory of the legislator, although drawing a list of nine exceptions, inter alia the principle of party autonomy and comity, as quoted in Yntema (above n 19) 22); U Huber, *De Conflictu Legum Diversarum in Diversis Imperiis* (1684). DJ Llewelyn Davies, 'The Influence of Huber's *De Conflictu Legum* on English Private International Law', (1937) 18 BYIL 49.

[65] Translated in Mann (above n 6) 26.

[66] B d'Argentré, *Commentarii in patrias Britonum leges seu consuetudines generales antiquissimi Ducatus Britanniae* (1660), art CCXVIII, glose VI, cited in Onclin (above n 20) 390.

[67] J Story, *Commentaries on the Conflict of Laws, Foreign and Domestic* (1834).

[68] Kassan (above n 2) 247.

international law only applied between Christian States and did not govern their relations with other States at the time, the perceived exception to the territoriality principle that consular jurisdiction embodied should be put in perspective.

(f) The 'continental European' view

Territoriality is an important principle of jurisdictional order in continental Europe. Under classical European jurisdictional theory, a State's power could not reach beyond its territory under international law, and acts were considered to only violate the law and authority of the territorial State. They were deemed *res inter alios acta* for other States.[69] Yet a number of criminal and political goals carved out numerous exceptions to the territoriality principle. For one thing, substantive justice and the desire to prevent impunity, a desire which reaches centuries back but was later fed by idealist German and Dutch thought, are goals of European criminal law which sit uneasy with procedural constraints. For another, the rise of nationalism in the nineteenth century caused continental European States to instrumentalize the law and apply it extraterritorially when doing so served their interests.[70] A State's own law was romanticized and presented as the best law available, a view which was, as will be seen in the chapters on extraterritorial economic jurisdiction, echoed in twentieth and twenty-first century US exceptionalism. Apparently, fears of reciprocal extraterritorial application of criminal law did not play a major role as a restraining factor. In continental Europe, bringing the truth to light, bringing perpetrators to account, and defending national interests, were considered to be more important than upholding the due process rights of the defendant. This explains for instance why, as of today, common lawyers have difficulties in understanding the exercise of universal jurisdiction by continental European countries. In the next section, it will be examined how the common law came to rely so heavily on the territoriality principle.

3.2 The Territoriality Principle in England

In England, territoriality occupies a very central position in the law of jurisdiction. This is so for historical reasons unrelated to the reasons why territoriality rose to prominence in continental Europe. Modern English adherence to the territorial principle, enunciated by a number of late nineteenth century court decisions,[71]

---

[69] Donnedieu de Vabres (above n 31) 12.

[70] Oehler (above n 1) 117–18.

[71] eg *R v Keyn*, LR 2 Ex D 63, 13 Cox CC 403 (1876) ('No proposition of the law can be more incontestable or more uniformly admitted that that, according to the general law of nations, a foreigner, though criminally responsible to the law of a nation not his own for acts done by him while within the limits of its territory, can not be made responsible to its law for acts done beyond such limits'); *MacLeod v Attorney-General for New South Wales* [1891] AC 455, 458 (Lord Halsbury LC)

harks back to mediaeval times, when criminal juries were summoned from the *locus delicti* (the jurymen originally being the eye and ear witnesses, with no formal witnesses being allowed at trial) and evidence was easiest to gather at the place where the crime occurred ('all crime is local').[72] A defendant was entitled to a trial by a local jury, because a jury summoned from another place was deemed to put the defendant at a disadvantage and subject him to arbitrariness.[73] Unlike in continental Europe, extraterritorial offences could therefore hardly be created, because they ran the risk of never being capable of being tried in England.[74]

In the nineteenth century, the justification for local juries somewhat lost its strength when formal witnesses were allowed in criminal trials,[75] but the territoriality principle remained the bedrock principle of jurisdiction in England.[76] Only in the courts of the Admiralty (which dealt with maritime law), did extraterritorial jurisdiction gain a foothold, notably in cases of piracy (the archetypical

---

('All crime is local. The jurisdiction over the crime belongs to the country where the crime is committed...'); *The Queen v Jameson* [1896] 2 QB 425, 430 (court stating that no State is allowed to apply its legislation 'to foreigners in respect of acts done by them outside the dominions of the sovereign power enacting. That is a rule based on international law, by which one sovereign power is bound to respect the subjects and the rights of all other sovereign powers outside its own territory'); *HM Advocate v Hall* (1881) 4 Couper 438 (Lord Young) ('The general rule is that criminal law is strictly territorial—so that a man subject only to the criminal law of the country where he is, and that his conduct there, whether by acting, speaking, or writing, shall be judged of as criminal or not by that law and no other'); *Cox v Army Council* [1963] AC 48, 67 ('Apart from those exceptional cases in which specific provision is made in respect of acts committed abroad, the whole body of the criminal law of England deals only with acts committed in England').

[72] A Levitt, 'Jurisdiction over Crimes', (1925) 16 J Crim L & Criminology 316, 327 (describing the taking of evidence in a homicide case as follows: '[T]he dead body of the victim of a homicide had to be before the jury if the jury was to adjudge an alleged offender to be a murderer. If the body of the victim was in another country the jury did not have all the facts before it. They could not say that the man was dead. They did not know. They had to view the victim before they would know. They could not see over a boundary line. Whatever happened outside of the territorial area of their community did not exist for them'). Also L Reydams, *Universal Jurisdiction* (2003) 202. The English approach unmistakably influenced the US approach, epitomized by Article 1, section 8 of the US Constitution ('In all criminal prosecutions, the accused shall enjoy the right to a speedy and public trial by an impartial jury of the state and district wherein the crime shall have been committed').

[73] Oehler (above n 1) pp 60–1, nrs 58–60.

[74] M Hirst, *Jurisdiction and the Ambit of the Criminal Law* (2003) 32–3; *R v Page* [1954] 1 QB 171, 175 ('One can see the procedural difficulty which would have occurred to the medieval lawyers who would be unable to understand how a jury consisting of persons drawn from the *vicinage* could have knowledge of crimes committed abroad, sufficient to present them to the Sovereign's court'). Donnedieu de Vabres has argued that England's 'splendid isolation' was particularly instrumental in extrapolating this domestic law of jurisdiction to the international level. Donnedieu de Vabres (above n 31) 14 (noting that a person prosecuted in England for an offence committed outside the territory could even plead not guilty, aside from arguing that the judge did not have jurisdiction).

[75] Hirst (above n 74) 32.

[76] eg England, *The Queen v Jameson* [1896] 2 QB 425, 430 (Court stating that no State is allowed to apply its legislation 'to foreigners in respect of acts done by them outside the dominions of the sovereign power enacting. That is a rule based on international law, by which one sovereign power is bound to respect the subjects and the rights of all other sovereign powers outside its own territory'). In *Amsterdam and others v Minister of Finance*, the Supreme Court of Israel defined the principle of territoriality as 'the cornerstone of the Anglo-American system', (1952) ILR 229, 231.

offence giving rise to universal jurisdiction), because these courts' procedure was civil law-based. As they could rely on testimony, they were not restrained by common law evidentiary rules.

While the strict jurisdictional view may to a great extent be explained by the doctrine of venue, which requires an offence to be tried by jury in the county where the offence occurred, it may also be explained by reference to the concept of crime in the common law. Whilst the civil law may emphasize a crime as an offence against the victim or against a natural order of justice, at least in recent times, the common law considers a crime to be an offence against the society in which it occurs or an affront to 'the King's (or Queen's) peace'.[77] As the great English political philosopher Thomas Hobbes held, a crime committed in another State is an offence against the order of that State ('the King' or 'the sovereign'), which then may exercise retribution.[78] The offence may be reprehensible, but it is not an offence against the United Kingdom's order.[79] If the offence does not implicate the order of the State, it is not amenable to English jurisdiction.

In the twentieth century, to the classical justification of territoriality—the ready accessibility of evidence and witnesses in the State where the crimes have been committed[80]—another justification, based on international law, was added: territoriality would be dictated by the principle of non-intervention in the domestic affairs of another State.[81] In one case, a court relied on international comity and stated that '[i]t would be an unjustifiable interference with the sovereignty of other nations over the conduct of persons in their own territory if we were to punish persons for conduct which did not take place in the United Kingdom and had not harmful consequences there'.[82] Nonetheless, English courts, when construing an act of Parliament, will usually presume that Parliament did not intend to

---

[77] Home Office, 'Review of Extra-Territorial Jurisdiction', Steering Committee Report, July 1996, p 2, § 1.2; M Kirby, 'Universal Jurisdiction and Judicial Reluctance: A New "Fourteen" Points', in S Macedo, ed, *Universal Jurisdiction. National Courts and the Prosecution of Serious Crimes under International Law* (2004) 247.

[78] T Hobbes, *Leviathan* (1688) Chapter 21, penultimate paragraph; WW Cook, 'The Application of the Criminal Law of a Country to Acts Committed by Foreigners Outside the Jurisdiction', (1934) 40 W Va LQ 303, 328. Contra J Locke, *Two Treatises of Government* (1689) 2. Treatise, nr 9 (propounding the personality principle when asking 'by what right any prince or state can put to death or punish any alien for any crime he commits in their country').

[79] Oehler (above n 1) p 59, nr 57 (contrasting the Continental European view with the English view as follows: 'Der Gedanke der materiellen Gerechtigkeit, dass ein Täter der Tat willen bestraft werden muss, oder eine schwere Tat um des Landes willen vor Gott nicht ungesühnt bleiben darf, is dem common law völlig fremd') (footnotes omitted).

[80] See Home Office, 'Review of Extra-Territorial Jurisdiction', Steering Committee Report (1996) p 4, § 1.9.

[81] G Gilbert, 'Crimes sans Frontières: Jurisdictional Problems in English Law', (1992) BYIL 416. Compare Levitt (above n 72) 327 (terming this the 'metaphysical foundation' of territorial jurisdiction, and stating that '[e]ach over-lord looked after his own domain and let the domain of another overlord severely alone', a notion which was backed up by the religious notion that 'the king rules by divine right and as the temporal representative of omnipotent deity').

[82] *Treacy v DPP* [1971] AC 537, 561. Contra Hirst (above n 74) 9, 35.

violate international law,[83] a canon of statutory construction that is also used in the United States.[84] Furthermore, the jurisdictional latitude left by international law, the PCIJ's 1927 *Lotus* judgment in particular, has surely boosted the statutory extension of the English law of jurisdiction over the last few decades.[85]

The primacy of the territorial principle in England does not imply that Parliament cannot extend the territorial ambit of the law. It surely can, the territoriality of the law being a concept of the common law which may be overridden by statute in specific instances. However, in the absence of an unambiguous and clearly stated intent of Parliament to extend the ambit of the law, statutes are presumed not to apply extraterritorially,[86] a presumption which is also employed by US courts.[87]

In light of the rapid growth of possibilities of transport and telecommunication and the ensuing international crime rate growth, however, the rigorous application of the territorial principle in England has been hollowed out,[88] as have the restrictions on the use of evidence.[89] This occurred especially in the latter part of the twentieth century, when England adopted legislation implementing a number of international conventions dealing with terrorist crimes, conventions which provided for obligatory extraterritorial jurisdiction.[90] It may be noted that the relaxation of the territoriality principle in the United States took place along similar lines. England still takes a rather strict view on extraterritoriality, however, as

---

[83]   eg *Mortensen v Peters* (1906) 8 F (J) 93.

[84]   *The Schooner Charming Betsy*, 6 US (2 Cranch) 64 (1804).

[85]   Hirst (above n 74) 45.

[86]   *Treacy v DPP* [1971] AC 537, 551 ('It has been recognized from time immemorial that there is a strong presumption that when Parliament, in an Act applying to England, creates an offence by making certain things punishable, it does not intend this to apply to any act done by anyone in any country other than England. Parliament, being sovereign, is fully entitled to make an enactment on a wider basis. But the presumption is well known to draftsmen, and where there is an intention to make an English Act or part of such an Act apply to acts done outside England, that intention is and must be made clear in the Act'); *Air India v Wiggins* [1980] 1 WLR 815; *R v Jameson* [1986] 2 QB 425. In *Lawson v Fox* [1974] AC 803, the House of Lords seemed to take the view that the presumption did not apply if an act caused effects in England ('There is a presumption . . . that Parliament, when enacting a penal statute, unless it uses plain words to the contrary, did not intend to make it an offence in English law to do acts in places outside the territorial jurisdiction of the English courts—at any rate unless the act is one which necessarily has its harmful consequences in England'); *Al Skeini v Secretary of State* [2007] UKHL 26, paras 27–33 (Lord Bingham of Cornhill) (dismissing claims arising from the deaths of six Iraqi civilians, and the brutal maltreatment of one of them causing his death, in Basra, Iraq, for which a member or members of the British armed forces could be held responsible, on the grounds that the Human Rights Act does not have extraterritorial application).

[87]   *Foley Bros, Inc, v Filardo*, 336 US 281, 285 (1949); *EEOC v Arabian Am Oil Co*, 499 US 244 (1991).

[88]   *Liangsiriprasert v US Government* [1991] 1 AC 225, 241 ('Unfortunately in this century crime has ceased to be largely local in origin and effect. Crime is now established on an international scale and the common law must face this new reality'); Hirst (above n 74) 56–7.

[89]   The availability of live video-links in particular may boost the number of extraterritorial prosecutions. Hirst (above n 74) 202.

[90]   Hirst (above n 74) 28 (arguing that 'international treaty obligations now represent by far the most common reason for the creation of new exceptions to the territoriality principle').

is apparent from the tests set forth in the 1996 Report of an Interdepartmental Steering Committee conducting a Review of Extraterritorial Jurisdiction, which ought alternatively to be satisfied before the ambit of English criminal law could legitimately be extended:[91]

(1) the offence is serious;
(2) by virtue of the nature of the offence, witnesses and evidence are likely to be available within the United Kingdom;
(3) there is international consensus as to the reprehensible nature of the crime and the need to take extraterritorial jurisdiction;
(4) the vulnerability of the victim makes it particularly important that offences are prosecuted;
(5) it is in the interests of the standing and reputation of the United Kingdom within the international community;
(6) there is a danger that such offences would not otherwise be justiciable.

3.3 The Territoriality Principle in the United States

Throughout the history of US law, US courts have time and again pointed out the importance of the territorial principle. While in some early cases, the territorial principle was predicated on 'the law of nations', more recent cases do not make reference to international law[92] but instead attempt to ascertain the intent of the US legislature. This development has cut the territorial principle loose from its origins and has given it a distinctively American flavour. In this subsection, first, under (a), territoriality as a US principle of jurisdictional restraint derived from international law will be discussed. In a second part (b), light will be cast on the presumption against extraterritoriality, pursuant to which US courts may only apply a statute extraterritorially if such was the unambiguous intent of the US Congress. It will be shown that exceptions to this presumption have recently been carved out, notably in the field of economic regulation and criminal law, and that, in the final analysis, international law may now often be the decisive factor and outer limit of jurisdictional reasonableness in the United States.

(a) Territoriality as a restraining principle derived from international law

The embrace of the territorial principle by the United States harks back to its very inception. Indeed, paragraph 21 of the 1776 Declaration of Independence denounced the English King George III, the nominal sovereign of British

---

[91] Home Office (above n 80), para 2.21.
[92] eg G Schuster, *Die internationale Anwendung des Börsenrechts* (1996) 51.

America, for '[t]ransporting us beyond Seas to be tried for pretended Offenses'. The drafters of the Declaration took the view that offences committed in the territory of the United States ought to be prosecuted in the United States and not abroad, not even in the courts of the colonizing State, England, which American citizens were subject to according to English law. This emphasis on territorial justice is however not merely a secession statement. Thomas Jefferson justified it by traditional common law arguments relating to evidence and fairness to litigants: only a local trial would guarantee that all relevant evidence be available and that litigants have access to familiar procedures.[93] In the Judiciary Article of the 1787 US Constitution, Article III, § 2, clause 3, the same emphasis on territoriality comes to the fore: 'The trial of all Crimes, except in Cases of Impeachment shall be...held in the State where the said Crimes shall have been committed'.[94] In spite of the apparent constitutional preference for territorial jurisdiction, there does however not seem to be a constitutional *bar* to the extraterritorial application of US laws.[95]

In a number of early nineteenth century judgments the US Supreme Court laid great emphasis on the territoriality principle. In *Rose v Himely* (1808), the Supreme Court held that 'legislation of every country is territorial'.[96] Four years later, in *Schooner Exchange v McFaddon* (1812), one of the most important early cases, the Supreme Court put forward the absolute and exclusive jurisdiction of the State within its own territory, a statement that was later echoed by the Permanent Court of Arbitration in *Island of Palmas* (1928):[97] 'The jurisdiction of the nation within its own territory is necessarily exclusive and absolute. It is susceptible of no limitation not imposed by itself. Any restriction upon it, deriving validity from an external source, would imply a diminution of its sovereignty to the extent of the restriction. All exceptions, therefore, to the full and complete

---

[93] T Jefferson, 'Draft of Instructions to the Virginia Delegates in the Continental Congress (1774)', in JB Boyd, ed, 1 *The Papers of Thomas Jefferson* (1950) 128. ('[W]ho does his majesty think can be prevailed on to cross the Atlantick for the sole purpose of bearing evidence to a fact?'); ibid 128–9 ('And the wretched criminal...stripped of his privilege of trial by peers, of his vicinage, removed from the place where alone full evidence could be obtained, without money, without counsel, without friends, without exculpatory proof, is tried before judges predetermined to condemn'). Also Resolution of 14 October 1774, in 1 *Journals of the Continental Congress* (1774) 62, 65 (deciding that the colonies are entitled 'to the great and inestimable privilege of being tried by their peers of the vicinage, according to the course of that law'). Quoted in GR Watson, 'Offenders Abroad: The Case for Nationality-Based Criminal Jurisdiction', (1992) 17 Yale J Int'l L 41, 45, nn 20–2.

[94] To be true, this sentence continues with the words: 'but when not committed within any State, the Trial shall be at such Place or Places as the Congress may by Law have directed'. 'Within any State' should, however, probably be construed as referring to *terrae nullius* or 'territories acquired or to be acquired by the United States', although it may not be excluded that the Framers also contemplated crimes committed in foreign States. AF Lowenfeld, 'U.S. Law Enforcement Abroad: The Constitution and International Law', (1989) 83 AJIL 880, 882.

[95] *US v Felix-Gutierrez*, 940 F 2d 1200, 1204 (9th Cir 1991), citing *Chua Han Mow v United States*, 730 F 2d 1309, 1311 (9th Cir 1984), *United States v King*, 552 F 2d 833, 850 (9th Cir 1976).

[96] 8 US (4 Cranch) 241, 279 (1808).

[97] Perm Ct Arb, *Island of Palmas* (US v Netherlands), (1928) 2 RIAA 829.

power of a nation within its own territories, must be traced up to the consent of the nation itself.'[98]

The US Supreme Court restated the *Schooner* dictum in *The Appolon* (1824), holding that '[t]he laws of no nation can justly extend beyond its own territories', that these 'can have no force to control the sovereignty or rights of any other nation, within its own jurisdiction', that extraterritorial jurisdiction would be 'at variance with the independence and sovereignty of foreign nations' and that such jurisdiction had 'never yet been acknowledged by other nations, and would be resisted by none with more pertinacity than by the Americans'.[99] The Court added that, 'however general and comprehensive the phrases used in our municipal laws may be, they must always be restricted in construction, to places and persons, upon whom the Legislature have authority and jurisdiction'.[100] In so stating, the Court tied the presumption of territoriality less to congressional intent than to the restrictions imposed by international law. A year later, in *The Antelope* (1825), the Supreme Court predicated the prohibition of extraterritorial legislation on the sovereign equality of nations, now widely accepted as one of the most basic principles of international law:[101] 'No principle of general law is more universally acknowledged, than the perfect equality of nations. [...] It results from this equality, that no one can rightfully impose a rule on another.'[102]

In early American conflict of laws and international law doctrine, the territoriality of jurisdiction was propounded with equal force. The great conflict of laws scholar Joseph Story held in 1834 that:

every nation possesses an exclusive sovereignty and jurisdiction within its own territory...He, or those, who have the sovereign authority, have the sole right to make laws...[W]hatever force or obligation the laws of one country have in another, depends solely on the laws, and municipal regulations of the latter...and upon its own express or tacit consent.[103]

Francis Wharton, probably the first public international law scholar in the United States, for his part held in 1887 that 'the authority of a nation within its own territory is absolute and exclusive'.[104]

---

[98] 11 US (7 Cranch) 116, 136 (1812). Compare Justice Blackmun, with whom Justice Brennan, Justice Marshall and Justice O'Connor joined, concurring in part and dissenting part, *Société Nationale Industrielle Aerospatiale v United States District Court for the Southern District of Iowa*, 482 US 522, 556–7 (1986), citing *The Schooner Exchange v McFaddon* ('Under the classic view of territorial sovereignty, each state has a monopoly on the governmental power within its borders and no state may perform an act in the territory of a foreign state without consent'). Also in the context of criminal law: *United States v Nord Deutscher Lloyd*, 223 US 512, 517–18 (1912) ('A local criminal statute has no extraterritorial effect and a party cannot be indicted in the United States for what he did in a foreign country').

[99] *The Appolon*, 22 US (9 Wheat) 362, 370–2 (1824).

[100] ibid 371.   [101] Article 2 (1) UN Charter.

[102] 10 Wheat 66 (1825).

[103] J Story, *Commentaries on the Conflict of Laws* (7th edn 1972) 19–21, 24.

[104] F Wharton, *A Digest of the International Law of the United States* (2nd edn 1887), vol 2, p 432, section 198.

The emphasis on the territorial principle during the early nineteenth century may be attributable to the United States' precarious existence as a fledgling nation that only recently wrought independence from the British Empire. The United States was particularly wary of foreign interference of the Great Powers of the time, such as the United Kingdom and France, in its own affairs. If the United States were not to uphold a strict reading of the territoriality principle, it would have deprived itself of the legal arguments to object to more powerful nations applying their laws in US territory.[105] Such might have harmed US interests to an extent that the perceived benefits of the extraterritorial application of US laws could never offset.[106]

When American power gradually rose in the late nineteenth and early twentieth century, a loosening of the territorial principle was not yet in sight, as the *Cutting Case*, the 1886 libel case in which the United States repudiated the passive personality principle,[107] and *American Banana*, the 1909 antitrust Supreme Court judgment which dismissed the effects doctrine, illustrate.[108] The United States only shed the strict interpretation of territoriality when it dominated the world stage by the end of the Second World War. In 1945, the Second Circuit famously held, in the *Alcoa* antitrust case, that US courts have jurisdiction over foreign conduct that affects the United States.[109]

---

[105] The principle of territoriality was indeed fine-tuned in light of incidents involving the application of foreign laws in US territory or to US vessels. In 1793, Secretary of State Thomas Jefferson vigorously defended the territorial principle when France claimed jurisdiction over vessels in US waters ('Every nation has, of natural right, entirely and exclusively, all the jurisdiction which may be rightfully exercised in the territory it occupies. If it cedes any portion of that jurisdiction to judges appointed by another nation, the limits of their power must depend on the instrument of cession'). (Letter from Mr Jefferson to Mr Morris (Aug 16, 1793), in W Lowrie and M St Claire, eds, *American State Papers* (1832) 167, 169, quoted in GB Born, 'A Reappraisal of the Extraterritorial Reach of U.S. Law', (1992) 24 Law & Pol Int'l Bus 1, 11). Between 1873 and 1875, the United States similarly protested the exercise of civil jurisdiction over disputes involving sailors on US vessels on the high seas, invoking principles of sovereignty, independence, exclusive jurisdiction, international comity, and the equality of States. See extensive references in Born, ibid 12, n 37).

[106] Compare *Hudson v Hermann Pfauter GmbH & Co*, 117 FRD 33, 38 (NDNY 1987) ('The "classic" view of territorial sovereignty was summarized by Chief Justice Marshall in 1812 [in *Schooner Exchange*], during a period in which our nation better understood the resentment that results when a more powerful nation shows disrespect for the sovereign integrity of a weaker state'). Also Born (above n 105) 11, n 33 ('The U.S. position was not unrelated to existing U.S. security and foreign policy concerns').

[107] JB Moore, *Report on Extraterritorial Crime and the Cutting Case*, reprinted in 1887 *Papers relating to the Foreign Relations of the United States* (1888) 757.

[108] In *American Banana v United Fruit Co*, the first case in which extraterritorial application of the Sherman (antitrust) Act was claimed, the Supreme Court ruled that only the territorial State could determine the legality of an act. In so doing, it excluded the exercise of extraterritorial jurisdiction: '[T]he general and almost universal rule is that the character of an act as lawful or unlawful must be determined wholly by the law of the country where the act is done. [. . .] For another jurisdiction, if it should happen to lay hold of the actor, to treat him according to its own notions rather than those of the place where he did the acts, not only would be unjust, but would be an interference with the authority of another sovereign, contrary to the comity of nations, which the other state concerned justly might resent' 213 US 347, 356 (1909).

[109] *United States v Aluminium Corp of America*, 148 F 2d 416 (2d Cir 1945). Although strict territoriality was abandoned in the field of antitrust law as early as 1945, the force of the territoriality

(b) Territoriality as a restraining principle derived from congressional intent: the presumption against extraterritoriality

1. Presumption against extraterritoriality

In more recent US history, the territorial principle has not been grounded upon international law, but rather on Congress's primary concern with domestic conditions.[110] Orphaned from its public international law origins, application of the territorial principle became merely a matter of US statutory construction. While US courts appeared to recognize that the demands of international commerce and globalization are prone to make inroads in the classical international law principle of territorial jurisdiction, they did not leave the last say on the legality of these inroads to the international community. Instead, legality was a function of clear statements to that effect of the democratically elected and accountable US legislature. Therefore, if Congress has deemed it wise to apply its laws abroad beyond what is customarily accepted in international law, the courts should not second-guess it: they should only ascertain the true intent of Congress.[111]

The Supreme Court repeatedly held that it is a long-standing principle of US law 'that legislation of Congress, unless a contrary intent appears, is meant to apply only within the territorial jurisdiction of the United States'.[112] Although in *EEOC v Arabian American Oil Co* (*Aramco*, 1991), the Supreme Court construed

principle did not entirely disappear from later antitrust court opinions. eg *Laker Airways Ltd v Sabena, Belgian World Airlines*, 731 F 2d 909, 921 (DC Cir 1984) ('[T]he territoriality base of jurisdiction is universally recognized. It is the most pervasive and basic principle underlying the exercise by nations of prescriptive regulatory power').

[110] *EEOC v Arabian Am Oil Co*, 499 US 244, 248 (1991). It has been noted that Congress's primary concern with domestic conditions does not necessarily reinforce the territorial principle, as domestic conditions 'may be substantially affected by conduct occurring outside U.S. territory' Born (above n 105) 74.

[111] Even the Supreme Court cannot overrule Congress in this regard. The Court has repeatedly upheld the extraterritorial application of US law against constitutional challenge. Born (above n 105) 3, references in n 6. In classical conflict of laws cases, however, the Supreme Court has held that the Constitution requires that contract and tort liability be determined by the law of the State where the contract was made or the conduct took place, thus excluding the extraterritorial application of US laws under US constitutional law. *Mutual Life Ins Co v Liebing*, 259 US 209, 214 (1922) ('[T]he Constitution and the first principles of legal thinking allow the law of the place where a contract is made to determine the validity and the consequences of the act'); *New York Life Ins Co v Dodge*, 246 US 357, 377 (1918) (application of US law to contract made abroad violates Fourteenth Amendment); *Western Union Telegraph Co v Brown*, 234 US 542, 547 (1914) (application of US tort law to conduct abroad violates Commerce Clause).

[112] *Foley Bros, Inc, v Filardo*, 336 US 281, 285 (1949); *de Atucha v Commodity Exchange, Inc* 608 F Supp 510, 519 (DCNY 1985) '[...] the laws of any jurisdiction apply only to activities within its borders unless there is some indication to the contrary'); *EEOC v Arabian American Oil Co* (*Aramco*), 499 US 244, 251 (1991) ('The intent of Congress as to the extraterritorial application of the statute must be deduced by inference from boilerplate language which can be found in any number of congressional Acts, none of which have ever been held to apply overseas'); *Hartford Fire Insurance Co v California*, 509 US 764, 814 (1993) (Scalia J, dissenting); *Kollias v D & G Marine Maintenance*, 29 F 3d 67, 70 (2d Cir 1994); *New York Central RR v Chisholm*, 268 US 29, 31 (1925) ('Legislation is presumptively territorial and confined to limits over which the law-making power has jurisdiction').

the presumption against extraterritoriality as protecting 'against unintended clashes between [U.S.] laws and those of other nations which could result in international discord',[113] and thus appeared to hint at an international law foundation, it appears that this protection against normative competency conflicts is not the *rationale* of the presumption against extraterritoriality, but rather its *consequence*. The courts do not decide whether or not to apply foreign law after weighing the sovereign interests concerned: they only trace the *intent of Congress*. Obviously, courts may welcome the effects in terms of international comity entailed by applying the presumption against extraterritoriality. Indeed, a mere application of the common sense idea that statutes 'stop at the border'[114] may avoid the politically sensitive weighing of governmental interests and the risk of embarrassing the political branches.[115]

In order to discern congressional intent, the Supreme Court set forth a three-factor test in *Foley Bros v Filardo* (a 1949 case the issue of which was the application of the Eight Hour Law[116] to the employment contract of an American citizen employed at US public works projects in Iran and Iraq): (a) the express language of the statute; (b) the legislative history of the statute; (c) administrative interpretations of the statute.[117] In *Aramco*, the Supreme Court only deemed the first factor to be instrumental in discerning congressional intent,[118] although in a later case, it held that congressional intent must be traced using 'all available evidence'.[119] The courts appear to ascertain congressional intent without regard to the express intent to have a similar statute applied extraterritorially.[120]

---

[113] *EEOC v Arabian American Oil Co*, 499 US 244, 248 (1991) (*Aramco*) (Congress later overruled the Supreme Court by adopting 42 USC section 2000(e) (Supp V 1993)).

[114] MD Ramsey, 'Escaping "International Comity"', (1998) 83 Iowa L Rev 893, 910.

[115] JR Paul, 'Comity in International Law', (1991) 32 Harv Int'l LJ 1, 60 (arguing that 'U.S. courts on occasion employ territorial analysis as a way of achieving the purposes of comity').

[116] 40 USC section 324 (1940).

[117] *Foley Bros, Inc, v Filardo*, 336 US 281, 285–90 (1949).

[118] 499 US 244, 248 (1991).

[119] *Sale v Haitian Ctrs. Council, Inc.*, 509 US 155, 177 (1993) (relying on legislative history, at 174–79); *Smith v United States*, 507 US 197, 204 (1993) (relying on legislative purpose). Also *Kollias v D & G Marine Maintenance*, 29 F 3d 67, 73 (2d Cir 1994) (rejecting a 'clear statement' rule—which would imply that the presumption against extraterritoriality cannot be overcome absent a clear statement in the statute itself—as identified by the dissent in *Aramco* (*EEOC v Arabian Am Oil Co*, 499 US 244, 261 (1991) (Marshall, J dissenting)); *Gushi Bros v Bank of Guam*, 28 F 3d 1535, 1542 (9th Cir 1994) (relying on legislative history). In 1992, Born had already argued that the presumption against extraterritoriality ought 'to permit consideration of all ordinary indicia of legislative intent'. Born (above n 105) 86.

[120] In *Aramco*, the Supreme Court refused to apply the Civil Rights Act extraterritorially, although in similar cases, Congress had overruled the courts' refusal to apply the Age Discrimination Law extraterritorially. *Aramco* itself was eventually overruled by Congress as well. MP Gibney and RD Emerick, 'The Extraterritorial Application of United States Law and the Protection of Human Rights: Holding Multinational Corporations to Domestic and International Standards', (1996) 10 Temple Int'l & Comp LJ 123, 133.

2. Clear versus unclear congressional intent

If Congress's intent to give extraterritorial effect to a particular statute is clear, the presumption against extraterritoriality will not avoid jurisdictional conflict. US courts will ordinarily not be in a position to prevent this. Once Congress has deemed it wise to enact an extraterritorial statute, the courts are not allowed to second-guess the legislature and review the statute in light of international law. Under US law, Congress is indeed not bound by international law: 'If it chooses to do so, it may legislate with respect to conduct outside the United States, in excess of the limits posed by international law'.[121] This is an application of the US doctrine that later statutory law prevails over prior international law.[122] It is rooted in Article I, section 8 of the US Constitution, which grants Congress the power to regulate commerce with foreign nations. US courts are 'bound to follow the Congressional direction unless this would violate the due process clause of the Fifth Amendment'.[123] This has obviously been denounced by the more internationalist-minded doctrine.[124]

---

[121] *United States v Pinto-Mejia*, 720 F 2d 248, 259 (2d Cir 1983). Also *The Over the Top*, 5 F 2d 838, 842 (D Conn 1925) (when congressional intent is clear, international law 'bends to the will of Congress'); *Tag v Rogers*, 267 F 2d 664, 666 (DC Cir 1959), *cert denied*, 362 US 904 (1960) ('There is no power in this Court to declare null and void a statute adopted by Congress or a declaration included in a treaty merely on the ground that such provision violates a principle of international law'); *United States v Quemener*, 789 F 2d 145, 156 (2d Cir 1986), *United States v Allen*, 760 F 2d 447, 454 (2d Cir 1985), *Am Baptist Churches v Meese*, 712 F Supp 756, 771 (ND Cal 1989) ('Congress is not constitutionally bound to abide by precepts of international law, and may therefore promulgate valid legislation that conflicts with or preempts customary international law'). Also Born (above n 105) 3. Contra *United States v Palmer*, 16 US (3 Wheat) 610, 641–2 (Johnson, J, dissenting) ('Congress cannot make that piracy which is not piracy by the law of nations, in order to give jurisdiction in its own courts over such offences').

[122] *Whitney v Robertson*, 124 US 190, 194 (1888). Obviously, this approach may lead to US responsibility for an internationally wrongful act vis-à-vis other States, if the conduct consisting of an action or omission is attributable to the US and constitutes a breach of an international obligation of the US.

[123] *United States v Pinto-Mejia*, 720 F 2d 248, 259 (2d Cir 1983). Also *United States v Kimbell Foods, Inc*, 440 US 715 (1979); *Federal Trade Commission v Compagnie de Saint-Gobain-Pont-à-Mousson*, 636 F 2d 1300, 1323 (DC Cir 1980) ('[C]ourts of the United States are [...] obligated to give effect to an unambiguous exercise by Congress of its [power to grant jurisdiction to agencies or to courts] *even if such an exercise would exceed the limitations imposed by international law*') (emphasis added); L Brilmayer and C Norchi, 'Federal Extraterritoriality and Fifth Amendment Due Process', (1992) 105 Harv L Rev 1217.

[124] eg Born (above n 105) 80. Born proposes an 'international law presumption' instead, but it remains to be seen whether his approach would make any difference. Indeed, he is adamant that 'the presumption should focus on *U.S.* understandings of international law', because '[t]his is the approach that US courts have historically taken, it is the treatment of international law in the United States of which Congress and the President are most aware, and which provides the natural background for actions by them', and 'to the extent that there are differences between US government on international law issues and those of foreign governments, separation of powers concerns at a minimum counsel strongly for judicial application of those norms recognized by the U.S. political branches'. ibid 82–3. In fact, Born does not propose to draw on multilaterally shaped norms of public international law, but on the provincial application of any such norms, and on US views of conflict of laws and comity as epitomized by section 403 of the Restatement (Third) of Foreign

In case of doubt, however, as the Supreme Court held in the seminal *Charming Betsy* case (1804), 'an act of Congress ought never to be construed to violate the law of nations if any other possible construction remains'.[125] This canon of statutory construction may limit the extraterritorial application of US law by US courts, by requiring them to construe an act of Congress in light of the customary international law of international jurisdiction (which is considered to be part of the common law[126]).[127] Accordingly, if congressional intent is ambiguous, statutory construction may still give a role to international law in assessing the limits of extraterritorial jurisdiction.[128] It is probably in this light that Justice Scalia's statement in his dissenting opinion in *Hartford Fire* ought to be viewed: 'In sum, the practice of using international law to limit the extraterritorial reach of statutes is firmly established in our jurisprudence'.[129] Ordinarily, however, international law is just another interpretive device to solve conflicts of jurisdiction,[130] alongside such devices as unambiguous congressional intent and arguments relating to public policy, welfare-enhancement, and procedural economy.

That the courts' assessment of the reach of US laws might be informed by rules of public international law under the *Charming Betsy* canon of statutory construction might appear a blessing. In reality, however, reliance on *Charming Betsy* may prove a sheep in wolf's clothing. International jurisdictional rules, the territoriality principle in economic law in particular, are not well-defined and thus extremely malleable for domestic purposes. The danger is real that international law, the *Lotus* precedent in particular, is used as a fig-leaf for an otherwise rationally hardly defensible extraterritorial application of US law. As Born has argued in this context, *Charming Betsy* only requires Congress 'not to overstep the bounds of *public* international law' and not to heed private international law rules.[131] The latter rules may limit the scope of US law, 'where public international law would

---

Relations Law and the *Timberlane/Mannington Mills* legacy. He basically intends to discard the presumption against extraterritoriality and to replace it by an interest-balancing test as the main method of addressing issues of extraterritoriality in the US.

[125] *Murray v Schooner Charming Betsy*, 2 Cranch 64, 118, 2 L Ed 208 (1804) (Marshall, CJ); *McCulloch v Sociedad Nacional de Marineros de Honduras*, 372 US 10, 21 (1963).

[126] JH Beale, 'The Jurisdiction of a Sovereign State', (1923) 36 Harv L Rev 241, 242 (stating that 'the principles [of international law] which give or withhold jurisdiction are... principles of our common law').

[127] Also § 114 of the Restatement (Third) of Foreign Relations Law (1987) ('Where fairly possible, a United States statute is to be construed so as not to conflict with international law or with an international agreement of the United States').

[128] Contra Born (above n 105) 10 (arguing that the international prohibition of extraterritorial application of national laws was very much a nineteenth century understanding).

[129] *Hartford Fire Ins Co v California*, 509 US 764, 818 (1993) (Scalia, J, dissenting).

[130] DC Langevoort, 'Schoenbaum Revisited: Limiting the Scope of Anti-fraud Protection in an International Securities Marketplace', (1992) 55 Law & Contemp Probs 241, 243 (stating that '[r]eferences to principles of international law... are not meant in their intended sense as limitations on the jurisdiction to prescribe, but rather for their heuristic role in helping think through the policy dilemmas posed in this setting').

[131] Born (above n 105) 86 (emphasis added).

permit U.S. law to apply'.[132] As the *Lotus* judgment may give States overbroad powers of extraterritorial jurisdiction, Born has proposed to use a canon of statutory construction which slightly differs from *Charming Betsy*: an act of Congress ought never to be construed to violate (the stricter) *US choice of law rules*.[133] In Chapter 5, we will return to these rules' useful role in mitigating jurisdictional excess.

Importantly, however, if it was Congress's intent not to give extraterritorial effect to a statute, and jurisdictional conflict or a violation of international law would not arise if Congress had the intent of applying the statute extraterritorially, the courts are not allowed to second-guess the legislature, swap the presumption against extraterritoriality for another test, and expand jurisdiction.[134] The presumption is then a matter of *Roma locuta causa finita*. It terminates the extraterritoriality analysis, and confines the reach of the statute to US territory. If, however, the presumption is rebutted after careful statutory analysis, techniques of jurisdictional restraint, eg interest-balancing informed by choice of law, may be used to limit the reach of the law. Put differently, the presumption against extraterritoriality serves as a threshold requirement. If it is overcome, other thresholds or hurdles may have to be overcome as well. If it is not overcome, the analysis ends, and the statute is not applied extraterritorially.

3. Economic justification

It has been argued that, from an economic perspective, the presumption against extraterritoriality guards against economically inefficient overregulation. Pursuant to the presumption, national courts are only authorized to exercise extraterritorial jurisdiction if Congress has exceptionally provided for the extraterritorial application of a statute. Congress will usually only provide for extraterritorial application as a sort of 'automatic correction mechanism' for flagrant instances of underregulation laid bare by particular cases.[135] Under this theory, Congress may be considered as being naturally inclined to correct judicial *under*regulation, while it would be disinclined to correct judicial *over*regulation in case the courts were not to employ a presumption against extraterritoriality. Congress may indeed be more willing to protect the interests of its own economy by extending the geographical scope of a statute, than it is to protect the interests of a foreign economy by scaling back the overbroad scope of a statute as defined by courts, unless, obviously, foreign States force them to do so.

---

[132] ibid.   [133] ibid.

[134] In *Foley Bros, Inc, v Filardo*, 336 US 281 (1949) for instance, it may be argued that international law would have allowed the extraterritorial application of the US Eight Hour Law to US companies employing US workers on US government projects, in view of the strong US nexus and interest, although Congress had the intent not to apply the statute extraterritorially. Ramsey (above n 114) 911–12 (stating that *Foley* is 'completely inexplicable as a decision based upon comity').

[135] AT Guzman, 'Choice of Law: New Foundations', (2002) 90 Geo LJ 883, 927.

Drawing on public choice theory, Dodge has argued, however, that this operation of the presumption against extraterritoriality, namely Congress stepping in when regulation is necessary, is actually a sham, since consumers, being the main beneficiaries of economic regulation, are too disorganized to bring pressure to bear on Congress to regulate.[136] In Dodge's view, courts are required to step in where Congress fails to protect the interests of US citizens, thus also when Congress has not made clear its intent to have its act applied extraterritorially. While the absence of a presumption against extraterritoriality might result in overregulation—as Congress is in that situation not inclined to restrict the geographical scope of a statute—Dodge, relying on Weintraub, argues that this is precisely a good thing, as it provides Congress with the bargaining chips to bring about a far more efficient international regime through international negotiations.[137]

This argument is flawed in two respects. For one thing, it supposes that traditional processes of popular democracy do not work adequately and that citizens had better turn to the courts as the ultimate guardians of the interests of the people. In a time when judicial activism is widely denounced, this argument does not seem particularly persuasive. As far as the tendency of the absence of a presumption against extraterritoriality toward multilateral negotiations is concerned, while broad assertions of extraterritorial jurisdiction may indeed at times have furthered negotiations, there does not seem to be solid evidence that this will always be the case. On the contrary, there is quite some evidence that assertions of extraterritorial jurisdiction precisely sour international relations and may diminish the prospect of ever reaching an international agreement.

The presumption against extraterritoriality serves as an interpretive device that guarantees the democratic legitimacy of the extraterritorial application of US laws. Courts arguably ascertain the true intent of Congress, which they do not substitute for their own idiosyncratic views of the desired scope of application of statutes. However, although courts claim to merely ascertain the explicit or implicit will of Congress, it has been submitted that Congress has in most cases not thought about any possible extraterritorial application of the laws it enacts, so that there may be no will to interpret.[138] It is indeed no exaggeration to say that, as far as establishing jurisdiction is concerned, the courts are often legislating from the bench, apparently with tacit approval of congressional representatives,[139]

---

[136] WS Dodge, 'An Economic Defense of Concurrent Antitrust Jurisdiction', (2003) 38 Tex Int'l LJ 27, 34.

[137] ibid 34–5; RJ Weintraub, 'The Extraterritorial Application of Antitrust and Securities Laws: An Inquiry Into the Utility of a "Choice-of-Law" Approach', (1992) 70 Tex L Rev 1799, 1817.

[138] MP Gibney, 'The Extraterritorial Application of U.S. Law: The Perversion of Democratic Governance, the Reversal of Institutional Roles, and the Imperative of Establishing Normative Principles', (1996) 19 BC Int'l & Comp L Rev 297, 310. Also Gibney and Emerick (above n 120) 123 (referring to 'an intellectual dishonest search for congressional intent where there seldom is any').

[139] However see Age Discrimination in Employment Act, 29 USC section 623(f)(1) (1988) (overturning the territorial application of this Act by the courts in *DeYoseo v Bell Helicopter Textron, Inc*, 785 F 2d 1282 (5th Cir 1986); *Pfeiffer v Wm. Wrigley Jr Co*, 755 F 2d 554 (7th Cir 1985); *Cleary v United States Lines*, 728 F 2d 607 (3d Cir 1984)), Civil Rights Act Pub L No

the constitutionally designated lawmakers who are accountable to the people. In reality, US courts are the de facto lawmakers in the field of extraterritorial jurisdiction. It has therefore been argued, quite convincingly, that a realignment of institutional roles is overdue, with the political branches clearly setting out the beacons of extraterritorial jurisdiction and the judiciary applying clear statements of Congress in this regard.[140] Nonetheless, even if Congress (re)claims the higher ground, democratic objections will persist, not from a US constitutional perspective, but from a global perspective. Indeed, the basic concept of extraterritoriality—the application of laws to persons located abroad—runs counter to the principle that those who are subject to the law should have a say in its making.

In some fields of the law, notably in antitrust and securities law, courts have rejected the presumption against extraterritoriality. They have applied statutes extraterritorially in the absence of affirmative congressional intent, and subsequently employed other doctrines of jurisdictional restraint. In so doing, they in effect rejected the idea that the presumption against extraterritoriality serves as a threshold analysis.[141] The question arises why this has happened in the field of economic law, and not in other fields of the law, notably in labour and employment standards legislation (the extraterritorial application of which was at issue in the seminal *Foley Bros* and *Aramco* cases), and environmental legislation. Although the shift from rejecting extraterritoriality in the employment *Aramco* case (1991) to finding extraterritoriality in the antitrust *Hartford Fire* case (1993) may be attributable to the different facts of the case (both the majority and minority in *Hartford Fire* conducting the same reasonableness analysis as in *Aramco*, but reaching another outcome),[142] there is arguably more at stake. The application of the presumption against extraterritoriality to some statutes and not to others is often not premised on a different congressional intent, but is rather underpinned by the courts' own policy considerations. Indeed, as pointed out above, in the absence of clear congressional intent, the courts have promoted themselves to the de facto lawmakers in the field of extraterritoriality.

It has been argued that violations of antitrust and securities legislation, unlike violations of labour and employment legislation, produce general social harm, and that, accordingly, extraterritorial application of the former legislation in the

---

102-66, section 109 105 Stat 1071, 1077 (1991), codified at 42 USC section 2000e-n (Supp III 1991) (overturning the territorial application of his act by the Supreme Court in *EEOC v Arabian American Oil Co (Aramco)*, 499 US 244 (1991)).

[140] Gibney (above n 138) 297.

[141] Contra MD Vancea, 'Exporting U.S. Corporate Governance Standards Through the Sarbanes-Oxley Act: Unilateralism or Cooperation?', (2003–2004) 53 Duke LJ 833, 855 (arguing that the exemptions granted by US regulatory agencies such as the SEC, based on the fear of losing investment or listings of foreign companies, and on the fear of foreign retaliatory actions, make at any rate clear that these agencies are also willing to uphold the presumption against extraterritoriality in antitrust and securities cases).

[142] A-M Slaughter, 'Liberal International Relations Theory and International Economic Law', (1995) 10 Am U J Int'l L & Pol'y 717, 735 n 81.

absence of congressional intent would be justified.[143] Violations of US labour and employment standards, by contrast, would have a much more tenuous effect on the US economy than violations of US antitrust and securities laws. Such violations would be the primary concern of foreign nations, and courts would not be allowed to cast aside the presumption against extraterritoriality.

The stricter construction of the presumption against extraterritoriality may also be attributable to the fact that 'market extraterritoriality is less invasive on the sovereignty of foreign states', whilst labour and employment 'non-market' regulations are more politically sensitive.[144] International tensions stemming from the extraterritorial application of the latter regulations appear therefore more likely to arise than in the context of the extraterritorial application of US antitrust and securities laws.

The discrepancy between the reach of US antitrust and securities laws and the reach of US labour and environmental legislation may not only be explained by the extent of social harm entailed by violations of the respective laws, or by a disparity in international conflict potential. It may be argued that US courts and regulators could harness the national interest to a much greater extent in the field of antitrust and securities than they could in the field of labour or environmental laws, since violations of the latter laws invite the formation of transnational solidarity groups much more than violations of the former laws do.[145]

Extraterritorial violations of labour and environmental laws will usually pit labour or environmental groups (ie civil society) against multinational corporations and foreign governments. A US court will usually face an uphill struggle in identifying 'the' national interest, as all these actors somehow represent the national interest. In light of the complicated transnational solidarities, the court may tend *not* to apply a statute extraterritorially (although in so doing it actually furthers the interests of a particular group).

Extraterritorial violations of antitrust and securities laws will usually not involve the sort of class struggle caused by violations of labour and environmental laws. To be true, violations of antitrust and securities laws may pit corporations

[143] W Estey, 'The Five Bases of Extraterritorial Jurisdiction and the Failure of the Presumption Against Extraterritoriality', (1997) 21 Hastings Int'l & Comp L Rev 177, 187 n 60. US courts do not always decide against the extraterritorial application of labor regulations. In *Vermilya-Brown*, 335 US 377 (1948), the Supreme Court applied the Fair Labor Standards Act (FSLA, Act of 25 June 1938, section 3, 52 Stat 1060, ch 676, 29 USC section 201) to all employees, US or foreign, on a military base in Bermuda which the United States leased from the United Kingdom. In light of the facts of the case however—involving a *territory* leased by the US government—the case is not representative of typical extraterritorial cases. Yet even in *Vermilya-Brown*, dissenting Justice Jackson argued against the application of US laws to foreign employees of the military base ('Thus it was settled American policy . . . that . . . we should acquire no such responsibilities as would require us to import to those islands our laws, institutions and social conditions beyond the necessities of controlling a military base and its garrison, dependents and incidental personnel'). ibid 394.

[144] J Turley, 'When in Rome: Multinational Misconduct and the Presumption Against Extraterritoriality', (1990) 84 Nw U L Rev 598. Also Vancea (above n 141) 855.

[145] Cf X, 'Constructing the State Extraterritorially, Jurisdictional Discourse, the National Interest, and Transnational Norms', (1990) 103 Harv L Rev 1273, 1293.

against consumers, or issuers against investors, but this conflict is less outspoken, since corporations are often consumers as well, and issuers often investors as well, and vice versa. Persons may indeed belong to different 'classes' at the same time, also domestically, which may prevent them from claiming transnational allegiances. As they may identify with their supposed adversaries, they may form the overarching class of the national economic establishment defending its interests against encroachment by other States, or by asserting its interests through the forum State. If internal dissent and competing claims of national interest are silenced, courts and regulators of the forum State will no longer face substantial difficulties in identifying 'one' national interest. Weighing this strong national interest against the interests of the foreign State, they will tend to prefer the national over the foreign interest, thereby expanding the reach of the law.

At bottom, the extraterritorial application of US laws is not a function of the presumption against extraterritoriality, but of the pursuit of the US national interest, although, as shown above, it may at times be difficult to discern this interest. The refusal of the United States to apply its laws to extraterritorial non-market cases may either be attributable to these cases having only a tenuous effect on the US economy, or to the fact that extraterritorial application of US laws might provoke a diplomatic backlash, but in either case, the perceived national interest might be the deciding factor.[146] As far as market cases are concerned, it may be submitted that the spread of the free market is coterminous with the pursuit of American interests. This ideologically charged statement will not be elaborated on here, but, assuming it is true, one should not fail to observe that the free market purpose is not always served by the extraterritorial application of US market laws, and that, thus, US interests may not be served.

For instance, in the antitrust field, the rationale of the extraterritorial application of the 1890 Sherman Act and the 1982 Federal Trade Antitrust Improvement Act is to break up foreign market-distorting conspiracies that harm US consumers or exporters, and thus to promote a free and competitive market. However, the United States is singularly reluctant to use this stated free market creed to the detriment of its own (corporate) citizens. Under the 1918 Webb-Pomerene Act, it refuses to apply the Sherman Act to US conspiracies that cause market-distorting effects abroad, because exercising jurisdiction over such conduct would arguably not serve the US interest. Similarly, the United States does not apply the Sherman Act to the anticompetitive policies of US governmental entities.[147] By applying

---

[146] Cf Gibney (above n 138) 304–5 (adding that the United States often does not apply its laws to the conduct of its corporations abroad to enable them to compete in a global market, ie a refusal to apply US laws extraterritoriality in light of the national interest). The perceived national interest may not always correspond to the genuine national interest as more legitimately construed by Congress.

[147] In *FTC v Ticor Title Ins Co,* 112 S Ct 2169 (1992), the Supreme Court restated that immunity from federal antitrust law is conferred out of respect for ongoing regulation by the state, provided that the restraint must be one clearly articulated and affirmatively expressed as state policy, and that the policy must be actively supervised by the State itself. Also S Weber Waller, 'Can U.S. Antitrust Laws Open International Markets?' (2000) 20 Nw J Int'l L & Bus 207, 222.

the Sherman Act to foreign export cartels and, certainly after the *Hartford Fire* antitrust judgment (1993),[148] casting aside permissive cartel-friendly policies by foreign governmental entities, the United States may obviously stand accused of applying a double standard.[149] Moreover, the application of US extraterritorial regulation to foreign economic actors may precisely have the effect of restraining the development of a free market instead of promoting it, as corporations are burdened with layers of conflicting or non-conflicting governmental regulation. The application of wide-ranging corporate governance requirements set forth in the 2002 Sarbanes-Oxley Act to foreign issuers and their audit firms is a case in point.[150] If economic actors shun the United States for fear of being subject to US regulation, it may seriously be doubted whether US interests are served.

4. The Bowman *criminal law exception to the presumption*

The aforementioned explanations of the abandonment of the presumption against extraterritoriality in some fields of the law are of a doctrinal nature. They have not explicitly been mooted by the courts. In the field of criminal law, however, the US Supreme Court has carved out, and justified, an exception to the presumption against extraterritoriality, implicitly relying on norms of permissive extraterritorial jurisdiction of public international law. In *US v Bowman* (1922), the Supreme Court held that Congress need not expressly provide for extraterritorial jurisdiction over crimes of which the government is a victim; such jurisdiction could be inferred from the nature of the offence.[151] In order to overcome the presumption against extraterritoriality in this situation, the Court seemed to draw on a combination of both a broad protective principle and the classical active personality principle under public international law, addressing offences impairing 'the right of the government to defend itself against obstruction, or fraud wherever perpetrated' (ie protective jurisdiction) provided that a US person is the perpetrator ('especially if committed by its own citizens, officers, or agents') (ie active personality jurisdiction).[152]

---

[148] *Hartford Fire Insurance Co v California*, 509 US 764 (1993).

[149] In *FTC v Ticor Title Ins Co*, 112 S Ct 2169 (1992), the Supreme Court had restated that immunity from federal antitrust law is conferred out of respect for ongoing regulation by the state, provided that the restraint must be one clearly articulated and affirmatively expressed as state policy, and that the policy must be actively supervised by the state itself.

[150] Act to protect investors by improving the accuracy and reliability of corporate disclosures made pursuant to the securities laws, and for other purposes, Public Law 107–24, 30 July 2002, 116 Stat 745, in particular section 102(a) ('It shall be unlawful for any person that is not a registered public accounting firm to prepare or issue, or to participate in the preparation or issuance of, any audit report with respect to any issuer'). The concept 'issuer' is defined in section 2(a)(7) of the Act, in conjunction with 15 USC 78c (Securities Exchange Act 1934).

[151] *United States v Bowman*, 260 US 94, 97–8 (1922). Also, *a contrario*, *American Banana v United Fruit Co*, 213 US 347, 357 (1909) ('The foregoing considerations would lead, in case of doubt, to a construction of any statute as intended to be confined in its operation and effect to the territorial limits over which the lawmaker has general and legitimate power. "All legislation is prima facie territorial"').

[152] MB Krizek, 'The Protective Principle of Extraterritorial Jurisdiction: A Brief History and an Application of the Principle to Espionage as an Illustration of Current United States Practice', (1988)

Courts have interpreted the *Bowman* standard rather liberally, according to Podgor even 'without regard to the government being a victim and without regard to the government being affected by the conduct's criminality'.[153] This led her to advocate a return to genuine *Bowman*-style 'defensive territoriality'.[154] She nevertheless made an exception for 'conduct of United States businesses, deliberately occurring outside the United States for the purpose of avoiding United States jurisdiction',[155] conduct of which the government thus need not be a victim.

5. International law trumping the presumption

A statute almost never explicitly provides for its extraterritorial application.[156] Under the presumption against extraterritoriality, statutes should thus only

6 BU Int'l LJ 337, 345 (stating that 'since the defendants in the *Bowman* case were U.S. citizens, the Court specifically chose not to address the issue of whether it could exercise jurisdiction over alien defendants who had committed crimes abroad'). The Court appeared reluctant to solely rely upon the protective principle, because this principle was historically mistrusted by US courts. ibid 340.

[153] ES Podgor, '"Defense Territoriality": a New Paradigm for the Prosecution of Extraterritorial Business Crimes', (2002) 31 Geo J Int'l & Comp L 1, 28. For cases relying on *Bowman*, eg *Chuan Han Mow v United States*, 730 F 2d 1308, 1311 (9th Cir 1984) (relying on *Bowman* so as to permit the extraterritorial application of drug laws); *United States v Zehe*, 601 F Supp 196, 200 (D Mass 1985) (relying on *Bowman* and ruling that '[g]iven Congress' failure to distinguish between citizens and noncitizens when repealing the territorial restriction, the Court sees no reason to infer that the [Espionage] Act does not continue to apply to both citizens and noncitizens. Therefore, the Court finds that the legislative record . . . does indicate that Congress meant the Act to apply extraterritorially to noncitizens as well as citizens'); *United States v Thomas*, 893 F Ed 1066, 1068 (9th Cir 1990) ('[T]he exercise of [extraterritorial jurisdiction] may be inferred from the nature of the offenses and Congress' other legislative efforts to eliminate the type of crime involved', quoting *United States v Baker*, 609 F 2d 134, 136 (5th Cir 1980); *United States v Felix-Gutierrez*, 940 F 2d 1200 (9th Cir 1991) (concluding 'that the crime of "accessory after the fact" gives rise to extraterritorial jurisdiction to the same extent as the underlying offense [a drug offense in case, over which extraterritorial jurisdiction could be established under *Bowman*]', since '[l]imiting jurisdiction to the territorial bounds of the United States would greatly curtail the scope and usefulness of the accessory after the fact statute in cases in which extraterritorial crimes occur'); *United States v Vasquez-Velasco*, 15 F 3d 833, 837, 840 (9th Cir 1994) (relying on *Bowman* so as to permit the extraterritorial application of violation crimes in aid of a racketeering enterprise, 18 USC § 1959); *United States v Bin Laden*, 92 F Supp 2d 189, 193 (SDNY 2000) (holding that the extraterritorial application of US criminal law is not allowed 'unless such an intent is clearly manifested', quoting *Sale v Haitian Ctrs. Council, Inc*, 509 US 155, 188 (1993)); *United States v Plummer*, 221 F 3d 1298, 1305 (11th Cir 2000) (holding that 'courts in this Circuit and elsewhere have routinely inferred congressional intent to provide for extraterritorial jurisdiction over foreign offenses that cause domestic harm').

[154] Podgor (above n 153) 28. A 'correct' application of the *Bowman* doctrine may possibly be found in *Gillars v United States*, 182 F 2d 962, 979 (DC Cir 1950) (holding that the 'usual presumption against extraterritorial application of the criminal law does not apply to treason'). See also *Kollias v D & G Marine Maintenance*, 29 F 3d 67, 71 (2d Cir 1994) ('[T]he holding in Bowman should be read narrowly so as not to conflict with these more recent pronouncements on extraterritoriality. Reading Bowman as limited to its facts, only criminal statutes, and perhaps only those relating to the government's power to prosecute wrongs committed against it, are exempt from the presumption').

[155] Podgor (above n 153) 29.

[156] For some rare examples: Pub L No 101-298, 104 Stat 201, codified at 18 USC section 175 (Biological Weapons Anti-Terrorism Act) ('There is extraterritorial federal jurisdiction over an offense under this section committed by or against a national of the United States'); Maritime

rarely be given extraterritorial application. However, some courts have tended to distort the presumption by relying on the observation that a statute almost never rules out its extraterritorial application either.[157] They appear to take the view that the classical presumption is obsolete in light of technological and economic developments that have reduced the importance of State borders and the necessity of strict State sovereignty.[158] In the absence of prohibitive wording in the statute, they have relied upon policy considerations to assess the desired reach of the statute. In the *Alcoa* antitrust case for instance, the Second Circuit might, in order to legally justify its effects-based jurisdiction, have construed the intent of Congress when enacting the Sherman Act in light of the objective territorial principle under international law,[159] or even simply have replaced congressional intent by broad international law authorization.

The bottom line of this approach is that, if Congress did not want a statute to be applied extraterritorially, it would have explicitly stated so. This argument links up with international law where it denounces a strict presumption against extra-territoriality for being over-inclusive when no conflict between US and foreign law exists,[160] or when laws are not given the extraterritorial reach that rules of public international law might authorize. Indeed, courts often only pay lip-service to the territoriality presumption and rely upon public international law rules such as the effects doctrine and the protective principle as principles that *permit* extraterritorial jurisdiction.[161] The presumption against extraterritoriality then becomes a presumption in favour of extraterritoriality, as vague public international law rules hardly serve as restraining devices.[162] Accordingly, and ironically, (customary) *international* law starts serving as a vehicle for promoting the *national* interest.[163]

Drug Law Enforcement Act, 46 USC app section 1903(h) (1988) ('This section is intended to reach acts of possession, manufacture, or distribution committed outside the territorial jurisdiction of the United States').

[157] For a rare example: Fair Labor Standards Act, 29 USC section 213 ('The provisions of sections 206, 207, 211, and 212 of this title shall not apply with respect to any employee whose services during the workweek are performed in a workplace within a foreign country').

[158] Born (above n 105) 53, with references in notes 273 and 274.

[159] DJ Gerber, 'The Extraterritorial Application of German Antitrust Laws', (1983) 77 AJIL 756, 759.

[160] Id, at 77 (citing the absence of any conflict between Saudi and US law in *Aramco*).

[161] Born (above n 105) 53, with references in notes 273 and 274. Case citations of § 403 through June 2004, available at <http://www.lawschool.westlaw.com>, eg *United States v Vasquez-Velasco*, 15 F 3d 833, 841 (9th Cir 1994) (court not applying the usual presumption against extraterritoriality to violent crimes committed in aid of a racketeering enterprise, instead holding that it is 'convinced that extraterritorial application of [18 USC § 1959] to violent crimes associated with drug trafficking is reasonable under international law principles. Because drug smuggling is a serious and universally condemned offense, no conflict is likely to be created by extraterritorial regulation of drug traffickers').

[162] Podgor (supra n 153) 26 (arguing that, in the field of criminal law, '[b]y using "objective territoriality" in a globalized world, the presumption of not permitting extraterritorial conduct in criminal cases has become a presumption in favour of permitting these prosecutions').

[163] J Goldsmith and E Posner, 'A Theory of Customary International Law', (1999) 66 U Chi L Rev 1113, 1169 ('When the court is confident of which course of action is in the national interest, it will use [customary international law] to rationalize the result').

3.4 Territorial Jurisdiction Over Cross-border Offences

The contours of territorial jurisdiction are not as clear as might appear at first glance. Offences do not necessarily occur wholly within one State. A crime may be initiated in State X, and consummated in State Y. A person may make a criminal attempt from State X directed at State Y. Person A may participate in State X in a crime committed by person B in State Y. Cross-frontier offences raise the question of where exactly the *locus delicti* is, and thus, which State may legitimately exercise jurisdiction over the crime. According to Oehler, writing in 1983, this question is even the single most important issue in international criminal law,[164] a law which nevertheless, as Fitzmaurice, writing in 1957, pointed out, does not 'very satisfactorily delimit...the respective spheres of competence of States in cases of this kind'.[165]

In international criminal law, it is commonly accepted that it is necessary and sufficient that one constituent element of the act or situation has been consummated in the territory of the State that claims jurisdiction. This solution was propounded as early as 1622 in *De criminibus*, an influential work by the Dutch criminal jurist Matthaeus,[166] who defended it on the ground that it prevented impunity.[167] The constituent elements approach is, however, problematic under international law, as it is not international law, but municipal law which defines the constituent elements of a particular offence.[168] International law seems therefore to have satisfied itself with requiring that either the criminal act or its effects have taken place within a State's territory for the State to legitimately exercise territorial jurisdiction, irrespective of the municipal characterization of the act or the effects (in practice usually the effects) as a constituent element of the offence.

---

[164] Oehler (above n 1) p 201, nr 226 ('Es gibt im internationalen Strafrecht kaum einen Punkt, der selbst innerhalb des einzelnen Landes mehr umstritten ist, als das Merkmal des Tatorts').

[165] G Fitzmaurice, 'The General Principles of International Law', (1957-II) 92 RCADI 1, 214.

[166] Matthaeus (above n 13) l xlvii, c 5, No 6 ('Let us see what must be said if murder has been committed on a border and the judges of both territories vie for the inquiry.... There is also a third opinion of those who think that both [States] can hold a trial but the dispute must be resolved as follows, namely that he who is already busy with the accused ie he who has anticipated the other, is to be preferred. And this third opinion seems to me the more correct'). ibid No 7 ('[O]bviously, he who has arrested him ought to have the stronger case. If, however, neither has arrested him, in that case precedence can also be achieved by laying a charge'). ibid No 8 (arguing that the commentators of Roman law 'say that...the judges of either territory can punish.'). ibid No 9 ('[A] crime begun in the territory of one magistrate and completed in the territory of another is rightly said to have been committed in both, because a crime cannot be divided into parts'). Also PCIJ, *SS Lotus*, PCIJ Reports, Series A, No 10 (1927), 23 and 30; Hirst (above n 74) 45–6.

[167] Matthaeus (above n 13) l xlvii, c 5, No 8 ('[W]e must see to it lest, by wanting to refer the enquiry to only one court, we open up a road for the accused to escape'). ibid No 9 ('Public utility ought to override niceties of argumentation lest while the jurisdiction is being debated, an escape is provided for the offender').

[168] HD Wolswijk, *Locus delicti en rechtsmacht* (1998) 45.

Because domestic law rather than international law defines what a constituent element of a crime is, and a jurisdictional assertion over a cross-border offence is lawful under international law if a constituent element of the offence has occurred in the territory of the forum, it would be beyond the scope of this study to examine how national systems have interpreted 'constituent elements'. It suffices here, for a good understanding of the remainder of the argument that, in doctrinal writings, so-called 'objective territoriality' and 'subjective territoriality' are ordinarily distinguished in respect of cross-border crime.[169] A State can exercise jurisdiction if the act has been initiated abroad, but completed in its territory (objective territoriality).[170] Conversely, a State can exercise jurisdiction if the act has been initiated in the territory, but completed abroad (subjective territoriality).[171]

3.5 Territorial Jurisdiction Over Transnational Antitrust Violations

It remains to be seen whether these criminal law concepts—handbooks typically cite the example of the firing of a gun across a frontier—are fully applicable to less clear-cut non-penal acts, such as foreign restrictive business practices producing domestic effects. In relation to such antitrust or anticompetitive practices, US Judge Learned Hand, in the 1945 *Alcoa* case, reasoned that they indeed are, holding that:

> it is settled law [. . .] that any state may impose liabilities [may exercise jurisdiction over], even upon persons not within its allegiance [foreigners], for conduct outside its borders that has consequences [effects] within its borders which the state reprehends, and these liabilities other states will ordinarily recognize.[172]

It was, and is, believed to be economically rational to employ the effects prong of the constituent elements approach in the field of antitrust law as well, in view of

---

[169] The subjective and objective theories of territoriality were introduced in conventional international law in Article 9 of the Convention for the Suppression of Counterfeited Currency, 112 LNTS 2624, 20 April 1929, and Articles 2 and 3 of the Convention for the Suppression of the Illicit Traffic in Dangerous Drugs, 198 LNTS 4648, 26 June 1936. They were apparently first used in 1887 by JB Moore in his 'Report on Extraterritorial Crime and the Cutting Case', US For Rel 575, 770 (1887) (distinguishing the 'objective principle' and the 'subjective principle').

[170] ibid 757, 771 ('The principle that a man who outside of a country willfully puts in motion a force to take effect in it is answerable at the place where the evil is done, is recognized in the criminal jurisprudence of all countries'). In this sense, the *Lotus* judgment may be premised on the objective territorial principle. Also A Cassese, 'Is the Bell Tolling for Universality?', (2003) 1 JICJ 589, 591.

[171] Harvard Research on International Law, 'Draft Convention on Jurisdiction with Respect to Crime', (1935) 29 AJIL 439, 484–7. Akehurst observed that at the beginning of the twentieth century, the arguments in favour of subjective and of objective territoriality were 'so evenly matched that it was eventually realized that there was no logical reason for preferring the claims of one State over the claims of the other'. M Akehurst, 'Jurisdiction in International Law', (1972–1973) 46 BYIL 145, 152. Also Harvard Research on International Law, ibid 487.

[172] *United States v Aluminium Corp of America*, 148 F 2d 416, 443 (2d Cir 1945).

the adverse domestic effects of foreign-based conspiracies, and the tendency of the territorial State not to clamp down on conspiracies that are mainly export-oriented.[173] In fact, every assertion of sovereign power in the form of sanctions, such as fines, penalties, and confiscation of property, even if these sanctions are strictly speaking non-criminal, may be justifiable under the effects doctrine.[174] Other States have sometimes resisted using the effects principle in antitrust matters. Most notably, while the European Commission considers 'effects' in the Community to be sufficient so as to make the effects-causing foreign anticompetitive conduct amenable to EC jurisdiction, the European Court of Justice has not conclusively approved of effects-based jurisdiction in cartel cases. Instead, it still nominally applies the 'implementation doctrine', which is a variation on the subjective territorial principle.[175] On the basis of this doctrine, jurisdiction obtains on the basis of the territorial implementation of a conspiracy, rather than its territorial effects. In practice, the differences between the effects and the implementation doctrine are small, however. Moreover, in antitrust merger cases, the European Court of First Instance has not shrunk from applying the effects doctrine.[176] There surely is not much evidence of the EC objecting to the assertions of effects-based jurisdiction on international law grounds.[177] In the chapter on reasonableness, we will return to the issue of jurisdiction over antitrust violations, when we attempt to identify a customary norm that obliges States to exercise their 'territorial' jurisdiction over antitrust violations reasonably.

3.6 Territorial Jurisdiction Over Transnational Securities Transactions

Another major field of economic law where 'extraterritorial' assertions of jurisdiction which in fact have a territorial nexus have arisen, is the field of securities

---

[173] At length C Ryngaert, *Jurisdiction over Antitrust Violations in International Law* (2008).
[174] Akehurst (above n 171) 190.
[175] Joined Cases 89, 104, 114, 116, 117 and 125 to 129/85, *A Ahlstrom Osakeyhtio v Commission*, [1988] ECR 5193 ('Wood Pulp'). The ECJ observed in para 16 that, 'an infringement of Article 85 [of the EC Treaty], such as the conclusion of an agreement which has had the effect of restricting competition within the common market, consists of conduct made up of two elements, the *formation* of the agreement, decision or concerted practice and the *implementation* thereof. If the applicability of prohibitions laid down under competition law were made to depend on the place where the agreement, decision or concerted practice was formed, the result would obviously be to give undertakings an easy means of evading those prohibitions. The decisive factor is therefore the place where it is *implemented*.' It held in para 18 that, since the implementation of anticompetitive agreement concluded abroad was territorial, the anticompetitive conduct 'is covered by the territoriality principle as universally recognised in public international law'.
[176] CFI, Case T-102/96, *Gencor Ltd v Commission*, [1999] ECR II-753.
[177] Ryngaert (above n 173).

law.[178] Securities law, a branch of financial law, governs transactions in certificates attesting the ownership of stocks. The field of securities law lends itself to broad assertions of jurisdiction. Indeed, an economic activity as global and interconnected as trade in securities almost inevitably entails ripple effects across borders. States may want to exercise their jurisdiction over a securities transaction either on the basis of territorial conduct or territorial effects relating to a securities transaction (ie on the basis of respectively the subjective and the objective prong of the territoriality principle). Notably the United States has aggressively tackled transnational securities fraud, such as insider-trading, on a unilateral basis.[179] At times, it could only advance rather tenuous territorial links. Disquietingly, US courts, in particular in private suits, do not usually rely on comity or reasonableness (see Chapter 5 for these concepts) to limit US jurisdiction over securities transactions. Foreign protest against US assertions has nevertheless remained fairly mute, although it may be only a matter of time before conflicts erupt.[180]

The securities antifraud provisions are but a small part of the corpus of securities laws. Securities laws writ large may also impose extensive disclosure requirements,[181] they may protect investors holding securities in targets of a takeover by other investors (takeover law),[182] they may prohibit issuers from engaging in corrupt practices,[183] and they may require issuers to set up corporate governance structures that ensure the transparency and fairness of their corporate dealings.[184] The reach of such securities laws is typically more modest than the reach of the securities antifraud provisions. It is conceptually also less developed. As regulators rather than courts supervise the enforcement of non-antifraud-related provisions, a principled framework is often lacking, and solutions are reached on the basis of a case-by-case analysis and on the basis of transnational interagency cooperation. Regulators generally keep the long arm of their takeover and corporate governance laws within reasonable boundaries, yet sometimes only because foreign nations and issuers have urged them to. We will revert to reasonableness, also in the context of jurisdiction over securities transactions, in Chapter 5.

---

[178] At length G Schuster, 'Extraterritoriality of Securities Laws: An Economic Analysis of Jurisdictional Conflicts', (1994) 26 Law & Pol'y Int'l Bus 165; Schuster (above n 92).

[179] Also H Kronke, 'Capital Markets and Conflict of Laws', (2000) 286 RCADI 245, 272.

[180] eg Langevoort (above n 130) 241, 242 (1992) (arguing that 'it will only be a matter of time before cases arise that more visibly involve standards of fiduciary responsibility and similar conduct restraints where the potential for implicit conflicts in legal cultures is strong').

[181] Notably 15 USC §77e and §77l. From a practical perspective: B Black, 'Entering the U.S. Securities Markets: Regulation of Non-U.S. Issuers', (2004:4) 1 International Journal of Baltic Law.

[182] C Ryngaert, 'Cross-Border Takeover Regulation: a Transatlantic Perspective', (2007) European Company and Financial Law Review 434.

[183] eg US Foreign Corrupt Practices Act, 15 USC §§ 78dd-1 (Exchange Act § 30A) and 78dd-2; Exchange Act § 13.

[184] eg the reach of the US Sarbanes-Oxley Act, Public law 107-24, 30 July 2002, 116 Stat 745. For an appraisal of this act from an international and Belgian perspective: C Ryngaert, 'De verenigbaarheid van de Amerikaanse Sarbanes-Oxley Act met internationaal en Belgisch recht', (2004) Tijdschrift voor Rechtspersoon en Vennootschap 3.

3.7 Territoriality and Orders for Discovery Abroad

In transnational disputes over which States exercise substantive 'extraterritorial'—but in fact territorial—jurisdiction, valuable documents that could serve as evidence are often located abroad. In order to bring the truth to light before the court hearing the dispute, a mere exercise of prescriptive jurisdiction over the subject matter of the dispute does not suffice: courts may have to order, usually at the request of one of the parties, the production of documents held by one party abroad, or the deposition of witnesses residing abroad. The traditional method of getting hold of foreign-based evidence is international judicial cooperation. To that effect, the Hague Convention on the Taking of Evidence Abroad in Civil and Commercial Matters was concluded in 1970.[185] Another method consists of ordering a defendant over which a State has personal jurisdiction, possibly by means of a subpoena, to produce documents held abroad by that person, his employer, or a person controlled by the former. While the former method, based on international cooperation, does not raise jurisdictional issues, the latter clearly does: court orders to produce foreign-based documents subject such documents to the laws and procedures of a State other than the State where they are located.[186]

European States appear to rely exclusively on international cooperation so as to get hold of foreign-based evidence. Their position does not give rise to jurisdictional concerns.[187] US courts, by contrast, have often considered international cooperation to be too cumbersome and disadvantageous to plaintiffs. Instead, they have applied the domestic rules of discovery (evidence-taking) to transnational litigation, and unilaterally ordered defendants to produce foreign-based materials under threat of a subpoena. As document disclosure is subject to territorial legislation as well, and even more, as the disclosure of certain documents is sometimes prohibited under foreign law, discovery orders by US courts with extraterritorial effect have regularly met with stiff foreign opposition, especially from European States. This has occurred most notably in international antitrust proceedings, where the outcome often depended on evidence of business restrictive practices located abroad,[188] and where the underlying assertions of

---

[185] Hague Convention on the Taking of Evidence Abroad in Civil and Commercial Matters, 18 March 1970, 847 UNTS 231.

[186] HL Buxbaum, 'Assessing Sovereign Interests in Cross-Border Discovery Disputes: Lessons From *Aérospatiale*', (2003) 38 Texas Int LJ 87. However C Day Wallace, 'Extraterritorial Discovery: Ongoing Challenges for Antitrust Litigation in an Environment of Global Investment', (2003) J Int'l Econ L 353, 355 (arguing that 'these procedures are by no means universally agreed to be "extraterritorial" in fact'). Compare cmt a to § 442 of the Restatement (Third) of US Foreign Relations Law (stating that '[d]iscovery . . . is an exercise of jurisdiction').

[187] RA Trittmann, 'Extraterritoriale Beweisaufnahmen und Souveränitätsverletzungen im deutsch-amerikanischen Rechtsverkehr', (1989) 27 Archiv des Völkerrechts 195.

[188] Day Wallace (above n 186) 353.

prescriptive jurisdiction were also contested.[189] It is against this backdrop that one ought to understand reporter's note 1 to § 442 of the Restatement (Third) of the Foreign Relations Law of the United States (1987), which states that '[n]o aspect of the extension of the American legal system beyond the territorial frontier of the United States has given rise to so much friction as the request for documents associated with investigation and litigation in the United States'.

US courts have traditionally premised their orders for the production of documents located abroad on the *territoriality* principle. In the US view, the principle of non-intervention would only prohibit the United States from ordering discovery *within foreign territory*,[190] such as ordering the inspection of a plant located abroad, without the consent of the foreign State. In contrast, it would not prohibit US courts from ordering the production of documents located abroad or the presence of foreign parties or witnesses to present themselves before US courts, if need be by issuing a subpoena. Arguably, the territoriality principle would be respected, since the foreign acts to give effect to a US discovery order are merely preparatory, whilst the main acts (the document production in a US court, a deposition in the United States) take place *within US territory*.[191] In the US view, the application of US discovery orders to foreign documents or witnesses is thus considered to be an aspect of territorial indirect enforcement jurisdiction,[192] and an aspect of US territorial judicial sovereignty which foreign States are expected to respect.[193] In fact, pursuant to the US view, the law of the forum, and no other

---

[189] eg United Kingdom, brief as *amicus curiae* in litigation between *Westinghouse Electric Corp.* and *Rio Algom Limited et al*, July 1979, (1979) BYIL 355 ('Because of the basic disagreement over the international legality of assertions in antitrust cases of jurisdiction based on the "effects" test there have been well known disagreements over the proper scope of discovery requests and remedy orders issued by U.S. courts in international antitrust cases').

[190] DJ Gerber, 'Extraterritorial Discovery and the Conflict of Procedural Systems: Germany and the United States', (1986) 34 Am J Comp L 745, 776.

[191] eg *Adidas Canada v SS Seatrain Bennington*, F Supp 1984 WL 423, 2 (SDNY 1984), with respect to a US discovery order relating to French witnesses and documents ('The discovery here sought does not involve any such intrusion on French sovereignty or judicial custom. No adverse party will enter on French soil to gather evidence (or otherwise). No oath need be administered on French soil or by a French judicial authority. What is required of Les Toles on French soil is certain acts preparatory to the giving of evidence. It must select appropriate employees to give depositions in the forum state: likewise it must select the relevant documents which it will reveal to its adversaries in the forum state. These acts do not call for French judicial participation. If Les Toles were preparing to bring litigation against United States adversaries in the United States courts, it would perform the same acts of selecting employee witnesses and evidentiary documents from its files without participation by any French judicial authority. In no way do those acts affront or intrude on French sovereignty'); *In re Anschuetz & Co*, 754 F 2d 602, 611 (5th Cir 1985) (with respect to a US discovery order relating to a German corporation); *Graco, Inc v Kremlin, Inc*, 101 FRD 503 (ND Ill 1984) (with respect to a US discovery order relating to a French corporation).

[192] Cf FA Mann, 'The Doctrine of Jurisdiction Revisited after Twenty Years', (1984-III) 186 RCADI 9, 49.

[193] eg *United States v Bank of Nova Scotia I*, 619 F 2d 1384, 1391 (11th Cir 1982) ('The judicial assistance procedure does not afford due deference to the United States' interests. In essence, the Bank asks the court to require our government to ask the courts of the Bahamas to do something lawful under United States law. We conclude such a procedure to be contrary to the interests of our nation and outweigh the interests of the Bahamas'). Cf Buxbaum (above n 186) 93, who

law, governs procedure and evidence-taking.[194] Requiring recourse to international judicial assistance, in contrast, would, as the US Court of Appeals for the Fifth Circuit put it, 'make foreign authorities the final arbiters of what evidence may be taken from their nationals, even when those nationals are parties properly within the jurisdiction of an American court'.[195]

Foreign States, European States in particular, have, after the adoption of the Convention, not surprisingly often argued that the execution of US discovery orders for the production of documents located within their territory is not in keeping with the territoriality principle, runs afoul of international law, and violates their judicial sovereignty if their consent was not previously obtained.[196] This narrower, European view on judicial sovereignty takes into account the sovereignty of States other than the forum State deciding on a discovery request.[197] In this view, absent consent by the territorial State, any US order for the production of documents or the deposition of witnesses located abroad violates the basic principles of the foreign legal system (*ordre public*)[198] and hence, the sovereignty of the foreign State and the international law principle of non-intervention,[199] even if the documents are only disclosed or the witnesses only deposed in the United States.[200] Europeans tend to argue that only voluntary bilateral assistance requests, and not unilateral discovery orders, will duly respect foreign States' sovereignty, or as Professor Mann wrote in 1964: 'If, for the purpose of civil litigation pending in the forum State, it is necessary to *take evidence* in a foreign country, this cannot normally be done otherwise than with the assistance of the competent authorities of the foreign State'.[201] More moderate European voices may at times approve of unilateral discovery by the United States, but none will be found who does not take issue with discovery in case of foreign sovereign compulsion, notably when a European State has enacted legislation blocking the execution of US discovery orders, or when European courts otherwise prohibit the transmission of evidence.[202]

only defines the general sovereign interest of civil law countries in limited discovery as 'judicial sovereignty'.

[194] AF Lowenfeld, 'International Litigation and the Quest for Reasonableness', (1994-I) 245 RCADI 9, 254. Also *SEC v Banca della Svizzera Italiana*, 92 FRD 111 (1981) ('It would be a travesty of justice to permit a foreign company to invade American markets, violate American laws if they were indeed violated, withdraw profits and resist accountability for itself and its principals for the illegality by claiming their anonymity under foreign law').

[195] *In re Anschuetz & Co*, 754 F 2d 602, 612 (5th Cir 1985). Also reporters' note 1 to § 442 (1) (c) of the Restatement (Third) of US Foreign Relations Law.

[196] Also cmt c to § 442 (1) (c) of the Restatement (Third) of US Foreign Relations Law.

[197] Lowenfeld (above n 194) 254 (stating that '[p]ublic international law teaches that judicial functions can be carried out in a State only by officials of that State and with the State's consent').

[198] Gerber (above n 190) 778.

[199] Trittmann (above n 187) 195.

[200] Mann (above n 6) 137 (arguing that enforcing 'the attendance of a foreign witness [by a State] before its own tribunals by threatening him with penalties in case of non-compliance . . . runs contrary to the practice of States in regard to the taking of evidence as it has developed over a long period of time').

[201] ibid 136.   [202] Schuster (above n 92) 591.

Accordingly, the United States and Europe both rely on the territoriality principle in order to support their positions, which are actually 'based on assumptions which derive from [their own] domestic legal system and correspond to [their] own interests'.[203] A uniform public international law perspective on extraterritorial discovery is thus conceptually not very developed.[204] Europeans may consider the protection of their own interests as based on the international law principle of non-interference and the prohibition of extraterritorial enforcement jurisdiction as set forth in the PCIJ's *Lotus* case.[205] Americans may retort that foreign nations' concerns are sufficiently accommodated by ordering documents to be produced in the United States, and not abroad, and by flying foreign residents to the United States to testify in a US court. They may add that it would be unfair to US persons to exempt foreign persons benefiting from doing business in the United States from the application of US discovery laws (ie the argument of equal treatment or waiver by conduct).[206]

It may be noted that considerations of reciprocity, which often spontaneously lead to a convergence of State interests and to the crystallization of a norm of customary international law, may play a smaller role in the international law debate over discovery. Only the United States engage in the sort of liberal discovery conducted by private attorneys, for domestic reasons related to the emphasis put on full disclosure of facts in the US litigation process. Because of the narrow view on evidence-taking taken by European States, who subject evidence-taking by parties to stringent relevancy requirements and reserve a prominent role for the judge, the odds of European courts upsetting the United States by ordering the production of US-based materials are doubtless lower than in the situation of US courts ordering the production of Europe-based materials. Nonetheless, one would be hard-pressed to deny that the traditional European preference for multilateral solutions to international problems does not underlie European reliance

---

[203] Gerber (above n 190) 779.

[204] Day Wallace (above n 186) 391 ('The present state of international law is inadequate to fully cope with disputes of this nature or to provide international judicial or alternative dispute settlement procedures'). The International Law Association addressed the issue in 1964, arguing that there was no international law providing authority for extraterritorial discovery. It did however not cite any international law authority *prohibiting* extraterritorial discovery. In fact, it merely described the divergent views of the United States and other States: 'It is difficult to find any authority under international law for the issuance of orders compelling the production of documents from abroad. The documents are admittedly located in the territory of another State. To assume jurisdiction over documents located abroad in advance of a finding of effect upon commerce raises the greatest doubts among non-Americans as to the validity of such orders' (International Law Association, Report of the Fifty-First Conference (1964) 407).

[205] Day Wallace (above n 186) 356–7.

[206] *United States v The Bank of Nova Scotia II*, 740 F 2d 817 (11th Cir 1983). Also KA Feagle, 'Extraterritorial Discovery: a Social Contract Perspective', (1996) 7 Duke J Comp & Int'l L 297, 302 and 311 (noting that, '[w]hile use of the comity analysis did quell international complaints about U.S. discovery, it ultimately created just as many domestic ones', and complaining that 'the United States has guaranteed to all litigants in U.S. courts an opportunity for broad discovery, but routinely denies litigants this opportunity if they are unfortunate enough to sue or be sued by a party with relevant evidence located in a foreign country').

on international judicial assistance with respect to evidence-taking. Europeans may indeed reason that arguments of reciprocity counsel against unilateral assertions of jurisdiction in the field of the law of evidence. Although such assertions may confer short-term litigation benefits, such benefits may be outweighed by the burdens of future unilateral assertions of jurisdiction by other States.[207]

3.8 Concluding Observations

In this section, we have discussed the territoriality principle and its applications in various fields of the law. It has been shown that, in the criminal law, common law countries have put far more emphasis on the territoriality principle than continental European countries. Because in the latter countries, substantive justice has historically been considered as more important than evidentiary due process standards—the latter requiring that the offender be tried where he committed his crime—extraterritorial jurisdiction is uncommon in the common law. The grounds of extraterritorial jurisdiction (principles of nationality, security/protection, and universality), will be discussed in the next chapter. It will be seen that civil law countries provide more statutory opportunities for exercising extraterritorial jurisdiction.

Because territoriality has been the cornerstone of jurisdictional order in the common law, and extraterritorial jurisdiction has been shunned, it comes as no surprise that common law countries, the United States in particular, have construed the territorial principle rather broadly in order to get to grips with the challenges posed by transnational crime and economic globalization. Drawing on the criminal law constitutive elements approach, US jurisdiction in the antitrust and securities fields has been found as soon as some territorial effects or some territorial conduct could be discerned, even absent a clear statement of Congress regarding the territorial scope of the antitrust and securities laws. US jurisdictional assertions outside the criminal law have, as a result, been generally perceived as broader than those of other States. Sometimes they are denoted as assertions of 'extraterritorial' jurisdiction, in spite of their often being based, albeit loosely, on the territorial principle.

Such broad assertions may engender international conflict, notably when another State believes it has a stronger interest in the situation over which jurisdiction is exercised. A second-level rules-based framework of permissible

---

[207] However also cmt c to § 442 of the Restatement (Third) of US Foreign Relations Law (1987) ('In making the necessary determination of the interests of the United States . . . the court or agency should take into account not merely the interest of the prosecuting or investigating agency in the particular case, but the long-term interests of the United States generally in international cooperation in law enforcement and judicial assistance, in joint approach to problems of common concern, in giving effect to formal or informal international agreements, and in orderly international relations').

jurisdiction assertions may thus be called for. This framework of 'jurisdictional reasonableness' is the subject of Chapter 5. Reasonableness requires that not only the exercise of jurisdiction be based on a permissive principle such as the territorial principle, but also that such exercise take into account the regulatory interests of other States. Before jurisdictional reasonableness is discussed, however, the other permissive principles of jurisdiction will be examined in Chapter 4. It should be kept in mind that, like a jurisdictional assertion based on territoriality, a State's assertion of jurisdiction predicated on one of the other principles may only be presumptively valid. If a reasonableness analysis makes clear that another State could present a more legitimate jurisdictional case, in view of its connections to and interests in the regulatory situation, the former State may want to, or have to, defer. The exact legal status of a purported rule of reason will be further explored in Chapters 5 and 6.

4

The Principles of Extraterritorial Criminal Jurisdiction

In Chapter 3, the scope of the principle of territorial jurisdiction has been set out. In the customary international law scheme of jurisdiction, the territoriality principle serves as the basic principle of jurisdiction. Exceptionally, however, national laws may be given extraterritorial application, provided that these laws could be justified by one of the recognized principles of extraterritorial jurisdiction under public international law: the active personality principle, the passive personality principle, the protective principle, or the universality principle. In this chapter, the extraterritorial reach of the law will be discussed.

It will be shown how continental European and common law countries exercise, to various extents, extraterritorial jurisdiction. While the active personality and the protective principles (sections 4.2 and 4.4 respectively) are generally deemed uncontroversial, the same cannot be said of the passive personality and the universality principles (sections 4.3 and 4.5 respectively). Notably the universality principle has gained a remarkable but contested ascendancy recently. In section 4.5, it will be ascertained whether the exercise of universal jurisdiction, ie, the exercise of jurisdiction without a direct link to the forum State, is lawful under international law, and if so, what limits international law attaches to it. In general, it will be seen that continental European countries will more readily exercise extraterritorial criminal jurisdiction than common law countries, which, for various reasons, lay more emphasis on the territoriality principle (see sections 3.2 and 3.3).

4.1 Continental Europe v The Common Law Countries

Most continental European criminal codes feature introductory provisions dealing with the geographical scope of application of domestic criminal laws. These provisions draw on the classical principles of criminal jurisdiction. The structure of most codes is such that they affirm at the outset the irreducible importance of the territoriality principle, and subsequently set out the scope of other jurisdictional principles. They ordinarily state that domestic criminal law is applicable to all offences within the territory,[1] and that offences are considered to have been committed within the territory where one of its constituent elements was committed within that territory.[2] Importantly, they do not set forth territorial exclusivity, in the sense that domestic criminal law would apply to territorial offences to the exclusion of foreign criminal law.[3] Instead, they allow the exercise of jurisdiction on other, non-territorial grounds. These grounds are ordinarily based upon the classical principles of jurisdiction under international law. In addition, continental-European criminal codes provide for special jurisdiction over foreign aircraft, provided that a link with the forum State can be established,[4] over offences committed by persons subject to military laws,[5] or over offences committed abroad when extradition proves impossible (vicarious jurisdiction).[6]

The very fact of having *general* provisions dealing with the scope of application *ratione loci* of domestic laws attests to the important role that continental European countries have reserved for extraterritorial criminal jurisdiction. Criminal codes in England and the United States, by contrast, do not have introductory provisions on jurisdiction. England and the United States have only allowed extraterritorial jurisdiction for specific offences. This may be explained by the high premium that these countries historically put on the territoriality principle.

The emphasis on territoriality is related to the strict evidentiary rules employed in the common law criminal process. Notably common law countries' mistrust of hearsay evidence and emphasis on cross-examination (and their concomitant unwillingness to receive deposition testimony) may prevent them from successfully applying their laws to situations arising abroad. Aside from a different tradition of evidence-gathering, some other reasons for common law countries' reluctance to exercise extraterritorial jurisdiction may be discerned. For one, their geographical features—the United Kingdom and the United States having mostly sea boundaries—may reduce the prevalence of transboundary crime, and

---

[1] eg article 113-2 of the French Code Pénal (French CP); article 2 of the Dutch Penal Code; § 3 StGB; articles 3–4 of the Belgian Penal Code.

[2] eg article 113-2 of the French CP; § 9 (1) StGB. Offences on board or against ships flying the flag of a particular State or aircraft registered in a particular State are usually considered to be offences committed within the territory, wherever these ships or aircraft may be and whatever the nationality of the offender or victim. eg article 113-3 French CP; articles 3 and 7 of the Dutch Penal Code; § 4 StGB. Compare Harvard Research on International Law, 'Draft Convention on Jurisdiction with Respect to Crime', (1935) 29 AJIL 439, 509–10 ('Ships and aircraft are not territory. It is recognized, nevertheless, that a State has with respect to such ships or aircraft a jurisdiction which is similar to its jurisdiction over its territory.' . . . 'And the jurisdiction which became well established with respect to ships was extended by analogy to include aircraft when the development of aviation made the jurisdiction of aircraft a practical problem').

[3] Contra eg article 113-3 *in fine* French CP (providing that French criminal law 'is the only applicable law in relation to offences committed on board ships of the *national navy*, or against such ships, wherever they may be') (emphasis added).

[4] eg article 113-11 French CP; article 4, 7° Dutch Penal Code.

[5] eg article 10*bis* PT Belgian CCP.

[6] Cf section 4.5 on universal jurisdiction.

thus obviate the need for extraterritorial jurisdiction. For another, common law countries may emphasize retribution over prevention as a purpose of the criminal law. In a retributive conception of the criminal law, criminal acts are considered to be offences against the territorial sovereign. Criminal acts done abroad are offences against a foreign sovereign and therefore in no need of punishment by another sovereign. In a preventive or 'cosmopolitan' conception of the criminal law,[7] in contrast, as emphasized in continental European countries, the criminal law is 'a means of selecting persons in need of remedial treatment, or of permanent detention where "cure" is impossible',[8] irrespective of the place where these persons have perpetrated their acts. In such a conception, it may be incumbent upon any State, obviously within certain limits, to apply its criminal laws to offenders it might catch, even if they have committed their acts abroad.

Over the years, common law countries have somewhat relaxed their exclusive jurisdictional reliance on the territorial principle, yet they have, unlike continental European countries, not done so in a systematic way.[9] Instead of subsuming crimes under a general head of jurisdiction, they have extended the scope of application of particular crimes in a piecemeal fashion. The ambit of the law is typically part of the definition (*actus reus*) of the crime.[10] The common law legislative technique is such that the substantive provision at the same time defines the crime *and* sets forth its scope *ratione loci* (at least if the crime could be prosecuted if committed abroad), ie an 'offence-specific' type of extraterritorial jurisdiction.[11] In continental Europe, in contrast, the crime is usually listed under a particular head of jurisdiction in a separate jurisdictional chapter. Needless to say, the common law approach, lacking general jurisdictional guidance and principles, spawns incoherence, which the English doctrine has not failed to criticize.[12] The introduction of general provisions has been proposed in England,[13] as it has in the United States,[14] yet these proposals have hitherto fallen on deaf ears.

The crime of torture, which in both common law and continental European countries is subject to universal jurisdiction, may serve as an example. In England,

---

[7] Cf the intellectual groundwork for the 'cosmopolitan' theory of criminal justice: H Grotius, *De Jure Belli ac Pacis Libri Tres* (2005) ch 20, § 40.

[8] WW Cook, 'The Application of the Criminal Law of a Country to Acts Committed by Foreigners Outside the Jurisdiction', (1934) 40 W Va LQ 303, 329.

[9] Cf GR Watson, 'Offenders Abroad: The Case for Nationality-Based Criminal Jurisdiction', (1992) 17 Yale J Int'l L 41, 52 (writing about a 'patchwork' of nationality-based jurisdiction).

[10] M Hirst, *Jurisdiction and the Ambit of the Criminal Law* (2003) 2–3.

[11] ibid 202.

[12] ibid 7; P Arnell, 'The Case for Nationality-Based Jurisdiction', (2001) 50 ICLQ 955 (stating that '[c]riminal jurisdiction in the United Kingdom is in a muddle').

[13] Draft Criminal Code 1989, Law Commission No 177, vol 1, para 3.13 ('The Code must contain general provisions relating to the jurisdiction of the criminal courts, that is to say, the definition of the territory of England and Wales for criminal purposes, and ... Part 1 [of the Code] was the appropriate place for them'); Hirst (above n 10) 326 (arguing that a Criminal Jurisdiction Act is needed, which could later be incorporated within a Criminal Code).

[14] § 208 of the Final Report of the National Commission on Reform of Federal Criminal Laws (1971), available at <http://wings.buffalo.edu/law/bclc/codein.htm>.

pursuant to section 134 of the 1988 Criminal Justice Act, it is a crime under English law if '[a] public official or person acting in an official capacity, whatever his nationality, commits the offence of torture if in the United Kingdom or elsewhere he intentionally inflicts severe pain or suffering on another in the performance or purported performance of his official duties'.[15] In continental European countries, however, the crime of torture is usually defined in a chapter dealing with substantive crimes, whereas the scope *ratione loci* of the crime is set out in a jurisdictional chapter, sometimes by means of an 'enabling clause', ie an open-ended statutory provision that grants prosecutors and courts universal jurisdiction over any offence which international (treaty) law requires them to prosecute.[16]

In the following sections, the scope of the jurisdictional principles (the personality, protective, universality, and vicarious principles of jurisdiction) in the United States, England, and continental Europe will be discussed. It will be noted that, while the criminal codes of continental European countries feature general jurisdictional provisions, these provisions do not set forth a wholesale assumption of personality, protective, or universality jurisdiction. Indeed, these States ordinarily predicate the exercise of extraterritorial jurisdiction on a number of restrictive conditions. Conversely, while common law criminal codes do not feature general jurisdictional provisions, this has not prevented common law countries from providing for extraterritorial jurisdiction over an increasing number of offences. Recent times have thus witnessed a convergence of practices of extraterritorial criminal jurisdiction in continental Europe and common law countries.

4.2 Active Personality Principle

Under the nationality or active personality principle, a State is entitled to exercise jurisdiction over its nationals, even when they are found outside the territory,[17] and even when the perpetrator is no longer a national or has only become a national after committing the crime.[18] It is hardly contested that a State can base

---

[15] Also the criminalization of torture and the attendant extension of US jurisdiction in 18 USC §2340A(b)(2), '[t]here is jurisdiction over [torture] if [...] the alleged offender is present in the United States, irrespective of the nationality of the victim or alleged offender'.

[16] For enabling clauses: article 12*bis* of the Belgian Code of Criminal Procedure, article 23.4 (g) of the Spanish Organic Law of the Judicial Power, and article 6, § 9 of the German Criminal Code. See for a separation between explicit substantive incrimination and jurisdiction: section 2 (jurisdiction) *juncto* section 8 (incrimination) of the Dutch International Crimes Act, and article 689-2 of the French Code of Criminal Procedure (jurisdiction) *juncto* article 222–1 of the Criminal Code (incrimination).

[17] In private international law, national law often follows the national outside the territory as far as his personal status is concerned. Hence, courts may apply foreign law provided it does not violate domestic police laws or public order. In criminal law, the nationality principle rather refers to the jurisdiction to adjudicate: can a State adjudge crimes committed abroad?

[18] Harvard Research on International Law (above n 2) 532 (justifying this extension by arguing that, in the former case, '[w]ere the rule otherwise, a criminal might escape prosecution by change of nationality after committing the crime', and that in the latter case, 'if a contrary rule were followed, impunity might result from naturalization in a State which refuses extradition of its nationals').

its criminal jurisdiction on the nationality of the accused.[19] In fact, some authors, and the US Supreme Court, have argued that a State's treatment of its nationals is not a concern of international law.[20] Others have even argued that exercising active personality jurisdiction may be a State's *duty* under international law.[21]

Also if the accused's conduct is not punishable in the territorial State, active personality jurisdiction might be legitimate. In that case, however, it may signal the inadequacy of territorial legislation and thereby raise sovereignty concerns.[22]

It may be noted that active personality jurisdiction may cover all crimes committed abroad. Yet national legislation incorporating the active personality principle typically only covers serious offences, on the basis of a variety of legislative techniques.[23] The limitation of the principle to serious crimes does nevertheless not seem to be required by international law.[24] While quite a few crimes are amenable to the exercise of active personality-based jurisdiction, punishment may in practice often be lighter than for territorial crimes, because the harm to a State's public order might be smaller in case of extraterritorial offences.[25]

---

[19] ibid 519 ('The competence of the State to prosecute and punish its nationals on the sole basis of their nationality is universally conceded'); M Akehurst, 'Jurisdiction in International Law', (1972–1973) 46 BYIL 145, 156.

GR Watson, 'The Passive Personality Principle', (1993) 28 Tex Int'l LJ 1, 2; JH Beale, 'The Jurisdiction of a Sovereign State', (1923) 36 Harv L Rev 241, 253. It was long unclear whether domicile or residence would afford an adequate basis for jurisdiction under international law, although Scandinavian countries traditionally used it. Harvard Research on International Law (above n 2) 533 (no adequate basis). In light of the fact that quite some States that did not use domicile or residence as a sufficient nexus, have recently expanded the ambit of their criminal law to include some offences committed by resident aliens abroad, it may be submitted that domicile or residence probably represents an adequate jurisdictional basis.

[20] Harvard Research on International Law (above n 2) 519; *Blackmer v United States*, 284 US 421, 437 (1932) ('With respect to such an exercise of authority, there is no question of international law, but solely of the purport of the municipal law which establishes the duties of the citizen in relation to his own government').

[21] C Scott, 'Translating Torture into Transnational Tort: Conceptual Divides in the Debate on Corporate Accountability for Human Rights Harms', in C Scott, ed, *Torture as Tort* (2001) 55 (arguing, in the context of sex tourism abroad, that international law may not only authorize, but also *require*, the application of US law to US nationals abroad).

[22] Watson (above n 9) 77 (arguing that '[t]he dearth of state practice makes it premature to infer a dual-criminality requirement for all such prosecutions. If anything, international practice suggests the opposite conclusion'). ibid 79 (even noting that 'not all states find it unacceptable to provide assistance in prosecuting a crime not included in their domestic criminal code').

[23] Legislation may make punishable all offences which are also punishable by the *lex loci delicti*; all offences of a certain degree; offences against co-nationals; or certain enumerated offences only: Harvard Research on International Law (above n 2) 523.

[24] Harvard Research on International Law (above n 2) 531 ('It is believed, however, that [limitations on the exercise of active personality jurisdiction] are matters which each State is free to determine for itself. Both the crimes abroad for which it will punish its nationals and the circumstances under which it will punish its nationals and the circumstances under which it will exercise jurisdiction are matters which international law leaves each State free to decide according to local needs and conditions').

[25] eg article 5 of the Italian Penal Code of 1889, which reduced the punishment by a sixth if the offence had been committed abroad. HFA Donnedieu de Vabres, *Les principes modernes du droit pénal international* (1928) 64.

The concept of active personality jurisdiction draws on the conception of a State as a group of persons, wherever located, who are subject to a common authority.[26] Outside the field of criminal law, this concept has been particularly influential in the field of international family law.[27] A variety of explanations traditionally underpin active personality jurisdiction, such as the need to prevent nationals from engaging in criminal activity upon their return to their home State, and from enjoying scandalous impunity in the eyes of the domestic public, the impossibility of locating an offence,[28] the representation of the territorial State in case the perpetrator could not be extradited (a number of States traditionally do not extradite their own nationals),[29] and the need to protect a State's reputation from being blemished by the conduct of its nationals abroad. As far as the latter justification is concerned, it has been argued that active personality jurisdiction is in fact a compensation for the diplomatic protection that the State offers to its nationals abroad (the so-called 'allegiance theory').[30] As States often refuse to extradite their own nationals, active personality jurisdiction may even be necessary if offenders are not to go unpunished. The territorial State might arguably welcome the exercise of jurisdiction by the State of nationality of the offender, as this may relieve it of the task of harnessing its resources to prosecute the offence.[31]

Historically, the active personality principle was already recognized at the time of Bartolus by the medieval city States of northern Italy.[32] It was first codified in the legislation of the states of the German Confederation, the Swiss cantons, Sardinia and Tuscany, in the mid-nineteenth century.[33] In the Anglo-Saxon countries, which have a strong territorial system, active personality jurisdiction was traditionally underdeveloped.[34] As these countries are willing to extradite their own nationals, there is in fact no compelling need for such jurisdiction. In some countries, active personality jurisdiction has been used as a political instrument. In Italy, for instance, where it was known as 'the nationality doctrine',

---

[26] ibid 77.   [27] ibid 80.

[28] An offence may sometimes be difficult to locate because it was committed on board a train or a plane, when it was committed upon the crossing of a border, or when it was committed in disputed territory. Donnedieu de Vabres, a product of his time, even added: 'Il peut arriver aussi que le crime ait été commis sur un territoire que ne régit aucune souveraineté effective: territoire inhabité, ou habité par des populations d'une civilization inférieure.' ibid 81.

[29] ibid 115; F Desportes and F Le Gunehec, *Le nouveau droit pénal*, vol 1 (7th edn 2000) 328.

[30] Donnedieu de Vabres (above n 25) 63; Desportes and Le Gunehec (above n 29) 328; Watson (above n 9) 68 (arguing that 'the state provides its national the benefits of nationality, including protection at home and abroad, in exchange for the national's obedience').

[31] Watson (above n 9) 69–70 (pointing out that '[t]he State Department has argued that [the] indictment of a U.S. national for a crime committed abroad might actually benefit bilateral relations, because it might reduce pressure on host states to prosecute').

[32] ibid 57.   [33] ibid 60 and 63.

[34] Only the extraterritorial offences causing the greatest scandal in England have historically been subject to active personality jurisdiction. Murder and manslaughter (Act of 1541, 33 Henry VIII, c 23; Act of 1813, 43 George III, c 113; Act of 1861, 24 and 25 Victoria, c 100), bigamy and anarchist offences (Act of 1883, 46 Victoria, c 3) can be cited in this context.

it was tied to Italian irredentism, a nationalist movement that advocated the annexation to Italy of territories inhabited by an Italian majority but retained by Austria after 1866.[35]

Control theory

In the field of economic law, the active personality principle may also play a role. States could rely on it to justify their jurisdiction over the business dealings of their corporations abroad. Difficulties relating to the application of the national-ity principle may arise, however. For one, the 'nationality' of a corporation may not always be readily established. Corporations could have different nationalities, since their nationality could be based on the State of incorporation, shareholder nationality as well as other corporate links to the forum.[36] For another, even if the nationality of a corporation could be established, the question may arise whether a State could exercise jurisdiction over foreign corporations *controlled* by its nationals or corporations. Notably US lawmakers and courts have at times sub-jected foreign undertakings controlled by US persons (ordinarily shareholders) to US laws for reasons related to foreign policy objectives, or out of reputational concerns.[37] Foreign subsidiaries of US corporations have tended to comply with US regulations (even if they could possibly be exempted under administrative requirements of the US Office of Foreign Assets Control).[38]

The 'control theory' is prima facie not in line with international law, which considers nationality, and not control, as controlling. Indeed, as the ICJ held in the *Barcelona Traction* case:

Separated from the company by numerous barriers the shareholder cannot be identified with it. The concept and structure of the company are founded on and determined by a firm distinction between the separate entity of the company and of the shareholder, each with a distinct set of rights.[39]

The ICJ's rejection of the piercing of the corporate veil theory in *Barcelona Traction*, which was admittedly a diplomatic protection case, is generally considered to be

---

[35] Donnedieu de Vabres (above n 25) 63.

[36] *Laker Airways v Sabena*, 731 F 2d 909, 936 (DC Cir 1984); comment a to § 414 of the Restatement (Third) of US Foreign Relations Law (1987) (stating that '[multinational] enterprises may not be nationals of one state only and their activities are not limited to one state's territory').

[37] G Schuster, 'Extraterritoriality of Securities Laws: An Economic Analysis of Jurisdictional Conflicts', (1994) 26 Law & Pol'y Int'l Bus 165, 185. The United States first relied on the control theory in 1942, when the US Treasury included in the category 'persons subject to the jurisdiction of the United States' set forth in the Trading with the Enemy Act of 1917 'any corporation or other entity, wherever organized or doing business, owned or controlled by [U.S.] persons'. Section 5(b) of the Trading with the Enemy Act of 1917, 40 Stat 411. US Treasury Public Circulary No 18, 30 March 1942, 7 Fed Reg 2503 (1 April 1942).

[38] J Lee and J Slear, 'Beware of Ofac', IFLR (September 2006) 58, 59.

[39] ICJ, *Barcelona Traction, Light and Power Co Ltd* (Belgium v Spain), ICJ Rep 4, § 41 (1970). See also § 213 of the Restatement (Third) of Foreign Relations Law ('For purposes of international law, a corporation has the nationality of the state under the laws of which the corporation is organized').

good law in the field of international jurisdiction.[40] Also from an economic perspective, it appears rational not to accept the control theory, since the costs of identifying and initiating proceedings against US-controlled foreign undertakings (ie enforcement costs) may outweigh any perceived benefits.[41] Control-based jurisdiction may, however, be acceptable under international law, if limited to foreign branches, as opposed to foreign subsidiaries, of domestic corporations, since foreign branches are legally closer to the State of the parent corporation.[42]

The control theory does not pose significant problems provided that prescriptive jurisdiction could duly be established on the basis of an accepted principle of jurisdiction under international law, such as the territoriality or protective principle.[43] Jurisdiction could thus obtain over foreign subsidiaries that have actively participated in a conspiracy involving a domestic parent,[44] if the conduct of the foreign subsidiary causes substantial effects on domestic commerce,[45] or if the conduct of the foreign subsidiary jeopardizes national security.

4.3 Passive Personality Principle

It is unclear whether the nationality of the victim, which certainly constitutes a legitimate interest of the State,[46] also constitutes a sufficient jurisdictional link under international law.[47] It is, quite likely, the most aggressive basis for extraterritorial jurisdiction (if universal jurisdiction *in absentia* is discounted).[48] Several dissenting opinions in the *Lotus* case rejected the passive personality principle.[49] Donnedieu

[40] A Bianchi, Reply to Professor Maier, in KM Meessen, ed, *Extraterritorial Jurisdiction in Theory and Practice* (1996) 74, 94 (stating that, 'for the time being, state practice indicates that there is a strong presumption in favour of the separate entity of foreign subsidiaries', although conceding that 'in the future . . . newly developed criteria [justifying the exercise of control jurisdiction] might be applied as "generally recognized principles of law"').

[41] Schuster (above n 37) 186.

[42] Cmt b to § 414 of the Restatement (Third) of US Foreign Relations Law (1987).

[43] ibid cmt a *in fine*.

[44] Schuster (above n 37) 186; Bianchi (above n 40) 94.

[45] *a contrario* AV Lowe, 'The Problems of Extraterritorial Jurisdiction: Economic Sovereignty and the Search for a Solution', (1985) 34 ICLQ 724, 734 (arguing that jurisdictional assertions on the basis of the control theory 'represent a much deeper penetration of municipal laws into the affairs of foreign States than do claims based on the effects doctrine, and it should not be expected that the two kinds of claims would be tolerated on the same conditions').

[46] Watson (above n 19) 18.

[47] FA Mann, 'The Doctrine of Jurisdiction in International Law', (1964-I) 111 RCADI 1, 39; Harvard Research on International Law (above n 2) 579 (stating that the principle of passive personality has 'been more strongly contested than any other type of competence').

[48] E Cafritz and O Tene, 'Article 113-7 of the French Penal Code: the Passive Personality Principle', (2003) 41 Colum J Transnat'l L 585, 599; Watson (above n 19) 1; Harvard Research on International Law (above n 2) 579 (naming the passive personality principle 'the most difficult [principle] to justify in theory', because accepting it 'would only invite controversy without serving a useful objective').

[49] Eight Turkish nationals were killed as a result of the collision of *Lotus*, the French vessel, with the *Boz-Kourt*, the Turkish vessel. The Turkish penal code actually provided for jurisdiction over

de Vabres forcefully criticized passive personality jurisdiction as a solution that would, unlike the universality principle, not correspond to the way the judicial system is domestically organized, would not close an enforcement gap, and would lack any social aim of repression. Instead, it would merely be predicated on the egoism of States, and increase competency conflicts between States.[50]

It is submitted that, seen from the perspective of the perpetrator's rights, under a jurisdictional system partly based on the passive personality principle, the perpetrator cannot anticipate what State's laws he will be subjected to, as he will usually not know the victim's nationality.[51] In case double criminality is not required, such a system may subject an individual to foreign criminal law if she unwittingly encounters a foreigner.[52] Under the *active* personality principle, by contrast, individuals might reasonably be expected to be informed about the law applicable to their behaviour. They will not be surprised, as they know beforehand that, aside from the law of the territory that they enter, they are also subject to the law of their national State, wherever they go.[53] Since individuals will be surprised about the applicable law if jurisdiction is exercised under the passive personality principle, the principle will not have major deterrent effects. It is deterrence which is a classical aim of criminal law. If a provision of substantive, procedural, or jurisdictional criminal law fails to deter criminality, such as a rule that confers passive personality jurisdiction on a State's courts, it arguably fails to serve its purpose.[54]

Also from a sovereignty perspective the application of a foreign State's criminal law in a given territory raises concerns.[55] It indeed adds a regulatory layer and 'blurs the accepted standards of conduct' within the territorial State.[56] The great

---

'[a]ny foreigner who...commits an offence abroad to the prejudice of Turkey or of a Turkish subject'. PCIJ, *SS Lotus*, PCIJ Reports, Series A, No 10 (1927) 14–15, quoting article 6 of the Turkish Penal Code. Cf dissenting opinions *Lotus*, diss op Loder 36, diss op Finlay 55–8, diss op Nyholm 62, and diss op Moore 91–3. Also Watson (above n 19) 7–8.

[50] Donnedieu de Vabres (above n 25) 170.

[51] J Meyer, 'The Vicarious Administration of Justice: An Overlooked Basis of Jurisdiction', (1990) 31 Harv Int'l LJ 108, 114.

[52] Department of State, 'Report on Extraterritorial Crime and the Cutting Case', (1887) US Foreign Rel L 751, 840 (arguing that the passive personality principle would subject individuals 'not merely to a dual, but to an indefinite responsibility' since they would be required to obey *any State*'s law). Also Cafritz and Tene (above n 48) 593. In a system of unlimited passive personality, any citizen would be required to be familiar with the criminal laws of every country. ibid 595 (conceding however that 'it is not unrealistic to assume that [average citizens] would realize that committing *violent acts* might subject them to foreign prosecution') (emphasis added).

[53] Watson (above n 9) 79 (stating that '[i]f a state imposes high standards of conduct on an individual and presumes that the individual is aware of those standards, then it is not unreasonable to expect the individual to abide by the same standards when abroad, even if the standards in the foreign country are lower').

[54] Watson (above n 19) 19 (arguing that 'the very uncertainty of the passive personality remedy may enhance its deterrent effect').

[55] It may be conceded here, to be true, that a potential offender may, in case of doubt about the nationality of a potential victim, refrain from targeting the victim. Cafritz and Tene (above n 48) 597.

[56] Watson (above n 19) 16 (believing that 'it seems unlikely that the international legal system will ever approve of passive personality jurisdiction unless there is at least some element of "dual criminality" built into it').

theorist of jurisdiction, the late Professor Mann, therefore believed (in 1964) that '[passive personality jurisdiction] should be treated as an excess of jurisdiction'.[57]

In spite of calls to abandon the principle of passive personality,[58] recent State practice appears to consider jurisdiction on the basis of the passive personality principle to be reasonable, at least for certain crimes,[59] often linked to international terrorism.[60] *Aut dedere aut judicare* provisions in international conventions dealing with international terrorism, and later with torture, indeed authorize—but not compel—States to exercise passive personality jurisdiction.[61] The Restatement (Third) of US Foreign Relations Law (1987) took into account this evolution and, while stating that the passive personality principle 'has not been generally accepted for ordinary torts or crimes', it pointed out that it is 'increasingly accepted as applied to terrorist and other organized attacks on a state's nationals by reason of their nationality, or to assassination of a state's diplomatic representatives or other officials'.[62]

It was initially unclear whether passive personality jurisdiction could also be exercised if it was not in implementation of an international (antiterrorism) convention.[63] State practice nowadays shows that it probably could, if 'circumscribed by important safeguards and limitations'.[64] To be true, as few States have actually applied their laws, it is difficult to discern a customary norm of international law unambiguously *authorizing* passive personality jurisdiction, or more accurately,

---

[57] Mann (above n 47) 92.   [58] Meyer (above n 51) 114.

[59] ICJ, *Arrest Warrant* (Democratic Republic of Congo v Belgium), ICJ Rep 3 (2002) sep op Higgins, Kooijmans and Buergenthal, § 47 ('Passive personality jurisdiction, for so long regarded as controversial, is now reflected not only in the legislation of various countries, [..] and today meets with relatively little opposition, at least so far as a particular category of offences is concerned'); sep op Rezek, § 5 ('[D]ans la plupart des pays, l'action pénale est possible sur la base des principes de la *nationalité active* ou *passive*[.]'); sep op Guillaume, § 4 ('Under the law as classically formulated, a State normally has jurisdiction over an offence committed abroad only if the offender, *or at the very least the victim*, has the nationality of that State or if the crime threatens its internal or external security') (emphasis added).

[60] R Higgins, *Problems and Process: International Law and How We Use It* (1994) 66 (attributing the revived interest in the passive personality principle to the explosion of international terrorism). eg USC § 2331 (a)–(e) (1986).

[61] eg Article 4(b) of the Convention of Offences Committed on Board Aircraft, Tokyo, 14 September 1963, 220 UNTS 10106; Article 6(2)(b) of the Convention for the Suppression of Unlawful Acts Against the Safety of Maritime Navigation, Rome, 10 March 1988, 222 UNTS 29004; Article 5(1)(c) of the UN Torture Convention, New York, 10 December 1984, 1465 UNTS 85.

[62] Restatement (Third) of US Foreign Relations Law (1987), § 402, cmt g. In 1965, the Second Restatement still provided in an unqualified fashion that: '[a] state does not have jurisdiction to prescribe a rule of law attaching legal consequences to conduct of an alien outside its territory merely on the ground that the conduct affects one of its nationals'. (§ 30(2)). Cf Restatement (Third), § 421 ('States exercise jurisdiction to adjudicate on the basis of various links, including [...] the defendant's nationality [...] reliance on other bases, such as the nationality of the plaintiff or the presence of property unrelated to the claim, is generally considered as "exorbitant"'); B Stern, 'Can the United States Set Rules for the World? A French View', (1997:4) 31 JWT 17; I Brownlie, *Principles of Public International Law* (4th edn 1990) 303.

[63] AF Lowenfeld, 'U.S. Law Enforcement Abroad: The Constitution and International Law', (1989) 83 AJIL 880, 892.

[64] Harvard Research on International Law (above n 2) 579.

its scope.[65] However, if one draws on *Lotus*, the fact that international law does not explicitly authorize passive personality jurisdiction does not imply that international law outlaws it.[66] The lack of international protest against jurisdictional assertions based on passive personality may surely boost its legality.[67]

The absence of protest against passive personality jurisdiction is probably attributable to the restrictive conditions that usually surround its application, such as dual criminality, the requirement that only serious crimes are eligible for prosecution (certain classes of crime, eg murder, rape, felonious assault, or only crimes with a minimum degree of punishment),[68] the presence requirement,[69] or the requirement of executive consent.[70]

The impact of jurisdictional assertions based on the passive personality principle could further be soothed by premising jurisdiction on the request, the consent, or the acquiescence of the territorial State.[71] The unwillingness of the territorial State or the offender's home State to prosecute a particular crime against a foreign national does, however, probably not suffice for there to be jurisdiction that is respectful of the territorial State's sovereignty.[72] Indeed, it may be a territorial State's deliberate, sovereign and legitimate choice *not* to prosecute a crime, especially in States with a system of prosecutorial discretion. Admittedly, against this, it could be argued that preventing impunity is in the international community's systemic interest,[73] and that, thus, some State should be able to exercise jurisdiction. It remains, however, to be seen if this also holds true for common crimes, ie crimes which are not violations of obligations which any State owes to the international community (*erga omnes* obligations).

The myriad restrictive conditions accompanying the exercise of passive personality jurisdiction could not but undercut the efficiency of its exercise if the perpetrator is not present in the territory of the forum State. In order to bring about the perpetrator's presence, the custodial State's cooperation is ordinarily required. The

[65] Watson (above n 19) 13; JG McCarthy, 'The Passive Personality Principle and Its Use in Combatting International Terrorism', (1989–1990) 13 Fordham Int'l LJ 298, 318.

[66] W Berge, 'Criminal Jurisdiction and the Territorial Principle', (1931) 30 Mich L Rev 238, 268 ('It is submitted that if this type of jurisdiction is undesirable it should be outlawed by international agreement, but that, until this can be done, nations disapproving of such jurisdiction will have to tolerate its exercise by those nations which claim it').

[67] Higgins (above n 60) 69 (pointing out that '[p]rotests are not usually over the assertion of such (limited) passive-personality jurisdiction *as such*, but over something else—the forcible bringing of the alleged offender into the territory of the state of the victim…') (original emphasis).

[68] Watson (above n 19) 23 (1993); McCarthy (above n 65) 315.

[69] McCarthy (above n 65) 314.

[70] Cf Cafritz and Tene (above n 48) 597–8 (pointing out that in Greece, Finland, Norway, and Sweden, the double criminality requirement is a statutory precondition to passive personality jurisdiction, and that in Norway, Finland, Italy, and Sweden, executive (or the King's) consent is required for its application).

[71] Watson (above n 9) 52.   [72] ibid 21.

[73] ibid 44–5 (citing the reasonableness factors 'the importance of the regulation to the international political, legal, or economic system' and 'the extent to which the regulation is consistent with the traditions of the international system' in § 403 (2) (e)–(f) of the Restatement (Third) of Foreign Relations Law, so as to buttress the need for passive personality jurisdiction).

custodial State will often only cooperate and grant extradition if the requesting State bases its jurisdiction on a jurisdictional ground (and the restrictive conditions of its application) which the custodial State also recognizes in its domestic legal order. If the custodial State does not recognize the passive personality principle, it will usually not honour an extradition request by another State based on this principle. Also, if the custodial State imposes restrictive conditions on its own exercise of passive personality-based jurisdiction, it will expect the requesting State to impose equally restrictive conditions. Clearly, the efficiency of passive personality jurisdiction and international cooperation in criminal matters could benefit from a more uniform regime of passive personality jurisdiction.[74] An international streamlining and consolidation of the abovementioned restrictive conditions therefore appears desirable. In order to be successful, the international community could, for instance, first focus on crimes of which the heinous nature is generally accepted by States, such as terrorist crimes.[75]

4.4 Protective Principle

The protective principle protects the State from acts perpetrated abroad which jeopardize its sovereignty or its right to political independence. As such acts, such as the offence of treason, may not be punishable in the State where they originate, protective jurisdiction by the State at which the acts are directed, appears warranted.[76] For the operation of the protective principle, actual harm need not have resulted from these acts. This distinguishes it from the objective territorial principle (or effects doctrine).[77] Protective jurisdiction was already recognized in the city States of northern Italy in the thirteenth and fourteenth centuries. From the fifteenth

---

[74] McCarthy (above n 65) 319. Also C.L. Blakesley, 'Extraterritorial Jurisdiction', in MC Bassiouni, ed, *International Criminal Law II: Procedural and Enforcement Mechanisms* (2nd edn 1999) 105 (pointing out that coherence in grounds of jurisdiction is needed for purposes of extradition).

[75] McCarthy (above n 65) 321–7. However, even for terrorist crimes, consensus on the exercise of jurisdiction may prove elusive, if only because there is no agreement yet on what actually constitutes terrorism. *United States v Ramzi Ahmed Yousef and others*, 327 F 3d 56, 78–88 (2nd Cir 2003), citing *Tel-Oren v Libyan Arab Republic*, 726 F 2d 774 (DC Cir 1984) ('there continues to be strenuous disagreement among States about what actions do or do not constitute terrorism').

[76] MR Garcia-Mora, 'Criminal Jurisdiction Over Foreigners for Treason and Offenses Against the Safety of the State Committed Upon Foreign Territory', (1958) 19 U Pitt L Rev 567, 587 ('It is precisely because [territorial] States have failed to discharge adequately [their duty to prevent treasonable and other harmful activities from being carried on under the protection of their territorial sovereignty] that protective jurisdiction appeared as a necessary alternative thereby filling a gap in the international legal order'); Harvard Research on International Law (above n 2) 552 (explaining this lack of cooperation by reference to '[t]he traditional political liberalism of certain States', which 'has made them reluctant to lend any support to the protection or maintenance of régimes based upon principles different from their own').

[77] MB Krizek, 'The Protective Principle of Extraterritorial Jurisdiction: A Brief History and an Application of the Principle to Espionage as an Illustration of Current United States Practice', (1988) 6 BU Int'l LJ 337, 345. Cf *US v Evans et al.*, 667 F Supp 974, 980 (SDNY 1987) (stating that

and sixteenth centuries on, even before extradition became a common practice, European States committed themselves to surrendering the perpetrators of political offences.[78] Nowadays, given the widespread adoption of legislation based on the protective principle, the legality of protective jurisdiction is not in doubt.[79]

Continental European authors have traditionally considered the protective principle as deriving from a State's inherent right of self-defence.[80] Common law authors, however, in whose home countries protective jurisdiction was historically non-existent, have rejected this justification, primarily because it is conceptually fallacious and prone to politicization and abuse.[81] From a conceptual perspective, the self-defence justification has been criticized on the ground that protective jurisdiction is in fact exercised sometime *after* the (criminal) act has taken place. Self-defence is ordinarily only allowed as an inherent right when an armed attack actually occurs.[82] Defence against a *fait accompli* may appear paradoxical.[83] More importantly, because the justification of the protective principle is rooted in the concept of State sovereignty and political independence, which every State defines for itself, there is unmistakably a danger that States might abuse the protective principle.[84] The trial of a defendant accused of a crime against the security of the State (the category of crimes typically amenable to protective jurisdiction) would almost certainly be conducted in a climate of animosity and revenge which is bound to be detrimental to the fairness of the trial. This is anathema to the protection of individual human rights, such as the right to a fair trial.[85] The exercise of protective jurisdiction may also poison international relations and cause other States to retaliate, not only because other States might have concurrent jurisdiction over the crime, but also because crimes against the security of a State may, unlike common crimes, be supported or condoned by a foreign government. Claiming protective jurisdiction over the author(s) of the acts may imply passing

'international law permits jurisdiction under [the protective principle and the effects doctrine] even if the act or conspiracy at issue is thwarted before ill effects are actually felt in the target State').

[78] Donnedieu de Vabres (above n 25) 86.

[79] Harvard Research on International Law (above n 2) 556; CL Blakesley, 'United States Jurisdiction over Extraterritorial Crime', (1982) 73 J Crim L. and Criminology 1109, 1138.

[80] Donnedieu de Vabres (above n 25) 87. Also Krizek (above n 77) 339.

[81] Garcia-Mora (above n 76) 585 ('[B]eing essentially a political doctrine, self-defense is singularly exempted from any legal regulation and, consequently, its application to specific cases is likely to make for highly unjust decisions...Concurrently with...disturbing [political] forces is the fluid and shifting nature of the ordinary political exigencies, which render manifestly impossible any attempt to evaluate objectively concrete situations').

[82] eg Article 51 of the Charter of the United Nations (providing for 'the inherent right of individual or collective self-defence if an armed attack occurs against a Member of the United Nations').

[83] Garcia-Mora (above n 76) 585.

[84] ibid 583 (discussing the offence of treason and pointing out that 'the very nature of this offense inevitably lends itself to inadmissible extensions of State power...in view of the fact that the application of criminal jurisdiction reaches out to acts affecting the State in its supreme function, namely its external defense and its sovereignty'); Harvard Research on International Law (above n 2) 553 (arguing that underlying the controversy with respect to the propriety of protective legislation is 'a fear that its practical application may lead to inadmissible results').

[85] Garcia-Mora (above n 76) 588.

judgment on the acts of a foreign State and could possibly undermine the political independence of the latter State.[86] Therefore, in case a foreign State is involved in the perpetration of a crime against another State, State-to-State international dispute settlement on the basis of the rules of State responsibility may be preferable to the exercise of protective jurisdiction by the latter State.[87]

It appears desirable to adopt an international convention on protective jurisdiction. This convention would objectively determine the crimes that could give rise to protective jurisdiction, and put in place mechanisms of jurisdictional restraint.[88] Nonetheless, as in other fields of jurisdiction, such a convention might prove elusive in the face of tenacious State interests. As it actually presupposes a world order in which States consent to the future unilateral exercise of jurisdiction by other States over crimes in which they may be involved,[89] such a convention may appear utopian, or even if concluded, unlikely to be implemented in practice.[90] To be true, the flaws inherent in unilateral jurisdiction could be remedied by providing for an independent international tribunal competent to prosecute perpetrators of crimes against the security of the State, along the lines of the International Criminal Court. The prospects for the establishment of such a tribunal are, however, dim, as States will be reluctant to confer adjudicatory powers on an *international* tribunal over offences against *national* security. Especially in wartime, crimes of treason might yield important intelligence benefits for the warring parties.

In spite of the bias potentially displayed by courts when exercising protective jurisdiction, one could, however, take comfort in the fact that protective jurisdiction is in practice hardly exercised. When it is exercised, it proves hardly controversial. In ordinary circumstances, it is exercised over offences which the State where they took place does not condone or support, eg plotting the overthrow of a State with which the territorial State is not at war. Often, the territorial State

---

[86] Akehurst (above n 19) 159 (warning that the protective principle 'loses all its validity when it is used, not to safeguard the political independence of the State claiming jurisdiction, but to undermine the political independence of other countries' assuming of course that the author is not a State organ enjoying foreign sovereign immunity under international or domestic law).

[87] International Law Commission, Draft Articles on Responsibility of States for Internationally Wrongful Acts, 2001, Articles 3–11.

[88] Garcia-Mora (above n 76) 589. eg Article 7 of the Draft Convention on Jurisdiction with Respect to Crime Harvard Research on International Law (above n 2) 543 ('A State has jurisdiction with respect to any crime committed outside its territory by an alien against the security, territorial integrity or political independence of that State, *provided that the act or omission which constitutes the crime was not committed in exercise of a liberty guaranteed the alien by the law of the place where it was committed*') (emphasis added).

[89] Garcia-Mora (above n 76) 590 (arguing that 'there is a compelling need to develop a high degree of political integration of the international community. The fact, indeed, may have to be faced that future legal action in this area demands an overhaul of the basic principles upon which the international community has thus far rested').

[90] Harvard Research on International Law (above n 2) 553 ('In the present condition of the international community, it is doubtful whether substantial advance in this field through conventional agreement is to be anticipated').

will even exercise its own territorial jurisdiction over such offences.[91] Moreover, the protective principle is often invoked under not very dramatic circumstances, eg forgery or the counterfeiting of foreign currency,[92] making false statements to consular officials abroad in order to obtain a visa,[93] or drug smuggling.[94] In such cases, the exercise of protective jurisdiction is as uncontroversial as the exercise of active personality-based jurisdiction.

Secondary boycotts

The enactment of secondary boycotts may at times also be premised on the protective principle. Secondary boycotts are boycotts or embargoes which apply to foreign persons in their dealings with a boycotted State. They are extraterritorial measures in that they intervene in the commercial relations between actors who are not active within the territory of the regulating State. They universalize a primary boycott and reduce the foreign policy discretion that third States can exercise vis-à-vis the boycotted State.[95] They may be justifiable under the protective principle when they are aimed at the protection of the regulating State's national security interests.

---

[91] Under the US Neutrality Act (18 USC 1960), for instance, '[w]hoever, within the United States, knowingly begins or sets on foot or provides or prepares a means for or furnishes the money for, or takes part in, any military or naval expedition or enterprise to be carried on from thence against the territory or dominion of any foreign prince or state, or of any colony, district, or people with whom the United States is at peace, shall be fined under this title or imprisoned not more than three years, or both'. On the basis of this Act, in 2007 the US Department of Justice charged a number of defendants for conspiring on US soil to overthrow the (communist) government of Laos by force and violence. Press release DoJ, 4 June 2007, 'Operation Tarnished Eagle Thwarts Plot to Overthrow the Government of Laos', available at <http://www.usdoj.gov/usao/cae/press_releases/docs/2007/06-04-07JackPressRls.pdf>.

[92] eg article 10, 2° and 3° of the Preliminary Title of the Belgian Code of Criminal Procedure.

[93] *United States v Rodriguez*, 182 F Supp 479 (SD Cal 1960) (holding that 'entry by an alien into the United States secured by means of false statements or documents is an attack directly on the sovereignty of the United States'); *United States v Pizzarusso*, 388 F 2d 8, 10 (2nd Cir 1968), cert denied, 392 US 936 (1968) (defining the protective principle as '[the authority to] prescribe a rule of law attaching legal consequences to conduct outside [the State's] territory that threatens its security as a state or the operation of its governmental functions, provided the conduct is generally recognized as a crime under the law of states that have reasonably developed legal systems', and holding that lying to a consular officer constituted 'an affront to the very sovereignty of the United States [and had] a deleterious influence on valid governmental interests'); *United States v Khalje*, 658 F 2d 90 (2nd Cir 1981).

[94] *United States v Keller*, 451 F Supp 631 (DPR 1978); *United States v Newball*, 524 F Supp 715, 716 (EDNY 1981) (holding that 'for protective purposes, drug-smuggling threatens the security and sovereignty of the United States by affecting its armed forces, contributing to widespread crime, and circumventing federal customs laws').

[95] eg European Community: Note and Comments on the Amendments of 22 June 1982 to the Export Administration Act, Presented to the United States Department of State on 12 August 1982, (1982) 21 ILM 891, 895 ('The practical impact of the Amendments to the Export Administration Regulations is that E.C. companies are pressed into service to carry out U.S. trade policy towards the U.S.S.R., even though these companies are incorporated and have their registered office within the Community which has its own trade policy towards the U.S.S.R. The public policy ("ordre public") of the European Community and of its Member States is thus purportedly replaced by U.S. public policy which European companies are forced to carry out within the E.C., if they are not to lose export privileges in the U.S. or to face other sanctions. This is an unacceptable interference in the affairs of the European Community').

The Helms-Burton Act, for instance, a US Act (1996) which prohibits any person, whatever his nationality, from 'trafficking' in confiscated property belonging to Americans or Cubans who later acquired American citizenship, seemed to justify its jurisdictional assertions under the protective principle where it considered Cuba to be posing a national security threat to the US.[96] In fact, the law of the World Trade Organization authorizes trade restrictions, in which secondary boycotts result, by virtue of the national security exception of Article XXI of GATT.[97]

If the protective principle is invoked so as to justify a secondary boycott, sufficient evidence of a direct threat to national security should be adduced. As far as the lawfulness of the Helms-Burton Act is concerned, there is/was apparently no convincing evidence of terrorist activity sponsored by the Cuban government nor of the specific security threat posed by mass migration of Cubans to the United States.[98] It is difficult to sustain that a vaguely defined threat to the political independence or territorial integrity of the United States falls within the scope of the protective principle.[99] Possibly only in times of war may secondary boycotts be justified under the protective principle.[100]

4.5 Universality Principle

As seen in the previous sections, the exercise of jurisdiction is ordinarily premised on the presence of a nexus of the matter to be regulated with the regulating

---

[96] According to section 2 (28) of the Cuban Liberty and Democratic Solidarity Act, Public law 104th-114, 12 March 1996, 110 Stat 785, 22 USC §§ 6021–91, '[f]or the past 36 years, the Cuban government has posed and continued to pose a national security threat to the U.S.'. Therefore, the purposes of the Act are pursuant to section 3 (3) 'to provide for the continued national security of the United States in the face of continuing threats from the Castro government of terrorism, theft of property from United States nationals by the Castro government, and the political manipulation by the Castro government of the desire of Cubans to escape that results in mass migration to the United States'.

[97] Former US Trade Representative Mickey Kantor stated in this context, with respect to the Helms-Burton Act: 'I believe we're well within the obligations under NAFTA and the Uruguay Round'. Quoted in JL Snyder and S Agostini, 'New U.S. Legislation to Deter Investment in Cuba', (1996:3) 30 JWT 43, footnotes 37–38.

[98] Also M Cosnard, 'Les lois Helms-Burton et d'Amato-Kennedy, interdiction de commercer avec et d'investir dans certains pays', (1996) 42 AFDI 40.

[99] However *US v Evans et al.*, 667 F Supp 974 (SDNY 1987) (relying on the protective principle so as to exercise jurisdiction over defendants who had conspired to violate the Arms Control Act by re-exporting US-made defence articles).

[100] This explains why, for instance, the US Treasury Department's demand that Fruehauf, a French corporation controlled by US nationals, stop the execution of a sales contract with China in the early 1960s, may not be covered by the protective principle either. While this demand was based on the extension of the scope of application of the Trading with the Enemy Act to cover trade of US-controlled foreign corporations with China during the 1950–53 Korean War, when the demand was made, the US was technically speaking no longer at war with China. The Treasury Department's demands sparked a legal case in France, *Société Fruehauf Corp v Massardy*, 1968 DS Jur 147, 1965, 5 ILM 476 (1966) (Ct Appel Paris 1965). In this case, the Court decided that the contract of a US-controlled French corporation with China should be honoured, on the ground that the needs of the company's employees outweighed the personal interests of the American directors.

State. One jurisdictional principle, however, the universality principle, does not operate on the basis of a connecting factor linking up a situation with a State's interests. Instead, it is based solely on the nature of a crime 'without regard to where the crime was committed, the nationality of the alleged or convicted perpetrator, the nationality of the victim, or any other connection to the State exercising such jurisdiction'.[101] Under the universality principle, the nature of the act may in itself confer jurisdiction on any State. Admittedly, most States require some territorial link in the form of the presence of the suspect in its territory, yet it is unsure whether international law requires them to do so.

Before the 1990s, universal jurisdiction did not receive much doctrinal attention. Some conventions, anti-terrorism conventions in particular, provided for universal jurisdiction on the basis of an *aut dedere aut judicare* obligation.[102] Some States also provided in their criminal codes for unilateral, although usually uncontroversial, universal jurisdiction over sexual offences,[103] immigration offences,[104] corruption,[105] offences involving nuclear energy, explosions or radiation,[106] traffic

---

[101] Principle 1 (1) of the Princeton Principles on Universal Jurisdiction (2001), reprinted in S Macedo, ed, *Universal Jurisdiction* (2004) 21. The Princeton Principles are, according to the Commentary, a progressive restatement of international law, although they contain elements *de lege ferenda*. ibid 26. Also Principle 13 of the Brussels Principles Against Immunity and for International Justice, in *Combating Impunity: Proceedings of the Symposium Held in Brussels From 11 to 13 March 2002*, 149, 157, which defines universal jurisdiction as 'the right of a State to institute legal proceedings and to try the presumed author of an offence, irrespective of the place where the said offence has been committed, the nationality or the place of residence of its presumed author or of the victim'. Also International Law Association, *Final Report on the Exercise of Universal Jurisdiction in Respect of Gross Human Rights Violations* (2000) 2 ('Under the principle of universal jurisdiction, a state is entitled, or even required to bring proceedings in respect of certain serious crimes, irrespective of the location of the crime, and irrespective of the nationality of the perpetrator or the victim'); Institute of International Law, Resolution of the 17th Commission on universal criminal jurisdiction with regard to the crime of genocide, crimes against humanity and war crimes (2005) nr 1 ('Universal jurisdiction in criminal matters, as an additional ground of jurisdiction, means the competence of a State to prosecute alleged offenders and to punish them if convicted, irrespective of the place of commission of the crime and regardless of any link of active or passive nationality, or other grounds of jurisdiction recognized by international law'). Judge ad hoc Van den Wyngaert believed in her dissenting opinion in *Arrest Warrant* that '[t]here is no generally accepted definition of universal jurisdiction in conventional or customary international law', that '[m]any views exist as to its legal meaning', and that 'uncertainties [. . .] may exist concerning [its] definition.' ICJ, *Arrest Warrant* (above n 59) diss op Van den Wyngaert, §§ 44–46. Also Donnedieu de Vabres (above n 25) 135 ('Dans sa notion élémentaire, et son expression absolue, le système de la *répression universelle*, ou de l'*universalité du droit de punir* est celui qui attribue vocation aux tribunaux répressifs de tous les Etats pour connaître d'un crime par un individu quelconque, en quelconque pays que ce soit') (original emphasis).

[102] For domestic implementation laws: article 12*bis* PT Belgian CCP (referring to treaty law, customary international law and EU law); § 6, 9° StGB; articles 689 *et seq.* French CCP.

[103] Article 10*ter*, 1°–2° PT Belgian CCP.

[104] Article 10*ter*, 3° PT Belgian CCP.

[105] eg articles 10*ter* and 10*quater* PT Belgian CCP.

[106] § 6, 2° StGB.

in human beings,[107] distribution of narcotics,[108] distribution of pornography,[109] counterfeiting,[110] or subsidy fraud.[111] Only in the late twentieth century did universal jurisdiction gain international ascendancy, when 'bystander' States started prosecuting the perpetrators of such crimes as war crimes, genocide, crimes against humanity, and torture, committed in far-flung places.[112] Because the machinery of the State is often used in the commission of these crimes, international conflict over universal jurisdiction appeared bound to arise.

(a) Vicarious jurisdiction

A jurisdictional ground which resembles, but should nevertheless be distinguished from, universal jurisdiction is vicarious or representational jurisdiction.[113] Pursuant to this ground of jurisdiction, which is not widely used by States, States prosecute an offence as representatives of other States, if the act is also an offence in the territorial State and extradition is impossible for reasons not related to the nature of the crime.[114] Although the forum State represents the territorial State when it exercises vicarious jurisdiction, the forum State ordinarily applies its own laws and not the laws of the territorial State. In order not to distort the idea of representation too much, it is advisable then that the territorial State does not impose punishment in excess of what is allowed by the territorial State.[115]

It is submitted that vicarious jurisdiction draws upon a Kantian world view, pursuant to which crimes may be considered as attacks on individual interests and not as breaches of a territorially limited 'King's peace'.[116] If an individual is

---

[107] § 6, 4° StGB.

[108] § 6, 5° StGB. The legality of universal jurisdiction over distribution of narcotics is, however, controversial. German courts have therefore attempted to identify an additional nexus to Germany in particular cases. eg BGH, *Dost*, 20 October 1976, *BGHSt* 27, S 30 f; BGH, *Dost*, 9 April 1987, *BGHSt* 34, S 334 f (arguing that, in a case in which a Dutch national sold drugs to German nationals in the Netherlands, after which the Germans imported the drugs into Germany and sold them there, 'der Angeklagte die Voraussetzungen dafür geschaffen hat, dass eine gross Menge Hashisch in der Bundesrepublik verteilt werden können'). Also HD Wolswijk, *Locus delicti en rechtsmacht*, (1998) 48.

[109] § 6, 6° StGB.   [110] § 6, 7° StGB.   [111] § 6, 8° StGB.

[112] Although the legality of universal jurisdiction might not have been contested before the 1990s, in practice only Nazi war criminals were prosecuted under the universality principle (eg Eichmann). See D Orentlicher, 'Whose Justice? Reconciling Universal Jurisdiction with Democratic Principles', (2004) 92 Georgetown LJ 1057, 1073.

[113] J Meyer, 'The Vicarious Administration of Justice: An Overlooked Basis of Jurisdiction', (1990) 31 Harv Int'l LJ 108, 115–16.

[114] In a 1958 case, the Supreme Court of Austria defined representational jurisdiction as follows: 'The extraditing State also has the right, in the cases where extradition for whatever reason is not possible, although according to the nature of the offence it would be permissible, to carry out a prosecution and impose punishment, instead of such action being taken by the requesting State' (1958) 28 ILR 341, 342. Because of these restrictive conditions, petty or political crimes are not eligible for vicarious jurisdiction.

[115] Meyer (above n 113) 116 (although conceding that this view is not generally accepted).

[116] I Cameron, 'Jurisdiction and Admissibility Issues under the ICC Statute', in D McGoldrick, P Rowe and E Donnelly, eds, *The Permanent International Criminal Court. Legal and Policy Issues* (2004) 78–9.

harmed somewhere in the world, he is entitled to have his day in court anywhere in the world, provided that the harm is caused by an act which is a crime under both local and foreign law.

Although the Harvard Research on International Law (1935) considered the principle of vicarious jurisdiction not as an autonomous jurisdictional ground but as a modality of the universality principle,[117] it may be argued that the two types of jurisdiction have a different rationale. The main difference between universal jurisdiction and representational jurisdiction lies therein that States, when exercising representational jurisdiction, protect the interests of the territorial State, whereas, when exercising universal jurisdiction, they (supposedly) protect the interests of the international community. The rationale of acting on behalf of the territorial State renders the conditions of the exercise of representational jurisdiction by another State both more lenient and stricter. On the one hand, representational jurisdiction also applies to lesser crimes. On the other hand, its exercise is subject to the requirement of double criminality and the requirement that extradition proves impossible (the latter requirement actually implying the pre-eminence of the territorial or national State).[118]

Vicarious or representational jurisdiction took root in Germany and Austria in the nineteenth century. § 7 (2), 2° of the German StGB currently sets forth that all offences by foreigners committed abroad may be subject to German penal law, if the conduct is punishable under the legislation of the territorial State (or if no State has authority over the place where the conduct has taken place), if the offender is found in Germany, and—although the Extradition Law permits the extradition on the basis of the nature of the offence—he or she is not extradited because an extradition request has not been filed in a timely manner, because it has been refused, or because the extradition could not be executed.

In 2004, France adopted a law similar to the German law. France now applies its criminal law to any felony or misdemeanor subject to a penalty of at least five years' imprisonment committed outside France by an alien whose extradition to the requesting State has been refused by the French authorities because the offence for which the extradition has been requested is subject to a penalty or to a safety measure that is contrary to French public policy, or because the person in question has been tried in the aforesaid State by a court which does not

---

[117] Harvard Research on International Law (above n 2) 573 (Article 10. *Universality*—other crime: 'A State has jurisdiction with respect to any crime committed outside its territory by an alien . . . (a) When committed in a place not subject to its authority but subject to the authority of another State, if the act or omission which constitutes the crime is also an offence by the law of the place where it was committed, if surrender of the alien for prosecution has been offered to such other State or States and the offer remains unaccepted, and if prosecution is not barred by lapse of time under the law of the place where the crime was committed. The penalty imposed shall in no case be more severe than the penalty prescribed for the same act or omission by the law of the place where the crime was committed').

[118] M Inazumi, *Universal Jurisdiction in Modern International Law: Expansion of National Jurisdiction for Prosecuting Serious Crimes under International Law* (2005) 111–13; Meyer (above n 113) 116.

respect the basic procedural guarantees and the rights of the defence, or because the matter in question shows the characteristics of a political offence.[119] The same restrictive conditions as those applying to the operation of the personality principle apply.[120]

While only a few States provide for, and actually exercise, vicarious jurisdiction, vicarious jurisdiction has not been objected to by other States. This is largely due to its cooperative nature. The forum State indeed only exercises jurisdiction when extradition to the territorial State proves impossible, and thus in fact takes over the prosecution from the territorial State. Because of the absence of international protest against assertions of vicarious jurisdiction, such assertions appear as lawful under international law.

(b) *Aut dedere aut judicare*

Another principle that resembles the universality principle, but that nevertheless ought to be distinguished from it, is the principle (or the obligation) of *aut dedere aut judicare* (or *punire*). Pursuant to this principle, a State is required to establish its jurisdiction over any perpetrator of the offence present in its territory, if it does not extradite him. A number of conventions, in particular anti-terrorism conventions, feature an *aut dedere aut judicare* clause[121] (eg the 1970 Convention for the Suppression of Unlawful Seizure of Aircraft).[122]

Assertions of jurisdiction on the basis of such a clause are not necessarily assertions of universal jurisdiction. *Aut dedere aut judicare* clauses typically oblige States to either extradite or prosecute *any* person within their power suspected of committing the offence. If States do not extradite that person, they have to prosecute

---

[119] Article 113-8-1, para 1 French CP.

[120] ibid para 2.

[121] See for a doctrinal and historical analysis of the principle of *aut dedere aut judicare* C Maierhofer, *Aut dedere aut judicare. Herkunft, Rechtsgrundlagen und Inhalt des völkerrechtlichen Gebotes zur Strafverfolgung oder Auslieferung* (2006) (tracing the doctrinal origins of the principle to the fourteenth century Italian jurist Baldus de Ubaldis, a student of Bartolus's. ibid 62). In the twentieth century, some of the offences threatening State interests became the object of international conventions. These conventions typically featured a jurisdictional clause that required a State Party to exercise its jurisdiction over any perpetrator of the offence present in its territory, if it did not extradite him or her (*aut dedere aut judicare/punire*). Such a clause initially conditioned jurisdiction on the law of the forum State authorizing the exercise of extraterritorial jurisdiction, a requirement which was, however, abandoned in post-war anti-terrorism conventions containing such provisions. Also ICJ, *Arrest Warrant* (above n 59) sep op Guillaume, § 7 ('the obligation to prosecute was no longer conditional on the existence of jurisdiction, but rather jurisdiction itself had to be established in order to make prosecution possible'). Some of these conventions may have attained the status of customary international law.

[122] Article 7 Hague Hijacking Convention (1970). Also Article 5(2) Montreal Hijacking Convention (1971), Article 6(2) Convention against the Taking of Hostages (1979), Article 6(4) Terrorist Bombings Convention (1997), Article 7(4) Convention on Financing of Terrorism (1999). These conventions are often vague on whether the State Party is required to exercise its jurisdiction only after an extradition request has been filed, or also if such a request has not been filed.

him, or at least take the necessary measures to establish their jurisdiction, on the basis of either the territoriality, the personality, or the universality principle.[123]

It has been submitted that, if States premise their jurisdiction solely on the territorial presence of the perpetrator in accordance with their *aut dedere aut judicare* obligations, they do in fact not exercise universal jurisdiction. The operation of the *aut dedere* requirement is indeed limited to States Parties, which pool their sovereignty and explicitly authorize each other to exercise jurisdiction over crimes committed by their nationals or on their territory. As Higgins has argued, '[u]niversal jurisdiction, properly called, allows *any* state to assert jurisdiction over an offence'.[124]

The obligation of *aut dedere aut judicare* is a specific conventional clause relating to specific crimes. It is not an obligation under customary international law.[125] In principle, States that are not parties to the convention containing an *aut dedere aut judicare* obligation are not bound by it. Conventional *aut dedere aut judicare* clauses may only become mandatory upon *any* State if they crystallize as norms of customary international law.[126] Nationals of States not parties to the relevant convention are not necessarily exempt from the scope of jurisdiction under the *aut dedere aut judicare* principle, however. In the United States, for instance, federal courts have exercised universal jurisdiction over terrorists who were nationals of States not parties to relevant anti-terrorism conventions such as the Hostage-Taking Convention and the Hijacking Convention, without the latter States lodging formal complaints.[127] Morris has argued, in this context, that 'with sufficient

---

[123] Also Inazumi (above n 118) 122.

[124] Higgins (above n 60) 64. *See also* ICJ, *Arrest Warrant* (above n 59), joint separate opinion Higgins, Kooijmans and Buergenthal, §§ 22 and 39. *Aut dedere aut judicare*-based jurisdiction could in fact be conceived of as representational or delegated jurisdiction. eg A Poels, 'Universal Jurisdiction *In Absentia*', (2005) 23 Neth Q Hum Rts 65, 68.

[125] The ILC is now ascertaining whether there is an *aut dedere aut judicare* obligation under customary international law in relation to specific crimes. It is currently compiling State practice to that effect. See ILC Report, A/61/10, 2006, ch XI, paras 214–32.

[126] Also M Cosnard, 'La compétence universelle en matière pénale', in C Tomuschat and J-M Thouvenin, eds, *The Fundamental Rules of the International Legal Order. Jus Cogens and Obligations Erga Omnes* (2006) 355, 367; KC Randall, 'Universal Jurisdiction under International Law', (1998) 66 Texas L Rev 821 (arguing that *aut dedere aut judicare*-based jurisdiction may become genuine universal jurisdiction if the underlying crime is a violation of *jus cogens*). Contra M Halberstam, 'Terrorism on the High Seas: the Achille Lauro, Piracy and the IMO Convention on Maritime Safety', (1988) 82 AJIL 269, 272 (stating that 'limiting the application of anti-terrorist treaties to nationals of state parties would significantly undermine their effectiveness', and that '[i]t would mean that the community of states is essentially helpless to take legal measures against terrorists who are nationals of states that do not ratify the conventions'); M Scharf, 'The ICC's Jurisdiction over the Nationals of non-Party States: a Critique of the U.S. Position', (2001) 64 Law & Contemp Probs 67, 99–101.

[127] *United States v Yunis*, 681 F Supp 896 (DDC 1988); *United States v Yunis*, 924 F 2d 1086 (DC Cir 1991) (Lebanon not a party to the Hostage-Taking Convention). *United States v Rezaq*, 899 F Supp 697 (DDC 1995); *United States v Rezaq*, 134 F 3d 1121 (DC Cir 1998) (the Palestine Territories not a party to the Hijacking Convention); *United States v Wang Kun Lue*, 134 F 3d 79 (2nd Cir 1997); *United States v Lin*, 101 F 3d 760 (DC Cir 1996); *United States v Ni Fa Yi*, 951 F Supp 42 (SDNY 1997); *United States v Chen De Yian*, 905 F Supp 160 (SDNY 1995) (China not a party to the Hostage-Taking Convention). *See also United States v Marino-Garcia*, 679 F 2d 1373, 1386–7 (11th Cir 1982) (Honduran and Columbian crew members of stateless vessels

time and state practice, [*aut dedere aut judicare* based] universal jurisdiction over
[hostage-taking and hijacking] will pass into customary law', given the absence
of international protest against the exercise of such jurisdiction over nationals of
States not parties to the conventions criminalizing these offences.[128] The exercise
of universal jurisdiction over nationals of States that were not parties to the UN
Torture Convention, which features an *aut dedere aut judicare* clause in its Article
5(2), by contrast, has met with more criticism. A case on the issue is now pending
with the International Court of Justice (*Certain Criminal Proceedings in France,
Republic of Congo v France*, 2003–).

(c) Universal jurisdiction: justifications

Genuine universal jurisdiction is, as Higgins has hinted at,[129] jurisdiction that
may be exercised by any State over a (specific) offence, without the offence having
any link with the State (except perhaps for the presence of the offender). Genuine
universal jurisdiction may be exercised irrespective of extradition being requested
by, and refused to, the State having a stronger link with the offence.

The fact that, under the universality principle, a State may exercise jurisdiction
over any offence without regard to any connection to that State, or the interests
of other States, sits uneasy with the classical State-centered view of public international law. Some doctrine has therefore attempted to link up universal jurisdiction with the interests and goals of the State and the concept of statehood. Marks,
for instance, has predicated the exercise of universal jurisdiction on a 'common
interest rationale',[130] emphasizing the shared interests which States have in
exercising universal jurisdiction.[131] The 'common interest rationale' 'acknowledges that the conduct of those who perpetrate serious international crimes in
one State has an impact on other States: such conduct poses a potential threat to
all States and thus all States have an interest in prosecuting the wrongdoer'.[132]

---

prosecuted for trafficking in marijuana under the Law of the Sea Convention, although Honduras
and Columbia were not parties to this Convention).

[128] M Morris, 'High Crimes and Misconceptions: the ICC and non-Party States', (2001) 64
Law & Contemp Probs 13, 64.

[129] Cf section 4.5.b.

[130] JH Marks, 'Mending the Web: Universal Jurisdiction, Humanitarian Intervention and the
Abrogation of Immunity by the Security Council', (2004) 42 Col J Transnat'l L 445, 465–7. Also
the type of universal jurisdiction identified by Stern as 'somme d'intérêts propres identiques des
Etats', as opposed to 'l'intérêt unique partagé par tous'. B Stern, 'La compétence universelle en
France: le cas des crimes commis en ex-Yougoslavie et au Rwanda', (1997) 40 GYIL 280, 281.

[131] Compare I Kant, 'Perpetual Peace: A Philosophical Sketch', in H Reiss, ed, *Kant's Political
Writings* (1970) 107–8: 'The peoples of the earth have [...] entered in varying degrees into a universal community, and it has developed to the point where a violation of rights in one part of the
world is felt everywhere'. Quoted in Marks (above n 130) 465.

[132] ibid 465. Marks draws an interesting comparison with the Security Council, whose powers
extend to serious international crimes committed within the borders of one State since these might
be of interest to the international community as a whole. Acting under Chapter VII, the Security
Council established, for instance, the ICTR to adjudge crimes of genocide. ibid 466. Compare

Especially universal jurisdiction over crimes such as piracy, drug offences, hijacking, hostage-taking, and other terrorist acts, lends itself to justification under the common interest rationale. The common interest rationale is not very helpful to justify the exercise of universal jurisdiction over crimes against international humanitarian law (war crimes, genocide, crimes against humanity), however. Perpetrators of such crimes are not very likely to repeat their crimes, because those found their origins in the political, historical and social environment of a particular territory. This also explains why another pragmatic State-centered justification of universal jurisdiction—that offenders of extraterritorial crimes might cause trouble in a State's territory by their mere presence, given their propensity for criminal behaviour[133]—does not carry much suasion for these crimes.

It should nevertheless be observed that a refusal to grant impunity to criminals residing or found in the territory of the forum State may deter future violators who operate in, or from the home State: punishment may set an example to persons within the jurisdiction that certain crimes, irrespective of where they occurred, are so heinous as to not warrant any tolerance. While such persons may not commit crimes in the very specific political context in which the convicted person committed his crimes, the accountability signal which accompanies a criminal conviction may prevent them from ever engaging in similar criminal conduct, eg as servicemembers or mercenaries in foreign conflict zones. By sending this signal—'no impunity'—a State prevents future violations in other States, and serves the common interests of all States.

Aside from those pragmatic considerations of deterrence and prevention, it may, in addition, be submitted that States have an inherent mission to realize the ideals of justice, and not only to protect their own narrowly-defined interests. In idealist Kantian thought, criminal law is a categorical imperative informed by practical reason. Criminals ought to be punished, not because, from a utilitarian perspective, they breach the King's peace, but because they harm humanity as a whole.[134] From this viewpoint, some crimes are considered to be breaches of obligations *erga omnes*, owed to every State and which, thus, every State has an interest in prosecuting, even without a concrete link with the State. This justification

Flores v S Peru Copper Corp, 343 F 3d 140, 156 (2d Cir), a case arising under the US Alien Tort Statute (holding that 'official torture, extrajudicial killings, and genocide, do violate customary international law because the "nations of the world" have demonstrated that such wrongs are of "mutual ... concern," and capable of impairing international peace and security').

[133] Medieval Italian city States for instance grounded their right to exercise jurisdiction over the offenders of extraterritorial crimes present in their territory on this possibility. Donnedieu de Vabres, at 135–6 ('Néanmoins, il fut admis pendant tout le moyen âge, dans la doctrine italienne, et dans le droit qui gouvernait les rapports des villes lombardes, qu'à l'égard de certaines catégories de malfaiteurs dangereux [...] la simple présence, sur le territoire, du criminel impuni, étant une cause de trouble, donnait vocation à la cité pour connaître de son crime'). This justification has been criticized for arbitrarily and egoistically downplaying the *universality* of prosecution, by premising the jurisdictional intervention of the custodial State on it being harmed by the later presence of the offender instead of on the nature of the crime. ibid 142–3.

[134] ibid 151.

of universal jurisdiction appears to have become the dominant one: some acts are considered as so morally reprehensible that any State should be authorized, or even required, to prosecute them.

In practical terms, a State's exercise of universal jurisdiction is often fed by public outrage presented by the very presence in the forum State of a perpetrator of an international crime.[135] It is politically not expedient for States to condone the territorial presence of international criminals, even if these persons do not pose a public danger. In recent times, media pressure has considerably fed this indignation, with journalists, notably in the United Kingdom, sometimes tracking down presumed perpetrators living quietly in the territory of a bystander State.

(d) The historical trail of universal jurisdiction

Universal jurisdiction is not a new phenomenon. It already featured in an embryonic form in the sixth century *Codex Justiniani,* which, regulating the competence of the different governors of the Empire, granted jurisdiction to both the tribunal of the place where the crime was committed (*judex loci delicti commissi,* territorial jurisdiction), and the place where the perpetrator was arrested (*judex deprehensionis,* universal jurisdiction subject to the presence requirement).[136] Similarly, in the mediaeval city States of northern Italy, certain dangerous offenders could be prosecuted by any state where they could be found.[137] In the seventeenth century, ironically at the time when the territorial principle gained ascendancy, a number of Dutch scholars, such as Voet, Cocceji and, most importantly, Grotius, advocated universal jurisdiction over crimes that violated the law of nature and shocked the *societas generis humani.*[138] By 1928, Donnedieu de Vabres noted that the system of universal jurisdiction was recognized as a principle by the international community, but that it remained to be organized in practice.[139]

One crime over which universal jurisdiction was not merely a doctrinal construct, but was historically organized, is piracy, the classical crime giving rise to

---

[135] R Rabinovitch, 'Universal Jurisdiction *In Absentia*', (2005) 28 Fordham Int'l LJ 500, 518; ICJ, *Arrest Warrant* (above n 59) sep op Guillaume, para 4 (2002) (citing classical writers such as Covarruvias and Grotius).

[136] *Codex Justiniani,* C III, 15, *Ubi de criminibus agi oportet.* In civil law matters, embryonic universal jurisdiction could be gleaned from the Roman law practice of allowing the plaintiff to sue a vagrant defendant, ie a defendant without domicile, anywhere the plaintiff could find him (*ubi ti invenero ibi te judicabo*). On this practice J Plescia, 'Conflict of Laws in the Roman Empire', (1992) 38 Labeo 30, 47.

[137] Donnedieu de Vabres (above n 25) 136.

[138] H Grotius, (1925) 3 *De Jure Belli Ac Pacis* 504 (arguing that States have a right 'to exact Punishments, not only for Injuries committed against themselves or their Subjects, but likewise, for those which do not peculiarly concern them, but which are, in any Persons whatsoever, grievous Violations of the Law of Nature or Nations' and that 'any State would have the moral imperative to punish the perpetrators of *delicta juris gentium*', '[f]or [. . .] it is so much more honorable, to revenge other Peoples Injuries rather than their own [. . .] Kings, beside the Charge of their particular Dominions, have upon them the care of human Society in general').

[139] Donnedieu de Vabres (above n 25) 137.

universal jurisdiction under customary international law. Universal jurisdiction over piracy is premised on the legal fiction that pirates, as enemies of all mankind, are citizens of no country,[140] on the *res communis* nature of the high seas, and on enforcement difficulties.[141] Especially the latter two justifications make sense from a practical point of view: as the high seas do not belong to any State and pirates could easily leave the crime scene, the possibility of a jurisdictional vacuum looms large. Therefore, giving all States jurisdiction to punish piracy offenders would prevent impunity. In practice, however, piracy prosecutions based on the universality principle were extremely rare, as States were reluctant to '[confer] a benefit on many states while single-handedly shouldering all the costs'.[142] Universal jurisdiction over piracy was later codified in Article 19 of the Geneva Convention of 29 April 1958, and Article 105 of the Convention of Montego Bay of 10 December 1982 (UNCLOS).[143]

Universal jurisdiction adapted to the criminal-political agenda of the day. While in the seventeenth century, piracy was the scourge of sea-faring nations, the nineteenth century saw the emergence of such State-threatening offences as anarchist offences, counterfeiting, and the destruction of cables. These offences—the commission of which modern technology contributed to in no small measure—were considered as *delicta juris gentium*, and on that basis as eligible for universal jurisdiction.[144] Like piracy, they had a transnational element, were committed by non-State actors against State interests, and were not necessarily particularly heinous. As 'universal' jurisdiction over these offences did not protect *universal* interests (*'répression universelle'*) but rather interests that States have in common with *each other* (*'répression internationale'*), Donnedieu de Vabres preferred the term *'compétence réelle'* over *'compétence universelle'*.[145] By exercising such jurisdiction, States would not act as representatives of the international community but rather as representatives

---

[140] A Levitt, 'Jurisdiction over Crimes', (1925) 16 J Crim L and Criminology 316, 323–4.

[141] Kontorovich has argued that the *res nullius* argument makes no sense, because, while the high seas may be beyond the jurisdiction of a State, flag States could exercise territorial jurisdiction over their vessels, and States could exercise active or passive personality jurisdiction. Universal jurisdiction over crimes of piracy would thus not be premised on there being a jurisdictional lacuna, but its rationale would rather lie in problems of enforcement, as States had difficulties in policing the activities on the high seas. E Kontorovich, 'The Piracy Analogy: Modern Universal Jurisdiction's Hollow Foundation', (2004) 45 Harv Int'l LJ 183.

[142] E Kontorovich, 'Implementing *Sosa v. Alvarez-Machain*: What Piracy Reveals About the Limits of the Alien Tort Statute', (2004) 80 Notre Dame L Rev 111, 154.

[143] See for a recent prosecution of piracy under the universality principle, the prosecution of ten Somali pirates by a court in Mombasa, Kenya. *The Nation* (Kenya), '10 Somalis to Stand Trial in Piracy Case', 4 August 2006, available at <http://allafrica.com/stories/200608040092.html>.

[144] The Harvard Research on International Law (above n 2) 478–9 listed the following offences as *delicta juris gentium*: (1) slavery and the slave trade; (2) traffic in women and children for immoral purposes; (3) counterfeiting; (4) traffic in narcotics; (5) injury to submarine cables; (6) traffic in obscene publications; (7) liquor traffic; (8) illegal trade in arms. Harvard Research did not consider anarchistic crimes of violence to be *delicta juris gentium*.

[145] Donnedieu de Vabres (above n 25) 110 *et seq.*

of a foreign State. It may even be submitted that States exercised their jurisdiction for fear of being retaliated upon by foreign States,[146] which is a far cry from the sort of universal jurisdiction over crimes against international humanitarian law that States are precisely *reluctant* to exercise for fear of being retaliated upon by foreign States.

(e) Universal jurisdiction over 'core crimes' against international law

Nowadays, the main offences arguably amenable to universal jurisdiction are the so-called 'core crimes against international law', which include crimes against international humanitarian law and crimes of torture.[147] These crimes were historically not subject to universal jurisdiction,[148] and were often not even subject to international criminalization. Genocide eventually became the object of an international convention in 1948 (Genocide Convention), war crimes were internationally criminalized in 1949 and 1977 (the Four Geneva Conventions), and torture was prohibited as a matter of treaty law in 1984 (UN Torture Convention). Crimes against humanity have never become the object of a convention.

---

[146] ibid 111.

[147] Cosnard (above n 126) 358 (noting that the field of core crimes is 'à l'heure actuelle son champ d'application de prédilection, quoique non exclusif'). It is notable that proceedings involving crimes against international humanitarian law, mostly war crimes, largely outweigh proceedings involving crimes of torture, although only the UN Torture Convention unambiguously provides for universal jurisdiction. Kamminga has attributed this paradox to the fact that instruments addressing crimes against international humanitarian law, the Geneva Conventions in particular, were adopted earlier and have been more widely ratified than the UN Torture Convention. See MT Kamminga, 'First Conviction under the Universal Jurisdiction Provisions of the UN Convention Against Torture', (2004) NILR 439, 442, who admits that it is gratifying that the first torture conviction took only 20 years (Sebastien N, the Netherlands, 2004), whereas the first war crimes conviction took 45 years (Saric, Denmark, 1994). See on the prosecution of torture under the universality principle: C Ryngaert, 'Universal Criminal Jurisdiction over Torture: A State of Affairs after 20 Years UN Torture Convention', (2005) Neth Q Hum Rts 571.

[148] Donnedieu de Vabres (above n 25) 143 (identifying as crimes giving rise to universal jurisdiction: crimes against telegraph and telephone cables, counterfeiting, trafficking in Negroes, piracy, trafficking in women and children, and trafficking in obscene publications and toxic drinks). Although pre-war doctrine seemed to support universal jurisdiction over egregious human rights violations such as genocide and war crimes (ibid 47), before 1945 it was only established law that war crimes offenders could be tried by the belligerent party in whose hands they were (JW Garner, 'Punishment of Offenders Against the Laws and Customs of War', (1920) 14 AJIL 70, 71). The Versailles Treaty epitomized this restrictive view, which falls far short of universal jurisdiction as properly understood. Article 228 of the Treaty of Versailles, 28 June 1919, in Carnegie Endowment for International Peace, edn, 1 *The Treaties of the Peace 1919–23*, 1921 (1924) 3 ('The German Government recognizes the right of the Allied and Associated Powers to bring before military tribunals persons accused of having committed acts in violation of the laws and customs of war. Such persons shall, if found guilty, be sentenced to punishments laid down by law. This provision will apply notwithstanding any proceedings or prosecution before a tribunal in Germany or in the territory of her allies').

Only the Geneva Conventions,[149] and the UN Torture Convention,[150] provide for *aut dedere aut judicare*-based 'universal' jurisdiction. The exercise of universal jurisdiction over core crimes against international law could, however, be premised on customary international law. It has notably been argued that the PCIJ in *Lotus* left States a wide jurisdictional margin. Under *Lotus*, it ought to be proven that no rule prohibiting the exercise of universal jurisdiction over core crimes has crystallized. Alternatively, it has been argued that States have the authority to exercise

[149] As far as grave breaches of the laws of war committed in international armed conflicts are concerned, Articles 49, 50, 129, and 146 of Geneva Conventions I, II, III, and IV, and Article 85(1) of Additional Protocol I to the Geneva Conventions stipulate that States should bring war criminals before their own courts. These provisions do not explicitly provide that war criminals should be tried extraterritorially. The *travaux préparatoires* and subsequent State practice contain, however, sufficient indications that the Conventions allow for universal jurisdiction. See L Reydams, *Universal Jurisdiction* (2003) 54–5. Kamminga, for his part, is convinced that the exercise of universal jurisdiction in the said articles of the Geneva Conventions is clearly mandatory. M Kamminga, 'Lessons Learned from the Exercise of Universal Jurisdiction in Respect of Gross Human Rights Offenses', (2001) 23 Hum Rts Q 940, 946. Mandatory universal jurisdiction over grave breaches may also have a customary character, so that States non-Parties to the Geneva Conventions may equally be bound by the said jurisdictional provisions. G Bottini, 'Universal Jurisdiction after the Creation of the International Criminal Court', (2004) 36 NYU J Int'l L & Pol 533; UN Commission on Human Rights, Resolution 1999/1, 16th meeting, 6 April 1999: the Commission '[r]eminds all factions and forces in Sierra Leone that in any armed conflict, including an armed conflict not of an international character, the taking of hostages, wilful killing and torture or inhuman treatment of persons taking no active part in the hostilities constitute grave breaches of international humanitarian law, and that all countries are under the obligation to search for persons alleged to have committed, or to have ordered to be committed, such grave breaches and to bring such persons, regardless of their nationality, before their own courts').

As far as non-grave breaches of the laws of war are concerned, the Geneva Conventions may not provide for obligatory universal jurisdiction. It has been argued, however, that States have a right, although not a duty, under customary international law to exercise universal jurisdiction over these breaches. Bottini (above n 149) 534; Scharf (above n 126) 92.

As far as war crimes committed in internal armed conflicts—that are not violations of common Article 3 of the Geneva Conventions—are concerned, the situation is similarly unclear. Article 6 of Additional Protocol II 1977, dealing with war crimes committed in internal armed conflicts, provides for penal prosecutions, but does not delineate its geographical scope of application, possibly because of the weight attached to the principle of non-intervention in these matters. In *Tadic*, however, the ICTY Appeals Chamber held that 'the logical and systematic interpretation of Article 3 [of the Geneva Conventions 1949] as well as customary international law' impelled it to exercise 'jurisdiction over the [war crimes] alleged in the indictment, regardless of whether they occurred within an internal or international armed conflict. Thus, to the extent that Appellant's challenge to jurisdiction under Article 3 is based on the nature of the underlying conflict, the motion must be denied.' Case No IT-94-1, *Tadic*, Appeals Chamber, Decision on the Defense Motion for Interlocutory Appeal of the Jurisdiction, 2 October 1995, para 137. Although *Tadic* only dealt with the jurisdiction of the ICTY, its findings could be extrapolated to universal jurisdiction, as it generally referred to individual criminal responsibility for violations of Article 3 of the Geneva Conventions and national legislation designed to implement the Geneva Conventions (paras 128–36). Also C Ryngaert, 'Universal Jurisdiction over Genocide and Wartime Torture in Dutch Courts: an Appraisal of the Afghan and Rwandan cases', (2007:2) Hague Justice Journal 13–36.

[150] Article 5(2) of the UN Torture Convention. This provision sets forth an *aut dedere aut judicare* obligation, pursuant to which States, even in the absence of an extradition request, are obliged to prosecute anyone suspected of torture if they do not extradite him. JH Burgers and H Danelius, *The United Nations Convention Against Torture* (1988) 133; A Cassese, *International Criminal Law* (2003) 286.

universal jurisdiction over core crimes on the basis of the *jus cogens* character of the prohibition of 'core crimes'. It has even been submitted that the prosecution of violations of *jus cogens* is itself endowed with the status of *jus cogens*.[151] A related argument has it that sovereignty entails responsibility, and that States are under an obligation not to become a safe haven for perpetrators of human rights violations, because in becoming so, they would actually acquiesce in these very violations.[152]

Against the *jus cogens* justification, it could be argued that violations of *jus cogens* are not per se amenable to universal jurisdiction.[153] On the one hand, Article 53 of the Vienna Convention on the Law of Treaties, in which the concept of *jus cogens* is enshrined, only sets forth that treaties could not derogate from the *jus cogens* obligations incurred by a State, and does not provide that States have the duty or authority to prosecute violations of *jus cogens*.[154] On the other hand, the international community could decide to have international tribunals, instead of national courts, investigate and prosecute such violations,[155] or even opt for non-criminal law mechanisms to deal with them (countermeasures, international sanctions, ...).[156] The fact that not many States have acted upon the purported obligation to exercise universal jurisdiction over violations of *jus cogens*, nor actually acted upon conventional obligations to exercise universal jurisdiction over such violations, clearly illustrates that States have not considered

---

[151] JJ Paust, *International Law as Law of the United States* (1996) 300; MC Bassiouni, 'Universal jurisdiction for International Crimes: Historical Perspectives and Contemporary Practice', (2001) 42 Va J Int'l L 81, 148–9; MC Bassiouni and EM Wise, *Aut Dedere Aut Judicare: The Duty to Extradite or Prosecute in International Law* (1995) 20–5. Also *Prosecutor v Furundzija*, ICTY Case No IT-95-17/1-T, Judgment paras 155–6 (10 December 1998) ('[I]t would seem that one of the consequences of the jus cogens character bestowed by the international community upon the prohibition of torture is that every State is entitled to investigate, prosecute and punish or extradite individuals accused of torture, who are present in a territory under its jurisdiction'); MS Myers, 'Prosecuting Human Rights Violations in Europe and America: How Legal System Structure Affects Compliance with International Obligations', (2003) 25 Mich J Int'l L 211, 222 (arguing that 'all nations are now considered bound by customary international law to prosecute crimes that have achieved *jus cogens* status'; drawing the customary international law duty to prosecute all *jus cogens* offences from the conventional law duty to prosecute particular *jus cogens* offences); Bottini (above n 149) 517 ('Customary international law recognizes universal jurisdiction for offenses involving *jus cogens* violations'); Investigating Judge Brussels, ordonnance of 6 November 1998, *Pinochet*, (1999) Journal des Tribunaux 308–11 (stating that *jus cogens* authorizes 'les autorités étatiques nationales à poursuivre et à traduire en justice, en toutes circonstances, les personnes soupçonnées de crimes contre l'humanité').

[152] Inazumi (above n 118) 144.

[153] eg Cosnard (above n 126) 358–9 (stating that 'la qualification d'une règle « fondamentale de l'ordre juridique international » n'exerce aucune influence juridique directe sur l'établissement d'une competence universelle en matière pénale').

[154] A Zimmermann, 'Violations of Fundamental Norms of International Law and the Exercise of Universal Jurisdiction in Criminal Matters', in Tomuschat and Thouvenin (above n 126) 335, 337.

[155] Bottini (above n 149) 517–19; Higgins (above n 60) 62 (stating that 'the fact that an act is a violation of international law does not of itself give rise to universal jurisdiction', thereby taking issue with a comment to § 404 of the Restatement (Third) of Foreign Relations Law which states that '[a]n international crime presumably subject to universal jurisdiction'); A Cassese, *International Law* (2001) 264.

[156] Cosnard (above n 126), 355–6.

themselves to be under an obligation to exercise universal jurisdiction over violations of *jus cogens*.[157] Even if they have exercised universal jurisdiction, they have
ordinarily done so by attaching a string of restraining conditions (most notably
the presence requirement), and by excluding the principle of mandatory prosecution. This is a *modus operandi* which appears at loggerheads with the obligation to
prosecute any violation of *jus cogens* on the basis of the universality principle.[158]

Inferring from the *jus cogens* prohibition of international crimes that States
could, or even should, prosecute these crimes under the universality principle
clearly requires a moral leap.[159] This moral justification, however, has become
the dominant legitimizing discourse of universal jurisdiction over core crimes
against international law.[160] Underlying this discourse is the idea that States
may, if not be *obliged*, at least be *authorized*, to exercise universal jurisdiction over
violations which are so reprehensible as to shock the conscience of mankind.[161]

---

[157] Also ibid 363.   [158] ibid 367–71.

[159] Cf ibid 355 ('Règles substantielles d'une part, règles procedurales d'autre part, le rapproche-
ment des deux notions n'est guidé par aucune nécessité intrinsèque, et ne peut s'imposer que par
une operation intellectuell extérieure').

[160] ibid 361 ('Le caractère fondamental d'une norme, dont le *jus cogens* est le degré ultime,
n'aurait donc d'autre function que d'en quelque sorte « doper » la justification de l'établissement
d'une competence universelle'), and 364 ('La contrariété des actes incriminés avec les intérêts fon-
damentaux de la communauté internationale intervient vraisemblablement comme motif (motiv-
ation?) de l'Etat posant une règle relative à la compétence universelle, mais il n'y a pas de raison
logique d'y voir un lien d'exclusivité').

[161] eg ICTY, *Tadic*, Case No IT-94-T (10 August 1995), para 28 (holding that the crimes listed in
the ICTY Statute 'are considered so horrific as to warrant universal jurisdiction'); Inazumi (above n
118) 142. Compare the generals terms of the preamble of the ICC Statute: 'The most serious crimes
of concern to the international community as a whole must not go unpunished and [...] their
effective prosecution must be ensured at the national level'. See also Principle 14 (1) of the Brussels
Principles Against Impunity and for International Justice ('By virtue of international law, any state
has the obligation to exercise universal jurisdiction in relation to the presumed author of a serious
crime from the moment the said presumed author is present on the territory of that state'); Articles
8, 9, 17, 18, and 20 of the Draft Code of Crimes Against the Peace and Security of Mankind Report
of the International Law Commission on the Work of its 48th Session, UN Doc A/51/10; ICTY,
Case IT-95-14-AR, *Blaskic* (29 October 1997), § 29; Report on the Work of the 43rd Session of the
International Law Commission, UN Doc. A/51/10, *ILC Yearbook* 1996, vol. II(2), 29 (ILC pro-
posing to give the ICC inherent jurisdiction over the crime of genocide because of 'the character of
the crime of genocide as a crime under international law for which universal jurisdiction existed as
a matter of customary law for those States that were not parties to the Convention'). See specifically with respect to genocide: ICTR, Case No ICTR-90-40-T, *Ntuyahaga* (18 March 1999); ICJ,
Application of the Convention on the Prevention and Punishment of the Crime of Genocide (Bosnia
and Herzegovina v Serbia and Montenegro), ICJ Rep 235, 435 (1993) sep op Lauterpacht (ground-
ing permissive universal jurisdiction on Article I of the Genocide Convention, pursuant to which
'[t]he Contracting Parties confirm that genocide, whether committed in time of peace or in time
of war, is a crime under international law which they undertake to prevent and to punish'); ICJ,
Application of the Convention on the Prevention and Punishment of the Crime of Genocide (Bosnia and
Herzegovina v Yugoslavia), ICJ Rep 594, para 31 (1996) (stating that Article VI of the Genocide
Convention does not entail any territorial limitation of the obligation under international law to
punish the crime of genocide); Higgins (above n 60) 59 (invoking the trial of *Eichmann* by Israel
as a justification for universal jurisdiction over genocide, yet adding that the special circumstances
of this trial may diminish the value of it as a precedent); Scharf (above n 126) 86 (2001) (stating
that 'Article VI [of the Genocide Convention] ... has been interpreted as merely establishing the

These moral underpinnings of universal jurisdiction are emphasized by what is termed the 'normative universalist position' by Bassiouni[162], the 'standard account' by Slaughter,[163] or the 'Manichean rationale' by Marks.[164] According to this position, core moral values of the international community, derived from religion or natural law, prevail over territorial limits on the exercise of jurisdiction.[165] Any State would have the right, or even obligation, to prosecute core international crimes without the consent of the territorial or national State. In so doing, such a 'bystander' State would not exercise its own sovereignty, but act as an agent of the international community enforcing international law in the absence of a centralized enforcer of the core values of that community.[166] The 'unilateral limited universality principle', as defined by Reydams, may also fit in this category. Under this principle, *any* State may unilaterally exercise its jurisdiction over certain offences *with an international character*, even *in absentia*.[167] This international character is not explicable in legal terms, but derives directly from a moral source: the international community considers certain offences of such an abhorrent nature that any State may prosecute them. If territorial or national States let these offences go unpunished, they lose a portion of their 'total sovereign bundle' to the international community as a whole,[168] and forfeit their

minimum jurisdictional obligation for states in which genocide occurs [*ie*, the obligation to exercise territorial jurisdiction]').

[162] MC Bassiouni, 'The History of Universal Jurisdiction and Its Place in International Law', in Macedo (above n 101) 42.

[163] A-M Slaughter, 'Defining the Limits: Universal Jurisdiction and National Courts', in Macedo (above n 101) 184–7. Also D Orentlicher, 'The Future of Universal Jurisdiction in the New Architecture of Transnational Justice', in Macedo (above n 101) 232, who finds the core justification for universal jurisdiction over inhumane crimes a moral claim. As a practical matter, universal jurisdiction steps in in case of lack of punishment in the territorial State.

[164] Marks (above n 130) 463–4. Marks criticizes this position as 'it must doubted whether there is any role for the concept of "evil" in any modern legal system'. ibid 464. He proposes to recast it as the 'harm rationale', 'a rationale based upon the enormity of the harm caused by the perpetrators of serious international crimes, rather than on concepts of good and evil'. ibid 469.

[165] Cf ICJ, *Arrest Warrant* (above n 59) diss op Van den Wyngaert § 46 ('Despite uncertainties that may exist concerning the definition of universal jurisdiction, one thing is very clear: the *ratio legis* of universal jurisdiction is based on the international reprobation for certain very serious crimes such as war crimes and crimes against humanity. Its *raison d'être* is to avoid impunity, to prevent suspects of such crimes finding a safe haven in third countries'). Also KL Boyd, 'Universal Jurisdiction and Structural Reasonableness', (2004) 40 Tex Int'l LJ 1, 38 (stating that 'any defense of universal jurisdiction must admit to the existence of a priori principles to which positive law is held accountable').

[166] Kontorovich (above n 142) 144 (adding that, as a nation is not exercising its own sovereignty, it could not prosecute a crime that is already adjudicated under 'the multiple sovereignties principle'); B Stephens, 'Translating Filartiga: A Comparative and International Law Analysis of Domestic Remedies for International Human Rights Violations', (2002) 27 Yale J Int'l L 1, 37 (pointing out that '[c]ommentators have long stressed the role of national courts in enforcing international law: in the absence of an international judiciary, most such enforcement necessarily comes through domestic judicial systems fulfilling a dual role as both national and international agents').

[167] Reydams (above n 149) 38–42.

[168] Sammons, 'The Under-Theorization of Universal Jurisdiction: Implications for Legitimacy on Trials of War Criminals by National Courts', (2003) 21 Berkeley J Int'l L 111, 127–31.

right of protest against the exercise of universal jurisdiction by bystander States. Driven to its extreme, this position implies that the courts of bystander States could exercise universal jurisdiction even in the absence of domestic enabling legislation.

(f) Lawfulness of universal jurisdiction over core crimes against international law

Core crimes against international law, such as genocide, war crimes, crimes against humanity, and torture, are, given their heinousness, generally considered to be the gravest offences imaginable. They are subject to international criminalization, often by means of an international convention. They are violations of *jus cogens*, and on that basis arguably subject to universal jurisdiction. Because any State is expected to prevent and punish such crimes, their being amenable to universal jurisdiction may not spark international protest.[169] As argued in section 2.2.c, the lawfulness of a jurisdictional assertion is often a measure of the amount of foreign protest levelled at it. If there is no protest, because no State feels harmed in its interests, universal jurisdiction over core crimes will be lawful.

Conceptually, all States may indeed consider perpetrators of core crimes as *hostes humani generis*, and have no qualms about them being prosecuted by any State. In practice, however, qualms may abound. Because core crimes are typically committed by State actors using the State's machinery, they often have a highly *political* connotation. States may have a strong interest in not having their State actors hauled before foreign courts, and not having foreign courts indirectly pass judgment on their policies. Often, adjudication of core crimes by bystander States carries the suspicion of politicized prosecution. States may fear that their military strategy will be second-guessed by ill-disposed foreign courts

---

[169] It is against his background that one has to understand Reydams's justification of universal jurisdiction on the basis of the cooperative (limited) universality principle. Reydams (above n 149) 28–38. Under this cooperative principle, the custodial State (ie the State where the foreign offender is present) acts on behalf of the territorial State in punishing an offender who seeks refuge in the former State, and who is not extradited to the territorial State for whatever reason. Initially, as Reydams pointed out, cooperation was strictly applied in that offenders were only prosecuted by a custodial State if they had turned down an extradition request (which conveys the willingness of the requesting State to have the offender prosecuted). Later, this negative *aut dedere aut judicare* approach gradually gave way to an independent positive right of the custodial State to prosecute absent an extradition request, an evolution which hollowed out the cooperative foundation of the universality principle. Under the cooperative principle, the legitimate expectations of the offender who left the territorial State are not frustrated provided that the principles of double criminality, *ne bis in idem* and the application of the *lex mitior* are respected. Moreover, as the territorial State arguably wanted to have the offender prosecuted anyway (in the early form of the cooperative principle given its extradition request, and in its later form given the heinous nature of the offence), a prosecution by the custodial State should not constitute an unwarranted interference in the domestic affairs of the territorial State.

that are ready to violate the sacrosanct principles of sovereign equality and non-interference.[170]

Because foreign protest against assertions of universal jurisdiction is not unlikely, the *jus cogens* rationale in itself provides insufficient justification for the lawfulness of universal jurisdiction. State practice and *opinio juris* in favour of universal jurisdiction ought to be specifically ascertained. Obviously, as for any exercise of jurisdiction, the lawfulness of universal jurisdiction may be traced to the *Lotus* judgment (1927),[171] in which the PCIJ ruled in favour of a broad grant of jurisdiction under customary international law.[172] Under *Lotus*, universal jurisdiction is presumptively lawful as long as no prohibitive rule to the contrary has crystallized. The bar for a finding of *unlawfulness* under *Lotus* is high, since uniformity of State practice as to the unlawfulness of universal jurisdiction has to be established. Since *Lotus*, however, as set out in section 2.2, a large part of international legal practice and doctrine has approached the law of jurisdiction on the basis of a more conservative permissive principles approach. Under this approach, a jurisdictional assertion is lawful if it is justified under a generally accepted principle authorizing the exercise of jurisdiction. Only to the extent that there is uniformity of State practice as to the *lawfulness* of the exercise of universal criminal jurisdiction over core crimes could a State establish such jurisdiction.

So far, the International Court of Justice has not explicitly addressed the lawfulness of universal jurisdiction, or the modalities of its exercise. In the 2002 *Arrest Warrant* judgment, relating to an exercise of universal jurisdiction *in absentia* by Belgium over crimes against international humanitarian law, it could have done so, yet it was able to sidestep the issue by focusing on functional immunity.[173]

---

[170]   Bassiouni (above n 162) 39.

[171]   PCIJ, *Lotus*, PCIJ Rep Series A, nr 10 (1927).

[172]   Contra C Kress, 'Universal Jurisdiction over International Crimes and the *Institut de Droit international*', (2006) 4 JICJ 561, 572. Kress argues that 'the *raison d'être* of true universal jurisdiction renders [the *Lotus*] principle inapplicable', implying that *Lotus* concerned State interests, and universal jurisdiction concerns the interests of the international community. Arguably, however, the *Lotus* principle concerns *any* unilateral exercise of jurisdiction by States, irrespective of whether these States act in their self-interest, or whether they act as agents of the international community when asserting jurisdiction.

[173]   Although the Democratic Republic of Congo (DRC) initially challenged the legality of a Belgian arrest warrant against the DRC Minister of Foreign Affairs issued on the basis of the universality principle, arguing that Belgium's claim to exercise universal jurisdiction violated the international law of jurisdiction, it eventually limited the legal grounds which it invoked before the ICJ to the question of immunity. The ICJ admitted that, as a matter of logic, it should first address the legality of universal jurisdiction before addressing jurisdictional immunity, 'since it is only where a state has jurisdiction under international law in relation to a particular matter that there can be any question of immunities in regard to the exercise of that jurisdiction'. ICJ, *Arrest Warrant* (above n 59) § 46. However, it refused to address the question of jurisdiction in view of the DRC's final submissions and assumed that Belgium indeed *had* universal jurisdiction. It has therefore been submitted that *Arrest Warrant* may be construed as upholding the general presumption of the legality of non-territorial jurisdiction, in line with the *Lotus* judgment. Inazumi (above n 118) 202. While the majority opinion did not deal with the legality of universal jurisdiction over core international crimes, several separate and dissenting opinions did. Judge Guillaume for instance argued that 'there can only be immunity from jurisdiction where there is jurisdic-

It may be hoped that it will soon provide long overdue clarification in another case relating to universal jurisdiction, namely the one initiated by the Republic of Congo against France, which had asserted universal jurisdiction over torture offences allegedly committed by a number of Congolese officials, in spite of the Republic of Congo not being a State Party to the UN Torture Convention.

Most doctrine argues that, in view of the widespread State practice as to the exercise of universal jurisdiction over core crimes, such jurisdiction is lawful under customary international law.[174] Quite a few States indeed provide for the exercise of universal jurisdiction over one or more core crimes against international law.[175] All in all, however, only a minority of States provide for, or actually exercise, universal jurisdiction over core crimes. Nonetheless, protest against the

tion'. ICJ, *Arrest Warrant* (above n 59) sep op Guillaume § 1. He found the question of universal jurisdiction of such importance and controversy, that clarification of it was in the interest of all States. Similarly, Judges Higgins, Kooijmans and Buergenthal held that '[i]mmunity depends on pre-existing jurisdiction'. ICJ, *Arrest Warrant* (above n 59) §§ 3–4 (also holding that '[w]hether the Court should accommodate this consensus [ie between Belgium and the DRC] is another matter'), while Judge Ranjeva pointed out that '[l]es considérations de logique auraient dû amener la Cour à aborder la question de la compétence universelle, une question d'actualité et sur laquelle une décision en la présente affaire aurait nécessairement fait jurisprudence'. ICJ, *Arrest Warrant* (above n 59), sep op Ranjeva § 2. Ad hoc Judge van den Wyngaert, dissenting, held the same, and was the only judge to vigorously defend the legality of universal jurisdiction as epitomized by the issuance of the Belgian arrest warrant against the DRC Minister of Foreign Affairs. ICJ, *Arrest Warrant* (above n 59) diss op Van den Wyngaert §§ 50–1 ('I believe that Belgium, by issuing and circulating the warrant, violated neither the rules on prescriptive jurisdiction nor the rules on enforcement jurisdiction'; 'I believe that there is no prohibition under international law to enact legislation allowing it to investigate and prosecute war crimes and crimes against humanity committed abroad'). In what follows, reference will on several occasions be made to these opinions.

[174] Also Zimmermann (above n 154) 351 ('the exercise of universal jurisdiction regarding the three core crimes—genocide, crimes against humanity and war crimes—is indeed based on broad State practice'). Courts typically exercise universal jurisdiction on the basis of statutory authorization, eg Cosnard (above n 126) 371. The legislature rather than the courts have thus considered universal jurisdiction to be authorized by customary international law. Among all decisions by European courts and magistrates involving the exercise of universal jurisdiction, just one was directly based on international law: in 1998, a Belgian investigating magistrate- based universal jurisdiction over crimes against humanity on customary international law, in the absence of a domestic statute authorizing such jurisdiction. See Juge d'instruction de Bruxelles, ordonnance, 6 November 1998, (1999) Rev dr pén crim 278, 288. Legislatures have conferred universal jurisdiction on the courts on the basis of detailed legal provisions, while others resorted to general enabling clauses authorizing national courts to exercise universal jurisdiction if the State is under an international obligation to do so. States which expressly provided for universal jurisdiction over specific offences have typically been more active in the prosecution of such offences under the universality principle than States which relied on a general enabling clause.

[175] eg section 1 of the German Code of Crimes against International Law 2002 (violations of international humanitarian law); article 23.4 of the Spanish Organic Law of the Judicial Power (genocide); article 7 of the Belgian Act on the punishment of grave violations of international humanitarian law (adopted in 1993 and expanded in 1999, repealed on 5 August 2003); French Laws No 96-432 of 22 May 1996 and No 95-1 of 2 January 1995 (crimes against international humanitarian law committed in the Rwanda and the former Yugoslavia); article 689-2 of the French Code of Criminal Procedure (torture); section 2,1(a) of the Dutch International Crimes Act 2003 (crimes against international humanitarian law and torture); section 134 of the UK 1988 Criminal Justice Act (torture); section 6(1) of the Canadian Crimes Against Humanity and War Crimes Act (2000) (crimes against international humanitarian law); 18 USC §2340A(b)(2) (1994) (torture).

exercise of universal jurisdiction has hardly arisen.[176] As argued in section 2.2.d, the absence of protest boosts the lawfulness of a jurisdictional assertion, because acquiescence may also count as relevant State practice.

Admittedly, it has been submitted that US 'reluctance...to assert universal jurisdiction underscores the premise that this doctrine is not part of well-established customary international law'.[177] Nonetheless, while the United States may be loath to exercise universal criminal jurisdiction, it need therefore not per se take issue with other States' assertions of universal jurisdiction. The United States opposed the universality principle during the drafting process of the 1948 Genocide Convention, but there have been no official declarations by the United States rejecting the universality principle as a matter of international law in the context of core crimes ever since.[178] Domestic concerns may go a long way in explaining the non-application of the universality principle to the prosecution of core crimes. And when the United States virulently opposed the Belgian Universality Act in 2003 (which eventually led the Belgian Parliament to repeal the Act), it may have taken issue with the conditions of the exercise of universal jurisdiction (the mechanism of civil party petition in particular) rather than with the principle itself. In fact, there are indications of active US support for universal jurisdiction over core crimes. The United States occasionally encouraged other States to exercise universal jurisdiction over core crimes,[179] and was one of the main promoters of the universal jurisdiction clause in the UN Torture Convention.

The dearth of active State practice as to the exercise of universal jurisdiction is nevertheless reason for concern. How could State practice in favour of a permissive rule truly be uniform if only a handful of States provide for universal jurisdiction? In fact, it could, if one espouses a more 'modern' view of customary international law formation. Kress,[180] drawing on Simma and Paulus,[181] has in this respect proposed using a more human rights-informed, 'modern positivist' understanding of customary international law formation. In this understanding, customary international law may also develop on the basis of general principles and 'verbal' State practice, and not only on the basis of States' assertions of universal jurisdiction. One may argue that the international community's desire not to let core crimes

---

[176] Also Zimmermann (above n 154) 353 ('it seems that no State has with regard to the exercise of universal jurisdiction concerning genocide, crimes against humanity or war crimes, so far acted as a persistent objector').

[177] G Bykhovsky, 'An Argument against Assertion of Universal Jurisdiction by Individual States', (2003) 21 Wisconsin J Int'l L 161, 168.

[178] Admittedly, during the drafting process of the ICC Statute, the United States rejected the exercise of universal jurisdiction by the ICC. This need however not imply that it would also take issue with the exercise of universal jurisdiction by bystander States. Morris (above n 128) 30 (stating that 'states would have reason to be more concerned about the political impact of adjudication before an international court than before an individual state's courts').

[179] Zimmermann (above n 154) 348.

[180] Kress (above n 172) 573.

[181] B Simma and A Paulus, 'The Responsibility of Individuals for Human Rights Abuses in Internal Conflicts: a Positivist View', (1999) 93 AJIL 302.

go unpunished—a desire which has been translated in the international criminal-ization of heinous acts and in widespread State support for international criminal tribunals, notably the ICC—may, 'be seen as a strong indication in favour of a customary state competence to exercise universal jurisdiction'.[182]

The lawfulness of universal jurisdiction may, as noted, further be boosted by the absence of protest against assertions of universal jurisdiction. In addition, the fact that some States do not provide for universal jurisdiction may not imply that these States consider universal jurisdiction to be unlawful under international law. Their reluctance may instead be informed by a lack of prosecutorial resources, the desire not to upset powerful foreign States, or evidentiary constraints. This is not to say that the universality principle in relation to the prosecution of core crimes is uncon-troversial. Yet the controversy may focus rather on the modalities of its application. It is, indeed, not yet settled what restraining principles should be applied so as to render actual assertions of universal jurisdiction reasonable,[183] nor is it settled what crimes against international humanitarian law (eg only grave breaches of the laws of war, or again minor breaches) are precisely amenable to universal jurisdiction.[184]

(g) Universal jurisdiction *in absentia*

Under the classical understanding of universal jurisdiction, which is in fact informed by the principle of *aut dedere aut judicare*, States only exercise universal jurisdiction over offenders present in their territory.[185] Universal jurisdiction is then the negation of the right of States to grant asylum to offenders.[186] The ques-tion arises whether States could also exercise universal jurisdiction over offenders who are not (yet) present in their territory (ie *in absentia*).

No treaty features an explicit legal basis for universal jurisdiction *in absentia*.[187] However, at the same time, no treaty excludes the exercise of such jurisdiction.[188]

---

[182] Kress (above n 172) 573.

[183] Also Cosnard (above n 126) 364.

[184] Institute of International Law (above n 101) nr 3(a), states that '[u]niversal jurisdiction may be exercised over crimes identified by international law as falling within that jurisdiction *in matters such* as genocide, crimes against humanity, grave breaches...' (emphasis added). The Institute thus seems to imply that *not all* crimes of genocide, crimes against humanity, and grave breaches of the law are amenable to universal jurisdiction. Kress (above n 172) 571.

[185] Inazumi (above n 118) 103; B Van Schaack, 'Justice Without Borders: Universal Civil Jurisdiction', (2005) ASIL Proc 120, 121.

[186] Donnedieu de Vabres (above n 25) 138.

[187] ICJ, *Arrest Warrant* (above n 59) sep op Guillaume § 9 and § 12 (stating that none of the con-ventions 'has contemplated establishing jurisdiction over offences committed abroad by foreigners against foreigners when the perpetrator is not present in the territory of the State in question' and that only the 'very special case' of Israel appeared to exercise universal jurisdiction *in absentia*). ibid sep op Rezek, § 6 ('L'activisme qui pourrait mener un Etat à rechercher hors de son territoire, par la voie d'une demande d'extradition ou d'un mandat d'arrêt international, une personne qui aurait été accusée de crimes définis en termes de droit des gens, mais *sans aucune circonstance de rattachement au for*, n'est aucunement autorisé par le droit international en son état actuel') (original emphasis).

[188] ibid sep op Higgins, Kooijmans and Buergenthal § 57 (asserting that the apparent restric-tion to the custodial State 'cannot be interpreted *a contrario so as to exclude* a voluntary exercise of a

Similarly, while most States providing for universal jurisdiction require the presence of the presumed offender,[189] this need not imply that a norm of customary international law has emerged that *prohibits* the exercise of universal jurisdiction *in absentia*.[190] State practice on the subject is too scarce and inconsistent to reach a conclusive answer.[191]

Universal jurisdiction *in absentia* is controversial, and the doctrine is often reluctant to endorse it.[192] Whereas traditional universal jurisdiction, which requires the presence of the offender in the forum State, is still somehow based on classical notions of territorial sovereignty—a State's territorial jurisdiction extending to all individuals within their territory, even with respect to acts done outside the territory before entering it[193]—universal jurisdiction *in absentia* can

---

universal jurisdiction') (original emphasis); ibid diss op Van den Wyngaert § 61 (holding that the conventions do 'not exclude any criminal jurisdiction exercised in accordance with national law').

However, with respect to the Geneva Conventions: ibid § 32 ('As no case has touched upon this point, the jurisdictional matter remains to be judicially tested. In fact, there has been a remarkably modest corpus of national case law emanating from the jurisdictional possibilities provided in the Geneva Conventions or in Additional Protocol I'). Also Poels (above n 124) 76; Inazumi (above n 118) 104. Treaties such as the Geneva Conventions 1949 (Articles 49, 50, 129, and 146 respectively of GC I, II, III, and IV) and the Torture Convention (Article 5(3)) do not explicitly prohibit the exercise of universal jurisdiction *in absentia*. O'Keefe has pointed out that inferring from the restriction of mandatory jurisdiction in the said treaties to instances of the offender being present in the territory, that universal jurisdiction *in absentia* is impermissible is not warranted, because the pertinent provisions containing this reference to the custodial State are tailored to the criminal procedure systems of common law States for whom trials *in absentia* are, unlike for civil law States, unknown. If the restriction to 'the custodial State' had not been inserted, the legal tradition of common law States would have precluded them ratifying the treaties. O'Keefe therefore concluded that 'the territorial precondition serves as a universally acceptable lowest common denominator'. R O'Keefe, 'Universal Jurisdiction: Clarifying the Basic Concept', (2004) 2 JICJ 735, 751.

[189]   In practice, while most States that explicitly provide for universal jurisdiction set forth the presence of the offender before jurisdiction could obtain, it is unclear whether this restriction applies only to the trial stage or also to the pre-trial stage. There may thus be quite some domestic leeway for prosecutors and investigators to conduct investigatory acts *in absentia*.

[190]   ICJ, *Arrest Warrant* (above n 59) diss op Van den Wyngaert, §§ 54–5 (arguing that there is no rule of conventional nor customary international law to the effect that universal jurisdiction *in absentia* is prohibited, espousing a teleological interpretation of the 1949 Geneva Conventions, and citing States that do not require the presence of the offender). It is indeed debatable whether concerns over the exercise of universal jurisdiction *in absentia* rise to the level of an *opinio juris* against the exercise of such jurisdiction, since States may sometimes reject universal jurisdiction on practical rather than legal grounds. ibid § 56. From the *travaux préparatoires* of the Scottish International Criminal Court Act 2001, for instance, concerns of overburdening the courts, the desire not to become a global prosecutor, reservations as to the practicability of evidence-gathering, and the fear of political repercussions are apparent. Scottish Parliament Official Report, cited in O'Keefe (above n 188) 758.

[191]   Rabinovitch (above n 135) 511.

[192]   eg International Law Association, *Final Report on the Exercise of Universal Jurisdiction in Respect of Gross Human Rights Violations* (2000) 2 ('The only connection between the crime and the prosecuting state that may be required is the physical presence of the alleged offender within the jurisdiction of that state').

[193]   ICJ, *Arrest Warrant* (above n 59), sep op Higgins, Kooijmans and Buergenthal, § 41 (discussing the *aut dedere aut judicare* provisions contained in some international treaties, and holding that, in view of the fact that these provisions set forth the presence of the offender in the territory of the prosecuting State, '[b]y the loose use of language [this] has come to be referred to as 'universal

no longer be justified on grounds of such (broadly construed) notions. Instead, being 'pure' universal jurisdiction, it derives its entire legitimacy from the interest of the international community in punishing perpetrators of crimes against international law.[194]

It is argued that authorizing universal jurisdiction *in absentia* strains foreign relations more than 'territorial' universal jurisdiction does. 'Territorial' universal jurisdiction does indeed not become operative as long as the perpetrator does not travel to States willing to bring their universal jurisdiction laws to bear.[195] By contrast, if universal jurisdiction *in absentia* were exercised, any perpetrator of an international crime, wherever he resides, in a safe haven or not, may be the subject of investigation and prosecution (although, admittedly, the perpetrator may prevent extradition or territorial enforcement acts from taking place as long as he remains in a safe haven). Because universal jurisdiction *in absentia* may reach anyone anywhere, it has been argued that it creates 'judicial chaos',[196] and that it violates the classical principle of non-intervention in the internal affairs of another State.[197]

Universal jurisdiction *in absentia* may also be at odds with due process rules, which inter alia require a suspect to know what laws he or she is subjected to. Pursuant to the classical concept of universal jurisdiction, jurisdiction is only exercised over a suspect who voluntarily enters the territory of the custodial State, and thus, who knows what laws he or she is subject to. Pursuant to universal jurisdiction *in absentia*, however, the forum is arbitrarily determined, which renders it difficult, if not impossible, for a suspect to foresee what laws will govern his conduct.[198] This objection should not be overstated, though. While it is true that in a system of universal jurisdiction *in absentia*, suspects could not know beforehand to what legal system and unfamiliar legal procedure they will be subjected, they

---

jurisdiction', though [it] is really an obligatory territorial jurisdiction over persons, albeit in relation to acts committed elsewhere').

[194] Cf Inazumi (above n 118) 104.

[195] This has also been used as an argument *against* the exercise of universal jurisdiction. Bykhovsky (above n 177) 182 (pointing at 'a serious risk of undermining traditional means of diplomacy and freedoms of international travel').

[196] ICJ, *Arrest Warrant* (above n 59) sep op Guillaume, § 15 ('But at no time has it been envisaged that jurisdiction should be conferred upon the courts of every State in the world to prosecute such crimes, whoever their authors and victims and irrespective of the place where the offender is to be found. To do this would, moreover, risk creating total judicial chaos. It would also be to encourage the arbitrary for the benefit of the powerful, purportedly acting as agent for an ill-defined 'international community'. Contrary to what is advocated by certain publicists, such a development would represent not an advance in the law but a step backward').

[197] eg Rabinovitch (above n 135) 521; *Regina v Bartle and the Commissioner of Police for the Metropolis and Others, ex parte Pinochet* [1999] 2 All ER 97 (HL) (Lord Millett) ('[T]he limiting factor that prevents the exercise of extra-territorial criminal jurisdiction from amounting to an unwarranted interference with the internal affairs of another State is that, for the trial to be fully effective, the accused must be present in the forum State'). Cf Donnedieu de Vabres (above n 25) 160 (rejecting universal jurisdiction *in absentia* 'puisque l'Etat entre les mains duquel il se trouve actuellement est, de ce chef, mieux qualifié pour connaitre de son affaire').

[198] Inazumi (above n 118) 147.

know beforehand that their heinous conduct is criminal under international law and that they could be hauled before any court.

Proponents of universal jurisdiction *in absentia* emphasize the important role which it could play in the fight against international impunity. They argue that, if the presence of the presumed offender is required, he will arguably go unpunished as long as he does not enter the territory of a State which is willing to either prosecute him, or extradite him to another State willing to prosecute. Roht-Arriaza has submitted in this context that '[t]o require that the defendant be present...changes the nature of universal jurisdiction from a doctrine providing for prosecution and punishment, to a doctrine that does little more than eliminate safe havens'.[199] Under the system of universal jurisdiction *in absentia*, victims are more likely to have their day in court, given the wide range of possible fora.[200] Moreover, universal jurisdiction *in absentia* could help prevent the axe of statutes of limitation from falling.[201] Bystander States could prosecute the perpetrator directly after he committed his heinous acts, and would not have to wait for the perpetrator to be (voluntarily) present in their territory.

This study supports the reasonable exercise of universal jurisdiction *in absentia*, on the ground that the fight against impunity demands that as wide a prosecutorial net as possible be cast. Unlike what its critics believe, the sweep of universal jurisdiction *in absentia* is not overbroad. While on the basis of an authorization to exercise universal jurisdiction *in absentia*, any State may in theory initiate proceedings against perpetrators of international crimes, wherever committed, any forcible measures against these perpetrators are necessarily tied to their presence in the territory of the forum State. Alleged offenders cannot be deposed or interrogated, let alone arrested or imprisoned in their absence, unless consent of the territorial State could be obtained. No forcible measure can be taken without the alleged offender being voluntarily present in the territory or being extradited by the requested State where he could be found. States can only take non-forcible, pre-trial measures *in absentia*, such as compiling information, hearing witnesses, pre-trial seizure of assets, issuing an arrest warrant with a view to securing the territorial presence of the offender (without any certainty that the alleged offender will effectively be arrested),[202] and, exceptionally (if domestic law allows for it),

---

[199] N Roht-Arriaza, comment on Spanish Constitutional Court, *Guatemala Genocide* case, (2006) 100 AJIL 207, 212.

[200] Poels (above n 124) 78 ('Universal jurisdiction *in absentia* is without doubt the most effective instrument against criminal impunity [...] the ultimate translation of [the international community's] reprobation of the most serious crimes').

[201] ibid 79.

[202] It may be submitted that an international arrest warrant is a purely domestic act with no actual extraterritorial effect, if the warrant could not be and is not executed in the country where it is issued or in the countries to which it is circulated. ICJ, *Arrest Warrant* (above n 59) § 80. An international arrest warrant will however *have* an extraterritorial effect when it is intended to be immediately executed, *quod plerumque fit*. In practice, only international immunities will remove the actual extraterritorial effect. It nevertheless remains true that an arrest warrant ordinarily only envisages the arrest of the alleged perpetrator in the territory of the issuing State or the arrest in a

conduct a trial *in absentia*.[203] The alleged offender need not be physically too embarrassed by such measures, as long as he stays in or travels to a State which will not extradite him. The exercise of universal jurisdiction *in absentia*, if limited to investigative acts, need therefore not interfere in the domestic affairs of a foreign State any more than the exercise of universal jurisdiction does.[204]

The encroachment of universal jurisdiction *in absentia* upon the principle of non-intervention appears, certainly in light of the grave character of the offences amenable to universal jurisdiction, negligible. Yet the stigmatic and deterrent effect of the initiation of investigations, in combination with the possibility of freezing assets, may provide considerable relief to the victims of core crimes.[205] Although the chances of a trial and the eventual imprisonment of the perpetrator may be slight because of his absence in the territory (extradition often being impossible), the exercise of universal jurisdiction *in absentia* may thus serve an important redemptive goal.[206] Furthermore, States that have or obtain custody of the perpetrator may benefit from the preparatory work done by a bystander State investigating the case *in absentia*. A bystander State's amassing of evidence ineluctably pointing to guilt of the offender may even serve as a wake-up call for

third State at the discretion of the State concerned. While an international arrest warrant may have an extraterritorial effect, it constitutes a territorial measure. In their joint separate opinion, three ICJ judges held that the aim of the arrest warrant 'would in principle seem to violate no existing prohibiting rule of international law'. ICJ, *Arrest Warrant* (above n 59), joint sep op Higgins, Kooijmans and Buergenthal, § 54. Third States can assist the exercise of universal jurisdiction *in absentia* by the forum State by extraditing the alleged perpetrator to the latter State. This does not seem to violate international law either. ibid § 58.

[203] In common law countries, trials *in absentia* are normally not authorized. In France, however, such trials are possible. In 2005, a French court convicted Ely Ould Dah, a Mauritanian torturer, in his absence. The rejection of a trial *in absentia* does not reflect a desire to comply with the international law of jurisdiction, but the desire to guarantee the right of a fair trial, enshrined inter alia in Article 6 ECHR and Article 14.3 ICCPR, the latter provision giving every person the right to be tried in his presence. Also ICJ, *Arrest Warrant* (above n 59), joint sep op Higgins, Kooijmans and Buergenthal, § 56. Rabinovitch for his part, while admitting that trials *in absentia* may be comply with human rights standards, has forcefully argued against them, pointing out that juries may 'draw the inappropriate inference that because the accused may be absent he or she is a fugitive and therefore probably guilty', that the presence of the accused is an essential aspect of the adversarial criminal justice system, that the presence of the accused is an essential part of the punishment that he ought to suffer, and that trials *in absentia* may bring the judicial system of the forum State into disrepute. Rabinovitch (above n 135) 528–9. Cf Kress (above n 172) 583 (arguing that 'if trials *in absentia* are considered as inappropriate in *international* criminal proceedings, the same should apply to those national proceedings that are based solely on the exercise of true universal jurisdiction'). Also Poels (above n 124) 73 (not condemning trials *in absentia*, but arguing that 'an at least formal notification of the initiation of criminal proceedings should be given to all concerned individuals', such as by the filing of an extradition request).

[204] In this sense also Kress (above n 172) 576–9.

[205] Also A Sanchez Legido, 'Spanish Practice in the Area of Universal Jurisdiction', (2001–2002) 8 Spanish Yb Int'l L 17, 36 ('[E]ven if merely a warning, allowing a pre-trial investigation and the activating of the mechanisms of international criminal cooperation can serve not only as a reminder to the suspect of the consequences that the international legal system attaches to crimes allegedly committed, but also a relief, a relative one of course, as regards the rights that this same legal system affords to the victims').

[206] See also Rabinovitch, at 520 (drawing a parallel with the ICTY's Rule 61 proceedings).

the State having custody of the offender (usually the territorial or national State), and even trigger a duty to prosecute.[207] Especially if a transnational network of information-sharing is put into place, as happened in the European Union,[208] far from wreaking havoc to the international legal system, limited possibilities for an exercise of universal jurisdiction *in absentia* actually further international cooperation in criminal matters. If the prosecution of the presumed offender in any other State—with which the investigating State has judicial cooperation agreements—could be anticipated, gathering evidence in the territory or accepting evidence submitted by civil parties, and hearing witnesses present in the territory should be deemed admissible.[209] Yet even if the prospect of international cooperation seems to be distant, investigatory acts *in absentia* should still be performed if the (voluntary) presence of the presumed offender in the territory of the forum State itself could be anticipated. Even if performed *in absentia*, they derive their anticipatory legality from the anticipated territoriality of a later full-fledged prosecution and possible trial. Investigations *in absentia* may even be necessary if a prosecution on the basis of the universality principle is to be successful: a person entering the territory only becomes a 'presumed offender', and could only be arrested, on the basis of a pre-existing dossier listing heinous acts allegedly perpetrated by him.[210] This appears in fact to be the message underlying the jurisdictional provisions of the Geneva Conventions, which require any State to 'search for' persons, whatever their nationality, suspected of committing grave breaches of the laws of war.[211]

While the argument in favour of universal jurisdiction *in absentia* is cogent, reasonableness requires that due consideration is given to the legitimate concerns of foreign States and their agents. It is often argued that the mere initiation of prosecutions *in absentia* may blemish the reputation of persons named in the complaint or act sparking the prosecution. This was actually the main grief of the United States against the Belgian 'Genocide Act', which, because it authorized the exercise of universal jurisdiction *in absentia* (as endorsed by the Court of

---

[207] Roht-Arriaza (above n 199) 212.

[208] On 13 June 2002, the Council of Ministers of the European Union decided to set up a European network of contact points in respect of persons responsible for genocide, crimes against humanity and war crimes. Council Decision [2002] OJ L 167/1–2. The 2002 Decision was complemented by a 2003 Decision pursuant to which Member States should assist one another in investigating and prosecuting these crimes, in particular through the exchange of information between immigration authorities. Council Decision [2003] OJ L 118/12–14. The Member States should have taken the necessary measures by 8 May 2005 (Article 7 of the 2003 Decision).

[209] In this sense also Institute of International Law (above n 101) nr 3 (b) ('*Apart from acts of investigation and requests for extradition*, the exercise of universal jurisdiction requires the presence of the alleged offender in the territory of the prosecuting State ... or other lawful forms of control over the alleged offender') (emphasis added).

[210] Cosnard (above n 126) 369.

[211] Kamminga (above n 149) 954 (implying that States Parties to the Geneva Conventions are not only authorized, but even *obliged* to exercise universal jurisdiction *in absentia* over grave breaches).

Cassation on 12 February 2003 in the *Sharon* case) upon civil party petitions by victims (groups), was repealed on 5 August 2003 after intense US pressure.

It could be argued that any initiation of criminal proceedings, be it in a domestic or international setting, could blemish the reputation of persons. It is precisely the task of prosecutors and investigating magistrates to unveil the truth, and by so doing possibly restore the name and integrity of the investigated person. Admittedly, complaints alleging core crimes against international law tend to be mediatized, which might result in condemnation by public opinion and thus jeopardize the impartiality of the investigation and the eventual trial. This need not undercut the case for universal jurisdiction *in absentia*, however. If a prosecutor or investigating magistrate could speedily dispose of a case, citing admissibility grounds, the damage to the persons named and the concomitant political fall-out may be limited. This may be illustrated by the complaint against a number of American high-ranking officials and service-members filed by the American Center for Constitutional Rights with the German Federal Prosecutor against, inter alia, the former US Secretary of Defence, relating to abuses allegedly committed at the US prison complex at Abu Ghraib (Iraq), a complaint that the prosecutor handily disposed of, to US satisfaction.[212] A speedy disposal of a complaint is not always possible or justified, however. States may therefore possibly want to provide that complaints (alleging international crimes) are inadmissible if they are released to the public prior to or at the moment of their filing. They could even provide for fines for the complainants if the complaint is released subsequent to the filing. This might discourage complainants from filing complaints to merely capture media attention instead of genuinely seeking legal accountability for the alleged perpetrators. No State appears to have contemplated such drastic measures, which may possibly run counter to freedom of information legislation.[213] Alternatively, one may, as Cassese has proposed, limit the exercise of universal jurisdiction *in absentia* to low-key perpetrators, and abolish it for high-ranking officials,[214] since the former class of offenders may presumably have less legitimate international reputational concerns.

---

[212] Under section 153f (1) of the German Code of Criminal Procedure, German prosecutors and courts could exercise universal jurisdiction *in absentia*, if the presence of the presumed offender can be anticipated. In a decision dated 5 April 2007, the German Federal Prosecutor decided that the accused persons cannot be expected to be present in Germany, and that Germany could therefore not exercise jurisdiction. The Prosecutor General at the Federal Supreme Court, *Re Criminal Complaint against Donald Rumsfeld et al.*, 5 April 2007, 3 ARP 156/06-2.

[213] Curbing the right to civil party petition, ie, the right of victims to seize an investigating magistrate who is obliged to act upon their petition, as happened in Belgium, may not be very useful if the stated aim is to limit media exposure of the person(s) named in the petition. Indeed, victims could always file complaints with a prosecutor. While the prosecutor may not be obliged to act upon the compliant, the damage may be done if the victims manage to capture media attention—which is often even their main objective.

[214] A Cassese, 'The Twists and Turns of Universal Jurisdiction: Foreword', (2006) 4 JCIJ 559.

(h) Universal tort jurisdiction

The universality principle is typically invoked in a criminal law context, regarding the prosecution of heinous crimes. Universal jurisdiction is therefore often equated with universal *criminal* jurisdiction.[215] However, not only may a State's criminal courts be willing to establish universal jurisdiction, so may also a State's *civil* courts. A State may allow its courts to hear complaints for damages by victims of serious infringements of international law, typically gross human rights violations, wherever these violations may have occurred. This jurisdiction may be characterized as universal *tort* or *civil* jurisdiction. Like universal criminal jurisdiction, universal tort jurisdiction may be solely premised on the heinous nature of a particular violation, without a territorial or personal nexus to the forum being required.[216]

Thanks to the peculiar features of the US procedural system, universal tort jurisdiction appears as a distinctly American phenomenon. Federal courts in the United States, especially since the early 1980s, have received numerous human rights complaints by aliens on the basis of the Alien Tort Statute (ATS), a statutory instrument which confers 'original jurisdiction of any civil action by an alien for a tort only, committed in violation of the law of nations or a treaty of the United States'.[217] In contrast, outside the United States, even in Western States, universal tort jurisdiction is an unknown quantity. This discrepancy might not be fatal to the lawfulness of assertions of universal tort jurisdiction. While non-US State practice may be scarce, such need not signal international opposition to universal tort jurisdiction on legal grounds. In fact, only few States actually *oppose* the exercise of universal tort jurisdiction. Continental European States may prefer criminal remedies for gross human rights violations, but do not necessarily deem civil remedies of the sort US law provides for to be unlawful. European States appear to countenance the principle of universal tort jurisdiction under international law, and to limit themselves to reminding the United States to remain *reasonable* in their jurisdictional assertions.

---

[215] eg J Terry, 'Taking *Filàrtiga* on the Road: Why Courts Outside the United States Should Accept Jurisdiction Over Actions Involving Torture Committed Abroad', in Scott (above n 21) 109.

[216] In practice, in tort cases under the universality principle, personal jurisdiction over the defendant will ordinarily not be established if the defendant has no minimal *territorial* contacts with the forum. This does, however, not require that the defendant reside in, or be a national of, the forum State. Transient or tag presence may suffice. See on the minimum contacts requirement for purposes of personal jurisdiction in the United States notably *International Shoe Co v Washington*, 326 US 310, 315 (1945).

[217] 28 USC section 1350. Under the ATS, claims brought by US nationals, as opposed to foreign nationals, are not admissible. There is no nationality requirement for the defendants, in contrast. In fact, *US* corporations were sued in many ATS cases. eg *Doe I v Unocal Corp*, 963 F Supp 880 (CD Cal 1997); *National Coalition Government of the Union of Burma v Unocal*, 176 FRD 329 (CD Cal 1997); *Doe v Unocal Corp*, 27 F Supp 2d 1174 (CD Cal 1998), aff'd 248 F 3d 915 (2001); *Doe I v Unocal Corp*, 110 F Supp 2d 1294 (CD Cal 2000); *Doe I v Unocal Corp* 395 F 3d 3932 (9th Cir 2002); *Aguina v Texaco*, 142 F Supp 2d 534 (SDNY 2001), aff'd 303 F 3d 470 (2d Cir 2002); *In re 'Agent Orange' Prod Liab Litig*, 304 F Supp 2d 404 (EDNY 2004).

In the final analysis, some legal systems may be more conducive to the development of one specific justice or accountability perspective with respect to international crimes or gross human rights violations. The reparations perspective may find fertile ground in the systems that value tort litigation, such as the US system. The punishment and moral condemnation perspectives, for their part, may rather be developed in systems that value criminal justice, such as the European system. No perspective may be better than the other. While some legal systems may admittedly be better suited for the development of one perspective, in fact, however, all legal systems where the universality principle has taken hold, have integrated *both* perspectives. European criminal proceedings *also* allow for victim participation and reparation, whereas US tort judgments may *also* allow for punishment and the international community's moral condemnation, notably by awarding high damages to the plaintiffs and by declaring the perpetrator responsible for the violation.

Rather than tussling over whether States should exercise universal criminal or universal tort jurisdiction, or both, over gross human rights violations, the international community may want to focus its efforts on ensuring that at least some international accountability for such violations is provided for in 'bystander' States' courts. The international community may want to see to it that at least one modality of the universality principle, either the criminal or the tort one, is applied by States.[218]

4.6 Concurrent Jurisdiction and Normative Competency Conflicts

As might be clear from this chapter, States could rely upon a variety of jurisdictional grounds regarding one and the same situation. In the case of a citizen of State X committing a crime in State Y against a citizen of State Z, all three States may have jurisdiction, on the basis of the territoriality principle, the active personality principle, or the passive personality principle. What is more, if the crime is an international crime that gives rise to universal jurisdiction, every single State may have jurisdiction, irrespective of a nexus with the crime. In the field of economic law, given the integration of the global economy, restrictive business practices and fraudulent securities transactions may produce worldwide effects, and cause several States to assert effects-based jurisdiction.

The system of jurisdiction, in both criminal and economic matters, is, accordingly, one of *concurrent* jurisdiction. This may be problematic, and spark normative competency conflicts between States. For instance, in the field of criminal law, only the State that could gain custody of the presumed offender, and put him or her on trial, will be able to effectively exercise its jurisdiction. Other States,

---

[218] See at length on universal tort jurisdiction under international law: C Ryngaert, 'Universal Tort Jurisdiction over Gross Human Rights Violations', (2007) NYIL 3.

who could also rely on a legitimate ground to exercise prescriptive jurisdiction, may resent this. They may argue that, in fact, *their* jurisdictional assertions are *more* legitimate, notably in view of the stronger link which they entertain with the crime or the criminal. Somewhat similarly, in the field of economic law, it may happen that States clamp down on a restrictive business practice and impose fines pursuant to the territorial principle—while other States may contend that they, in fact, have a stronger territorial link with the practice, and, on that basis, they are entitled to allow the practice without regulatory intervention by other States.

It is not a given that, in a situation in which different States are authorized to exercise jurisdiction, they will as a matter of course defer to the State that first exercises its jurisdiction. Because jurisdiction under international law is concurrent, conflicts over which State's jurisdictional assertions are most legitimate in a given case may surely arise. As to universal jurisdiction, for instance, the State on whose territory an international crime has been committed may argue that its right to establish jurisdiction (and to either prosecute or not prosecute) prevails over bystander States' right to do so. By the same token, as to antitrust jurisdiction, the State on whose territory a cartel was formed may argue that its right to establish jurisdiction (and to either condone or dismantle the cartel) prevails over the regulatory claims of States where any adverse territorial effects may be felt.

In order to solve conflicts of jurisdiction, some writers and courts have asserted the paramountcy of territoriality, on the ground that territoriality is the basic rule of jurisdiction, and other grounds of jurisdiction the exceptions.[219] In fact,

---

[219] eg Mann (above n 147) 90 ('In a large number of cases the local law will have to be allowed to prevail, for every other solution would be destructive of justice and international intercourse'); Beale (above n 19) 252 (arguing that 'any exercise of [active personality jurisdiction] must be subject to the higher authority of the act of the sovereign within the jurisdiction of whose law it is done'); G Fitzmaurice, 'The General Principles of International Law', (1957-II) 92 RCADI 1, 212 ('The territorial and the personal jurisdictions … are concurrent, not mutually exclusive jurisdictions, although there are limits, both natural and formal, to the extent to which they can be simultaneously *exercised* or enforced—and in this respect it is the personal that, in the nature of the case, defers to the territorial'); ibid 216 (concluding that 'the supreme principle of penal jurisdiction is territorial'); AV Lowe, 'Blocking Extraterritorial Jurisdiction: the British Protection of Trading Interests Act, 1980', (1981) 75 AJIL 257, 266 (noting that while 'the notion of "paramountcy" of jurisdiction is difficult to pin down … general principles of international law, and to some extent state practice, would suggest that there were a doctrine of "paramountcy" to be accepted, priority would be given to states claiming territorial jurisdiction …' (footnotes omitted); Inazumi (above n 118) 179–81 (citing the extradition law practice of requested States refusing to extradite the perpetrator of a crime committed in their territory, while at the same time noting the practice of requested States refusing to extradite their own nationals); Watson (above n 19) 17 (pointing out that 'the host state's interest in preserving order at home [under the territoriality principle] outweighs the interests of either the victim's or offender's home state in regulating conduct abroad', while noting that '[w]hen resolving jurisdictional disputes, states sometimes put nationality jurisdiction on a par with territorial jurisdiction'); European Court of Human Rights, *Bankovic and others v Belgium and 16 other Contracting States*, Application No 52207/99, 12 December 2001, § 60 ('[A] State's competence to exercise jurisdiction over its own nationals abroad is subordinate to that State's and other States' territorial competence'); *Laker Airways Ltd v Sabena*, 731 F 2d 909, 935–6 (DC Cir 1984) ('The purported principle of paramount nationality is entirely unknown in national and international law. Territoriality, not nationality, is the customary and preferred base

however, the international law of jurisdiction does not seem to prioritize the bases of jurisdiction.[220] There is no rule prohibiting States from establishing concurrent jurisdiction over one and the same situation on the basis of territoriality, nationality, or universality.[221] Nor may there appear to be a rule obliging States to exercise their jurisdiction reasonably.[222] The classical doctrine of international jurisdiction, a doctrine which defines 'the legally relevant point of contact' as 'indicating the State which has a close, rather than the closest, connection with the facts',[223] is not concerned with exclusivity of jurisdiction, and may thus fail to prevent the outbreak of jurisdictional conflicts.[224]

Moreover, even if territoriality were to be seen as being the paramount principle of jurisdiction, normative competency conflicts could not be excluded. Four

of jurisdiction.' [...] 'In fact, international law recognizes that a state with a territorial basis for its prescriptive jurisdiction may establish laws intended to prevent compliance with legislation established under authority of nationality-based jurisdiction.' [...] 'It would be difficult or impossible to determine when the nationality of a corporation is sufficiently strong that legitimate territorial contacts should be nullified').

A further question is whether objective territoriality prevails over subjective territoriality. It may be argued that States affected by extraterritorial acts have a greater interest in regulation than the State from whose territory the harmful effects originate. Maier, however, has argued against this reasoning that '[t]he nation that is the *situs* of the acts necessarily has a similar self-interest in determining whether the acts in question should be reprehended. That self-interest is defined by the *situs* state's freedom as an independent sovereign to govern its own society within its territory.' HG Maier, 'Jurisdictional Rules in Customary International Law', in KM Meessen, ed, *Extraterritorial Jurisdiction in Theory and Practice* (1996) 64, 69.

[220] See *Laker Airways Ltd v Sabena*, 731 F 2d 909, 935 (DC Cir 1984) ('[N]o rule of international law or national law precludes an exercise of jurisdiction solely because another state has jurisdiction', citing Restatement (Third) § 402 comment b); KM Meessen, 'Antitrust Jurisdiction Under Customary International Law', (1982) 78 AJIL 783, 801 (arguing, in the context of extraterritorial antitrust, that 'state practice has not yet resulted in consistency on jurisdictional priorities such as "paramount nationality"'); AV Lowe, 'Blocking Extraterritorial Jurisdiction: the British Protection of Trading Interests Act, 1980', (1981) 75 AJIL 257, 267 (arguing that the supposed 'paramountcy' of territoriality may be no more than a 'principle of comity'); A Bianchi, Reply to Professor Maier, in KM Meessen, ed, *Extraterritorial Jurisdiction in Theory and Practice* (1996) 74, 84 (arguing that 'the presumption of state sovereignty, underlying the *Lotus* case, implies the logical impossibility of setting priorities among conflicting sovereign prerogatives') (footnotes omitted). Contra ICJ, *Arrest Warrant* (above n 59) sep op Higgins, Kooijmans, and Buergenthal, § 59, advocating the primacy of national jurisdiction over universal jurisdiction ('A State contemplating bringing criminal charges based on universal jurisdiction must first offer to the national State of the prospective accused person the opportunity itself to act upon the charges concerned'); Inazumi (above n 118) 128; RS Clark, 'Offenses of International Concern: Multilateral State Treaty Practice in the Forty Years Since Nuremberg', (1988) 57 Nordic J Int'l L 59 (arguing that, given the order of the heads of jurisdiction in the conventions providing for universal jurisdiction, nationality, or territoriality jurisdiction prevails over universal jurisdiction); Blakesley (above n 74) 82.

[221] *Laker Airways Ltd v Sabena*, 731 F 2d 952 ('There is no principle of international law which abolishes concurrent jurisdiction').

[222] ibid ('There is [...] no rule of international law holding that a "more reasonable" assertion of jurisdiction mandatorily displaces a "less reasonable" assertion of jurisdiction as long as both are, in fact, consistent with the limitations on jurisdiction imposed by international law'). The DC Circuit in *Laker Airways* did not see 'neutral principles on which to distinguish judicially the reasonableness of the concurrent, mutually inconsistent exercises of jurisdiction [...]'. ibid 953.

[223] Mann (above n 147) 46.   [224] ibid 10.

examples will be given here: the first in the field of antitrust law, the second in the field of export controls, the third in regard of universal jurisdiction over violations of international humanitarian law, and the fourth in regard of a home State's regulation of the activities of 'its' corporations abroad (ie in a host State).

In the field of antitrust law, jurisdictional conflicts could arise if different States are allowed to rely on a broadly construed territorial principle (either conduct- or effects-based) in order to justify their jurisdictional assertions over one and the same restrictive business practice, and one State condones the practice (invoking its jurisdictional right *not* to regulate practices originating in its territory), while another censures it (invoking its right to clamp down on practices adversely affecting its territory). It is against that background that the United Kingdom, especially in the 1960s and 1970s, vehemently protested against US assertions of effects-based jurisdiction over restrictive practices originating in foreign States. Eventually, it adopted, in the wake of the *Uranium* Litigation, the British Protection of Trading Interests Act in 1980 (an Act which is still applicable) to ward off any encroachment of British business interests through US enforcement of its antitrust laws, including discovery orders.[225]

The law of export controls is another field of the law where major jurisdictional conflicts have broken out.[226] Again, the conflict was mainly transatlantic in character. Over the last decades, the US attempted several times to impose US export controls on foreign corporations to promote US foreign policy objectives, the fight against communism and terrorism in particular. Often, the United States was forced to back down after intense, mainly European, protest. In the 1960s, for instance, after the US Department of the Treasury prohibited Fruehauf, a French corporation under US control, from exporting to China under the US Trading with the Enemy Act,[227] a French lower court and an appeals court decided that the US order was no bar to Fruehauf's right as a French corporation to honour its contract with China, on the grounds that the needs of the company's employees outweighed the personal interests of the American directors.[228] When, in the 1980s, the United States prohibited the export to Russia of equipment produced abroad by foreign subsidiaries of US undertakings and by any company using technology licences granted by US undertakings ('Soviet Pipeline Regulations'), a Dutch court held that such export controls violated international law.[229] What is more, the European Community, whose companies bore the brunt of the Regulations, condemned them in the strongest words as contrary to

---

[225] This Act and the *Uranium Litigation* is elaborated on at length in C Ryngaert, *Jurisdiction over Antitrust Violations in International Law* (2008) 49 and 185–92.

[226] eg HL Clark, 'Dealing with US Extraterritorial Sanctions and Foreign Countermeasures', (2004) 25 U Pa J Int'l Econ L 455, 457.

[227] Trading With the Enemy Act of 1917, 50 App USCA § 10; Fed Reg 2503–04 (1942).

[228] *Société Fruehauf Corp v Massardy*, 1968 DS Jur 147, 1965, 5 ILM 476 (1966) (Ct Appel Paris 1965).

[229] *Compagnie européenne des Pétroles SA v Sensor Nederland BV*, District Court, The Hague, 17 September 1982, 22 ILM 66 (1983) 72.

international law and normal commercial practice.[230] In the 1990s then, in a last volley of secondary boycotts, the United States prohibited foreign corporations, even if not owned by US corporations, from trading in goods confiscated from US nationals by the Cuban government in the 1960s, and from trading with such 'terrorist' States as Iran.[231] The EU, which had major commercial interests in these States, reacted swiftly and fiercely, and even filed a WTO lawsuit against the United States.[232] In all these cases, the United States eventually backed down on political rather than legal grounds.[233]

The early 2000s saw serious jurisdictional conflicts over the exercise of universal jurisdiction over violations of international humanitarian law by a number of Western States. In this context, the fate of the liberal Belgian universality law is well-known. The law, adopted in 1993 and amended in 1999, authorized the filing of a civil party petition with an investigating judge (as a result of which the opening of a criminal investigation is mandatory) in the absence of any link with Belgium (even in the absence of the perpetrator on Belgian soil). After civil parties (ab)used the law to file (frivolous) complaints against current and former high-ranking US persons, the United States brought intense pressure to bear on Belgium to scale down the law.[234] Within a few months, in August 2003, the law was repealed.[235] Apart from Belgium, the United Kingdom has also been the

[230] European Community: Note and Comments on the Amendments of 22 June 1982 to the Export Administration Act, Presented to the United States Department of State on 12 August 1982, 21 ILM 891, 893–4 ('The U.S. measures as they apply in the present case are unacceptable under international law because of their extra-territorial aspects. They seek to regulate companies not of U.S. nationality in respect of their conduct outside the United States and particularly the handling of property and technical data of these companies not within the United States. They seek to impose on non-U.S. companies the restriction of U.S. law by threatening them with discriminatory sanctions in the field of trade which are inconsistent with the normal commercial practice established between the U.S. and the E.C. In this way the Amendments of 22 June 1982, run counter to the two generally accepted bases of jurisdiction in international law; the territoriality and the nationality principles') (footnotes omitted).

[231] Cuban Liberty and Democratic Solidarity Act, Public law 104th-114, 12 March 1996, 110 Stat 785, 22 USC §§ 6021–91; Iran Libya Sanctions Act, Pub L. 104–72, 5 August 1996, 110 Stat 1541 (50 USC 1701).

[232] EU Common Position, 2 December 1996, [1996] OJ L322. Council Regulation (EC) No 2271/96, Protecting Against the Effects of the Extraterritorial Application of Legislation Adopted by a Third Country, 36 ILM 125 (1997). The United Kingdom applied the British Protection of Trading Interests Act 1980 as a response to the Helms-Burton Act and the Iran Libya Sanctions Act; KJ Kuilwijk, 'Castro's Cuba and the U.S. Helms-Burton Act. An Interpretation of the GATT Security Exemption', (1997) 31 JWT 49–61.

[233] For further reading on the *Fruehauf* case: AF Lowenfeld, *Trade Controls for Political Ends*, New York, Bender, 1983, at 91–105 and 268–306; Soviet Pipeline Regulations: R Ergec, *La compétence extraterritoriale à la lumière du contentieux sur le gazoduc euro-sibérien* (1984); Helms-Burton Act and Iran Libya Sanctions Act: Understanding between the EU and the United States on US extraterritorial legislation of 11 April 1997, available at <http://www.eurunion.org/partner/summit/summit9712/extrater.htm>.

[234] 'U.S. Threatens NATO Boycott over Belgium War Crimes Law', The Guardian, 13 June 2003, available at <http://www.guardian.co.uk/nato/story/0,12667,976499,00.html>.

[235] For further reading, and for information on jurisdiction in the post-2003 era: J Wouters and C Ryngaert, 'De toepassing van de (Belgische) wet van 5 augustus 2003 betreffende ernstige

target of criticism regarding the reach of its universality laws. On 10 September 2005, a UK Senior District Judge issued, at the request of a number of Palestinian victims, a warrant for the arrest of Israeli Major General (retired) Doron Almog on suspicion of committing a grave breach of the Fourth Geneva Convention 1949 in the occupied Palestinian Territory. The arrest warrant provoked Israeli protest, and the British Foreign Secretary had to apologize. Subsequently, it was suggested to restrict the rights of (foreign) victims to seek an arrest warrant in the UK in order to prevent jurisdictional conflicts.[236]

States, ordinarily the home State or the territorial State, that protest against the exercise of universal jurisdiction over crimes with political overtones, such as war crimes, typically claim the primary right to investigate and prosecute the alleged perpetrator, because they fear that foreign courts will be biased and mete out undue or excessive punishment. The exercise of extraterritorial jurisdiction over common crimes on the basis of the nationality, passive personality, or protective principle, may be challenged on similar grounds. Yet in regard to common crimes, protest may be more mute given their often apolitical character, and thus the absence of a State interest worth of protection. When common criminals are put on trial in hostile States, or in States with poor human rights or due process records, the odds of foreign protest are obviously higher.

The next frontier of jurisdictional conflicts may be found in relation to calls for enhanced transnational corporate social responsibility. Home States of multinational corporations, typically Western States, are under rising pressure to regulate the latter's activities in host States, typically developing States. Since the latter are often unable or unwilling to impose or enforce high standards relating to human rights, health and safety, or the environment, a regulatory vacuum looms large. It has been proposed that this vacuum be filled by the corporation's home State.[237] If the home State were to regulate its corporations' overseas activities, eg by imposing higher standards on overseas corporate activities or by providing

---

schendingen van het internationaal humanitair recht', (2007) *Nullum Crimen*, special issue April 2007.

[236] See <http://www.hickmanandrose.co.uk/news05.html>. The victims had requested the issuance of an arrest warrant by the magistrate because the War Crimes Unit of the Metropolitan Police was unable to take a decision on the arrest or prosecution of Almog. Almog managed to take his flight back from Heathrow Airport to Israel before the arrest warrant could be executed. The UK Foreign Secretary thereupon apologized for the incident. The matter was also discussed by the Israeli and British prime ministers at a meeting of the UN in New York. V Dodd, 'UK Considers Curbing Citizens' Right to Arrest Alleged War Criminals', The Guardian, 3 February 2006. In June 2006, the UK Attorney-General paid a visit to Israel so as to resolve the issue of Israeli generals visiting the United Kingdom risking being arrested. New Statesman, 26 June 2006.

[237] M Anderson, 'Transnational Corporations and Environmental Damage: Is Tort Law the Answer?', (2002) 41 Washburn LJ 399, 409; O De Schutter, 'Les affaires *Total* et *Unocal* : complicité et extraterritorialité dans l'imposition aux entreprises d'obligations en matière de droits de l'homme', (2006) Annuaire français de droit international 1, 41. To that effect, the US Alien Tort Claims Act could for instance be used. 28 USC § 1350, pursuant to which '[t]he district courts shall have original jurisdiction of any civil action by an alien for a tort only, committed in violation of the law of nations or a treaty of the United States'.

a forum for tort or criminal complaints, however, it may well draw the ire of the host State.[238] The host State may indeed have deliberately employed lower regulatory standards to lure foreign investors and boost the local economy, or may more generally believe that Western States have no legitimate interest in regulating matters outside their territory.[239] In this context, accusations of Western imperialism or protectionism will often be made.

The foregoing examples make it clear that even if a State can point to the existence of an internationally accepted ground of jurisdiction, this will not pre-empt international protest. Foreign States that have a strong interest in a matter, irrespective of whether it is an interest in regulation (eg prosecuting the presumed perpetrator of a crime themselves), or an interest in non-regulation (eg the interest in not regulating a business practice), will tend to raise their heads, and claim that their interest outweighs the interest of the jurisdictionally active State. Clearly, for such situations, a second-level rule of jurisdictional reasonableness, which aims at identifying the State with the strongest connection to or the strongest interest in (non-)regulation of the matter, may be desirable. It is such a rule which will be the subject of the next chapter.

---

[238] eg D Mzikenge Chirwa, 'The Doctrine of State Responsibility as a Potential Means of Holding Private Actors Accountable for Human Rights', (2004) 5 Melbourne J Int'l L 1, 35; T Morimoto, 'Growing Industrialization of our Damaged Planet. The Extraterritorial Application of Developed Countries' Domestic Environmental Laws to Transnational Corporations Abroad', (2005) 1 Utrecht Law Review 134, 149 (discussing sovereignty concerns over the extraterritorial application of developed home States' environmental regulations).

[239] eg South African President Thabo Mbeki's stinging criticism of ATCA lawsuits in the US against South African corporations: Worldpress.org, 'Moment of Truth. South Africa's Truth and Reconciliation Commission Closes its Doors', 2 March 2003, available at <http://www.worldpress. org/Africa/1077.cfm> ('We consider it completely unacceptable that matters that are central to the future of our country should be adjudicated in foreign courts').

5

A Reasonable Exercise of Jurisdiction

In the previous chapters, it has been shown how jurisdictional assertions of different States over one and the same situation or person could be justified on different jurisdictional grounds. The classical grounds of jurisdiction are all based on *a link* or contact with a State. Yet this system does obviously not exclude that *different* States might entertain a link. As discussed in section 4.6, this may give rise to international conflict, and highlight the need for an *additional* contact-based analysis. In fact, the permissive principles approach merely guarantees reasonableness at a first, rather rough level. A more intricate second-level reasonableness analysis is called for. This analysis should arguably be aimed at identifying the State with the *stronger* link to the situation.

Two methods to render jurisdictional principles more efficient in delimiting spheres of competence, and thus to render the exercise of jurisdiction more reasonable at a more intricate level, could be conceived of. Either States agree upon a convention that precisely sets out on what ground, for what purpose, and under what conditions they could exercise jurisdiction. Alternatively, the principles of jurisdictional restraint are strengthened under customary international law. In *Lotus*, the first approach was advocated:

[I]t is in order to remedy the difficulties resulting from [the great variety of rules] that efforts have been made for many years past, both in Europe and America, to prepare conventions the effect of which would be precisely to limit the discretion at present left to States in this respect by international law, thus making good the existing lacunae in respect of jurisdiction or removing the conflicting jurisdictions arising from the diversity of the principles adopted by the various States.[1]

While over the ensuing decades, conventions have been signed, treaty law could never account for all areas of the law where jurisdictional tension could arise. Most notably

---

[1] PCIJ, *SS Lotus* (France v Turkey), PCIJ Rep Series A, No 10 (1927) 19. The PCIJ appeared to play down the importance of the classical principles of jurisdiction ('the diversity of the principles') such as the territoriality, nationality, universality and protective principle: these principles would be randomly applied by the various States and would possibly not be anchored in international law. The random application of the principles of jurisdiction may explain why the PCIJ did not rely on the passive personality principle, and did not emphasize the links of the case with Turkey, most notably the fact that Turkish nationals had died as a result of the collision on the high seas. It neglects the said principles and confines itself to stating that 'prohibitive rules' (without clarifying which) may limit extraterritorial jurisdiction in certain cases.

in tax matters, bilateral and multilateral treaties indeed remedy jurisdictional conflicts. In the fields of criminal law, antitrust law, and securities law, however, a multilateral framework with clear rules and supervisory mechanisms is still largely lacking. For these fields, a framework based on customary international law may be required.

As we write, it is unclear whether customary international law indeed provides guidance. As far as State practice is concerned, States undeniably exercise jurisdictional restraint, as, at times, they appear to defer to other States. But do they do so because an international legal rule obliges them to?

In classical criminal jurisdiction (jurisdiction exercised on the basis of the territoriality, personality, and protective principles), restraint has undeniably played a role in designing the ambit of a State's laws. Over the centuries, States have found ways to accommodate each other's sovereign interests through limiting the exercise of active personality, passive personality, protective, and representational jurisdiction, eg by requiring double criminality, intervention of the highest prosecutors, or complaints of the victim or the foreign State, limiting the exercise of jurisdiction to certain (classes of) offences, or excluding civil party petition. There is, however, no evidence that these limitations correspond to a hard duty under international law. In the field of economic jurisdiction, as will be elaborated upon in this chapter, the same holds true.

Maier therefore believed that international law does not inform a practice of jurisdictional restraint or reasonableness. In his view, solutions to conflicts of international jurisdiction are not found in international law, but 'in an accommodation process operating outside the limits of formal international law...described by the principle of international comity'.[2] Bianchi similarly argued that solutions are developed 'by resorting to an equitable balance of equally legitimate claims'.[3]

§ 403 of the Restatement (Third) of US Foreign Relations Law (1987), has given 'international comity', or 'the balance of claims' a more rigorous character as 'jurisdictional reasonableness' or 'the rule of reason'. Pursuant to this rule, assertions of jurisdiction that are based on the classical grounds of jurisdiction, discussed in Chapters 3 and 4, are merely prima facie valid. Only to the extent that they survive a subsequent *reasonableness* analysis, could they be considered as appropriate, and even lawful under international law. The rule of reason is supported in this study, since, as long as concurrent jurisdiction exists, in the field of both criminal and civil/economic law, there should be a method of designating the State which has, objectively, the best case for exercising jurisdiction.

Structure of this chapter

As noted, the system of international jurisdiction allows for the exercise of concurrent jurisdiction by more than one State. Especially in the field of economic law,

---

[2] HG Maier, 'Jurisdictional Rules in Customary International Law', in KM Meessen, ed, *Extraterritorial Jurisdiction in Theory and Practice* (1996) 64, 69.
[3] A Bianchi, Reply to Professor Maier, in ibid 74, 84.

this system may yield unsatisfactory outcomes. Because restrictive or fraudulent practices may wreak worldwide havoc, several States that have *some* connection to the practice may start exercising jurisdiction and may claim regulatory primacy. Rules may therefore have to be devised on the basis of which jurisdiction is conferred on the State with a strong, or even better, the strongest link with the matter to be regulated.

In a first section, it will be shown that, in order to restrain assertions of jurisdiction, courts and regulators could rely on the principle of international comity. In its jurisdictional version, this principle limits the reach of a State's laws by requiring that States (and their courts and regulators) recognize the laws of States with a stronger link with the case, and thus, that States with a weaker link with the case do not apply their own laws (section 5.1). Comity is, however, essentially a discretionary concept, and not a—binding—norm of customary international law. Attempts have therefore been made to elevate comity to an international law status. This has most notably occurred in § 403 of the US Restatement (Third) of Foreign Relations Law. § 403 proposes a rule of reason which States have to abide by, not as a matter of comity, but as a matter of *international law* (section 5.2). The actual customary international law status of the jurisdictional rule of reason is nevertheless in serious doubt (sections 5.4 and 5.6). Indeed, in Europe in particular, a standard of reasonableness, and its attendant requirement of balancing interests, may run counter to basic tenets of the continental system of judicial jurisdiction and private international law (section 5.5). The relationship between the rule of reason and the presumption against extraterritoriality may be equally fraught with problems. Ordinarily, if it is the intent of Congress to apply a statute extraterritorially, courts are not entitled to second-guess it in light of a 'rule of reason', whether this rule constitutes international law or not (section 5.3).

5.1 Comity as a Discretionary Principle of Jurisdictional Restraint

Black's Law Dictionary defines comity of nations or *comitas gentium* as:

the recognition which one nation allows within its territory to the legislative, executive, or judicial acts of another nation, having due regard both to international duty and convenience and to the rights of its own citizens or of other persons who are under the protection of its laws.[4]

Comity is a traditional diplomatic and international law concept used by States in their dealings with each other. Short of legal obligation, States respect each

---

[4] *Black's Law Dictionary* (6th edn 1990) 267. In general, the principle of (judicial) comity refers to courts of one state or jurisdiction giving effect to laws and judicial decisions of another state or jurisdiction, not as a matter of obligation but out of deference and mutual respect.

other's policy choices and interests in a given case,[5] without inquiring into the substance of each others' laws.[6] Comity is widely believed to occupy a place between custom and customary international law.[7]

In a jurisdictional context, comity means that States limit the reach of their laws, and defer to other States that may have a stronger, often territorial nexus to a situation. Comity may ensure that the exercise of jurisdiction remains *reasonable*, and accords due regard to the sovereignty of other States. A useful distinction could be made here, in the words of US Supreme Court Justice Scalia in his dissenting opinion in the *Hartford Fire* antitrust case, between 'comity of the courts' (judicial comity) and 'prescriptive comity'. While the latter refers to 'the respect sovereign nations afford each other by limiting the reach of their laws',[8] the former refers to the discretion that the courts enjoy to 'decline to exercise jurisdiction over matters more appropriately adjudged elsewhere [...]'.[9]

When US courts exercise judicial comity, they generally rely on the Supreme Court's opinion in *Hilton v Guyot* (1895).[10] In this case, the Court held that comity is and must be an uncertain rule, which depends on a variety of circumstances.[11] This implies that comity is not considered to be a hard rule of law. As will be shown in section 5.3, however, it has been argued, again in the United States,

---

[5] B Pearce, 'The Comity Doctrine as a Barrier to Judicial Jurisdiction: A U.S.-E.U. Comparison', (1994) 30 Stan J Int'l L 525, 529 (1994). Pearce described comity as 'a friendly gesture of reciprocity or even unilateral goodwill not required by international law', but he also observed that comity and international law are separated by a 'revolving door' in that 'a non-binding norm may transcend the jurisprudential purgatory of comity and enter the higher realm of international law; by the same token, disregarding a norm of international law may cause it to descend to comity's less lofty domain'. ibid 529–30.

[6] KA Feagle, 'Extraterritorial Discovery: a Social Contract Perspective', (1996) 7 Duke J Comp & Int'l L 297, 301.

[7] J Schwarze, 'Die extraterritoriale Anwendbarkeit des EG-Wettbewerbsrechts—Vom Durchführungsprinzip zum Prinzip der qualifizierten Auswirkung', in J Schwarze, ed, *Europäisches Wettbewerbsrecht im Zeichen der Globalisierung* (2002) 55; G Schuster, *Die internationale Anwendung des Börsenrechts* (1996) 677 (arguing that the boundary between comity and customary international law is a thin one). Contra FA Mann, 'The Doctrine of Jurisdiction Revisited after Twenty Years', (1984-III) 186 RCADI 9, 87 ('In truth "comity" is only another word for international law'). As far as case law is concerned, the German *Kammergericht* pointed out, in the *Morris/Rothmans* case, that comity had not reached the status of customary international law, and that the use of comity to solve jurisdictional disputes was not warranted, in that comity would lead to a situation in which no State would be able to act, or in which the interests of the protesting State would be unilaterally heeded. KG WuW/E OLG 3051, 3059. No claim has ever been brought before an international tribunal alleging that a State violated the principle of comity. JR Paul, 'Comity in International Law', (1991) 32 Harv Int'l LJ 1, 10.

[8] *Hartford Fire Insurance Co v California*, 509 US 764, 817 (1993) (Scalia, J, dissenting).

[9] ibid.

[10] *Hilton v Guyot*, 159 US 113, 163–4 (1895) ('"Comity," in the legal sense, is neither a matter of absolute obligation, on the one hand, nor of mere courtesy and good will, upon the other. But it is the recognition which one nation allows within its territory to the legislative, executive, or judicial acts of another nation, having due regard both to international duty and convenience, and to the rights of its own citizens, or of other persons who are under the protection of its laws').

[11] ibid 164. Also *Saul v His Creditors*, 5 Mar (ns) 569, 596 (La 1827) (stating that 'comity is, and ever must be, uncertain').

that comity, in a jurisdictional context, is nowadays just a by-word for international law. Comity then becomes a binding *international rule of reason*.

It may be noted that in the jurisdictional practice of *European* States, comity plays only a marginal role. Although comity is not unknown in Europe, it is generally not used by the courts as a jurisdictional concept in the adjudication of transnational disputes,[12] nor has it been used by European States and regulators to limit the reach of their laws and regulations. Rather, the executive and legislative branches use comity as a concept denoting non-binding diplomatic good manners. In its strict public international law version, comity is known in continental Europe as *comitas gentium*, 'courtoisie internationale', or 'Völkercourtoisie'.[13] If it is used in its judicial version, this happens mostly out of concern 'for the consistency of the status of individual nationals and residents', rather than out of respect for foreign sovereigns.[14]

Historical transformation of comity

The comity principle was originally not resorted to in order to circumscribe the reach of a State's laws or jurisdictional assertions, rather on the contrary. In fact, it urged States to apply *another State's laws* in their own territory, or, put differently, to give these laws extraterritorial application. Because the rule of reason, which is the subject of this chapter, is based on the modern version of comity, it is appropriate to explore the transformation of the comity principle from a principle geared to *expanding* the reach and the effects of a State's laws abroad to a principle geared to *limiting* this reach and these effects.

Although comity as a judicial doctrine is nowadays almost exclusively applied by US courts, and not in Europe, it has its roots in seventeenth century Dutch conflict of laws thinking. The ideas of the Dutch school, of Ulrik Huber in particular, travelled first to Scotland—Scottish students often went to Holland to deepen their legal knowledge—and from there to England[15] and the United States in the second half of the eighteenth century.[16] Dutch-style comity was

---

[12] Paul has traced a number of European cases decided on comity grounds. Paul (above n 7) 30–1. These cases typically deal with public international law themes such as foreign sovereign immunity or diplomatic immunity, and not with private disputes. Even in England, a common law country like the US, the use of comity is not widespread and not used in private international law cases. Discussing a number of English cases, Paul submits that it is used as 'a synonym for tolerance or substantive justice, diplomatic immunity, sovereign immunity, or most commonly, public international law in general', or as a means of 'fencing out intrusive U.S. jurisdiction rather than limits [English] jurisdiction'. ibid 42–3 (footnotes omitted). Comity and interest-balancing may not play a great role in England's practice of jurisdiction, as England is reluctant to assert extraterritorial jurisdiction in the first place. Schuster (above n 7) 671.

[13] Pearce (above n 5) 527.

[14] ibid 550.

[15] *Robinson v Bland*, 1 W Bl 234, 256, 96 Eng Rep 120, 141, 2 Burr 1077, 97 Eng Rep 717 (KB 1760) (citing Huber and a general principle of conflicts law established *ex comitate et jure gentium*).

[16] KH Nadelmann, 'Introduction to H.E. Yntema, The Comity Doctrine', (1996) 65 Mich L Rev 1, 2 (pointing out that Huber was first quoted in the United States in 1788, in *Camp v Lockwood*, 1 Dall 393, 398 (Phila County, Pa, CP 1788)).

first referred to by the US Supreme Court in 1827 in *Ogden v Saunders*.[17] It gained widespread acceptance in the United States after being espoused by Story—in his *Commentaries on the Conflict of Laws* in 1834[18]—who believed comity to be at the root of the system of conflict of laws:

> The true foundation on which the administration of international law must rest is that the rules which are to govern are those which arise from mutual interests and utility, from a sense of the inconveniences which would result from a contrary doctrine, and from a spirit of moral necessity to do justice, in order that justice may be done to us in return.[19]

Comity fell on fertile soil in the United States and quickly gained ascendancy as a method of adjudicating private disputes, partly because of the federal structure of the United States. As Pearce has noted, since American federal judges were '[l]ong accustomed to adjudicating competing jurisdictional demands of the [American] states', they 'should be relatively well suited to the type of international interest balancing that comity often requires'.[20] US courts traditionally placed limits on the exercise of jurisdiction on the basis of the constitutional principle of due process, which requires weighing the adjudicatory interests of the plaintiff, the defendant, and the State. Weighing the interests of a *foreign State* for the purpose of establishing personal jurisdiction as well, ie applying comity, then merely stands 'on the shoulders of due process'.[21]

The comity doctrine as a method to solve conflicts of laws did not originate in seventeenth century Holland by chance. As Yntema has pointed out, the seven Dutch Provinces that wrested independence from Spain at the end of the sixteenth century lacked a central authority and provided thus a fertile field for conflicts of laws.[22] At the same time, the needs of commerce made the Netherlands remarkably open to foreigners.[23]

Comity was introduced in an embryonic form by Paulus Voet, a professor at the Academy of Utrecht, who listed it as one of the exceptions to the principle of territoriality of statutes. Voet held that 'at times, when a people wishes to observe the customs of a neighboring people in comity and in order that many valid transactions may not be disturbed, it is customary for statutes to apply beyond the territory of the legislator'.[24] In Voet's writings, comity appears as a discretionary act of a State giving legal effect to acts done outside its territory. Comity does not so much operate as a constraint on the (extraterritorial)

---

[17] *Ogden v Saunders*, 25 US (12 Wheat) 212 (1827).

[18] J Story, *Commentaries on the Conflict of Laws, Foreign and Domestic* (1834) section 33, at 33 (Chapter II).

[19] ibid section 35, at 34

[20] Pearce (above n 5) 571–2.

[21] ibid at 573.

[22] HE Yntema, 'The Comity Doctrine', (1966) 65 Mich L Rev 1, 18.

[23] ibid 19, noting that the idea of comity may be implicitly discerned in Article XVII of the Union of Utrecht (1579), in which the Provinces undertook 'to administer good law and justice to foreigners and citizens alike'.

[24] P Voet, *De Statutis eorumque Concursu* (1661), as translated in Yntema (above n 22).

application of a forum State's laws (as it would later become in regulatory cases), but rather as a constraint on the exclusive territorial application of the forum State's laws. Put differently, comity was synonymous with a willingness to apply *ex comitate* a foreign State's laws in the forum State's territory, an application which is 'extraterritorial' from the perspective of the foreign State. Importantly, a State was not to apply a foreign sovereign's laws in its territory 'as of right, but on the grounds of utility by custom or treaty'.[25] This obviously conferred a distinctively discretionary character on the concept of comity, which it still has today.[26]

Ulrik Huber, a professor at the Academy of Franeker in Friesland, elaborated on the comity concept and gave it a foundation in a rational natural law of nations (*jus gentium*), which was developed a few decades earlier by his compatriot Hugo Grotius:[27]

[E]ven if not required by treaty or by reason of subordination, the reason of the common practice among nations nonetheless compels mutual indulgence in this respect. For if one nation were to refuse to recognize in any way the laws of another, an infinite number of acts and contracts would each day become of no effect, nor could commerce by land and by sea subsist.[28]

Huber precisely inferred from the absolute sovereignty of a State within its territory that 'the laws of each nation exercised within its territory, are effective everywhere, insofar as the interests of another State or its citizens are not prejudiced'.[29] This implies that transactions that are done in a State where they are valid ought to be given legal effect in another State, unless there is an overriding interest of the forum (*ordre public*). Conversely, if transactions are null in the State where they are done, a foreign State should not give them legal effect, unless it can assert an overriding interest to do so.[30]

It is a small step from stating, as Huber did, that territorial laws are effective everywhere, if there are no prohibitive rules to the contrary, to stating that international law leaves States a wide measure of discretion in extending the application of their laws and the jurisdiction of their courts to persons, property, and acts outside their territory, which is only limited in certain cases by prohibitive rules, as the Permanent Court of International Justice (PCIJ) did in the *Lotus* case. The outcome of the *Lotus* case, while seemingly at odds with the

---

[25] ibid 24.
[26] ibid 28 (noting that 'today as then, it is assumed that it is for each State to determine, as a matter of domestic law, the extent to which effect is given to foreign laws and judgments').
[27] Notably H Grotius, *De Jure Belli ac Pacis Libri Tres* (2005).
[28] As translated in Yntema (above n 22) 25–6.
[29] ibid 26.
[30] ibid 26–7. If one were to apply this concept to modern-day extraterritorial antitrust law, this would imply that a State should not apply its own laws to a foreign conspiracy that is legal in the territory where it has been entered into, unless that State can assert overriding public interests, such as the extent of the conspiracy's effects on its domestic economy (the *effects* doctrine).

intuitively felt presumption against extraterritoriality, may therefore be considered to be directly based on Huber's concept of territorial sovereignty.[31]

For our purposes, it is important to note that Huber, as did later the PCIJ in *Lotus*, recognized the possible existence of limits to the application of a forum State's laws in another State's territory. Indeed, States are only expected to apply another State's laws *ex comitate*. In Huber's theory, it is, however, unclear in what situations States should give effect to a foreign State's law. Put differently, a legal standard that sets out clear limits on the application of a foreign State's law appears to be lacking. As his definition of an overriding interest of the forum—limiting the extraterritorial application of a foreign State's law—is left entirely to the forum invoking it, Huber's comity remains a discretionary concept.[32]

In the field of general private international law, an intricate set of conflict of laws rules was later developed, not always successfully,[33] to make comity less malleable and more systematic and predictable for international actors. Similarly, in the field of criminal law, a rule-based framework of international jurisdiction was put in place, either based on prohibitive rules (*Lotus*) or on permissive rules (the principles of jurisdiction under customary international law). Comity, in its pristine purity, fell nonetheless somewhat into oblivion as a principle of solving jurisdictional conflicts. Toward the end of the twentieth century, however, it made a remarkable comeback, especially in the United States. Comity was not only rediscovered, but at the same time transfigured into a jurisdictional rule of reason *under public international law* in section 403 of the Restatement (Third) of US Foreign Relations Law.

As pointed out, in Huber's concept, comity remained discretionary. Nonetheless, in his writings Huber already referred to the international law foundations of his comity concept. This ought to imply that comity has intersubjective, and not only discretionary, meaning. Comity would have contours which all States could agree on, including the scope of an 'overriding interest of the forum'. Huber failed, however, to clarify, at a conceptual level, what the international law character of comity precisely was. In the twentieth century, courts and legal scholars, especially in the United States, and to a lesser extent in Germany, picked up the thread of comity from where it had been left by Huber. Challenged by jurisdictional conflict in the field of antitrust law, they objectivized comity, and baptized it 'the jurisdictional rule of reason'. The rule of reason restrains the exercise

---

[31] Maier (above n 2) 69–70 (noting that Huber's concept 'comports with the conclusion, reached centuries later in the *Lotus* case, that there is no compulsion external to the forum to give effect to the laws or decision of the foreign state').

[32] Cf Yntema (above n 22) 30–1 ('[I]n the last analysis the solution of conflicts of laws is a prerogative of sovereign authority, in the views of some exercised primarily to protect the local governmental interest and, where it seems expedient in this interest, to satisfy the requirements of international commerce', not so much referring to Huber, but rather to the progeny of Hobbes, Pufendorf and Voet).

[33] Cf ibid 31 (calling to 'resurrect the *jus gentium* of the Seventeenth Century in the guise of transnational law or the general principles of law' and referring to international custom as a source of law).

of jurisdiction through weighing the interests and connections of the case with the States and individuals involved. Unlike comity, the rule of reason is not a subjective rule, but—purportedly—an objective norm of customary international law by which all States have to abide.[34]

5.2 'Reasonable Jurisdiction' under International Law

The Restatement (Third) of US Foreign Relations Law believes that reasonableness—which requires weighing the different interests involved in the situation, as discussed in a later section—is not merely a requirement of comity, but a rule or principle of *public international law*.[35] This would mean that States, when they exercise prescriptive jurisdiction pursuant to an accepted principle of jurisdiction, are under an obligation to conduct an additional reasonableness analysis and possibly restrain their jurisdictional assertions because international law says so.

It is, however, debatable whether this is indeed the present state of international law.[36] Most authors take the view that the rule of reason is *not* a principle of international law (which need obviously not imply that these authors take issue with the rule of reason as a norm of *US* law).[37] Other authors are somewhat

---

[34] The difference between comity and the rule of reason lies herein that the former 'reflects— [*Lotus*-style—] *the state's freedom* under the law to choose the path most likely to encourage reciprocal action by other states in later situations', whereas the latter reflects 'the limitations of *international law*'. Maier (above n 2) 72 (emphasis added).

[35] § 402, cmt k ('Since international and other foreign relations law are the law of the United States, under the Supremacy Clause of the Constitution, an exercise of jurisdiction by a State that contravenes the limitations of §§ 402-403 is invalid [...]'); § 403, cmt a ('The principle...has emerged as a principle of international law as well. [...] Some United States courts have applied the principle of reasonableness as a requirement of comity. [...] This section states the principle of reasonableness as a rule of international law').

[36] To some, it is even unclear whether it actually represents real law. AF Lowenfeld, 'Public Law in the International Arena: Conflict of Laws, International Law, and Some Suggestions for Their Interaction', (1979-II) 163 RCADI 311, 400 (explaining the lack of success of the propositions of Professor Kingman Brewster, the intellectual father of the rule of reason in the field of antitrust).

[37] Pro LE Kruse and RH Benavides, 'Federal Subject Matter Jurisdiction in Federal Courts in International Cases', in DJ Levy, ed, *International Litigation* (2003) 149. Somewhat pro D Vagts, Panel Discussion on the Draft Restatement, (1982) 76 ASIL Proc 184, 205 ('[T]he new Restatement reflect[s] the way the law [is] going, and...it [reflects] at least an emerging consensus'). Somewhat contra Maier (above n 2) 72–3 (arguing that the jurisdictional sections of the Restatement are 'a blend of international law and the principle of comity', and that 'the exercise of state authority is, as in all international law, conditioned by the requirement that one state may not act in an unreasonable manner toward another', although at the same time pointing out that '[e]vidence of an international legal rule requiring [interest-balancing] is sparse. At best one can argue that the courts of several nations do in fact employ this interest balancing technique, but there is little evidence that they do so because they believe, that this approach is required as a customary practice accepted as law'). Contra WS Dodge, 'Extraterritoriality and Conflict-of-Laws Theory: An Argument for Judicial Unilateralism', (1998) 39 Harv Int'l LJ 101, 137, note 224 ('Section 403's balancing approach is not required by international law'); SB Burbank, 'Case Two: Extraterritorial Application of United States Law Against United States and Alien Defendants (Sherman Act)', (1995) 29 New Eng L Rev 588, 591 ('[F]ew people other than those who drafted

circumspect. Meessen, for instance, considered the rule of reason to be 'too open a rule to be operable on the level of international law'[38]—although, at the same time, he argued that a rule of reason is workable *de lege ferenda*, if it is limited to the balancing of sovereign interests.[39] Somewhat similarly, Schuster, a fellow German, believed that uniformity and consistency are still lacking for interest-balancing to constitute a norm of customary international law, but that such a norm may be *in statu nascendi*.[40] It does not come as a surprise that German authors such as Meessen and Schuster take a more nuanced view of the international law character of the rule of reason, as it is precisely in Germany, as will be seen in subsection 5.4.c.6, that interest-balancing has gained traction.

There is only one authoritative international law source, apart from the doctrine, that believes that the principle of jurisdictional reasonableness/restraint/moderation, whatever its content, represents international law. In *Barcelona Traction*, Judge Fitzmaurice wrote in his separate opinion

> that under present conditions, international law does not impose hard and fast rules on States delimiting spheres of national jurisdiction... It does however... involve for every State an obligation to exercise moderation and restraint as to the extent of the jurisdiction assumed by its courts in cases having a foreign element, and to avoid undue encroachment on a jurisdiction more properly appertaining to, or more appropriately exercisable by another State.[41]

the relevant sections of the Restatement (Third)... believe that section 403 states rules of customary international law'); PR Trimble, 'The Supreme Court and International Law: The Demise of Restatement Section 403', (1995) 89 AJIL 53, 55 ('[T]here is no such general principle and hence no customary international law like that advanced in section 403...'); CJ Olmstead, 'Jurisdiction', (1989) 14 Yale J Int'l L 468, 472 ('[I]t seems implausible that section 403 rises to the level of... "a principle of international law"'); CJ Olmstead, in 'Panel Discussion on the Draft Restatement of the Foreign Relations Law of the United States', (1982) 76 ASIL Proc 184, 201 ('whether this concept has matured into a rule of law seems dubious'); KM Meessen, 'Conflicts of Jurisdiction Under the New Restatement', (1987-III) 50 Law & Contemp Probs 47, 59 ('No way exists to accept the Restatement's claim for qualifying reasonableness as a rule of international law if the standard of reasonableness is interpreted by reference to an independent international law standard based on the common denominator of a widely diverging state practice'); Mann (above n 7) 20 ('There is... outside the United States no support for [the theory of interest-balancing] to be found in any of the traditional sources of international law, and it should be firmly rejected'); J-M Bischoff and R Kovar, 'L'application du droit communautaire de la concurrence aux entreprises établies à l'extérieur de la Communauté', (1975) 102 JDI 675, 696 (arguing that, as soon there are certain effects of a foreign restrictive business practice within the Community, EC jurisdiction may legitimately obtain under public international law, and that public international law is not concerned with finding solutions to problems of concurrent jurisdiction, such as those put forward under a rule of reason).

[38] KM Meessen, 'Antitrust Jurisdiction under Customary International Law', (1984) 78 AJIL 783, 802.

[39] ibid 803–8.

[40] Schuster (above n 7) 665.

[41] ICJ, *Barcelona Traction, Light and Power Company, Ltd* (Belgium v Spain), ICJ Rep 3, 105 (1970), sep op Fitzmaurice. Also AF Lowenfeld, 'International Litigation and the Quest for Reasonableness', (1994-I) 245 RCADI 9, 77 (arguing that *moderation* and *restraint*, *undue encroachment* and *appropriate* exercise of jurisdiction 'can be summed up in the term reasonableness').

Judge Fitzmaurice did not cite much international law to support his case for restraint. Nonetheless, a number of international legal concepts may inform the interest-balancing-informed rule of reason set forth in § 403 of the US Restatement.[42] Although these concepts have not been used so as to solve conflicts of international jurisdiction, they may clearly support a jurisdictional rule of reason by providing an *opinio juris*.[43] It may in fact be argued that foreign nations' familiarity with these principles of international law has informed the absence of foreign protest against the US rule of reason. In this section, such international law principles as non-intervention, genuine connection, equity, proportionality, and abuse of law, all of them bearing resemblance to a rule of reason requiring interest-balancing, will be discussed.

(a) Principle of non-intervention

Pursuant to the principle of non-intervention, States are prohibited from intervening in the domestic affairs of other States.[44] If this principle were to be strictly applied in the law of prescriptive jurisdiction, it may give rise to a finding of any jurisdictional assertion that reaches beyond a State's boundaries being in violation of international law. This is clearly not what the international community has opted for. As argued in Chapter 2, neither the PCIJ in *Lotus* nor the permissive principles approach has considered the principle of non-intervention as precluding the exercise of 'extraterritorial' prescriptive jurisdiction. Only the exercise of extraterritorial enforcement jurisdiction— the carrying out of certain material acts on another State's territory—has been deemed to infringe upon the principle of non-intervention and, thus, on the sovereignty of a foreign State.[45]

---

[42] For a legal-philosophical perspective on how *the international judge* should give shape to 'reasonableness' (particularly from a French perspective): O Corten, *L'utilisation du 'raisonnable' par le juge international* (1997).

[43] ibid 677.

[44] The principle was developed primarily in a *military* context: it precluded States from using force on the territory of another State. eg Declaration on Principles of International Law concerning Friendly Relations and Co-operation among States in accordance with the Charter of the United States, United Nations General Assembly Resolution 2625 (XXV), 24 October 1970, principle I ('The principle that States shall refrain in their international relations from *the threat or use of force* against the territorial integrity of political independence of any State, or in any other manner inconsistent with the purposes of the United Nations') (emphasis added). Also ICJ, *Case concerning Military and Paramilitary Activities in and against Nicaragua*, ICJ Rep 14 (1986).

[45] A solution which gives States quite some discretion to exercise prescriptive jurisdiction, and does not reserve a prominent role for the principle of non-intervention appears as justified from an historical perspective. Indeed, in older times, because inter-State contacts were less frequent than they are today, States hardly felt the need to apply their laws to foreign situations, nor, accordingly, did they feel the need to expand the protective purpose of the principle of non-intervention beyond protecting States' territorial integrity from military, 'material' encroachment by other States. J Kaffanke, 'Nationales Wirtschaftsrecht und internationaler Sachverhalt', (1989) 27 Archiv des Völkerrechts 129, 150–2.

This is not to say that the principle of non-intervention may not have a role to play in restraining the law of jurisdiction. It surely has, and a very important one. Yet it is a given that a particular jurisdictional assertion does not of itself violate the principle of non-intervention.[46] In this respect, it has been proposed to use an *interest-balancing test* so as to ascertain whether the principle of non-intervention is respected in a given case.[47] Only if the asserting State's interests in having its laws applied to a foreign situation outweigh the interests of another involved State will a jurisdictional assertion respect the principle of non-intervention. This is, in fact, exactly the solution advanced by § 403 of the US Restatement, which advocates interest-balancing to solve conflicts of jurisdiction. Accordingly, the principle of non-intervention under international law may be said to support the jurisdictional rule of reason as set forth in the US Restatement. As much has in fact been pointed out by the US Supreme Court in its 2004 opinion in the *Empagran* antitrust case. In this case, the Court ruled that, pursuant to the customary international law principle of non-interference in the internal affairs of another State, it is to be assumed that Congress takes 'the legitimate sovereign interests of other nations into account'[48] when assessing the reach of US law, and avoids extending this reach when such would create a 'serious risk of interference with a foreign nation's ability independently to regulate its own commercial affairs'.[49]

Obviously, it is unclear at what point a jurisdictional assertion precisely intervenes in another State's sovereignty. It is notably questionable whether an inherently vague interest-balancing test may confer sufficient legal certainty on international acts and transactions regarding the permissibility of jurisdictional assertions. Admittedly, the principle of non-intervention is in itself an extremely vague principle, certainly in an economic context. One could, therefore, only welcome a method that could render the principle of non-intervention more operational at the practical level. Yet whether there is sufficient evidence of interest-balancing being the internationally accepted method of ascertaining whether the principle of non-intervention is upheld, remains to be seen.

(b) Genuine connection

In the *Nottebohm* case, a case before the International Court of Justice (ICJ) in 1955, the Court required, in order for a State to exercise diplomatic protection

---

[46] Cf Max Planck Institut for Comparative Public Law and International Law, *Encyclopedia of Public International Law* (1992–2001) 621 ('Concerning economic 'interference', the principle of non-intervention reflects the helplessness of international law in general').

[47] KM Meessen, *Völkerrechtliche Grundsätze des internationalen Kartellrechts* (1975) 199 ('Das Problem des Schutzes der Souveränität ausländischer Staaten muss durch die Gegenüberstellung der Interessen des handelnden und des betroffenen Staates gelöst werden...'); Kaffanke (above n 45) 153.

[48] *F Hoffman-La Roche Ltd et al. v Empagran SA et al.*, 124 S Ct 2359, 2366 (2004).

[49] ibid 2367.

over its nationals abroad, that 'the legal bond of nationality accord with the individual's *genuine connection* with the State which assumes the defence'.[50] In the 1970 *Barcelona Traction* case, the Court refined this doctrine in the context of diplomatic protection over corporate entities, holding: '[N]o absolute test of the "genuine connection" has found general acceptance. Such tests as have been applied are of a relative nature, and sometimes links with one State have had to be weighed against those with another.'[51]

The concept of 'genuine connection' may have a role to play in restraining jurisdictional assertions.[52] The jurisdictional rule of reason indeed requires that a significant nexus between the regulated matter and the regulating State be discerned in order for that State to be authorized to exercise its jurisdiction. The concept of 'genuine connection' in the law of diplomatic protection may, however, not prevent more than one State from exercising diplomatic protection. Individuals or corporations could indeed have a genuine connection with more than one State. Similarly, a situation, act, event, or person could have a genuine connection with more than one State, and different States could thus be entitled to exercise their jurisdiction. Use of the concept of 'genuine connection' may weed out a number of extravagant jurisdictional assertions, but may eventually not entirely prevent normative competency conflicts. The rule of reason in fact goes further than the concept of 'genuine connection', since it is aimed at identifying the 'most genuine connection', on the basis of weighing the regulating State's own connections and interests with those of other States involved. Because the rule of reason goes further than the concept of 'genuine connection' as used in the law of diplomatic protection, 'genuine connection' only partially supports the rule of reason under international law.

(c) Equity

Another international law concept that might provide support for a jurisdictional rule of reason under international law is 'equity', a general principle of law that corrects the law in the interests of justice.[53] In a number of continental shelf cases, the ICJ pointed out that equity requires that substantive justice be administered

---

[50] ICJ, *Nottebohm* (Liechtenstein v Guatemala), ICJ Rep 4 *et seq.* (1955) (emphasis added).

[51] ICJ, *Barcelona Traction* (Belgium v Spain), ICJ Rep 42 (1970).

[52] It should be noted that the law of diplomatic protection and the law of jurisdiction are related in that both govern the operation of the acts of a State outside its territory. Schuster (above n 7) 41. Solutions in the field of diplomatic protection could therefore possibly be extrapolated to the field of jurisdiction. Notably B Grossfeld and CP Rogers, 'A Shared Values Approach to Jurisdictional Conflicts in International Economic Law', (1983) 32 ICLQ 931, 945, consider the genuine link concept to be one of the main limits on the extraterritorial reach of law.

[53] Equity may arguably be one of 'the general principles of law recognized by civilized nations' applied by the International Court of Justice in accordance with Article 38(1)(c) of the ICJ Statute. Equity so understood would then be a source of international law. EPIL 110. For a study on equity: CR Rossi, *Equity and International Law. A Legal Realist Approach to International Decisionmaking* (1993).

in order to solve a dispute.[54] Continental shelf cases resemble international jurisdiction cases in that both address the basic question of how to delimit a State's power. In both categories of cases, solutions are used that weigh the connections of a particular situation with the State claiming its rights to that effect, and dismiss jurisdiction when another State's rights are unduly encroached upon. In the *North Sea Continental Shelf* case, for instance, the ICJ held that 'the continental shelf of any State must be the natural prolongation of its land territory and must not encroach upon what is the natural prolongation of another State'.[55] In order to ensure that that one State's 'natural prolongation' does not encroach upon another State's natural prolongation, the ICJ advocated weighing (a possibly indefinite number of) connecting factors:

In fact, there is no legal limit to the considerations which States may take into account for the purpose of making sure that they apply equitable procedures, and more often than not it is the balancing-up of all such considerations that will produce this result rather than reliance on one to the exclusion of all others. The problem of the relative weight to be accorded to different considerations naturally varies with the circumstances of the case.[56]

More generally, Article 38(2) of the ICJ Statute, a provision which grants the ICJ the power to decide *equitably* if the parties want to, provides that the ICJ may 'decide a case *ex aequo et bono*, if the parties agree thereto'. This provision arguably means that 'the Court may reach a fair compromise in *balancing the interests of the parties*'.[57]

In the law of international jurisdiction, it is similarly attempted to develop rules that balance the interests of the respective States involved in a situation, through a variety of relevant factors varying with the circumstances of the case. This balancing act prevents States from exercising jurisdiction over situations if such would encroach upon the regulatory prerogatives of another State. It could be objected that it is one thing to confer the application of the principle of equity on an *international court* such as the ICJ, and quite another to confer the application of an equity-informed rule of reason on a *national court* or regulator (the impartiality of which may be in serious doubt).[58] This is no doubt true. Reference to the equity principle here, however, only serves to illustrate that weighing connections and interests is not an unknown quantity in classical public international

---

[54] In particular ICJ, *North Sea Continental Shelf Cases* (Fed Rep of Germany v Denmark; Fed Rep of Germany v the Netherlands), ICJ Rep 3, 47 (1969); ICJ, *Case Concerning the Continental Shelf* (Tunisia v Libya), ICJ Rep 18, 60 (1982) ('Equity as a legal concept is a direct emanation of the idea of justice. The Court whose task is by definition to administer justice is bound to apply it. ... Moreover, when applying positive international law, a court may choose among several possible interpretations of the law one which appears, in the light of the circumstances of the case, to be closest to the requirements of justice'). The principle was pioneered by Judge Hudson in PCIJ, *Meuse Case* (Belgium v Netherlands), Series A/B, No 70, p 73 (1937).

[55] *North Sea Continental Shelf Cases* (above n 54) 48.

[56] ibid 50.   [57] EPIL 109.

[58] Schuster (above n 7) 55.

law. The fact that equity informed by interest-balancing is an international law principle in its own right, may in fact bolster the case for understanding the international law principle of non-intervention (discussed in (a)) as a principle that requires weighing the interests of the different States involved in a situation.

(d) Proportionality

Another international law principle that may support reasonableness in the international law of jurisdiction is the principle of proportionality. Under the principle of proportionality, a measure used to achieve an objective should be proportionate, ie, properly related in size or degree to that objective. In international law, the principle of proportionality may be invoked in the law of war, which prohibits States from mounting 'an attack which may be expected to cause incidental loss of civilian life, injury to civilians, damage to civilian objects, or a combination thereof, which would be excessive in relation to the concrete and direct military advantage anticipated'.[59] It may also play a role in the field of countermeasures,[60] and the law of the World Trade Organization.[61]

The principle of proportionality has so far not explicitly been applied in the law of jurisdiction, although it surely lends itself to it. Proportionality may require that one State's jurisdictional assertion not encroach upon the interests of another State to an extent that is disproportionate to the object or aim of that assertion. In fact, like equity-informed interest-balancing, proportionality may clarify the principle of non-intervention in the law of jurisdiction. While construed very strictly, the principle of non-intervention may prohibit a State from asserting its jurisdiction over a situation arising in another State lest it unjustifiably intervene in that State's domestic affairs, the principle of proportionality *allows* interference, yet only if it is not excessive.

In European law, the principle of proportionality plays a very important role. As a general principle of European law, it prohibits the European institutions from taking a measure which is not proportionate to the object or aim of that measure.[62] One could argue that the European institutions may also be bound by the principle of proportionality in the field of the EU's external relations.[63] Proportionality would then prohibit the institutions, when exercising

---

[59] In particular Article 51(5)(b) of Additional Protocol I to the Geneva Conventions (1977).

[60] E Cannizzaro, 'The Role of Proportionality in the Law of International Countermeasures', (2001) 2 EJIL 889.

[61] A Desmedt, 'Proportionality in WTO Law', (2001) 4 J Int'l Econ L 441.

[62] Article 5, § 3 of the Treaty Establishing the European Community ('Any action by the Community shall not go beyond what is necessary to achieve the objectives of this Treaty'). For discussions of the principle: G de Bùrca, 'The Principle of Proportionality and its Application in EC Law', (1993) 13 Yb Eur L 105; N Emiliou, *The Principle of Proportionality in European Law—a Comparative Study* (1996).

[63] A Layton and AM Parry, 'Extraterritorial jurisdiction—European Responses', (2004) 26 Houston J Int'l L 309, 322–3 ('It is possible that various doctrines inherent in E.U. law, particularly proportionality, may be invoked to water down the most extreme examples of extraterritoriality').

jurisdiction, eg, in international competition matters, from interfering with the interests of a third country to an extent that is disproportionate to the object or aim of that measure.[64] Bourgeois has applied this rule to the field of merger control and pointed out that it 'could justify a Commission decision not to prohibit an international merger, where the aim of such prohibition, ie, protecting the competitive structure in the Community, could reasonably be achieved by parallel action against such merger by another State'.[65] While the Commission may, inter alia pursuant to the 1998 US-EU Positive Comity Agreement relating to competition matters,[66] defer to other States in cases in which these have a stronger interest, there is no evidence, however, that the Commission considers itself to be *bound* by the principle of proportionality to do so.[67] Neither have the European courts relied on the principle when determining the reach of Article 81 ECT (prohibition of cartels) and of the Merger Control Regulation.[68]

Clearly, the international law principle of proportionality may be a useful principle of jurisdictional restraint. Because its field of application has so far been rather limited, it may possibly not qualify as a general principle of international law *de lege lata* which States have to abide by when exercising jurisdiction.[69] Nonetheless, like the principle of equity, the principle of proportionality shows that interest-balancing—weighing one State's gain caused by a jurisdictional assertion against the burden imposed on another State by this assertion—is

---

[64] JHJ Bourgeois, 'EEC Control over International Mergers', (1990) 10 Yb Eur L 103, 126.

[65] Ibid.

[66] Agreement between the European Communities and the Government of the United States of America on the Application of the Positive Comity Principles in the Enforcement of their Competition Laws, [1998] OJ L 173/28.

[67] Bourgeois (above n 64) 128 (noting that '[i]t does not appear possible to use a well known rule of Community law [the rule of proportionality] to give a more precise content to the international law principle of "non-interference"').

[68] Possibly, European institutions may believe that the principle of proportionality is only designed to protect *European* interests (of governmental or private nature) from excessive regulation by the institutions. Pursuant to the maxim *pacta tertiis non prosunt*, they may submit that foreign governments could not borrow rights from the ECT that could limit the EU's international sphere of action. It appears, however, that, in view of the principle *in foro interno, in foro externo*, European institutions may also be required to apply the principle of proportionality when exercising their powers at the international level. In one case, the ECJ seemed willing to limit the EC's sphere of action when the interests of third States were implicated. In *Poulsen and Diva Navigation*, 24 November 1992, C-286/90, [1992] ECR 1992, I-6019, the Court applied EC fisheries law to a Danish ship flying a Panamian flag of convenience, holding that Danish authorities could seize the fish caught in violation of EC fisheries law, even though the fish were caught outside EC waters. However, recognizing the importance of the flag State under international law, and, on that basis, the freedom of shipping on the high seas and the exclusive economic zone, and the right of innocent passage in territorial waters, the Court also held that Danish authorities could only do so because the ship had called at a Danish port after catching the fish but before selling it (outside the Community). Because the Court put such a high premium on the rights of the flag State (Panama), it may be said to have respected the sovereignty of a third State when determining the reach of EC fisheries law. J Vanhamme, *Volkenrechtelijke beginselen in het Europees recht* (2001) 298.

[69] Bourgeois (above n 64) 127 (1990) (stating that '[t]here is no general rule of international law . . . which could come into play as a proportionality test', and that '[t]he most that could be said is that non-respect for a third country's legislation or policies may in certain cases be unlawful under international law as violating the principle of non-interference').

known in public international law. It may bolster the credentials of the jurisdictional principle of reasonableness as a principle of international law.

(e) Abuse of rights

Developed national legal systems know a doctrine of abuse of rights (*abus de droit*), pursuant to which legal persons are not to exercise awarded rights in a manner detrimental to the rights and interests of other legal persons. The doctrine of abuse of rights is also used in international law,[70] where it assumes a similar function as in national legal systems: it prohibits States from making use of their rights under international law in ways that do not serve a 'legitimate social goal',[71] or, put differently, disproportionately encroach upon the rights of other States.[72] What a legitimate social goal exactly is, is unclear.[73] This should not necessarily subtract from the usefulness of the doctrine of abuse of rights as

---

[70] eg ICJ, *Case Concerning the Gabcikovo-Nagymaros Project* (Hungary v Slovakia), ICJ Rep 95 (1997) sep op Weeramantry (terming abuse of rights a 'well-established area of international law'); WTO Appellate Body, United States—Import Prohibition of Certain Shrimp and Shrimp Products), WTO Doc WT/DS58/AB/R (1998) ('The chapeau of Article XX [GATT] is, in fact, but one expression of the principle of good faith. This principle, at once a general principle of law and a general principle of international law, controls the exercise of rights by states. One application of this general principle, the application widely known as the doctrine of *abus de droit*, prohibits the abusive exercise of a state's rights and enjoins that whenever the assertion of a rights "impinges on the field covered by [a] treaty obligation, it must be exercised bona fide, that is to say, reasonably". An abusive exercise by a Member of its own treaty rights thus results in a breach of the treaty rights of other Members and, as well, a violation of the treaty obligation of the Member so acting'). On abuse of rights from a doctrinal point of view: N-S Politis, 'Le problème des limitations de la souveraineté et la théorie de l'abus de droits dans les rapports internationaux', (1925) 1 RCADI 1; H-J Schlochauer, 'Die Theorie des abus de droit im Völkerrecht', (1933) 17 Zeitschrift für Völkerrecht 373; ERC van Bogaert, *Het rechtsmisbruik in het volkenrecht: een rechtstheoretische verhandeling* (1948); A-C Kiss, *L'abus de droit en droit international* (1952). For a treaty-based prohibition of abuse of rights: Article 300 of the UN Convention on the Law of the Sea, for instance, provides that 'States Parties shall fulfil in good faith the obligations assumed under this Convention and shall exercise the rights, jurisdiction and freedoms recognized in this Convention *in a manner which would not constitute an abuse of right*' (emphasis added).

[71] PJ Kuyper, 'European Community Law and Extraterritoriality: Some Trends and New Developments', (1984) 33 ICLQ 1013, 1015.

[72] Compare Politis (above n 70) 81 ('[I]l y a abus si l'intérêt général est lésé par le sacrifice d'un intérêt individuel très fort à un autre intérêt individuel plus faible'); L Oppenheim, H Lauterpacht, ed, *International Law: A Treatise* (8th edn 1955) 345 (stating that there is abuse of rights 'when a State avails itself of its rights in an arbitrary manner in such a way as to inflict upon another State an injury which cannot be justified by a legitimate consideration of its own advantage'); P Guggenheim, 'La validité et la nullité des actes juridiques internationaux', (1949) 74 RCADI 195, 250 ('Une règle comme celle qui confère la souveraineté à l'Etat indépendant donne lieu à un abus lorsqu'elle est appliquée dans le but de nuire à autrui ou dans un autre but que pour celui pour lequel le droit international a établi cette règle').

[73] M Byers, 'Abuse of Rights: An Old Principle, a New Age', (2002) 47 McGill LJ 389, 404 (noting that '[t]he principle of abuse of rights has not yet been studied and codified by the ILC; its content and scope of application remain unresolved'). However also ibid 417 (submitting that 'it may be impossible to develop specific rules for every situation in which excessive or abusive exercises of rights might require limitation').

a doctrine of mediating between various State claims and interests in an inter-dependent world in which the discretionary exercise of rights is increasingly undesirable.[74]

Assuming that States enjoy a wide margin of discretion in exercising juris-diction, in keeping with the *Lotus* judgment, or in keeping with an ill-defined territorial effects doctrine, the doctrine of abuse of rights implies for the law of jur-isdiction that States may not assert their jurisdictional freedom if such would not actually serve their legitimate interests, but instead disturb the peace of another State. Akehurst held in this respect that abuse of rights in a State's exercise of prescriptive (legislative) jurisdiction would occur 'if the legislation is designed to produce mischief in another country without advancing any legitimate interest of the legislating State', or 'if legislation is aimed at advancing the interests of the legislating State illegitimately at the expense of other States'.[75]

The doctrine of abuse of rights appears related to the principle of good faith, a well-known principle of international law,[76] although it is unclear whether bad faith is actually required for the principle to be relied upon, or whether abuse of discretion (eg the wide margin of jurisdictional discretion that States enjoy under the *Lotus* judgment) suffices.[77] Applied to the law of jurisdiction, the doc-trine of abuse of rights comes close to the principle of proportionality. They both fine-tune the principle of non-intervention, and allow States to exercise juris-diction over foreign situations, provided that the exercise of jurisdiction serves a legitimate social goal that does not abrogate other States' legitimate rights to pursue social goals for themselves.

---

[74] Cf Schlochauer (above n 70) 378–9 ('Je enger sich die vielmaschigen internationalen Beziehungen knüpfen, desto weniger frei und ungehemmt werden die Staaten ihre "Rechte" nach subjektivem Ermessen ausüben können. Est is eine notwendige Folge der Entwicklung von der "indépendence des états" zur "interdépendence", zum Ausbau der "communauté internationale", dass sich der ursprünglich rein individualistische Charakter der Völkerrechtsordnung zu einem sozialen wandelt…'); V Lowe, 'The Politics of Law-making: Are the Method and Character of Norm Creation Changing?', in M Byers, ed, *The Role of International Law in International Politics* (2000) 207, 212; Byers (above n 73) 431 ('In an international society that itself continues to experi-ence rapid and far-reaching change, long-standing general principles of law such as abuse of rights help to extend legal controls to previously unregulated areas, and to fill new gaps as they appear').

[75] M Akehurst, 'Jurisdiction in International Law', (1972–1973) 46 BYIL 145, 189.

[76] Cf Byers (above n 73) 411 (arguing that the principle of abuse of rights is 'supplemental to the principle of good faith: it provides the threshold at which a lack of good faith gives rise to a viola-tion of international law, with all the attendant consequences'). On good faith in international law inter alia JF O'Connor, *Good Faith in International Law* (1991); R Kolb, *La bonne foi en droit inter-national public* (2000). The principle of good faith has also been invoked as an international law and European Community law principle by the European Court of First Instance, which linked it to the principle of legitimate expectations. CFI, Case T-115/94 *Opel Austria GmbH v Council* [1997] ECR II-39, § 93 ('[T]he principle of good faith is the corollary in public international law of the principle of protection of legitimate expectations which, according to the caselaw, forms part of the Community legal order. Any economic operator to whom an institution has given justified hopes may rely on the principle of protection of legitimate expectations').

[77] Pro the bad faith interpretation: HJ Schlochauer, ed, *Wörterbuch des Völkerrechts* (1962) 69–70; Byers (above n 73) 412.

(f) Responsibility or duty to protect

The principles discussed in sections 5.3.a through 5.3.e are all geared to limiting jurisdictional overreaching. None of them is geared to ensuring that States actually *do* exercise jurisdiction when such would be in the interest of the international community. It may be argued that States do at times have a responsibility, or even a duty to exercise jurisdiction: they may have a responsibility or duty to *protect* either other States or fundamental values of the international community.

The responsibility/duty to protect has been developed in international relations thinking about sovereignty and intervention. Two principles underlie the concept:

(1) State sovereignty implies responsibility, and the primary responsibility for the protection of its people lies with the state itself.

(2) Where a population is suffering serious harm, as a result of internal war, insurgency, repression or state failure, and the state in question is unwilling or unable to halt or avert it, the principle of non-intervention yields to the international responsibility to protect.[78]

In a jurisdictional context, the concept of protection could be used to require a State to exercise jurisdiction over gross human rights violations committed on its territory, and to authorize, or even oblige, bystander States to assume their responsibility to bring to justice the perpetrators of such violations.[79] Outside the field of human rights protection, it could be resorted to to require States to exercise jurisdiction over internationally harmful activities originating in their territory. If the territorial State fails to assume its responsibility, other States could, by default, step in to protect their own interests or even the interests of the international community.

There is nevertheless not much evidence of the responsibility or duty to protect having crystallized as a norm of international law, in the field of *jus ad bellum* nor in the field of jurisdiction. It remains an ethical concept aspiring to international law status.

The responsibility to protect is closely linked to the principle of 'subsidiarity'. This principle implies that, if the State entertaining the strongest link to a situation does not assume its jurisdictional responsibility, it may forfeit its right to protest against other States' jurisdictional assertions over that situation. The concepts of 'responsibility to protect' and 'subsidiarity' will be elaborated upon when a new jurisdictional theory, *de lege ferenda*, is presented in section 6.6. It may suffice here to say that, pursuant to these concepts, sovereignty should no longer be used as a shield to fend off unwelcome jurisdictional assertions. Instead, sovereignty ought to entail jurisdictional responsibility for States: the responsibility to bring

---

[78] Report of the International Commission of Intervention and State Sovereignty, *The Responsibility to Protect*, 2001, Basic Principles (A) and (B), available at <http://www.iciss.ca/>.
[79] Also section 4.5 on universal jurisdiction.

their laws to bear on internationally harmful situations with which they entertain a strong connection. Then, jurisdictional reasonableness may not require a State to *restrain* its assertions, but, on the contrary, to *expand* its assertions.

5.3 The Jurisdictional Rule of Reason of § 403 of the Restatement (Third) of US Foreign Relations Law (1987)

It has been shown that a number of international law principles may support the jurisdictional rule of reason, which requires States to restrain the reach of their laws in view of the legitimate interests of foreign States. These principles, however, have typically been developed and applied in other fields of international law. While they may inform a duty of jurisdictional reasonableness in international law, it may be submitted that an obligation of States to apply a jurisdictional rule of reason, as a norm of customary international law or as a general principle of international law, will only crystallize if specific evidence, in terms of State practice and *opinio juris*, with respect to such an obligation could be found.

Before we embark on such an analysis in section 5.4, we will first discuss the practical operation of the jurisdictional rule of reason, as was notably proposed in § 403 of the Restatement (Third) of US Foreign Relations Law (1987). It will be shown in this section that the origins of the rule of reason could be found in US antitrust law, and that § 403 is grafted upon reasonableness-informed considerations by US courts hearing private antitrust cases (5.3.a–b). Because the rule of reason has been developed in private cases, private interests feature prominently in § 403. Although public international law ordinarily only concerns itself with public or sovereign interests, taking private interests into account should in itself not be problematic, as States could commit themselves to heeding all sorts of interests. It raises the interesting question, however, how a conflict between private and sovereign interests ought to be decided (5.3.c). The rule of reason also raises other questions. One may notably wonder how jurisdictional assertions that are all reasonable are arbitrated (5.3.d). Also, it is unclear how a conflict should be solved between the rule of reason and a clear congressional statement that casts that rule aside (5.3.e). The biggest question surrounding § 403—whether it represents international law or not—will, as noted, be tackled extensively in section 5.4.

(a) Antitrust origins of the rule of reason

In 1945, the US Supreme Court had held in the *Alcoa* antitrust case, that the United States could exercise its jurisdiction over foreign antitrust violations provided that these violations caused domestic effects.[80] Since foreign nations also

---

[80] *United States v Aluminium Corp of America*, 148 F 2d 416 (2d Cir 1945).

started to take a keen interest in antitrust policy after the Second World War, US effects-based jurisdiction over corporations' foreign business restrictive practices seemed bound to give rise to international tension. US antitrust courts soon qualified the effects doctrine by requiring direct, substantial, and reasonably foreseeable effects. In spite of this jurisdictional restraint, conflict potential did not appear to subside. Therefore, toward the end of the 1970s, courts superimposed another test of jurisdictional restraint.[81] This test required antitrust courts to inquire 'whether the interests and the links to the United States—including the magnitude of the effect on American foreign commerce—are sufficiently strong vis-à-vis those of other nations, to justify an assertion of extraterritorial authority'.[82] This interest-balancing test soon found its way to the jurisdictional provisions of the draft for a new Restatement of US Foreign Relations Law. In 1987, the new Restatement was adopted, and the interest-balancing test featured prominently in § 403 as a general rule of jurisdictional restraint under international law, the application of which admittedly grew out of, but was no longer limited to international antitrust cases.

(b) § 403 of the Restatement

As a preliminary matter, before discussing § 403 of the Restatement, it may be useful to recall that a Restatement is not an official document of the United States. It is drawn up by the American Law Institute (ALI), an unofficial influential body of leading legal practitioners and academics, established in 1923 to promote the 'clarification and simplification of the law and its better adaptation to social needs'.[83] Thus, it is a doctrinal work. Its content does not necessarily reflect American foreign relations law or general international law, although, as an authoritative document, it might, in view of a US court hearing a case involving the law of jurisdiction, contain the 'principles derived from international law, for determining when the United States may properly exercise regulatory (or prescriptive) jurisdiction over activities or persons connected with another state'.[84]

In § 402, the Restatement (Third) lists the classical grounds of jurisdiction which render a (US) jurisdictional assertion presumptively lawful (see also the discussion in Chapters 3 and 4). In § 403, however, the eventual lawfulness of the

---

[81] *Timberlane Lumber Co v Bank of America*, 549 F 2d 597 (9th Cir 1976); *Mannington Mills v Congoleum Corp*, 595 F 2d 1287 (3d Cir 1979). In the context of the enforceability of forum selection clauses by US courts, the US Supreme Court had emphasized jurisdictional reasonableness as early as 1972, when it stated in *M/S Bremen v Zapata Off-Shore Company*, 407 US 1 (1972) that the US 'cannot have trade and commerce in world markets and international waters exclusively on our terms, governed by our laws and resolved in our courts'.

[82] *Timberlane*, 549 F 2d 613.

[83] GC Hazard, Jr, foreword to Restatement (Third), at xi.

[84] *United States v Nippon Paper Indus Co*, 109 F 3d 1, 11 (1st Cir 1997) (Lynch, J, dissenting), *cert denied*, 522 US 1044 (1998).

assertion is conditional upon it being exercised *reasonably*. § 403 (1) indeed obliges the United States to refrain from exercising prescriptive jurisdiction which it may have under § 402 'with respect to a person or activity having connections with another State when the exercise of such jurisdiction is unreasonable'.[85] Drawing on § 6 of the Restatement (Second) of Conflicts and on the Third Circuit's 1979 *Mannington Mills* decision, it set forth, in § 403(2), the following criteria that determine the reasonableness of the exercise of jurisdiction:

Whether exercise of jurisdiction over a person or activity is unreasonable is determined by evaluating all relevant factors, including, where appropriate:

(a) the link of the activity to the territory of the regulating state, i.e., the extent to which the activity takes place within the territory, or has substantial, direct, and foreseeable effect upon or in the territory;

(b) the connections, such as nationality, residence, or economic activity, between the regulating state and the person principally responsible for the activity to be regulated, or between that state and those whom the regulation is designed to protect;

(c) the character of the activity to be regulated, the importance of regulation to the regulating state, the extent to which other states regulate such activities, and the degree to which the desirability of such regulation is generally accepted;

(d) the existence of justified expectations that might be protected or hurt by the regulation;

(e) the importance of the regulation to the international political, legal or economic system;

(f) the extent to which regulation is consistent with the traditions of the international system;

(g) the extent to which another state may have an interest in regulating the activity; and

(h) the likelihood of conflict with regulation by another state.

Conspicuously, while § 40 of the Restatement (Second) of US Foreign Relations Law still emphasized States' pre-existing jurisdiction—which States may be required to moderate in case of a direct conflict—§ 403 emphasizes that any actual exercise of jurisdiction is subject to the requirement of reasonableness, even when there is only a potential or no conflict at all.[86]

---

[85] The rule of reason may arguably draw on the prohibition of *unreasonable* search and seizure in the American Bill of Rights. remarks by A Lowenfeld, in 'Panel Discussion on the Draft Restatement of the Foreign Relations Law of the United States', (1982) 76 ASIL Proc 184, 192 (citing the use of the rule of reason in the Bill of Rights in support of its being elastic but not meaningless). § 402 states that the US has jurisdiction on the basis of the classical principles of jurisdiction. It has been argued, quite convincingly, that the traditional theories are only factors to reasonableness, which is the actual basis of jurisdiction. CL Blakesley, 'Extraterritorial Jurisdiction', in MC Bassiouni, ed, *International Criminal Law II: Procedural and Enforcement Mechanisms* (2nd edn 1999) 41. The connecting factors (primarily territoriality and nationality) that underpin the classical principles are indeed factors used in the reasonableness analysis conducted under § 403 of the Restatement.

[86] Reporters' note 10 to section 403 (stating that reasonableness is 'an essential element in determining whether, as a matter of international law, States may exercise jurisdiction to prescribe'); Lowenfeld (above n 85) 194.

§ 403 sets forth a general framework for the application of the rule of reason to all fields of the law by courts and legislatures, as well as administrative agencies.[87] § 403 thus suggests a 'generic' rule of reason that could be applied across-the-board, regardless of the particular field of substantive law concerned.[88] Its use in selected contexts is elaborated upon in subsequent sections of the Restatement[89] (although the rule of reason referred to in these sections draws to a large extent on § 403). It should nonetheless be noted that the generic rule of reason is based on the use of the rule of reason in selected contexts (notably antitrust law), and not vice versa. It goes to the Restatement's drafters' credit that they devised a rule of reason from jurisdictional principles that lay scattered over different fields of substantive law.[90]

(c) Balancing sovereign and private interests

The essence of the rule of reason is that a legitimate US interest does not in itself justify an assertion of jurisdiction.[91] Only after 'evaluating all relevant factors' (not all factors may be relevant to any dispute) including foreign interests, and if US interests and contacts eventually outweigh foreign interests and contacts, could US law possibly apply to foreign situations.[92] It should indeed not be forgotten that, as one commentator has forcefully pointed out, 'a jurisdictional scheme is valid only insofar as it gives [the principles of comity and predictability] precedence over national interests'.[93] Thus, the rule of reason requires that a State balances the interests of any State affected by a possible jurisdictional assertion.[94]

---

[87] In practice, legislatures are not adepts of the rule of reason, since, as non-repeat-players, they may lack sensitivity about the extraterritorial effects of their legislation. Bianchi (above n 3) 86. It may also be argued that the legislature need not heed the rule of reason to the same extent as other actors do, as '[n]o one really cares before the law is implemented, at which point there is still occasion to call for restraint'. KM Meessen, 'Drafting Rules on Extraterritorial Jurisdiction', in Meessen (above n 2) 225, 226.

[88] X, Note, 'Predictability and Comity: Toward Common Principles of Extraterritorial Jurisdiction', (1985) 98 Harv L Rev 1310, 1321.

[89] These sections include tax (§§ 411–413), foreign subsidiaries (§ 414), antitrust (§ 415), securities (§ 416), foreign sovereign compulsion (§ 441) and transnational discovery (§ 442).

[90] *a contrario* X (above n 88) 1310 ('Because the doctrine of extraterritoriality has developed independently within different areas of substantive law, too little attention has been paid to devising a set of common principles that can guide the discussion').

[91] X (above n 88) 1320 (stating that '[t]he interests of a single country do not in themselves dictate the scope of its legitimate authority').

[92] For European supportive voices: Bischoff and Kovar (above n 37) 714 (stating that '[L]a mise en œuvre [of the principle of jurisdictional restraint imposes] une analyse contextuelle de tous les intérêts impliqués en la cause').

[93] X (above n 88) 1323.

[94] A jurisdictional assertion not only implies a finding that the forum State laws govern a particular situation, but also the remedial or punitive measures imposed after such a finding. It may be reasonable for a State to apply its laws to a situation, but unreasonable to impose certain measures to be executed by the foreign defendant (eg, industrial reorganization, divestitures,...). Compare Bischoff and Kovar (above n 37) 726 (stating that the American judge, in imposing certain measures on foreign defendants in the *ICI* and *Swiss Watchmakers* antitrust cases (105 F Supp 215 (SDNY

This implies, on the one hand, that the exercise of jurisdiction over foreign situations does not of itself run counter to the principle of non-intervention, but, on the other hand, that the asserting State is required to inquire into the strength of a foreign State's policy interests in not having another State dictate what laws ought to govern situations arising in its territory.[95]

Reporters' note 6 to § 403 provides guidance for a determination of competing State interests, stating that:

[i]n weighing the interests of a foreign state, a court in the United States may take into account indications of national interest by the foreign government, whether made through a diplomatic note, a brief *amicus curiae*, a declaration by government officials in parliamentary debates, press conferences, or communiqués.[96]

Foreign States need, however, not *explicitly* assert their interests by intervening in a given case. It may indeed be argued that courts and regulators have a duty to track foreign States' interests *proprio motu*.[97]

The factors set forth in § 403 are, conspicuously, not only aimed at mediating conflicts of jurisdiction *between States*. They are also aimed at providing legal certainty on *private actors'* conduct and transactions.[98] Notably 'the connections, such as nationality, residence, or economic activity, between the regulating state and the person principally responsible for the activity to be regulated',[99] and 'the existence of justified expectations that might be protected or hurt by the regulation'[100] may be cited in this respect. The rule of reason enshrined in § 403 thus appears as a remarkable hybrid that combines the purpose of public international law rules of prescriptive jurisdiction, aimed at delimiting States' sovereign spheres of action, *and* the purpose of private international law rules of judicial jurisdiction, aimed at conferring legal certainty on private actors' conduct and transactions by identifying the proper judicial forum for hearing private claims.

1952) and 1963 Trade Cas 70,600 (SDNY 1962), 1965 Trade Cas 71,352 (SDNY 1965)) 's'immisce dans le fonctionnement d'institutions qui échappent à son pouvoir de juger et de décider').

[95] Cf Kuyper (above n 71) 1021 (arguing that '[i]t is possible ... to prescribe conduct in a foreign country which goes against a policy of that country, but much would depend on how firmly that policy is integrated in the socio-economic order of that country as a whole').

[96] Also Meessen (above n 38) 806 (arguing that '[s]pecific statements of the domestic government and the foreign government are helpful, but they are not dispositive from the point of view of international law. They would have to be related to policy trends as laid down, for instance, in statutory enactments or in general pronouncements of policy').

[97] Schuster (above n 7) 676.

[98] On the burdens on private actors that may be caused by the exercise of 'extraterritorial' jurisdiction: Policy Statement of the International Chamber of Commerce, 'Extraterritoriality and business', 13 July 2006, Document 103-33/5 (on file with the author) ('The extraterritorial application of national laws frequently subjects companies to conflicting or overlapping legal requirements, fosters unpredictability, increases the risks involved in commercial activities, exposes companies to overly burdensome litigation in foreign jurisdictions, and inflates legal and other transactions costs'). For European support for balancing private interests: Bischoff and Kovar (above n 37) 713.

[99] § 403(2)(b) of the Restatement.   [100] § 403(2)(d).

Under public international law, private interests are ordinarily not relevant.[101] The public international law of jurisdiction indeed delimits States' spheres of competence with sole regard to States' interests.[102] Public international law does, however, not prevent States from consensually deciding to attach as much weight to foreign *individual* interests as to foreign *sovereign* interests. It may be noted that this is only to say that private interests should not a priori be excluded from the realm of public international law. It is not to say that States have *actually* reached the stage of consensus over *what* private interests should be relevant under the public international law of jurisdiction.

If private interests could be taken into account in an interest-balancing test alongside public interests, the risk may arise that, after weighing all relevant interests, a State might exercise jurisdiction under international law over a situation because such might serve the private interests of a particular individual rather than the sovereign interests of foreign States. A clash between private and sovereign interests is, however, not the order of the day in the law of jurisdiction. Indeed, there is often not much of a dichotomy between private and public interests, since it is not unusual that the interests of governments on the one hand, and individuals or corporations on the other hand, coincide, especially in the field of economic law. Corporations may represent an important part of the national economy. Foreign regulation then comes at a cost for corporations *and* their home States alike. Corporations will have to comply with foreign rules on top of domestic rules, which may reduce their profits, and thereby lower the tax income of their home States. Home States will thus have an incentive to support their corporations in opposing foreign regulation.

Large corporations are, moreover, often highly skilled in lobbying their governments in order for the latter to take a particular jurisdictional stance beneficial to the former. It may be noted that corporations may even have so much lobbying power that they are able to convince governments to take a particular position, even though, as Lowenfeld has argued, these governments 'may well have been

---

[101] Schuster (above n 7) 690.

[102] Relying on the public international law principle of non-interference which arguably undergirds the rule of reason, Meessen has argued in 1984 that, for purposes of the crystallization of a customary international law norm, only sovereign interests should be taken into account. Meessen (above n 38) 804. Meessen formulates the international law norm as follows: 'a state is prohibited from taking measures of antitrust law if the regulatory interests it is pursuing are outweighed by the interests of one or more foreign states likely to be seriously injured by those measures'. A child of his time, he argued that 'there is little room for individual hardship arguments in antitrust cases at a time when the very basis for human rights in customary international law is still insecure'. ibid 803. However, those days are long gone, and international law is nowadays no longer exclusively concerned with narrowly defined rights and obligations of States. Rights and duties under international law are gradually being extended, to other (non-State) actors, such as international organizations, non-governmental organizations, corporations, and individuals. In the field of human rights, the legality of individual liability for gross human rights violations is now firmly anchored in international law, as the spread of international criminal tribunals and the use of universal jurisdiction by national courts since the 1990s attest to.

sympathetic to the [positions of the State asserting its jurisdiction]'.[103] In this respect, an argument could conceivably, although hardly persuasively, be made that the concept of State sovereignty is endowed with *jus cogens* character, which would render it a concept that States are not allowed to tamper with at will, for instance by subordinating State interests to private interests. A more common sense approach, however, is that, in assessing foreign governmental protests, it may not be warranted for the State asserting its jurisdiction to deconstruct the opinion of the foreign government: sovereign protest is sovereign protest, even if it vindicates private interests to the detriment of the *actual* interests of the sovereign or the democratic constituency which it represents.

Although State interests and the interests of private persons residing in or incorporated in the State concerned are ordinarily aligned, in rare cases, it may nevertheless happen that a corporation welcomes foreign regulation, for instance because this increases its credibility in the eyes of foreign investors, while its home State opposes the regulation for patriotic or economic motives. It appears that under public international law, which is (in spite of the broadening of its sphere of relevant actors) still mainly concerned with State interests, the interest of the home State to be free from foreign regulation thrust upon subjects under its territorial jurisdiction (a legal interest which derives from the historical principles of State sovereignty and non-interference) should prevail over the corporation's interest.

Nonetheless, in some circumstances, the private interest may arguably prevail. It could for instance be argued that parties are, under private law, entitled to enter into a private contract featuring a clause stating that the contract will be governed by a foreign State's law, even if that law undermines important policies of one of the parties' home States. Furthermore, it seems that a party is entitled to voluntarily transmit materials for use as evidence in a foreign proceeding, because such action does, legally speaking, not amount to a measure of evidence-*taking* in which the party's home State has an interest.[104]

Whether foreign persons could automatically become subject to the criminal jurisdiction of another State by voluntarily surrendering to that State for trial purposes (ordinarily, the presence of an accused who is present abroad is forcibly brought about by means of extradition) is doubtful. If a State's jurisdictional assertion exceeds what is allowed under public international law, the accused could arguably not justify the overreach. He could not possibly be considered to have waived his home State's sovereign rights of protest against another State's exercise of jurisdiction by his mere act of voluntary submission to the latter State's jurisdiction. Professor Tomuschat's argument that, although the Spanish trial of the Argentine torturer Adolfo Scilingo under the universality principle (2005) appears controversial from the perspective of the international law of jurisdiction

---

[103] Lowenfeld (above n 36) 397.
[104] RA Trittmann, 'Extraterritoriale Beweisaufnahmen und Souveränitätsverletzungen im deutsch-amerikanischen Rechtsverkehr', (1989) 27 Archiv des Völkerrechts 195.

over core crimes against international law, Scilingo's 'decision of his own volition [to surrender to the Spanish judiciary] ultimately provides a sound jurisdictional basis for his conviction',[105] should therefore probably be rejected.

(d) Multiple reasonableness

It may happen that the jurisdictional assertions of several States could be considered reasonable on the basis of the factors set forth in § 403(2) of the Restatement. For these situations, § 403(3) states that each State then 'has an obligation to evaluate its own as well as the other state's interests in exercising jurisdiction, in light of all the relevant factors, including those set out in § 403(2)', and that a State should defer 'to the other state if that state's interest is clearly greater'. A comment to § 403(3) adds that the provision only comes into play in case of 'true conflict', ie when one State's law requires what another State's law prohibits, or vice versa.[106] § 403(3) does not seem to contemplate the situation where it would be reasonable for each of two States to exercise jurisdiction, but the two States' prescriptions are not in direct conflict. This might imply that both States could concurrently exercise their reasonable jurisdiction, which may obviously burden persons and corporations with two layers of, albeit non-contradictory, regulation.[107]

Regrettably, if § 403(3) of the Restatement only solves 'true' jurisdictional conflicts, conflicts between jurisdictions, rather than between laws, remain unsolved, for instance where one State has deliberately chosen not to put in place a regulatory framework, and another State applies its own regulations to activities taking place in the former States. In order to solve such conflicts, it could be argued that the standard of reasonableness in § 403(2) should be applied more strictly. If reasonableness is readily accepted, the purpose of the conflict rule enshrined in § 403—identifying the State with the most significant relationship to the matter—is indeed not adequately served. Alternatively, one could erase § 403(3)'s restriction of normative competency conflicts to 'true conflicts', so that in situations in which it is reasonable for more than one State to exercise jurisdiction without the respective jurisdictional assertions necessarily being in 'true' conflict (but nevertheless in conflict), the State with the smaller interests ought

---

[105] C Tomuschat, 'Issues of Universal Jurisdiction in the *Scilingo* Case', (2005) 3 JICJ 1074, 1081.
[106] § 403, cmt e.
[107] The Supreme Court in *Hartford Fire* seemed to rely on this 'loophole' in order to justify its true conflict doctrine (*Hartford Fire Insurance Co v California*, 509 US 764, 799 (1993)), without, however, first ascertaining whether it would be reasonable for the States concerned to exercise their jurisdiction. Justice Scalia has, in this study's view, in his dissenting opinion, correctly pointed out that § 403(3) comes into play only after § 403(1) and (2) have been complied with, ie after it has been determined that the exercise of jurisdiction by both of the two States is not 'unreasonable' (509 US 821). The majority replied to this objection that true conflict was 'the only substantial issue before the Court' (509 US 799, note 25), implying that it was irrelevant whether the US assertion of jurisdiction was reasonable under § 403(2). This reasoning wholly undermines the operation of the rule of reason.

nevertheless to defer to the State with the greater interest on the basis of the factors set forth in § 403(2) through application of § 403(3). Either way, while their methodology might somewhat differ, both approaches resort to an application of the interest-balancing factors set forth in § 403(2) in order to identify the State with the greater interest. At any rate, the confusion surrounding the relationship between § 403(2) and § 403(3) may cast doubt on the international law character of the specific operation of the rule of reason contemplated by the Restatement.[108] The characterization of the rule of reason as a rule of international law on the basis of actual State practice and *opinio juris* will be discussed below.

(e) Relationship of the jurisdictional rule of reason with the presumption against extraterritoriality

§ 403 of the Restatement does not mention the relationship between a clear statement of Congress (section 3.3.b) and the operation of the rule of reason. This is because the rule of reason is a rule which 'the State', which logically includes the courts, the executive branch, and the legislative branch, ought to comply with. For the drafters of the Restatement, Congress is not infallible if it comes to reasonableness. Put differently, the territorial scope of an Act is not necessarily reasonable because the Act is enacted by the legislature.

There are, nevertheless, traces of deference to a clear statement of Congress, unreasonable as it may be, discernible in the comments to § 403. Comment c, for instance, states that 'the reasonableness of the exercise of jurisdiction may differ with the level at which the decision is taken'. The drafters illustrate that statement with a comparison between a directive of Congress and a decision by the Securities and Exchange Commission (SEC) with the same content, pointing out that the directive of Congress may be considered reasonable and the SEC decision not. The drafters may have believed that an organ imbued with a higher measure of democratic legitimacy, such as Congress, is more likely to produce decisions containing *reasonable* assertions of jurisdiction than an administrative and hierarchically lower organ is. If this were indeed their belief, it is nonetheless often belied by the facts. Administrative agencies such as the SEC deal with foreign actors on a day-to-day basis, which makes them generally more accommodating to foreign concerns. A SEC decision is ordinarily more likely to contain reasonable jurisdictional assertions than a congressional act is. The exemptions granted by the SEC to the requirements of the extremely strict congressional Sarbanes-Oxley Act make this abundantly clear. Thus, somewhat surprisingly, a rule of inverse hierarchy may often go further in preventing jurisdictional conflict. Under this rule, the lower the hierarchical position of a State actor, the higher the odds of the actor exercising jurisdiction reasonably.

---

[108] Also Schuster (above n 7) 687.

Comment c on the chameleon role of the rule of reason—a rule taking a different colour depending on the institutional environment in which it is found—may be linked with comment g, another comment tangentially dealing with the presumption against extraterritoriality. In this comment, the drafters admit that, at times, a 'construction of a statute that accommodates the intent of Congress within the limits of [the] international law [rule of reason] is not fairly possible'. They deplore this, but in line with a string of precedents, they could only 'restate' that such a statute is valid. Comment c can be squared with comment g in that the drafters seem to believe that there is some international wiggle room for Congress (comment c) but that in spite of the elasticity of the rule of reason, some jurisdictional assertions of Congress are so outrageous that they can impossibly withstand the *Charming Betsy* test (with the rule of reason serving as the international law norm in light of which Congressional acts ought to be reviewed).

It appears that what might be unreasonable in the eyes of the international community might be reasonable from a domestic US perspective only because the Act containing the jurisdictional assertion originates from a democratically elected actor, whom other, less democratic actors, such as a perceived 'international community' or the judiciary, are not allowed to second-guess. Such a reading is obviously anathema to the sanctification of the rule of reason as a rule of international law (comment a to § 403). If the rule of reason is indeed a clearly defined international rule, all State actors should be bound by it to the same extent.

A final reference to the clear statement rule or presumption against extraterritoriality could be found in comment f to § 403. In this comment, the drafters state that 'the presence of substantial foreign elements will ordinarily weigh against application of [regulatory] criminal law (i.e., antitrust and securities criminal law)' and that, therefore, in such cases, 'legislative intent to subject conduct outside the state's territory to its criminal law should be found only on the basis of express statement or clear implication'.

By referring to 'express statement or clear implication', the drafters did not aim at restricting the three-pronged *Foley Bros* test to ascertain congressional intent supposedly prevailing at the time of the Restatement in criminal matters. Rather, they believed that in regulatory criminal law matters, courts should await congressional instruction and should not determine reasonableness *proprio motu*. It is unclear from the wording of comment f whether the courts should defer to the legislature in all criminal regulatory law cases, or only when foreign elements outweigh domestic elements.[109] The latter interpretation should probably be rejected, as, if foreign elements outweigh domestic elements, courts should anyway have dismissed the expansion of jurisdiction because the criteria of the rule of

---

[109] 'However, in the case of regulatory statutes that may give rise to both civil and criminal liability, such as United States antitrust and securities laws, the presence of substantial foreign elements will ordinarily weigh against application of criminal law. *In such cases*, legislative intent to subject conduct...' (emphasis added).

reason were not met. As also set forth in comment g, if extraterritorial application is deemed desirable, Congress could overrule the rule of reason by stating clearly that it intends to apply a criminal law extraterritorially even if foreign elements weigh against extraterritorial application. However, it could be argued that the former interpretation is not defensible either. There is no compelling argument to authorize courts to assess the reach of a criminal statute of a general nature pursuant to the rule of reason without ascertaining congressional intent, while prohibiting courts from applying the rule of reason when they assess the reach of a regulatory criminal statute. Not surprisingly, the criminal/civil divide was later rejected in antitrust matters.[110] Ever since, all civil and criminal regulation is arguably subject to the same jurisdictional principles, including the rule of reason (although it may be noted that the Supreme Court took a very restrictive view of reasonableness in the *Hartford Fire* case).

While the drafters of the Restatement may not have repudiated the presumption against extraterritoriality as a jurisdictional restraining principle informed by constitutional considerations (separation of powers), their scarce references to the presumption undercut its normative value. While it is not very plausible that the courts, relying on an *international* rule of reason, will overrule a clear statement of *domestic* congressional intent, one could easily imagine that the courts, in case of doubt, have their assessment of the reach of US laws informed by permissive rules of public international law. As already noted,[111] reliance on the rule of reason instead of on the presumption against extraterritoriality may be a recipe for jurisdictional overreaching, as international jurisdictional rules are not well-defined and thus extremely malleable for domestic purposes. The danger is real that international law, the *Lotus* precedent in particular, is used as a fig-leaf for an otherwise rationally hardly defensible extraterritorial application of US law.

5.4 The Problematic Character of the Jurisdictional Rule of Reason as an International Law Norm or Principle

The reasonableness-based international law concepts discussed in section 5.2 may inform the crystallization of a jurisdictional rule of reason. Reasoning by analogy does, however, not suffice. Given the peculiarity of the concept of jurisdiction under international law, a specific *jurisdictional* rule of reason is arguably in need of its own State practice and/or *opinio juris*. In this section, it will be analysed whether there are sufficient indications which indeed point to the existence of a rule of reason under international law. To that effect, US and European practice in particular will be ascertained. In section 5.5, conclusions as to the status of

---

[110] *United States v Nippon Paper Indus*, 109 F 3d 1, 9 (1st Cir 1997).
[111] Section 3.3.b *in fine*.

the jurisdictional rule of reason as a rule or principle of international law will be drawn on the basis of the analysis performed in this Section.

(a) The international law claim of § 403

§ 403 of the Restatement itself draws on almost no reasonableness-related State practice outside the United States to support its thesis that the rule of reason as articulated in § 403 constitutes international law. In reporters' note 3, only a 1983 decision by the German *Kammergericht* in *Philip Morris/Rothmans* is cited.[112] In this decision, the *Kammergericht* restricted the effect of an order by the German Cartel Office preventing the merger of international companies from applying to their German subsidiaries. The *Kammergericht*'s decision was informed by a § 403-like weighing of sovereign interests, and was explicitly based on international law as incorporated into domestic law via Article 25 of the German Constitution.

It can surely not be derived from the German example only that there is sufficient practice of States applying any sort of rule of reason, let alone a rule of reason as a requirement of international law.[113] Nonetheless, the crystallization of a norm of customary international law does not require that all States actively *apply* the norm: a consistent pattern of absence of protest against another State's jurisdictional assertion may suffice.[114]

There is no hard evidence that foreign States, European States in particular, have *denounced* the US jurisdictional rule of reason. On the contrary, some States have explicitly recognized it. In its *Statement of Interest* in the *Hartford Fire Insurance* antitrust case, for instance, the United Kingdom held:

Under international law and the principles of moderation and restraint as they have been applied in U.S. courts, the extraterritorial exercise of a U.S. court's jurisdiction to prescribe or to enforce *must always be reasonable*.[115]

---

[112] Decision of 1 July 1983, Kart 16/82. Admittedly, the reporters' note to § 403 of the Restatement also referred to the practice of other States, but it only did so to the effect of supporting its argument that these States had accepted the effects doctrine, rather than the rule of reason.

[113] Probably, without the advice of Professor Meessen, who served as an adviser to the American Law Institute when the jurisdictional provisions of the Restatement (Third) were drawn up, not even the German example would have featured in the reporters' notes.

[114] Section 2.2.d.

[115] Statement of Interest of the United Kingdom, (1990) BYIL 571 (emphasis added). The rule of reason was initially not greeted as a major improvement by the United Kingdom, however: the UK believed that the even 'reasonable' assertions of jurisdiction remained overbroad. United Kingdom Response to US Diplomatic Note concerning the UK Protection of Trading Interest Bill, 27 Nov 1979, (1982) 21 ILM 847, 849–50 ('[T]he U.S. courts claim subject matter jurisdiction over activities of non-U.S. persons outside the U.S.A. to an extent which is quite unacceptable to the U.K. and many other nations. Although in recognition of international objections to the wide reach of anti-trust law enforcement in civil cases, the U.S. courts have begun to devise tests which may limit the circumstances in which the remedy may be available, these tests remain within these wider claims to jurisdiction to which Her Majesty's Government object').

The rule of reason has certainly appeased foreign nations.[116] European States were most likely all too happy that US courts and regulators finally started to restrain their jurisdictional assertions by taking into account interests and connections of the matter to be regulated with foreign States. Yet the question arises whether they would also have expected the United States to go as far as adopting a rule of reason as a matter of law. Massey pointed out that European States did in fact not take issue with 'unreasonable' assertions of jurisdiction, but only with 'exorbitant' assertions.[117] Also, European States may have criticized the lack of a jurisdictional nexus with the United States (eg adverse economic 'effects' not qualifying as a sufficient nexus for the United States to exercise jurisdiction in antitrust matters) rather than the unreasonableness of jurisdiction.[118] Put differently, they may have believed that there was no jurisdiction under the classical principles of jurisdiction in the first place (set forth in § 402 of the Restatement), so that an application of the rule of reason (set forth in § 403 of the Restatement) did not come into play at all.

The argument that European States tolerated unreasonable assertions of jurisdiction does not seem entirely convincing. For one thing, the distinction between 'unreasonable' and 'exorbitant' jurisdiction is not explicitly made in the diplomatic protests themselves (in particular against the imposition of US export controls on foreign actors),[119] and may thus amount to *Hineininterpretierung*. Even assuming that European States indeed denounced US jurisdictional assertions for their 'exorbitance', there is no evidence that they would have tolerated 'unreasonable' assertions. The category of 'reasonableness' in the field of the law of jurisdiction was only defined by the Restatement in 1987, so that a semantic discussion about perceived differences between 'unreasonableness' and 'exorbitance' before 1987 appears inapposite. In addition, while the Restatement itself refers to 'exorbitant' jurisdiction, it does so precisely to justify the rule of reason, which lends credence to the thesis that 'unreasonable' and 'exorbitant' are interchangeable adjectives.

The argument that European States took aim at the very existence of an economic effects doctrine rather than at its scope of application is equally unconvincing. The distinction between the threshold question of whether economic effects

---

[116] Layton and Parry (above n 63) 313 ('These refinements may have been influential in keeping critical foreign states at bay').

[117] DP Massey, 'How the American Law Institute Influences Customary Law: The Reasonableness Requirement of the Restatement of Foreign Relations Law', (1997) 22 Yale J Int'l L 419, 429.

[118] ibid.

[119] In their comments on the US Regulations concerning Trade with the USSR (Soviet Pipeline Regulations), featuring the only pan-European denouncement of US extraterritorial jurisdiction before the adoption of the Restatement in 1987, the European Communities believed these regulations to contain '*sweeping* extensions of U.S. jurisdiction which are unlawful under international law' (21 ILM 891 (emphasis added)), and to be '*unacceptable* under international law because of their extra-territorial aspects' (ibid 893 (emphasis added)). The term 'exorbitant' appeared to be used only by the United Kingdom (Debates on the British Shipping Contracts and Commercial Documents) Bill, 1964, 698 Parl Deb HC (5th Ser) 1215 (1961); Debates on the British Protection of Trading Interests Act, 1980, 973 Parl Deb HC (5th Ser) 1535 (1979), cited in § 403 of the Restatement, reporters' note 1).

jurisdiction actually exist, and the question of whether its modalities of application are satisfied, should such jurisdiction exist, is blurred by the Restatement itself. In § 402(1)(c), the Restatement provides, in relevant part, that '[s]ubject to § 403 [ie the rule of reason], a state has jurisdiction to prescribe law with respect to . . . conduct outside its territory that has or is intended to have substantial effect within its territory'. § 402 makes any legitimate assertion of effects jurisdiction subject to the rule of reason, of which the first factors to be considered precisely relate to a sufficient nexus of the activity with the regulating State.[120] The requirement of a jurisdictional nexus is embedded in the rule of reason, and any criticism leveled at the lack of a jurisdictional nexus thus in effect implies that the critic believes that the reasonableness requirement is not met.

The argument that State practice and/or *opinio juris* as to the existence of a rule of reason under international law is lacking, carries more weight. It seems granted that, for the development of a customary rule of reason in the field of economic jurisdiction, there is no need for all States to have taken a position on the existence and exact contours of any such norm.[121] Indeed, only a limited number of States have an interest in or are affected by economic jurisdiction, the industrialized Western nations traditionally being the main protagonists. It remains therefore to be determined whether Western States indeed concur on the existence of a rule of reason.[122]

(b) US practice

§ 403 of the Restatement may have doctrinal authority, but it is not the law of the land in the United States. In fact, in the 1993 *Hartford Fire Insurance* case,[123] the US Supreme Court dealt a serious blow to the rule of reason in antitrust cases by only requiring deference pursuant to comity in case a foreign sovereign compels what the United States prohibit, or vice versa (although in the 2004 *Empagran* case it might have re-introduced it to a certain extent).[124] Nonetheless, US courts and regulators may cite § 403 as authority to solve jurisdictional conflicts, and

---

[120] The first two (out of eight) factors of the reasonableness test set forth by § 403 (2) are (a) the link of the activity to the territory of the regulating State, ie, the extent to which the activity takes place within the territory, or has substantial, direct, and foreseeable effect upon or in the territory; (b) the connections, such as nationality, residence, or economic activity, between the regulating State and the person principally responsible for the activity to be regulated, or between that State and those whom the regulation is designed to protect.

[121] Section 2.2.d.

[122] Cf Massey (above n 117) 430 (arguing that '[w]ithout the concurrence of the United States, a major power in the field of extraterritorial regulation, it is difficult for a custom in this area to come into being').

[123] *Hartford Fire Insurance Co v California*, 509 US 764 (1993).

[124] *F Hoffman-La Roche Ltd et al. v Empagran SA et al.*, 124 S Ct 2359 (2004). The Supreme Court cited the customary international law principle of non-interference in the internal affairs of another State, and stated that, therefore, it is to be assumed that Congress takes 'the legitimate sovereign interests of other nations into account' (at 2366) when assessing the reach of US law, and avoids extending this reach when such would create a 'serious risk of interference with a foreign nation's ability independently to regulate its own commercial affairs' (at 2367). See for a

thus conduct a reasonableness analysis.[125] Also, the US legislative and executive branches may roll back initially rather broad jurisdictional assertions, possibly after foreign protest. The question may, however, be asked whether jurisdictional restraint in these instances is based on an international obligation. When, for instance, in the 1970s and 1980s, the United States withdrew controversial US export controls regulations after protests by foreign States, there are no indications that it did so out of a sense of legal obligation.[126] This finding is, as Massey noted, reinforced by the later or simultaneous enactment of other export controls regulations with similar extraterritorial effects.[127]

If jurisdictional restraint is not informed by a sense of legal obligation on the part of the US political branches, the *opinio juris* required for the crystallization of an international law norm is lacking. US courts, for their part, when citing and relying on § 403, may surely act out of a sense of legal obligation. Yet the legal obligation may arise under domestic conflict of laws principles rather than under *international law*.

(c) European practice

As set out in the previous subsection, it is open to serious doubt whether the US application, if any, of the rule of reason arises out of a sense of legal obligation. Application of the rule of reason outside the United States, notably in Europe, is, however, even more problematic, because European States are generally uneasy with the very process of interest-balancing as a method of solving jurisdictional conflicts. While protests against US applications of the rule of reason have been largely absent, it surely does not help the crystallization of an international norm or principle of reasonableness if a legal system, such as the continental European one, appears to display an almost inherent bias against the procedure of weighing interests.

1. *Ordre public v comity*

The use of comity or reasonableness as a principle restraining assertions of jurisdiction is almost unknown in Europe.[128] In deciding private transnational

---

detailed discussion of this case: C Ryngaert, *Jurisdiction over Antitrust Violations in International Law* (2008) section 10.2.

[125] Section 3.3.b *in fine*.

[126] Massey (above n 117) 431–2 (citing the limitation of the application of the Trading with the Enemy Act to wartime situations (Act of 28 December 1977, Pub L No 95-223, title I, 91 Stat 1625, 50 USC §§ 1701–1706 (1994), and the withdrawal of the Soviet Pipeline Regulations).

[127] ibid (citing the enactment of the International Emergency Economic Powers Act, upon which the restrictions on foreign activities of US banks in Iran was premised, and the extension of the Export Administration Act of 1969 to prohibit exports from any country of goods or technology exported by foreign subsidiaries of US corporations, by the same Act of 28 December 1977 cited above, effectuated by the Iranian Assets Control Regulations, 31 CFR 535.329 (1980), and the Soviet Pipeline Regulations, 47 Fed Reg 27,250–2 (1982)).

[128] eg Blakesley (above n 85) 41 (pointing out that 'non-Anglo-American jurists have no historical or theoretical background or frame of reference from which to understand the term').

disputes, European courts may nevertheless use a concept that is related to comity: the private international law concept of *ordre public*. This concept, however, differs considerably from comity.[129] Before we analyse European uneasiness with interest-balancing, it may be useful to explain how *ordre public* operates, and how it relates to the concept of jurisdiction.

As Juenger writes, '[w]hile public policy involves the *lex fori* to ward off undesirable foreign law, comity is used to curtail unreasonable impositions of *forum* law'.[130] Comity thus serves as a doctrine of jurisdictional *restraint*, while *ordre public* serves as a doctrine of jurisdictional *expansion*. Using *ordre public*, European courts indeed apply domestic law to transnational disputes if the application of foreign law through conflict of laws rules would produce a result inconsistent with the fundamental principles of the political, moral, or economic order of the forum State. A second difference between comity and *ordre public* could be directly gathered from this definition: the concept of *ordre public* authorizes a European forum State to apply its laws to a transnational situation with strong and even stronger links to another State. Unlike comity, the concept of *ordre public* leaves no room for weighing links or sovereign interests. The concept may result in the application of European laws to a transnational situation, even if the interests of the foreign State outweigh these of the forum State. Under comity and the rule of reason, however, the interests of the foreign State and those of the forum State are balanced, and (the law of) the State with the stronger interest will prevail over (the law of) the State with the weaker interest.[131] Admittedly, the forum State's courts may suffer from a pro-forum bias and tend to underestimate the weight of the foreign State's interests. Yet such does not subtract from the conceptual basis of the rule of reason: the State with the weaker interest ought to defer to the State with the stronger interest.

Because courts do not weigh sovereign interests but apply the laws of the forum as soon as the forum's interests are jeopardized, an increased potential for international conflict could be inferred from the application of the European *ordre public* exception. Nevertheless, *ordre public* is rather used as a *defensive* legal device so as not to apply another State's (extraterritorial) laws, than as an aggressive tool to expand the scope *ratione loci* of the forum State's laws to foreign situations. As European States shy away from projecting their extraterritorial regulatory power abroad in the first place, and do not grant private plaintiffs the right to bring claims in regulatory cases to the same extent as the United States does ('the

---

[129] Contra, without further elaboration, however: Mann (above n 7) 23.

[130] FK Juenger, 'Constitutional Control of Extraterritoriality?: A Comment on Professor Brilmayer's Appraisal', (1987) 50 Law & Contemp Probs 39, 45.

[131] Cf A Bianchi, 'Extraterritoriality and Export Controls: Some Remarks on the Alleged Antinomy Between European and U.S. Approaches', (1992) 35 GYIL 366, 377 (arguing that 'traditional single-aspect methods of conflict of laws resolution, still prevailing in continental Europe, even if in a better position to provide certainty and predictability, would fall short of doing justice in many cases').

private attorney-general'), the concept of *ordre public* will, despite its inherent inflexibility, ordinarily not lead to the unwarranted expansion of State power.

2. Explaining European uneasiness with interest-balancing

European uneasiness with (judicial) comity is rooted in a belief that the courts are not diplomats and ought not to be granted too much discretionary power on the basis of such a fuzzy concept as comity, lest the State become a *'gouvernement des juges'*.[132] In Europe, courts are not expected to balance sovereign interests, but to apply mechanical and 'certain' jurisdictional rules (such as rules based on the defendant's nationality or domicile).[133] It is in this context that one has to understand Professor Brownlie's categorization of jurisdictional reasonableness or interest-balancing as an 'unhelpfully vague' concept.[134]

Continental Europe's uneasiness with comity as a discretionary concept may hark back to the French Revolution, an ideological watershed that common law countries never experienced. In the revolutionaries' view, the courts of the *Ancien Régime* had arrogated too much power to themselves, thereby sidelining the (representatives of the) people. Therefore, as Pearce has described, '[r]evolutionary laws were passed explicitly forbidding the judiciary to take part in the exercise of legislative power, or, at the risk of a judge's forfeiture of office, to interfere in the operation of public administration'.[135] The judiciary was supposed to be the *'bouche de la loi'*: it applied the laws enacted and codified by the legislature. For our analysis of jurisdiction, this implies that the courts were *not* authorized to disregard rules of jurisdiction adopted by the legislature, by, for instance, invoking the weighing of different interests involved in a dispute. Taking into account the interests of foreign sovereigns was considered as anathema to the nationalistic ethos of the time, an ethos that considered the people united in a territorially delimited 'nation' as the sovereign lawgiver.[136] As of today, the revolutionary legacy is discernible in EC Regulation 44/2001, which sets forth bright-line rules for

---

[132] Although Americans are more at ease with judicial interest-balancing, they may at times also deplore it, but often because it does not confer legal certainty rather than because it gives judges too much power. See, eg criticizing the doctrine of *forum non conveniens*, which involves a balancing of private and public interests in order to determine an appropriate adjudicatory forum: *Gilbert*, 330 US 501, 516 (1947) (Black, J, dissenting) (stating that '[t]he broad and indefinite discretion' granted by this doctrine 'will inevitably procude a complex of close and indistinguishable decisions from which accurate prediction of the proper forum will become difficult, if not impossible').

[133] It may be noted that a mechanical reliance on nationality or domicile may, in the absence of any other connecting factor to the forum, at times be even more exorbitant than US reliance on judicial discretion to establish jurisdiction. Pearce (above n 5) 562–5.

[134] I Brownlie, *Principles of Public International Law* (4th edn 1990) 308. Also Bianchi (above n 3) 74, 85.

[135] The unavailability of judicial review for instance attests to the secondary role that the courts were expected to play in the continental State's institutional design. Pearce (above n 5) 567.

[136] ibid 570.

judicial jurisdiction and does not, on its face, allow judicial comity to play a role as a discretionary concept.[137]

While comity-based interest-balancing may not dovetail well with the mechanical nature of the exercise of jurisdiction in Europe, its underlying aim, neutrally identifying, in the terminology of Savigny, the 'seat' of a transnational legal relationship (ie, a classical aim of private international law), may nonetheless ring a bell with Europeans.[138] The balancing of (territorial or personal) connections in order to identify the proper law may surely be palatable to a European legal mind, although possibly, black-letter legal guarantees will need to embody these connections.

However, the balancing of *interests* as a means of identifying the seat of a transnational legal relationship, as contemplated by § 403 of the Restatement, may be off-limits for Europeans. In Savignist theory, the proper law is identified through an analysis of private connections rather than sovereign interests.[139] The emphasis on interests by § 403 has therefore been considered by Professor Mann to represent a radical departure from the classical European jurisdictional framework of reasonableness based on what he terms a 'sufficiently close legal connection', usually territoriality or nationality, and which disregards anything short of genuine contacts,[140] such as 'mere political, economic, commercial or social interests'.[141] For scholars of classical international law, schooled in the European tradition, interest-balancing is not an acceptable legal tool, because it involves political rather than legal arguments.[142] As Mann put it:

The so-called balancing of interests is nothing but a political consideration: it is not the subjective or political interest, but the objective test of the closeness of connection, of a sufficiently weighty point of contact between the facts and their legal assessment that is relevant. The lawyer balances contacts rather than interests.[143]

---

[137] ibid 577–8 (arguing that it is 'likely that the relatively smooth functioning of [EC Regulation 44/2001] will make European courts and commentators grow ever more wary and weary of the American common-law approach to judicial jurisdiction of which comity is so emblematic', and that European judges may conclude that Regulation 44/2001 'better serve[s] the ends of systematic harmony and fairness that constitute comity's ultimate goal').

[138] FC von Savigny, *System of Modern Roman Law*, vol 8 (1849) (translated by W Guthrie, 1869), 89. Cf GB Born, 'A Reappraisal of the Extraterritorial Reach of U.S. Law', (1992) 24 Law & Pol Int'l Bus 1, 84 (1992) (arguing that European private international law frequently takes similar approaches as the Restatement (Second) of Conflict of Laws and the Restatement (Third) of Foreign Relations Laws).

[139] Bischoff and Kovar (above n 37) 713 (stating that 'la règle de conflit classique du type savignien est essentiellement fondée sur la nature du rapport de droit litigieux. Or cette considération, si elle n'est pas négligeable, reste cependant accessoire lorsqu'il s'agit en définitive de délimiter des souverainetés').

[140] FA Mann, 'The Doctrine of Jurisdiction in International Law', (1964-I) 111 RCADI 1, 44 ('The problem, properly defined, involves the search for the *State or States whose contact with the facts* is such as to make the allocation of legislative competence just and reasonable') (emphasis added).

[141] Mann (above n 7) 29.   [142] ibid 30–1.

[143] ibid 31. Also Bianchi (above n 3) 91 (stating that 'international customary international law makes the legality of extraterritorial jurisdictional claims dependent on the existence of an effective and significant connection between the regulating state and the activity to be regulated').

Under a *contact-*, rather than *interest*-based conception of jurisdiction, courts and regulators examine whether the defendant's contacts with the forum are sufficient and voluntary. The exercise of jurisdiction over the defendant is then grounded upon the defendant waiving the protection afforded by its own country's laws ('waiver by conduct').[144] In spite of Mann's repudiation of interest-balancing, the differences between Mann's European concept of jurisdiction and the US concept of jurisdiction should not be overstated. In fact, Europeans might subscribe to the grounds of jurisdiction enshrined in § 402 of the Restatement, as well as to quite a number of connecting factors of the rule of reason set forth in § 403. What they may not subscribe to is the balancing of interests included in the US-style rule of reason. For Europeans, the reasonableness, and on that basis possibly the lawfulness, of a jurisdictional claim is 'dependent on the existence of an *effective and significant connection* between the regulating state and the activity to be regulated',[145] rather than on the existence of regulatory *interests* which the regulating State may have.

The distinction between 'connection' and 'interest' is, at any rate, a subtle one. Interest may be defined as 'a common concern, especially in politics or business',[146] whereas both connection and contact denote 'a link or relationship' (with 'contact' possibly denoting a 'physical' relationship).[147] It is difficult to see how a State can be concerned about a situation if that situation has no link or relationship with it. As pointed out in subsection 2.2.c, States will ordinarily refrain from regulating a situation if they are not affected by it, ie, if they do not have a relationship with it. Consequently, if a State has an interest in regulating a situation, that situation affects that State, or put differently, that State has a connection with it. Therefore, more useful than brandishing the divisive words 'connection' and 'interest' probably is ascertaining *what* connections and *what* interests ought to be taken into account in a reasonableness analysis.

3. EC courts and comity/reasonableness in competition cases

In subsection 5.3.a, it has been explained that the rule of reason as set forth in § 403 of the US Restatement is derived from US jurisprudence on the reach of the antitrust Sherman Act. Because of the antitrust origins of the rule of reason, it is appropriate to examine whether, and to what extent, *European* courts hearing antitrust (competition) cases have heeded comity and reasonableness in assessing the reach of EC (and EC Member States') competition law.

---

[144] X (above n 88) 1322–3 (1985). This test of legislative or prescriptive jurisdiction comes close to the test that US courts employ so as to establish personal jurisdiction, be it that the emphasis in the former case lies on the *defendant's activities'* contacts with the forum rather than on the *defendant's* contacts.

[145] Bianchi (above n 3) 90 (original emphasis).

[146] J Pearsall, *Oxford Concise English Dictionary* (10th edn 2001) 737.

[147] ibid 302 and 306.

Clearly, European courts' unfamiliarity with interest-balancing may not bode well for the application of the rule of reason in antitrust proceedings with a transnational aspect. This unfamiliarity has indeed, not surprisingly, translated in the repudiation of comity or reasonableness in two high-profile EC competition cases, the *Wood Pulp* cartel case (European Court of Justice, 1988) and the *Gencor* merger case (European Court of First Instance, 1999). It will be shown, that, nevertheless, EC antitrust regulators may implicitly apply comity when assessing the appropriateness of initiating proceedings against foreign defendants—although they might not do so out of legal obligation. In addition, European doctrine seems to be largely in favour of an encompassing antitrust comity or reasonableness test.

4. *Wood Pulp and Gencor*

In *Wood Pulp*, the European Commission had imposed fines on a number of non-EC suppliers of wood pulp, as well as two of their trade associations, on the ground that they had fixed the price of wood pulp sales to purchasers in the Common Market. The European Court of Justice (ECJ) eventually upheld the Commission's jurisdiction over these suppliers' anticompetitive agreements on the basis of the 'implementation' doctrine.[148] If the Commission were to have jurisdiction over all agreements that were implemented, through sales, within the EC, irrespective of the possibly strong foreign interests involved, the reach of EC competition law could become overbroad. Comity and reasonableness could, as in the US, serve to limit this reach. The ECJ, however, held that heeding concerns of international comity in considering the reach of what was then Article 85 of the EC Treaty would 'amount...to calling in question the Community's jurisdiction to apply its competition rules to conduct such as that found in this case'.[149] As Alford has also argued, the ECJ in *Wood Pulp* in fact only examined whether the EC is authorized to exercise jurisdiction under the classical principles of international law, the territorial principle in particular (ie the analysis of section 402 of the US Restatement), but not whether the EC ought to exercise its jurisdiction in view of the interests of other States involved (ie the analysis of section 403 of the Restatement).[150] It is precisely a comity or reasonableness analysis that addresses this normative question: in case several States could exercise their

---

[148] Section 3.5.

[149] *Wood Pulp* [1988] ECR 5244. Cf *IBM v Commission*, [1981] ECR 2639 (ruling that comity should not be considered until after a decision had been made).

[150] RP Alford, 'The Extraterritorial Application of Antitrust Laws: The United States and European Community Approaches', (1992) 33 Va J Int'l L 1, 43. J Dutheil de la Rochère, 'Réflexions sur l'application «extra-territoriale» du droit communautaire', in X, *Mélanges M Virally. Le droit international au service de la paix, de la justice et du développement* (1991) 282, 293, however, argued that the Court did not find a concurring jurisdiction which was better founded than the Commission's jurisdiction ('Dans l'affaire «Pâte de bois», la Cour ne s'est pas attachée a examiner le principe de modération parce qu'elle n'a pas discerné l'existence d'une prétention de compétence concurrente susceptible d'être mieux fondée que la compétence du droit communautaire telle qu'elle l'avait affirmée').

(concurrent) jurisdiction, which State ought to defer to the other State in light of all (sovereign) interests involved?

Unlike the ECJ, however, the European *Commission* had previously seemed willing to apply comity or reasonableness to competition cases. In *Eastern Aluminium* (1985), for instance, it held that:

[t]he exercise of jurisdiction . . . does not require any of the undertakings concerned to act in any way contrary to the requirements of their domestic laws, nor would the application of Community law adversely affect important interests of a non-member State. Such an interest would have to be so important as to prevail over the fundamental interest of the Community that competition within the common market is not distorted . . . [151]

As the Commission inquired into the interests of non-member States, it espoused comity.[152]

Eastern Aluminium appeared to recognize that the EC is not only precluded from exercising its antitrust jurisdiction in case so doing would cause a 'true conflict' with foreign legislation, ie, when one State compels conduct that another States prohibits, or vice versa (this is in effect the US *Hartford Fire* approach, see subsection 5.4.b), but *also* if important interests of a foreign State would be affected and these interests outweighed the interests of the EC (the approach of section 403 of the Restatement).[153] The EC's two-pronged approach of *Eastern Aluminium* eventually yielded, however, to the ECJ's *Wood Pulp* approach. This approach betrays hostility to comity and may be largely synonymous with the *Hartford Fire* 'true conflict' or foreign sovereign compulsion doctrine. In the ECJ's view, comity would indeed only come into play, if at all, when foreign laws compelled anticompetitive conduct and where EC laws prohibited such conduct, or vice versa.[154] By terminating the comity/reasonableness analysis there, the

---

[151] European Commission, *Eastern Aluminium* [1985] OJ L 92/37, 48.

[152] Pearce (above n 5) 576. It may be noted that in a 1981 case before the ECJ, *IBM v Commission*, IBM, a corporation with headquarters in the United States, maintained that a number of measures taken by the Commission 'offend[ed] against the international legal principles of comity between nations and non-interference in internal affairs, principles which ought to have been taken into consideration by the Commission before it adopted the measures in question because the conduct of IBM which is the subject of complaint occurred in the main outside the Community, in particular in the United States of America where it is also the subject of legal proceedings'. The US Assistant Attorney General in charge of the Antitrust Division also reportedly denounced the extraterritorial effects of the Commission's order. Wall Street Journal, 31 March 1982, p 1, cited in DF Vagts, 'A Turnabout in Extraterritoriality', (1982) 76 AJIL 591, 593. The ECJ did eventually not pronounce itself on the comity argument, and dismissed the case as inadmissible. Case 60/81, *IBM v Commission* [1981] ECR 2639.

[153] It has however been noted that if, under *Eastern Aluminium*, 'a third country's interest must be "so important as to prevail over the fundamental interest of the Community that competiton within the Common Market is not distorted", there does not seem to be much room for taking either international law or third country's interests into account'. Bourgeois (above n 64) 114.

[154] The defendants in *Wood Pulp* invoked this doctrine, pursuant to which 'where two States have jurisdiction to lay down and enforce rules and the effect of those rules is that a person finds himself subject to contradictory orders as to the conduct he must adopt, each State is obliged to exercise its jurisdiction with moderation'. The Court replied to this defence that that there was no

Court undeniably espoused a very narrow understanding of comity/reasonableness.[155] This understanding nonetheless dovetails well with traditional European uneasiness with 'political' interest-balancing.[156] Indeed, the presence of a 'true' jurisdictional conflict is easy and mechanically identifiable, and does not require the court to genuinely balance the regulatory interests that different States might have in exercising their jurisdiction or not. This approach, which was later also taken by the US Supreme Court in the *Hartford Fire* case,[157] is a far cry from the broad rule of reason set forth in § 403 of the Restatement.

By the same token, in the field of EC merger control, comity was largely dismissed by European courts. In the 1999 *Gencor* merger case, in which South Africa had a strong interest, the European Court of First Instance held that it was not necessary to consider whether a rule of comity existed in international law, since it would suffice to note

that there was no conflict between the course of action required by the South African Government and that required by the Community, given that [...] the South African competition authorities simply concluded that the concentration agreement did not give rise to any competition policy concerns, without requiring that such an agreement be entered into.[158]

need 'to enquire into the existence in international law of such a rule since it suffices to observe that the conditions for its application are in any event not satisfied. There is not, in this case, any contradiction between the conduct required by the United States and that required by the Community since the [American] Webb Pomerene Act merely exempts the conclusion of export cartels from the application of United States anti-trust laws but does not require such cartels to be concluded'. ECJ, *Wood Pulp*, §§ 19–20. Cf European Commission, *Aluminium Imports from Eastern Europe* [1985] OJ L 92/1, holding that there was no reason to restrain the exercise of jurisdiction of Eastern European aluminium producers on comity grounds, as the parties were not being required to act contrary to their domestic law and the application of Community law did not adversely affect important interests of a non-member State.

[155] This narrow understanding was criticized by the doctrine. eg J Dutheil de la Rochère (above n 150) 294 (stating that in *Wood Pulp*, the ECJ should have more explicitly balanced the regulatory interests of the EC with the importance of procedures exempting export cartels from US anti-trust laws under the US Webb-Pomerene Act); L Idot, note *Wood Pulp* (1989) Rev trim dr europ 345, 355; Kaffanke (above n 45) 134–5; M.Schödermeier, 'Die vermiedene Auswirkung', (1989) 39 WuW 21, 28. However, in support of the ECJ's comity-unfriendly approach: H-W Knebel, 'Die Extraterritorialität des Europäischen Kartellrechts', (1991) 2 EuZW 265, 274. The need for a genuine comity analysis was already advanced in European doctrine *before* the 1972 *Dyestuffs* case (Case 48/69, *ICI v Commission (Dyestuffs)* [1972] ECR 619). B Goldman, 'Les effects juridiques extra-territoriaux de la politique de la concurrence', (1972) Rev marché commun 612, 617 (stating that 'l'application extra-territoriale des règles de fond du droit communautaire de la concurrence peut exiger une coordination avec l'application de règles de ces Etats, elle-même fondée sur la localisation territoriale de certains des effets des ententes internationales').

[156] Cf I Van Bael and J-F Bellis, *Competition Law of the European Community* (4th edn 2005) 159 ('Possibly, the Court of Justice regards the argument on comity as a political one, which raises no legal restraints on the Commission's power').

[157] eg W Sugden, 'Global Antitrust and the Evolution of an International Standard', (2002) 35 Vand J Transnat'l L 989, 1016 (2002) (stating that 'the United States and the European Union have expanded extraterritoriality at the expense of international comity').

[158] CFI, *Gencor* [1999] ECR 1999, II-00753, § 103, citing ECJ, *Wood Pulp*, § 20.

Interestingly, however, the CFI noted in *Gencor* that 'neither the applicant nor, indeed, the South African Government [...] have shown, beyond making mere statements of principle, in what way the proposed concentration would affect the vital economic and/or commercial interests of the Republic of South Africa'.[159] This consideration may betray a less strict application of the 'true conflict' doctrine, and thus a willingness to conduct a more substantial comity analysis.[160] If, *arguendo*, the proposed concentration had affected 'the vital economic and/or commercial interests' of South Africa, the CFI might have been willing to balance the interests of the Community and of South Africa.[161] Yet whether the CFI would, in the event of South African interests outweighing EC interests, eventually dismiss EC jurisdiction, remains an open question.[162]

5. Implicit reasonableness as applied by the European Commission

As pointed out in the previous subsection, jurisdictional reasonableness came somewhat to the fore in the European Commission's opinion in the *Eastern Aluminium* case. In other cases, however, the Commission has not explicitly applied the rule of reason. Nonetheless, the fact that the Commission does not apply European competition laws to *all* extra-European transactions somehow impinging on EC interests, may suggest the application of some sort of reasonableness rule in EC competition law practice.[163] However, such a rule appears to be deprived of a legal cloak: the Commission may indeed only exercise jurisdiction when such appears reasonable, but it does so *as a matter of discretion*, not out of legal obligation. From a legal perspective, there is no principled fall-back position for European regulators who are willing to apply a wider rule of reason than the true conflict rule hinted

---

[159] CFI, *Gencor*, § 105.

[160] Y van Gerven and L Hoet, '*Gencor*: Some Notes on Transnational Competition Law Issues', (2001) 28(2) Legal Issues of Economic Integration 195, 208–9; FE Gonzalez-Diaz, 'Recent Developments in EC Merger Control Law: The *Gencor* Judgment', (1999) 22(3) W Comp 3, 14.

[161] It could be argued that, in holding that the proposed concentration would not affect the vital economic and/or commercial interests of South Africa, the Court may have wished to distinguish this case from the *Boeing/McDonnell Douglas* case, in which vital US economic and/or commercial interests may have been at stake. L Idot, comment *Gencor*, (2000) JDI 513, 515 ('Implicitement, le Tribunal laisse entendre qu'aucune comparaison ne pouvait être faite avec l'affaire Boeing Mac Donnell Douglas à propos de laquelle les Etats-Unis avaient fermement invoqué des intérêts vitaux relatifs à leur stratégie de défense').

[162] Cf Layton and Parry (above n 63) 322, on the *Gencor* judgment ('[I]t is not clear whether the use of the effects doctrine is always to be considered in itself a proportionate response, or whether individual applications of the doctrine would be open to challenge on proportionality grounds').

[163] Bourgeois (above n 64) 114 ('The Commission does consider itself obliged to have regard to comity when exercising its jurisdiction in competition cases with a foreign element and is better equipped to do so than a court of law'); Van Bael and Bellis (above n 156) 158–9 (stating that, although 'the Commission has preferred to rely on the effects doctrine in its decisions, this does not mean that the Commission turns a blind eye to considerations of comity'). Also Meessen (above n 38) 789–90 (stating, as a general matter, that 'it could very well be concluded that the outcome of most international antitrust conflicts, perhaps of all of them, reflected the multifaceted *Timberlane* approach').

at by the ECJ and the CFI.[164] In Europe, reasonableness appears to be a matter of economic policy-makers assessing the *expediency* of the application of competition law to foreign practices and exercising administrative restraint,[165] rather than of lawyers applying well-established jurisdictional rules, or 'countervailing principles', as Meessen terms them, to limit the reach of antitrust law.[166]

In the United States, by contrast, *legality* may have more leverage in determining reasonableness in international antitrust law, since the US Department of Justice and the Federal Trade Commission are expected to apply a more principled rule of reason as set forth in both agencies' 1995 Antitrust Guidelines for International Operations (a rule of reason which draws on § 403 of the US Restatement).

The fact that reasonableness remains a discretionary concept in Europe is attributable, as described above, to traditional European uneasiness with balancing 'political' interests. In competition matters, it is probably also attributable to the limited availability of private antitrust enforcement in Europe. In the United States, the rule of reason was precisely developed by federal courts in private antitrust suits. While the US government, when bringing suits, often steers a settlement-based course based on non-legal policy considerations,[167] private plaintiffs do not. The US judiciary, being a legal institution and not an economic decision-maker, was therefore in need of a legal framework to deal consistently with these private suits. Almost all attempts at legally defining the contours of international antitrust jurisdiction have been made in the context of private antitrust suits. The enunciation of the rule of reason by the federal courts in *Timberlane* and *Mannington Mills* is no exception. It is notable that, in the wake of these decisions, the 'legalized' rule of reason gradually made its way to the enforcement policy of the US antitrust agencies. The 1987 Restatement gave it a general scope of application in § 415 (ie a scope of application encompassing both private and public antitrust enforcement), and the agencies, influenced by the Restatement, inserted it into their 1995 Guidelines for International Operations. Arguably, without the availability of private antitrust enforcement in the United States, the US framework of international antitrust jurisdiction might have been as undeveloped as it is in Europe.

---

[164] Also Bourgeois (above n 163) 128 ('[T]he Commission is bound to give to [the international law principle of non-interference] and to [the balance-of-interests] test a more precise content. It will probably do so on a case by case basis. Apart from the legal uncertainty which this approach implies, it is unlikely to prevent conflicts of jurisdiction with third countries').

[165] Meessen (above n 38) 797 (arguing that 'as an instrument of conflict avoidance, administrative restraint is more important than the choice of connecting factors', citing German, Swiss, EC and US governmental practice).

[166] ibid at 797–8. Cf Alford (above n 150) 29–30 (arguing that the European Commission has never actually undertaken a rule-of-reason-informed balancing approach).

[167] Meessen (above n 38) 795 (describing the complexity of techniques of settlement and diversity of results achieved).

6. Interest-balancing by German courts

Within Europe, only in German competition law does interest-balancing appear to be seen as a *legal obligation*. In the 1983 *Morris/Rothmans* merger case, the Federal Cartel Office and the *Kammergericht* held that the international law principle of non-intervention and the principle of abuse of jurisdiction required a balancing of interests.[168] The former would require balancing sovereign interests, whereas the latter would require balancing both sovereign and private interests, be it that only in case of 'crass disproportionateness' between the interests involved abuse of jurisdiction could be found.

7. European doctrine

Unlike EC courts, continental European doctrine, influenced by US doctrine and practice, has been remarkably enthusiastic about the balancing of interests or connections so as to solve problems of concurrent economic jurisdiction. Notably Meessen, Kaffanke, and Schuster in Germany,[169] and Bischoff and Kovar in France,[170] have advocated the use of the jurisdictional rule of reason (although they may believe that the rule of reason is not a hard and fast rule of international law). Bischoff and Kovar even pointed out that it is 'l'essence de la fonction première du juge, celle de dire le Droit (jurisdictio),'[171] and that '[i]l appartient au droit international de s'efforcer de résoudre les conflits susceptibles de naître d'une...pluralité de compétences.'[172] In contrast, English authors, spearheaded by Mann, whose views have been presented in subsection 5.4.c.2, have been largely hostile to interest-balancing. It may nonetheless be argued that this hostility actually masks a hostility to the effects doctrine rather than to a rule of reason. Lowe, for instance, rejected interest-balancing as a workable method, yet supported it 'in proper cases (i.e. cases of concurrent jurisdiction)'.[173] By all means, in European doctrine, opposition to a flexible, non-mechanical rule of reason is on the retreat.

---

[168] BKartA, WuW/E 1943, 1953 (*Morris/Rothmans*); KG, Case Kart 16/82, *Philip Morris Inc* v *Bundeskartellamt* [1984] ECC 393 (Kammergericht) (FRG), KG WuW/E OLG 3051.

[169] Meessen (above n 47); Schuster (above n 7); Kaffanke (above n 45) 146 (stating that section 403 of the Restatement 'weist sie doch in die richtige Richtung und lässt sich als Ausgangspunkt der weiteren Entwicklung ansehen').

[170] Bischoff and Kovar (above n 37) 675.

[171] ibid 712.   [172] ibid.

[173] AV Lowe, 'The Problems of Extraterritorial Jurisdiction: Economic Sovereignty and the Search for a Solution', (1985) 34 ICLQ 724, 746. The rule of reason set forth in section 403 of the Restatement only becomes operative when jurisdiction has been established under the classical grounds of jurisdiction in section 402, which include the territoriality principle. Section 403 solves competency conflicts resulting from concurrent jurisdiction based on that principle (conduct- and effects-based jurisdiction). It is the effects doctrine which Lowe takes issue with, rather than interest-balancing. He thus argues that there was not an acceptable basis of jurisdiction in the first place under section 402. ibid 735.

5.5 The Jurisdictional Rule of Reason as a Norm of International Law

Is the jurisdictional rule of reason indeed a norm of international law, as believed by the drafters of the Restatement (Third) of US Foreign Relations Law? In this final section of Chapter 5, it will be argued that, given the absence of uniform State practice and of *opinio juris*, the rule of reason does not qualify as a norm of customary international law (5.5.a). It will be submitted, however, that, despite a dearth of State practice as to the application of the rule of reason, the general principles of international law, discussed in section 5.2 (eg proportionality, abuse of rights) may subsume more specific principles of jurisdiction that could inform a practice of jurisdictional restraint or reasonableness on the part of States (5.5.b). Even if reasonableness were to be characterized as a general principle of law, with the attendant obligations which it imposes on States, it remains to be seen, however, how such a principle should, *in practice*, be operationalized. Different methods could be discerned: according right of way to the first-seized State, weighing the contacts and interests of the States involved (ie the method advocated by the Restatement), or performing an efficiency and justice analysis (5.5.c). As will be elaborated on in Chapter 6, this study prefers the latter method, but attempts to integrate elements of the second, by giving the State with the strongest connections and interests the primary right to exercise jurisdiction.

(a) Customary international law

In order for custom to come into being, a 'virtually uniform' and 'settled' practice that has gained 'sufficient expression in legal form' should be discerned.[174] In addition, this practice ought to be supported by an *opinio juris*, ie, by an international opinion that the practice is also legally binding. In light of the foregoing analysis, one cannot but conclude that, *de lege lata*, there is no uniformity of State practice regarding the reasonableness of jurisdictional assertions. Even when States, notably regulators (as opposed to courts), have exercised jurisdiction reasonably, they have failed in 'making known to other states to collaborate in the formation of customary law'.[175] When States exercise jurisdiction reasonably, they appear to do so as a matter of discretion, not out of legal obligation. Reasonableness, if any could be discerned, appears to be 'soft law' that need not guide future State behaviour as a matter of law.

---

[174] ICJ, *North Sea Continental Shelf*, ICJ Rep 43–4 (1969).
[175] H Meijers, 'On International Customary International Law in the Netherlands', in IF Dekker and HG Post, eds, *On the Foundations and Sources of International Law* (2003) 88.

Massey argued, however, that '[b]y the time the Restatement (Fourth) is published...there may be enough state practice supported by *opinio juris*, by the United States and others, to support the reasonableness requirement as customary law'.[176] He pointed out that the very adoption of § 403 may contribute to the development of a reasonableness norm, as the writings of learned authors—which the drafters of the Restatement undeniably were—are, in keeping with Article 38 of the Statute of the International Court of Justice, a 'subsidiary means for the determination of rules of law'.[177] Since the adoption of the Restatement (Third), § 403 has indeed been cited by US courts[178] and academia, and even by the US Government.[179] In due course, if foreign States also start to apply a rule of reason, the customary international law nature of § 403 may prove to be a self-fulfilling prophecy: in spite of there being no evidence that § 403 reflected customary law at the moment the Restatement (Third) was adopted in 1987, its wide-ranging influence may vindicate its initially *de lege ferenda* normative claim.

As we write, however, the insufficiency of State practice and the absence of *opinio juris* with respect to the rule of reason—in fact, only the 1982 German *Morris/Rothmans* decision and the 2004 US Supreme Court's *Empagran* decision could be cited as supporting such a rule—may inexorably lead to the conclusion that there is simply no clearly discernible norm of customary international law subjecting a State's jurisdictional assertions to a reasonableness requirement.

---

[176] Massey (above n 117) 445.

[177] ibid 442. Also Restatement, § 103(2)(c).

[178] ibid 438, citing *United States v Vasquez-Valesco*, 15 F 3d 833, 840–1 (9th Cir 1994) (holding that section 403 'has emerged as a principle of international law', and using it for purposes of the *Charming Betsy* canon of statutory construction); 170 BR 800 (SDNY 1994); *United States v Felix-Gutierrez*, 940 F 2d 1200, 1204 (9th Cir 1991) ('[C]ourts generally look to international law principles to ensure that an extraterritorial application of United States laws is "reasonable"'); *United States v Juda*, 46 F 3d 961, 967 ('We look to [international law] principles to ensure that an extraterritorial application of United States law is "reasonable"'); *United States v Javino*, 960 F 2d 1137, 1142–3 (2d Cir 1992) ('Though Congress may prescribe laws concerning conduct outside of the territorial boundaries of the United States "that has or is intended to have substantial effect" within the United States, it may not regulate such conduct "when the exercise of...jurisdiction is unreasonable", *Restatement* § 403(1)') (citations omitted); *Boureslan v Aramco*, 857 F 2d 1014, 1024 (5th Cir 1988) (King, J, dissenting) ('[B]ecause section 403 is a principle of international law, a statute may not be construed to violate the principle absent an explicit, affirmative expression of congressional intent compelling that construction'); *Neely v Club Med Management Services, Inc*, 63 F 3d 166, 183 (3d Cir 1995) ('[W]e "rely on the Restatement (Third) of Foreign Relations Law [including the jurisdictional provisions] for the relevant principles of international law"'). It may be noted, in this context, that the sections 18 and 40 of the 1965 Restatement of Foreign Relations Law (Second) were the sections of the Restatement mostly frequently cited by the courts (remarks by Lowenfeld (above n 85) 191).

[179] Department of State, Office of the Legal Adviser, Legal Considerations Regarding Title III of the Libertad Bill, reprinted in 141 Cong Rec S15106 (12 October 1995) ('[I]nternational law... requires a state to apply its laws to extra-territorial conduct only when doing so would be reasonable in view of certain customary factors'). Massey, however, argued that this memorandum does not constitute *opinio juris* as it is not an official position of the US Government and was only intended for intragovernmental policymaking. Massey (above n 117) 439.

(b) General principles of law

The rule of reason may not qualify as a norm of customary international law because uniform State practice and *opinio juris* seem to be lacking. However, as shown in section 5.2, there are a substantial number of principles of international law, such as non-intervention, proportionality, abuse of rights, equity, and genuine connection, that may be seen as buttressing an international rule of reason informed by interest-balancing. It could therefore be argued that the rule of reason is, short of being a norm of customary international law, a general principle of international law.

It is widely accepted that 'general principles of law recognized by civilized nations' are a source of international law.[180] While general principles will admittedly not be recognized in the absence of at least some supportive State practice, they are, unlike customary norms, not in need of *uniform* State practice. As Brownlie has noted, general principles of international law are 'primarily abstractions from a mass of rules and have been so long and so generally accepted as to be no longer *directly* connected with State practice'.[181] They may derive their legal character mainly from States' conviction that they represent law.

The question is whether the *jurisdictional* rule of reason *qua* general principle of international law has indeed 'long and generally been accepted as law'. In the antitrust field, some courts have, to a certain extent, relied on such general principles as non-intervention, proportionality, and abuse of law in order to restrain the exercise of jurisdiction. Yet other courts and enforcement authorities appear to have taken the view that jurisdiction legally obtains as soon as the requirements for the application of a permissive principle of jurisdiction are satisfied, both in the criminal and the regulatory field. EC courts, for instance, reason that the principle of non-intervention is respected on the sole basis of the territoriality of the implementation or the effects of a foreign anticompetitive agreement. In the field of criminal law, while most States have restrained their jurisdictional assertions by requiring, for instance, double criminality, territorial presence of the perpetrator, or initiation by the highest prosecutor as a matter of domestic law, there is no evidence that these restrictions were informed by general principles of international law requiring States to exercise their jurisdiction reasonably.

Confronted with this uneven practice, some authors have argued that there is no established principle of reasonableness which delimits spheres of jurisdiction. Instead, 'each state's regulatory interests seem to set the minimum requirements for a basis of . . . jurisdiction', with States choosing certain connecting factors, not as a matter of law, but as a matter of 'enlightened self-interest' and 'voluntary self-limitation'.[182] As regulatory interests differ from case to case, advocates of legal

---

[180] Article 38(1)(c) of the ICJ Statute.
[181] Brownlie (above n 134) 19.
[182] Meessen (above n 38) 800–1. Also Idot (above n 155) 355 (stating that a 'principe d'autolimitation ou de self-restraint . . . deviendrait d'application générale'); Bischoff and Kovar

certainty in matters of extraterritorial jurisdiction will face an uphill battle in formulating rules of reason with a general scope of application. Having picked up the thread of comity from where Ulrik Huber had left it in the seventeenth century, one may be compelled to admit that the rule of reason is, and may remain, a discretionary concept rather than a genuine norm or principle of international law.[183]

However, the fact that practice is uneven does not necessarily affect the legal force of general principles of law. As noted, uniformity of State practice is not an element constitutive of a general principle of law. Instead, the yardstick appears to be the 'expression in a legal form' of certain non-legal (moral, economic, humanitarian, political . . .) considerations.[184] It is to be noted, in addition, that a principle of law will be more readily identified when it could be situated within the existing legal framework, eg because it is linked to existing principles of law, or may be seen as an application of those principles in a specific context.[185] In section 5.2 of this study, a number of existing principles of international law that could usefully inform a principle of reasonableness have been discussed. Although these principles have not specifically been applied to the law of jurisdiction, the fluid nature of general principles makes it arguably possible to deduce specific principles of jurisdiction, in particular the duty to reasonably exercise jurisdiction, from the more general principles discussed above, such as the obligation not to abuse rights (subsection 5.2.d) or to apply them in a proportionate manner (subsection 5.2.e). It is indeed submitted that the said general principles of international law, while hitherto often applied to other fields of international law, could subsume the specific principles applicable to the law of jurisdiction. These specific principles are in turn informed by non-legal considerations, such as efficiency and welfare analyses (economic considerations), justice imperatives (moral considerations), or national sovereignty concerns (political considerations). It is therefore argued that reasonableness could be considered as a *legal* principle, albeit a vague one, with which States have to comply when asserting jurisdiction. Characterizing the jurisdictional principle of reasonableness as a principle of international law, with

(above n 137) 712 (speaking of 'autolimitation'); U Draetta, 'The International Jurisdiction of the EU Commission in the Merger Control Area', (2000) RDAI 201, 204 (stating that public international law does not contain unequivocal criteria for determining the extent of the national jurisdictions and that it only requires compliance with good faith principles).

[183] Also PC Mavroidis and DJ Neven, 'Some Reflections on Extraterritoriality in International Economic Law: A Law and Economics Analysis', *Mélanges en hommage à Michel Waelbroeck*, II (1999), 1297, 1322.

[184] eg in a human rights context: B Simma and P Alston, 'The Sources of Human Rights Law: Custom, *Jus Cogens* and General Principles', (1992) Australian Yearbook of International Law 82, 102 (submitting that 'what is required for the establishment of human rights obligations *qua* general principles . . . is not equated with State practice but is rather seen as a variety of ways in which moral and humanitarian considerations find a more direct and spontaneous "expression in legal form"').

[185] P Westerman and M Wissink, 'Rechtsgeleerdheid als rechtswetenschap', (2008) Nederlands Juristenblad 503, 504 (arguing that the legal scientist attempts to describe and interpret a new legal development by making use of existing legal principles and categories, and that consistency and coherence of the system of law are central to the legal discipline).

the attendant obligations imposed on States, may then confer sorely needed stability on international relations.[186]

The question may be asked, nonetheless, whether, in case the rule of reason were indeed endowed with international normativity, this makes any difference *in practice*. Put differently, is an internationally binding rule of reason in fact useful, in terms of conferring international stability?

In reality, the workings of power in international law might actually reduce such a rule to a legal shell, deprived of genuine normative content. While Slaughter has hailed the breakthrough of the interest-balancing test as a 'shift from a focus on power to a focus on interests' in the practice of extraterritorial jurisdiction,[187] State interests are, in fact, multifarious in nature and are hard to capture by formal jurisdictional criteria.[188] More mundane concerns of political and economic loss or expansion of power often masquerade as 'objective' legal grounds, such as factors determining jurisdictional reasonableness that are invoked so as to oppose or justify jurisdictional assertions. The problem with the reasonableness factors set forth for instance in § 403 of the Restatement as legal grounds under international law is that they are so malleable as to render them non-criteria in practice. Indeed, almost any jurisdictional assertion could be defended or opposed by invoking one or more reasonableness factors.

Accordingly, a requirement of reasonableness under international law may in fact fail to restrain the exercise of jurisdiction. Such a requirement may, moreover, discredit the very system of international law. In the current decentralized system of assessing the legality and reasonableness of jurisdictional assertions, States ascertain for themselves whether an assertion is reasonable. Given this system, it may be rather fanciful to think that States will perform an entirely objective analysis of all relevant interests.

(c) The unfinished quest for reasonableness

This study refuses to embrace a defeatist approach, however. It acknowledges that the current system of jurisdiction is not satisfactory, since it allows several States to claim regulatory rights over one and the same situation. This

---

[186] Cf DF Vagts, 'International Relations Looks at Customary International Law: A Traditionalist's Defence', (2004) 15 EJIL 1031, 1040 ('[T]he awareness that a pattern of state behaviour has settled into a rule of law introduces a new element into the situation, tending to make the pattern more stable and reliable').

[187] A-M Slaughter, 'Liberal International Relations Theory and International Economic Law', (1995) 10 Am U J Int'l L & Pol'y 717, 735–6 (arguing that '[f]rom a Liberal perspective, this focus on interests is likely to be more fruitful than a straightforward assertion of power at resolving the underlying conflict', while emphasizing the need to untie the rule of reason from territory and physical power).

[188] Meessen (above n 38) 791 (arguing that 'whether [foreign interests] are adversely affected would depend on how the foreign government happens to view its interests at any given moment [is] a matter that surely escapes any prior description in abstract terms').

may result in overregulation, which is harmful to the individuals over whom jurisdiction is exercised, and harmful to international relations. It is harmful to individuals, because these may be encumbered by several regulatory, at times contradictory, orders. It is harmful to international relations, because one State may want to regulate a transnational situation which another State precisely doess *not* want to regulate. Therefore, the quest for reasonableness deserves support.

One easy solution of the jurisdictional conundrum is according right of way to the State which addresses the situation first in time. This first-seized jurisdiction rule may nonetheless yield unjust results, and it is therefore proposed here to discard it. In the criminal law, it may translate in the jurisdictional claims of the State that first issues an arrest warrant prevailing over the claims of other States that have an interest in prosecution. The former State may, however, have a much more tenuous link to the situation, eg in the case of universal jurisdiction *in absentia*, than the latter States, eg the State of nationality, the State where the offence occurred, or the State on the territory of which the presumed offender is found. It appears utterly unreasonable to give right of way to the State that actively seizes itself of the situation *before* others do so, because such a rule fails to account for the strong territorial and national links with, or interests in the situation which other States might entertain. It may, for instance, invariably give 'bystander' States who manage to gain custody of the presumed perpetrator of an international crime, the right to prosecute, even when the State where the crime was committed proves itself willing to investigate and prosecute. As justice for international crimes may contribute to national reconciliation in the State where the crime occurred, and most evidence is typically located in that State, it appears reasonable to conduct trials there, and not in the bystander State that first asserted its jurisdiction.[189]

In the field of economic law, the first-seized jurisdiction rule may similarly fail to deliver just outcomes. In particular, it may disadvantage the State that refrains from regulating a business practice on the ground that self-regulation might do, or that the practice, despite appearing restrictive, in fact increases economic efficiency. Conversely, it may reward the State that aggressively brings its own laws to bear on the practice on the ground that it adversely affects its own economy. Accordingly, in economic law, the first-seized jurisdiction rule may injustifiably prefer a regulatory outlook that emphasizes strict and intrusive economic regulation over models of *laissez-faire* or voluntary regulation.[190] As condoning a practice, eg a merger, may at times be globally more efficient than prohibiting it,

---

[189] This is indeed the philosophy underlying Article 17 of the Rome Statute of the International Criminal Law, pursuant to which the ICC will only consider a case admissible if a State is unwilling or unable to genuinely investigate or prosecute it.

[190] For a critique of the 'vacuum' theory in antitrust law, a theory pursuant to which one State would be authorized to apply its laws to practices that go unregulated in another State: C Ryngaert, *Jurisdiction over Antitrust Violations in International Law* (2008), 90–1.

it appears unreasonable to accord right of way to the prohibiting, jurisdiction-ally active State.[191] However, unreasonableness would also be the outcome if the concept of 'exercising jurisdiction' were to be understood as also encompassing deliberate non-regulation by States. Under the first-seized jurisdiction rule, the non-regulating State could be accorded right of way because its choice *not* to regulate practices within its jurisdiction may be considered to precede the asser-tions of a jurisdictionally active State that precisely seeks to *regulate* those prac-tices. Such a rule, or at least the interpretation of it, would support a regulatory outlook that prefers non-regulation over regulation, even if regulation would be globally more efficient.

In lieu of a first-seized jurisdiction rule, in the next chapter, a fairer and more efficient rule of reason will be advocated. Under this rule, jurisdictional assertions ought to be scaled back when they *decrease* global welfare and justice (eg in the case of concurrent effects-based jurisdiction in the antitrust field). Conversely, jurisdictional assertions will be expanded when they *increase* global welfare and justice (eg in the case of jurisdiction over crimes against international law which States entertaining a strong nexus are unable or unwilling to prosecute). It will be argued that this abstract rule of reason could be put into practice by States and their courts when they develop governance and judicial networks with other State actors and private actors. Through low-level contacts and increased mutual understanding, reasonableness may spontaneously come into being; pro-forum bias may decrease, and regard for sovereign interests, which is central to the clas-sical reasonableness analysis, may yield to regard for genuinely *international* interests. If the interests of the international community are duly taken into account, a more just solution to the jurisdictional conundrum may be reached.

---

[191] ibid 148–9 (highlighting that national merger regulators ordinarily fail to espouse a *global* perspective, and instead merely focus on *national* efficiency or *national* consumer welfare gains).

6

A New Theory of Jurisdiction in International Law

In the final chapter of this study, the basic problem posed by the unilateral exercise of jurisdiction will be restated. It will be shown how in an era of economic and value globalization, the exercise of unilateral jurisdiction by States has become nearly inevitable (section 6.1). Unilateral jurisdiction, especially if exercised unreasonably, has its obvious discontents, in terms of foreign sovereignty being encroached upon, and the democratic choices of foreign citizens being sidelined (section 6.2). In view of these discontents, it may be expected that States would spontaneously scale down their jurisdictional assertions because not doing so might encourage other States to exercise jurisdiction in a manner detrimental to the former's interests. In practice, however, this reciprocity maxim does not serve as a built-in mechanism of restraint, due to discrepancies in power and regulatory level (section 6.3). Alternatively, it could be submitted that a multilaterally agreed upon substantive solution may be more appropriate. In section 6.4, the tenets of 'substantivism' will be set out. It will be argued there that, somewhat counterintuitively, internationally harmonized laws are, in terms of fairness, not necessarily preferable over the unilateral exercise of jurisdiction.

In sections 6.5 and 6.6, this study's *de lege ferenda* approach to solving jurisdictional conflict will be proposed. In Chapter 5, we discussed the jurisdictional rule of reason at length. This rule, as laid down in section 403 of the US Restatement (Third) of US Foreign Relations Law, may be a useful device to solve jurisdictional questions. As argued in Chapter 5, it does not seem to have crystallized as a rule of customary international law, however, although it could possibly be characterized as a general principle of international law. At any rate, the more important question probably is how reasonableness, either as a rule of international law or as a comity requirement, should work in practice. In section 403 of the Restatement, a number of connecting factors to be used in a reasonableness-informed interest-balancing test are put forward. These factors deserve support. This study would like to add that States, when contemplating the exercise of jurisdiction, should consult with relevant actors—both State and private actors—so as to be fully informed of foreign concerns over jurisdictional overreaching. Low-threshold consultations could take place through networks. The exercise of jurisdiction then becomes the exercise of networked governance (section 6.5).

While consultations may make for informed jurisdictional choices, they do not in themselves provide guidance as to the appropriateness of exercising jurisdiction. Section 403 of the Restatement suggests weighing contacts and interests with different States; the State with the strongest contacts and interests would enjoy jurisdictional priority. Aside from obvious practical implementation problems (notably pro-forum bias), this study largely concurs with this logical objective method. However, the method of section 403 may fail to do justice to the genuine interests of the international community, as it may unduly lay emphasis on *State* contacts and interests. A balancing of interests pursuant to section 403 risks resulting in a jurisdictional outcome that is harmful to the international community. A State may have the strongest connections to, or the strongest interests in regulating a situation but decide not to regulate. The absence of regulatory intervention may serve the interests of that State, but produces adverse effects at a global level. To prevent this undesirable outcome, this study proposes in section 6.6 that States act in accordance with the *subsidiarity* principle. This principle implies that States only apply their laws to a foreign situation which another State—with presumably the stronger nexus to that situation—fails to adequately deal with. Yet it also implies that a State, which also entertains a strong nexus with the situation, is *entitled* to exercise jurisdiction if the other State is unable or unwilling to tackle a situation that is, on aggregate, harmful to the regulatory interests of the international community. By putting emphasis on global economic and value interests, this principle of jurisdiction departs from the classical understanding of the law of jurisdiction as a law that protects the interests of sovereign States.

This study will see to it that legitimate sovereign interests are adequately taken into account. Yet arguably, sovereign interests are only internationally legitimate if other States' sovereign interests are not disproportionately trampled upon, *and* if they somehow transmit the global interest. In the current system of decentralized enforcement of international and cross-border law, States act de facto as global regulators of internationally relevant situations, so that it becomes of primary concern that they do not regulate parochially, but always with the global interest in mind. Sovereignty should no longer be an excuse or a shield, but a responsibility: every sovereign nation has a responsibility not to condone or encourage activities that are, from a global perspective, harmful.

Finally, in section 6.7, the threads of jurisdiction will be connected from a transatlantic perspective. This perspective has been a main research focus throughout the study, and therefore deserves a conclusion of its own. In this conclusion, it will be explained, in broad strokes, how the transatlantic gap over jurisdiction, in the field of economic law as well as international humanitarian and human rights law, has opened up, and how it has gradually diminished. It will be shown how differences in jurisdictional ambit between the United States and Europe are largely attributable to differences in substantive policy. As it exceeds the scope of this study to elaborate on substantive policy differences as to the societal role of antitrust policy, capital markets regulation, wide-ranging evidence-taking powers for private parties, or international criminal justice, no specific recommendations will be issued as to which direction the United States or Europe should steer. It will only be stated that if the United States or Europe decides to apply its laws to foreign situations (believing that this serves its policy interests), it should do so reasonably, and in full respect of the principle of subsidiarity.

6.1 Inevitability

In an era of globalization, the exercise of extraterritorial jurisdiction is often inevitable. The expansion of commercial and financial interstate links has increased the vulnerability of States to adverse domestic effects of foreign activities. Not infrequently, these activities are condoned or encouraged by the States in which they take place, because they further their interests. This may happen in the field of antitrust law, where States face an incentive not to clamp down on export cartels or on mergers in the export industry. It may also happen in the field of securities law, when States believe that setting low standards may attract certain issuers and investors. Sometimes, the territorial State does not consider a particular activity to be harmful. This could occur in the field of securities law, where, for legitimate economic reasons, some States do not for instance consider insider-trading to be an evil, or do not deem stringent corporate governance regulation to be necessary to ensure the smooth functioning of capital markets. It could also occur in the field of export controls, where some States, unlike others, fail to see merit in imposing an economic embargo upon a foreign State. In this part, a new method to solve conflicts arising from one State favouring regulation, and another opposing it, will be proposed.

It is not only in the economic field that the exercise of unilateral jurisdiction has become nearly inevitable. The twentieth century has seen the weaving of a web of transnational business links, but also the rise of an international human rights movement. Under pressure of this movement, the world's values have become increasingly globalized. Substantive international norms of human rights and international humanitarian law have been globally adopted. At the same time, the international community has seen to it that the transgression of the most basic of these norms would not go unpunished. It is generally accepted now that violations of *jus cogens* are amenable to universal jurisdiction, ie, jurisdiction exercised by a State without any nexus to the violation whatsoever. The breakthrough of morality in international law and the international community's desire to bring perpetrators of the gravest crimes to justice have made it almost inevitable that single States shoulder part of the enforcement burden by unilaterally exercising jurisdiction over these crimes.

Typically, the United States finds itself on the side that *wants* stricter regulation, and Europe on the side that *opposes* stricter regulation. This results in the United States exercising extraterritorial jurisdiction, or put differently, applying its own strict economic laws extraterritorially more frequently than European countries do. As far as extraterritorial liability for core crimes against international law is concerned however, the situation is different, and prima facie confusing. Both the United States and Europe intend to make sure that perpetrators of *jus cogens* violations do not go unpunished, yet the United States only provides for tort liability for such violations, and Europe only for criminal liability. In section 6.7, the transatlantic rift over extraterritorial jurisdiction will be further examined.

6.2 The Discontents of Extraterritoriality

Extraterritorial jurisdiction is the fruit of a deeply rooted international scepticism. It is based on a conviction that foreign States and international venues are unable to dispense justice in an acceptable manner. Often, extraterritoriality is informed by a vague sense of superiority or exceptionality of domestic law vis-à-vis foreign law. Especially in the economic field, States tend to rely on the exercise of extraterritorial jurisdiction because it confers benefits on them which could not be acquired through multilateral negotiations, which inherently compel them to make concessions and accommodate other nations. Because States, when unilaterally exercising jurisdiction, tend to disregard foreign nations' interests, protest by foreign States often ensues. In the worst case scenario, blocking statutes are adopted, economic pressure is brought to bear, and the state of international relations in general deteriorates.

Although the exercise of extraterritorial jurisdiction accords with the realities of economic and value globalization, it may violate some established principles of international law, such as sovereignty, non-intervention, comity, and sovereign equality. Foreign protests based on these principles reflect a sense of nonrepresentation in how these laws are shaped, or put differently reflect uneasiness about the democratic content of laws that are applied extraterritorially. It is interesting to look at extraterritoriality through the lens of democracy, because democracy is a principle that, unlike the other principles cited, protects the interests of individuals and not just sovereign States.[1] From the vantage point of democracy, assertions of extraterritorial jurisdiction impose laws on legal subjects who did not participate in the making or changing of these laws.[2] The makers of extraterritorial laws are thus not accountable to the people that are governed by

[1] On the democratic principle as a nascent principle of international law: J Wouters, B De Meester and C Ryngaert, 'Democracy and International Law', (2004) NYIL 137.

[2] eg G Bykhovsky, 'An Argument Against Assertion of Universal Jurisdiction by Individual States', (2003) 21 Wisconsin J Int'l L 161, 184; S Stevens, 'The Increased Aggression of the EC Commission in Extraterritorial Enforcement of the Merger Regulation and Its Impact on Transatlantic Cooperation in Antitrust', (2002) 29 Syracuse J Int'l L and Com 263 (pointing out that '[t]he particular problem posed by extraterritorial enforcement of merger controls is that the enforcing agency is by definition regulating the conduct of firms that are neither incorporated in nor established on its territory, *and who have significantly less political clout*') (emphasis added).

them.[3] From the perspective of foreign persons, these laws are mere commands lacking the communicative texture that makes laws legitimate.[4]

Nuance is however appropriate. For one thing, in the field of universal jurisdiction in particular, many States have consented to the exercise of universal jurisdiction over certain offences, either on a conventional or customary basis.[5] For another, States that condone or encourage activities on their territory that are harmful to another State's interests, eg terrorist activities aimed at the overthrow of a foreign regime, or business-restrictive practices that dislodge the economies of foreign States, could hardly be said to exercise their democratic rights. By failing to prohibit such activities, they in effect supplant a foreign State's own legitimate democratic choices with what they consider to be appropriate for that State.[6] It is defensible then to authorize the foreign State to clamp down on foreign harmful activities through the exercise of extraterritorial jurisdiction by default.

Both consent and bad faith undercut the objection that extraterritoriality is at odds with the principles of democracy and representation. Nonetheless, in typical cases of extraterritoriality, the territorial State has a legitimate interest in not prohibiting or investigating certain activities, eg it may clear an international merger on grounds of economic efficiency, it may prefer self-regulation by issuers and audit firms over government regulation, or it may grant amnesty to high-ranking alleged perpetrators of crimes against international humanitarian law because it believes that only a pledge of non-prosecution may cause them to lay

---

[3] MP Gibney, 'The Extraterritorial Application of U.S. Law: The Perversion of Democratic Governance, the Reversal of Institutional Roles, and the Imperative of Establishing Normative Principles', (1996) 19 BC Int'l & Comp L Rev 297, 306; MD Vancea, 'Exporting U.S. Corporate Governance Standards Through the Sarbanes-Oxley Act: Unilateralism or Cooperation?', (2003–2004) 53 Duke LJ 833, 834.

[4] J Habermas, transl W Rehg, *Between Facts and Norms: Contributions to a Discourse Theory of Law and Democracy* (1996).

[5] DF Orentlicher, 'Whose Justice? Reconciling Universal Jurisdiction with Democratic Principles', (2004) 92 Georgetown LJ 1057, 1133–4 (adding that 'clearly-framed mandates also empower courts to assert universal jurisdiction in circumstances where its legitimacy should not be doubted'). It may also be pointed out that the exercise of universal jurisdiction by bystander States may encourage the territorial State to come to terms with its past and facilitate a transition to democracy. See, on the effect of the *Pinochet* proceedings, inter alia in Chile itself: N Roht-Arriaza, The *Pinochet Effect: Transnational Justice in the Age of Human Rights* (2005).

[6] For Dodge, for instance, the argument that asserting extraterritorial jurisdiction is at loggerheads with the principle of democracy—which requires that citizens only be subject to laws enacted by their democratically elected representatives—carries less weight than the argument that States never regulate neutrally and, drawing on the theory of comparative advantages, naturally favour their own net exporters to the detriment of net importers by allowing the former to engage in business restrictive practices. WS Dodge, 'Extraterritoriality and Conflict-of-Laws Theory: An Argument for Judicial Unilateralism', (1998) 39 Harv Int'l LJ 101, 156–7 (also noting in note 322 that States representing the underregulated net exporters act as extraterritorially as States representing the net importers regulating the practices of the net exporters). From an economic perspective, a self-interested State with the strongest links to a certain activity, such as a merger, may indeed reasonably choose not to regulate that activity because it increases its own national wealth, although it decreases a foreign State's national wealth and possibly overall global wealth. Also AF Lowenfeld, Book Review of Ebb, International Business, Regulation and Protection, (1965) 78 Harv L Rev 1699, 1703–4.

down arms. Therefore, the democratic deficiencies of extraterritorial jurisdiction should be taken seriously.

The democratic deficit of extraterritoriality could possibly be overcome when legislatures, courts, and regulators embark on a dialogue with foreign corporations (the subjects of regulation), regulators, and courts, either through institutionalized channels, or through *amicus curiae* briefs or statements of interest, when exercising jurisdiction over foreign situations.[7] Traditionally, business regulators have day-to-day working contacts with their foreign counterparts, so that a measure of representation of foreign sovereign interests may seep into the regulators' decision to give extraterritorial application to domestic laws. Courts by contrast have sometimes displayed fervent judicial activism and failed to heed the democratic interests of foreign States, primarily because they do not have organized contacts with foreign States or their representatives. In section 6.5, a system of international jurisdiction will be propounded in which courts develop, through transnational judicial networks, a much more active working relationship with foreign regulators, courts, and private actors. Such a relationship might further reciprocal understanding of each others' concerns and organically restrain jurisdictional assertions.

6.3 The Reciprocity Maxim and its Limits

If States exercise extraterritorial jurisdiction, it seems to be a matter of common sense to state that when so doing, they ought to be guided by the maxim of reciprocity, pursuant to which one only does to another what one tolerates that the other would do to one.[8] Fear of reciprocity may inform a practice in which States and their organs restrain their jurisdictional assertions. It could be argued then that cooperative mechanisms and networks are superfluous, in that States, acting in their rational self-interest, will take foreign interests duly in account, because the tables might soon be turned and their nationals may find themselves subject to a similar jurisdictional assertion by another State.

In practice, however, reciprocity might not serve as a restraining principle.[9] Indeed, in spite of the formal equality of States, some States are much more powerful than others in terms of political, economic, and military clout. Powerful States may at times face (ineffective) protests by other States if they regulate

---

[7] Historically, legislatures, such as the US Congress, have not been very willing to increase the accountability of their extraterritorial acts, especially in the economic field, because they lack direct contacts with foreign corporations. Vancea (above n 3) 834 note 8.

[8] G Schuster, *Die internationale Anwendung des Börsenrechts* (1996) 692.

[9] eg JHJ Bourgeois, 'EEC Control over International Mergers', (1990) 10 Yb European Law 103, 128 ('[R]estraint on the part of the [European] Community to allow a merger that is in the interest of a trading partner of the Community might not be matched by the same restraint of its main trading partners *vis-à-vis* a merger that is in the interest of the Community').

extraterritorially, but differences in relative power ensure that they will almost never have to face extraterritorial regulation by other, weaker States. Moreover, because prescriptive jurisdiction could only be effective if it is matched with enforcement jurisdiction—which is under the current international law rules only permissible if *territorially* exercised—only States on whose territory considerable foreign assets are located, which could be seized if foreign corporations refuse to pay the compensation or fine imposed by the regulating State, will exercise extraterritorial jurisdiction.[10] States with considerable foreign assets are ordinarily large States that are open to foreign trade and investment. Accordingly, for powerful States (or groups of States) with a large and open economy, such as the United States and the European Union, the spectre of reciprocity does not serve as an incentive for restraining their jurisdictional assertions.[11]

Power, however, does not fully explain why reciprocity does not restrict extraterritorial jurisdiction in the field of economic law. Reciprocity also does not work there because States that regulate extraterritorially typically boast a higher level of regulation on a wide range of issues. It is logically impossible for States regulating extraterritorially to harbour fears for the extraterritorial application of another State's permissive regulatory framework. European issuers may fear the application of strict US disclosure standards in the field of international securities when they list on US stock exchanges. Yet obviously, US issuers are not afraid of relaxed European disclosure standards when they list on European stock exchanges, quite to the contrary. By the same token, Japanese antitrust conspirators fear the long arm of US antitrust laws, but US antitrust conspirators do not fear the application of more relaxed Japanese antitrust laws when they are already subject to stringent US regulation.[12] Especially when a State's economic regulation in its entirety is stricter than other States' regulation,[13] reciprocity does not serve as a powerful tool of jurisdictional restraint.[14] This explains why the United States tends to exercise extraterritorial jurisdiction more often than other States. To the workings of US power, another explanation is added: the fact that US economic regulation is stricter than foreign economic regulation. It will not

---

[10] WS Dodge, 'The Structural Rules of Transnational Law', (2003) 97 ASIL Proc 317, 318 (pointing out that '[t]his may explain why the United States has historically favoured the extraterritorial application of antitrust law, while other countries have been more resistant'); D Kukovec, 'International Antitrust—What Law in Action?', (2004) 15 Ind Int'l & Comp L Rev 1, 5. States could, however, conclude conventions on enforcing antitrust judgments abroad. See WS Dodge, 'Antitrust and the Draft Hague Judgments', (2001) 32 Law & Pol'y in Int'l Bus 363, 387–9.

[11] Gibney (above n 3) 306.

[12] Unless they are engaged in an export cartel, in which case they may be exempted from US antitrust laws.

[13] The application of strict rules in one field of the law may not inoculate a State against the reciprocal application of strict rules by a foreign State in another field of the law. The argument of reciprocity may thus carry force only if one does not focus on the content of one particular law, but instead rephrases reciprocity as a maxim pursuant to which a State only asserts its jurisdiction over a subject matter with a particular impact, if that State accepts the exercise of jurisdiction by another State over the same or *another* subject matter, but with a similar impact.

[14] Cf Schuster (above n 8) 692.

be examined here whether both explanations are somehow interrelated (whether strict economic regulation makes a State powerful, or whether a powerful State tends to set high standards of economic regulation).

Another explanation of why reciprocity does not work is that it is at times unlikely that the nationals of the State exercising extraterritorial jurisdiction over another State's nationals will ever be subject to the writ of the latter State's laws. This holds true in particular in the field of universal jurisdiction over core crimes. The enthusiasm with which European States have embraced the universality principle to bring perpetrators of core crimes committed in developing countries to account may partly be explained by the unlikelihood of European States' nationals ever being tried by developing nations' courts (because these courts purportedly lack the resources to do so, because European nations do not have that many troops—who typically commit core crimes—deployed overseas, or because it is believed that developing countries will fail to get hold of alleged perpetrators).

Although reciprocity is not as powerful a tool of jurisdictional restraint as an idealist might assume it is, it nonetheless plays a role in international practice. The US Government for instance has been far less gung-ho about universal jurisdiction, including universal tort jurisdiction exercised under the Alien Tort Statute, fearing that it may encourage other countries, developing and European countries alike, to put on trial US service members.[15] Moreover, in the field of economic law, powerful States have tended not to criticize other powerful States' jurisdictional assertions on grounds of their incompatibility with the international law of jurisdiction, because such might tie their own hands in the future.[16] Instead, criticism is typically couched in terms of substantive law requirements not being met, or in terms of economic policy and efficiency goals. An unfortunate consequence of States' reluctance to use international law arguments is obviously that, given the absence of relevant State practice and *opinio juris*, developing a customary

---

[15] Statement of Interest of the United States, filed in *Doe v Liu Qi* (an ATS case against a Chinese official), No C 02-0672 CW (EMC) (26 September 2002), available at <http://www.state. gov/documents/organization/57535.pdf> ('We ask the Court in particular to take into account the potential for reciprocal treatment of United States officials by foreign courts in efforts to challenge U.S. government policy. In addressing these cases, the Court should bear in mind a potential future suit by individuals (including foreign nationals) in a foreign court against U.S. officials for alleged violations of customary international law in carrying out their official functions under the Constitution, laws and programs of the United States (e.g., with respect to capital punishment, or for complicity in human rights abuses by conducting foreign relations with foreign regimes accused of those abuses). The Court should bear in mind the potential that the United States Government will intervene on behalf of its interests in such cases').

[16] Cf FA Mann, 'The Doctrine of Jurisdiction in International Law', (1964-I) 111 RCADI 1, 48 (noting 'the universality or mutuality of the character of jurisdiction', and pointing out that 'any contact believed to warrant application of a State's law to a foreign transaction will be an equally strong warrant for another State to apply its law to a transaction in the legislating State'); Schuster (above n 8) 73 (noting that 'diejenigen Staaten, die ihr Wirtschaftsrecht auf das Auswirkungsprinzip gestützt, sei es ausdrücklich oder der Sache nach, extraterritorial anwenden, sich gegenüber gleichem Verhalten anderer Staaten nicht auf den Standpunkt stellen können, dies sei völkerrechtswidrig').

international law-based jurisdictional framework is an uphill struggle.[17] If States do not oppose another State's jurisdictional assertion on public international law grounds, this ineluctably leads to the conclusion that the assertion is legal under international law. Yet it is not because an assertion is legal, that it is also appropriate or in the best interests of the international community. In sections 6.5 and 6.6, a solution for the problems posed by the apparent international legality of concurrent jurisdiction—several States being allowed under international law to exercise their jurisdiction over one and the same legal situation on the same or different jurisdictional grounds—will be proposed. In section 6.4, it will be examined whether a substantive (multilateral, cooperative, harmonization-oriented...) solution to transnational regulatory problems would not be preferable over a system of unilateral jurisdiction, however reasonable this might be.

6.4 Substantivism

If the reciprocity maxim does not inform jurisdictional restraint, the question arises how States could be impelled to restrict the geographical reach of their laws. For one thing, obviously, the lack of prosecutorial and judicial resources may cause them to do so.[18] States' patchy record of prosecution of core crimes against international law is surely attributable to insufficient political will to commit adequate resources to the investigation and prosecution of such crimes. While it has been submitted that core crimes violate obligations *erga omnes* which every State has an interest in upholding, States do in practice not consider it to be a function of the State to ensure that global justice is done. On the other hand, if foreign situations directly affect States' well-being or the well-being of their citizens, they may not feel very much constrained to apply their laws to these situations. This happens for instance if foreign price-fixing conspiracies raise consumer prices within their territory, if foreign securities fraud affects the interests of their investors, if other States do not go along with an economic boycott of a rogue State, if foreign-based materials could be used as evidence in a domestic proceeding, or if a crime has been committed outside its borders by or against one of its nationals. Jurisdictional restraint may only appear feasible if the foreign conduct over which jurisdiction could (or should) be claimed does not directly harm the forum State's interests.[19] In other situations, the political will to apply national laws extraterritorially,

---

[17] KM Meessen, 'Schadensersatz bei weltweiten Kartellen: Folgerungen aus dem Endurteil im Empagran-Fall', (2005) 55 WuW 1115, 1121.

[18] eg SE Burnett, 'U.S. Judicial Imperialism Post "Empagran v. F. Hoffmann-Laroche"?: Conflicts of Jurisdiction and International Comity in Extraterritorial Antitrust', (2004) 18 Emory Int'l L Rev 555, 616 (arguing that too liberal an exercise of antitrust jurisdiction over foreign conspiracies may strain the judicial system of the US).

[19] The international community's experience with universal jurisdiction, however, has shown that even when the forum State's interests are not directly harmed, jurisdictional restraint does not occur as a matter of course. This has at times angered foreign nations. Cf section 4.5.

informed by nationalist feelings, will often be mustered, even though, from a global perspective, the exercise of jurisdiction (unlike the exercise of jurisdiction over core crimes against international law) might not be desirable.[20]

Because assertions of extraterritorial jurisdiction are usually aimed at promoting national sovereign interests, and restraint is therefore difficult to impose (with the concomitant inconveniences for the international community), regulators and academia have recently shifted the emphasis from the exercise of unilateral jurisdiction to harmonization of economic laws, transnational cooperation in the enforcement of these laws, and even to the establishment of international regulators and institutions. It is claimed that this 'shift to substantivism' moves beyond the fruitless debate over sovereignty—a debate in which any State somehow affected by a situation, either positively or negatively, brandishes its own 'sovereignty' to fend off the other's assertions. It is also claimed that, if internationally standardized substantive rules and procedures are increasingly used, normative competency conflicts will soon belong to the past, and legal certainty for private actors will ensue.[21]

In this subsection, it will be argued that substantivism may fail to deliver all benefits ascribed to it because of the dubious process in which substantive international law may come into being (c). To put it differently, this subsection traces the *limits* of an approach that intends to supplant *procedural* international law, ie, a law based on delimiting States' spheres of competence (the law of jurisdiction), with *substantive* international law, ie, an international *jus commune* of substantive rules and procedures. It will be submitted that the international community, and its weaker members in particular, may, on balance, sometimes be better off with a rule-based framework of international jurisdiction than with common substantive rules and procedures oozing the interests of the powerful.[22] As will be set out in sections 6.5 and 6.6, this rule-based framework should be guided by the principle of subsidiarity, which ought to be given shape through transnational governance and judicial networks.

(a) The substantivist approach

Extraterritorial jurisdiction may not adequately work. Because State actors primarily defend the interests of their State of allegiance, they tend to exercise

---

[20] The exercise of universal jurisdiction over crimes against international humanitarian law may, from a global perspective, however, not always be desirable either, because it may discourage the territorial State from putting in place the rule of law, or because it may complicate long-term perspectives for peace and political reconciliation, to which amnesties could, amongst others, contribute.

[21] eg H Kronke, 'Capital Markets and Conflict of Laws', (2000) 286 RCADI 245, 380 ('In order to provide predicable and standard solutions for problems arising on truly transnational capital markets the development of uniform law ("hard" and "soft") solutions will be inevitable').

[22] Part of this section is forthcoming as C Ryngaert, 'The Limits of Substantive International Economic Law: In Praise of Reasonable Extraterritorial Jurisdiction', in E Claes, W Devroe and B Keirsbilck, eds, *Limits of the Law* (2008).

jurisdiction if such serves their narrowly-defined economic interests, regardless of global harm of the jurisdictional assertion. To justify their jurisdictional assertions, they invoke sovereignty-related links, typically based on territoriality, yet they may fail to take into account *other* nations' sovereignty-related links. They may either believe that public international law does not require them do so, or they may claim that, methodologically, they defer to the State with the stronger links (even if such is not always borne out in practice).

Ideally, to a particular transnational situation, the *best law* should be applied, irrespective of whether that situation could be tied, almost mechanically, to a particular sovereign. Buxbaum has termed the better law approach a 'substantivist approach', because it operates on the basis of 'a choice-of-law methodology whose goal is to select the better law in any given case' through an analysis of the substantive content of laws.[23] Admittedly, in disputes over the reach of a State's laws before national regulators and courts, substantive analysis may play a role, yet it will typically do so within the straitjacket based on sovereignty and territoriality. Under traditional public international law and choice-of-law theory, a situation is indeed tied to a sovereign on the basis of formal, essentially desubstantivized connecting (territorial) factors,[24] and the law of the sovereign with the strongest nexus will be applied. Substantivism however requires that 'the better law' be applied to a particular situation. The better law is not necessarily the law of the State with arguably the strongest link to the situation. It is not a particularized or *phenomenal* law, but a law which is, from an economic, social, cultural ... perspective, the best *noumenal* law to apply. The better law may not be found in existing legal systems, but is to be developed by concurring rational minds.

The better law approach requires policy choices for which courts are ill-equipped. For constitutional reasons (the separation of powers), they are indeed not allowed to apply what they believe is the best law for a situation. Under rules of private international law, they are only allowed to apply the law of the particular

---

[23] In particular HL Buxbaum, 'Conflict of Economic Laws: From Sovereignty to Substance', (2002) 42 Va J Int'l L 931, 957.

[24] Cf ibid 956–7. A unilateral jurisdictional approach would consider the substantive content of potentially applicable law to determine whether the law is applicable (ibid). Under this approach, the substantive content of the law is analysed through the lens of the interest of the sovereign in having the situation regulated by its own law. Either the legal situation implicates important regulatory interests of the sovereign embodied in its own law, and then this law is applied, or the situation does not implicate any such interests, and then the law is not applied, nor is any foreign law.

A multilateral jurisdictional approach weighs the relative interests of each sovereign in regulating the legal situation by, for instance, examining the extent to which another State may have an interest in regulating the activity (section 403(g) of the Restatement Third of US Foreign Relations Law) and the likelihood of conflict with regulation by another State (section 403(h) of the Restatement). This may require an analysis of the substantive content of the foreign regulation, if any, but such an analysis is not aimed at identifying the best law to govern the situation but only at identifying the best of the available laws of the States concerned by the legal situation, thus at identifying a particular jurisdiction the laws of which are applied to the exclusion of the laws of another jurisdiction.

State with which the situation has the strongest, usually territorial, nexus. In regulatory matters of antitrust and securities, the choice-of-law analysis moreover typically only yields the application of forum law, because one State does not apply another State's public laws.[25] Far from applying the best law, courts will then apply no law at all.[26] Arguably, adequate solutions to transnational regulatory problems should not be devised by courts, but by the political branches, by national regulatory agencies that have a day-to-day contact with their foreign counterparts, or by international institutions. Agencies may cooperate in the enforcement of their national laws and thus ensure that law is applied in a manner which is both effective and respectful of each involved State's substantive policy choices. In addition, if sufficient international support could be mustered, negotiations on the harmonization of national laws could be started, either on a bilateral basis, or on a multilateral basis, possibly in the framework of an international institution (eg OECD, WTO).[27] In practical terms then, substantivism may be defined as a method of developing and applying the best law through harmonization and cooperation efforts which de-emphasize rules of choice-of-law and jurisdiction informed by territorial linkage.[28]

(b) Substantivism in practice

A shift from jurisdiction to substantivism is clearly discernible in recent international practice. The doctrine as well has focused more on international economic cooperation than on international economic jurisdiction.[29] At the outset, it should be noted, however, that a substantivist approach will appeal to national authorities only if it serves their national interests. This explains why harmonization and cooperation have only occurred where harmonized

---

[25] *The Antelope*, 23 US (10 Wheat) 66, 123 (1825) (Marshall, CJ), ('The Courts of no country execute the penal laws of another'); *Guiness v Miller*, 291 F 769, 770 (SDNY 1923) ('[N]o court can enforce any law but that of its own sovereign'); *United States v Aluminium Corp of America*, 148 F 2d 416, 443 (2d Cir 1945) ('[A]s a court of the United States, we cannot look beyond our own law'). Dodge attributes the unwillingness to apply foreign law not only to the public law taboo, as epitomized by *The Antelope*, but also to the absence of a federal question in case US federal law does not apply—which deprives the federal courts of jurisdiction. Dodge (above n 6) 109 note 40. Against this received wisdom: AF Lowenfeld, 'International Litigation and the Quest for Reasonableness', (1994-I) 245 RCADI 9, 30. See for statutes that nonetheless provide for the application of another State's antitrust laws by the forum: article 137 of the Swiss Private International Law Code; article 99, § 2, 2° of the Belgian Private International Law Code.

[26] The court will dismiss the antitrust or securities case if it opines that another State's laws should apply. There is no guarantee that the case will be dealt with by the other State.

[27] eg U Draetta, 'The International Jurisdiction of the E.U. Commission in the Merger Control Area', (2000) RDAI 201, 208.

[28] Buxbaum (above n 23) 962–6. Also Kronke (above n 21) 377 ('[C]ommonality in the sense of harmonized substantive law would seem to be the proper choice if application of *one* domestic set of rules by virtue of its determination through conflicts rules over-stretches the conceptual bases of those substantive rules, for example because they are envisaging one physical location').

[29] S Weber Waller, 'The Twilight of Comity', (2000) 38 Colum J Transnat'l L 563, 579.

law sufficiently resembles domestic law,[30] or when the benefits obtained from harmonization and cooperation clearly outweigh the benefits of a traditional jurisdictional approach.[31]

Since the early 1980s, securities regulators have embarked upon a course that resolves international regulatory conflicts through cooperation and harmonization.[32] Antitrust regulators followed suit in the 1990s.[33] Typically, States entered into bilateral memoranda of understanding providing for information-sharing and mutual assistance. While these memoranda still recognize unilateral assertions of jurisdiction by States—as they are precisely aimed at making these assertions more efficient—they are an application of substantivist theory in that the particular law of a sovereign, while still nominally applied, unravels in the face of the reciprocal international enforcement framework set forth in the memoranda.

Outside the field of antitrust and securities law, the substantivist approach has largely failed so far, because international economic transactions may be 'too multifarious to be amenable to a comprehensive scheme of multilateral treaties'.[34] Yet antitrust and securities substantivism too has been limited. In practice, it only governs the relations between industrialized nations, and is

---

[30] Buxbaum (above n 23) 964.

[31] As a general matter, the United States will enter into international agreements if these agreements sufficiently reflect pre-existing domestic law (eg in the field of environmental law, N Purvis, 'Europe and Japan misread Kerry on Kyoto', International Herald Tribune, 5 April 2004), while European States will support international regimes because they protect them from the unilateralism of stronger States, the United States in particular (RA Kagan, *Of Paradise and Power: America and Europe in the New World Order* (2003)).

[32] For a detailed overview on international cooperation and assistance in the field of securities law MD Mann and WP Barry, 'Developments in the Internationalization of Securities Enforcement', Practising Law Institute, Corporate Law and Practice Handbook Series, PLI Order Number 3011, May 2004, 355, 365 *et seq*. The US Securities Exchange Commission (SEC) for instance partly relies on harmonized international accounting standards instead of on US standards, giving up the requirement of US GAAP reconciliation.

[33] In particular Agreement Regarding the Application of Competition Laws between the Government of the United States and the Commission of the European Communities, (1991) 4 CMLR 823; (1995) 30 ILM 1487, [1995] OJ L 132; Agreement Between the European Communities and the Government of the United States of America on the Application of the Positive Comity Principles in the Enforcement of their Competition Laws, [1998] OJ L 173/28; (1999) 4 CMLR 502. For an overview of US cooperative agreements and interagency cooperation: Burnett (above n 18) 629–36 (noting that by entering into formal and informal regimes, the US will bolster the efficiency of its own antitrust regulatory regime).

[34] X, Note, 'Predictability and Comity: Toward Common Principles of Extraterritorial Jurisdiction', (1985) 98 Harv L Rev 1310, 1322 and 1325–6. Also AT Guzman, 'Choice of Law: New Foundations', (2002) 90 Geo LJ 883, 933 ('Agreement over substantive areas of law has proven to be extremely difficult to achieve'). Also A Bianchi, Reply to Professor Maier, in KM Meessen, ed, *Extraterritorial Jurisdiction in Theory and Practice* (1996) 74, 81 (holding that conflicts of jurisdiction cannot always be resolved by means of international agreements); AV Lowe, 'The Problems of Extraterritorial Jurisdiction: Economic Sovereignty and the Search for a Solution', (1985) 34 ICLQ 724, 731 (stating that '[a]s long as there are important national policies which diverge to such an extent that harmonization is not possible, the problem [of extraterritorial jurisdiction] will remain').

mainly limited to information-sharing, positive comity,[35] and conditional reciprocity.[36] The outcome of bilateral cooperation between the United States and Europe, which is in the field of international merger review at an all-time high, is not per se in the interests of third countries. One could imagine a situation of US and European regulators clearing a transatlantic merger in the export industry which distorts competitive conditions in developing nations, without the opinion of these nations being heard in the joint review procedure. Substantive bilateral antitrust cooperation may then reduce global welfare.[37] A global antitrust regime has been advocated,[38] but has so far proved elusive because a negotiated solution will possibly only be achievable with transfer payments. The interests of developing and developed countries are indeed diametrically opposed, with developing countries having an interest in stringent antitrust regulation (having a lot of consumers, but few producers), and developed countries having no such interest (having a lot of producers, but relatively few producers).[39]

International humanitarian law is probably the only branch of the law examined in this study where substantivism seems to have largely succeeded. National humanitarian laws hardly differ from each other, as humanitarian law is, and has been, at least since the late nineteenth century, *international* humanitarian law.[40] Codified humanitarian law was thus since its very inception *substantive*

---

[35] Article 6 of the 1998 Comity Agreement between the United States and the European Union. Whereas negative comity refers to the regulating State refraining from exercising jurisdiction because another State's interests may be more important (ie the traditional comity concept of jurisdictional restraint), positive comity refers to the competition authorities of a requesting party 'requesting the competition authorities of a requested party to investigate and, if warranted, to remedy anticompetitive activities in accordance with the requested party's competition laws'. Cf Article 6 of the 1998 Comity Agreement between the United States and the European Union.

[36] Cf the exemptions from the Sarbanes-Oxley Act granted by the SEC and the PCAOB, and the exemptions to be granted under the EC Statutory Audit Directive. Commonality (full harmonization) in the field of capital markets law has actually been deemed illusive by one of its main advocates, who instead believed that only reciprocity would be feasible. Kronke (above n 21) 'Capital Markets and Conflict of Laws', (2000) 286 RCADI 245, 378.

[37] RE Falvey and PJ Lloyd, 'An Economic Analysis of Extraterritoriality', Centre for Research on Globalisation and Labour Markets, School of Economics, University of Nottingham (UK), Research Paper 99/3, p 15, available at <www.nottingham.ac.uk/economics/leverhulme/reserach_paper/99_3.pdf>; AT Guzman, 'The Case for International Antitrust', (2004) 22 Berkeley J. Int'l L. 355, 362 (noting that 'a decision on whether to bring a case in the United States or the EU may be quite different from what is in the interests of a developing country').

[38] eg P Torremans, 'Extraterritorial Application of E.C. and U.S. Competition Law', (1996) 21 EL Rev 280, 292; M Matsushita, 'International Cooperation in the Enforcement of Competition Policy', (2002) 1 Washington University Global Studies Law Review 463; K von Finckenstein, 'International Antitrust Policy and the International Competition Network', in B Hawk, ed, *International Antitrust Law & Policy* (2002) chapter 3; ME Janow, 'Observations on Two Multilateral Venues: The International Competition Network (ICN) and the WTO', in ibid, chapter 4; D Voillemot and A Thillier, 'WTO and Competition Rules', in B Hawk (ed), *International Antitrust Law & Policy* (1999) chapter 4.

[39] Guzman (above n 34) 936.

[40] The United States was the first State to codify the laws of war in the Lieber Code (1863), reprinted in D Schindler and J Toman, *The Laws of Armed Conflicts* (1988) 3–23. International

international law. A next substantivist step was undertaken when, toward the end of the twentieth century, *international* repressive mechanisms, applying the same substantive international law, were set up. The establishment of the permanent International Criminal Court (ICC) in particular constitutes a major breakthrough in the international enforcement of international humanitarian law. In the wake of the adoption of the Statute of the ICC, substantivism has been taken another step further, when States overhauled their national laws concerning humanitarian law, and inserted the bulk of the Statute's criminalizations into their domestic law.[41] This process has however not eased international tension regarding the extraterritorial or international application of international humanitarian law, primarily because some concepts of the law of war, such as necessity and proportionality, are open to (possibly abusive) interpretation. The emphasis is mainly put on *economic* law here, because substantive harmonization and coordination have not yet been fully achieved in that field of the law (because the substantive content of this law, unlike humanitarian law, differs widely among States in the first place), and as will be argued in the next subsection, not necessarily regrettably so.

(c) The limits of substantivism

If substantivism could not be achieved, only (extraterritorial) jurisdiction will ensure that a State's interests are sufficiently accounted for. The question arises, however, whether even if substantivism *could* be achieved, it should be preferred over the unilateral exercise of jurisdiction. International cooperation may seem desirable because it allows all States concerned to have their voice heard. Yet in practice, the glorification of the benefits of substantivism has obscured the reality that international consultation, or the emphasis put on it, may at times produce outcomes that hardly serve the interests of justice and equity. It may be wondered aloud whether, under some circumstances, the (reasonable) exercise of (extraterritorial) jurisdiction should not be maintained.

From an economic perspective, substantive solutions have the drawback that they are expensive. The transaction costs of the unilateral exercise of jurisdiction may be lower than these of multilateral solutions, because the exercise of

codification ensued in 1899, 1907, 1949, and 1977, when respectively the Hague and Geneva Conventions (including Additional Protocols) with respect to the laws of war were adopted. In 1948, a Genocide Convention was adopted. See for a chronological overview of efforts at codification of international humanitarian law: <http://www.icrc.org/ihl.nsf/INTRO?OpenView>.

[41] See notably German Code of Crimes against International Law, *Völkerstrafgesetzbuch*, 2002 *Bundesgesetzblatt* (BGBl) Teil 1, at 2254; English translation available at <http://www.iuscomp. org/gla/statutes/VoeStGB.pdf>; Dutch Act of 19 June 2003 containing rules concerning serious violations of international humanitarian law (*Wet Internationale Misdrijven*); Belgian Act of 5 August 2003 concerning grave violations of international humanitarian law, *Moniteur belge* 7 August 2003; English International Criminal Court Act 2001, full text available at <http://www. hmso.gov.uk/acts/acts2001/20010017.htm>.

jurisdiction does not require cumbersome interstate negotiations.[42] In the long run, the economic benefits of an encompassing substantive regime may possibly outweigh its initial inconveniences.[43] Yet if a particular regulatory controversy is insulated, eg a controversy over how the international community should respond to a global price-fixing conspiracy producing worldwide effects, enforcement costs could be considerably cut if one State is willing to shoulder the burden by establishing its jurisdiction over the conspiracy. If States were to gather around the negotiating table in search of a solution which is acceptable to all States concerned and which requires implementation and enforcement, costs will tend to soar.[44] The cost factor 'time' should not be overlooked either, not only from an economic viewpoint but also from the perspective of justice. In case of private enforcement of antitrust law for instance, asking the plaintiff to wait—possibly *ad calendas graecas*, until a multilateral solution has been worked out between the various States whose interests are affected—appears unjust, since this may violate the plaintiff's right to a hearing in a reasonable time, and amount to a denial of justice if a solution ultimately proves elusive. It is in this context that Professor Meessen has argued that, if negotiations fail, the courts should be able to exercise their jurisdiction.[45] It may even be submitted that, if an acceptable negotiated solution could from the outset not reasonably be expected, the courts should not stay their proceedings, but dispense justice as swiftly as possible, with due respect for foreign interests under the jurisdictional rule of reason.

Substantive solutions may also undercut justice at another level: at the level of fairness between States.[46] It has been argued that the exercise of extraterritorial jurisdiction may be an instrument of the powerful, because only powerful States do not have to brace themselves for retaliatory action by a foreign State upon asserting jurisdiction in a manner detrimental to that State. Powerful States also tend to ascribe the rise of their power to the quality of their own laws. Viewing these laws as exceptionally good, such States may, almost as missionaries, apply their laws extraterritorially, and impose them upon weaker, purportedly 'uncivilized' nations.[47] Reliance on harmonization and cooperation, however, may at

---

[42]   Schuster (above n 8) 683.

[43]   Kronke (above n 21) 377 (supporting substantivism on the ground that 'the absence of predictability because of lacking (harmonized or uniform) substantive rules tends to increase transaction costs').

[44]   By the same token, it may appear efficient to allow *one State* instead of a variety of States to exercise jurisdiction over a transnational situation. HL Buxbaum, 'Transnational Regulatory Litigation', (2006) 46 Va J Int'l L 251, 272.

[45]   KM Meessen, 'Antitrust Jurisdiction under Customary International Law', (1984) 78 AJIL 783, 806.

[46]   Buxbaum (above n 23) 973–6.

[47]   Notably in the field of securities laws the United States has behaved as a benevolent hegemon taking on a duty to stamp out the universal evil of securities fraud. See JD Kelly, 'Let There Be Fraud (Abroad): A Proposal for a New U.S. Jurisprudence With Regard to the Extraterritorial Application of the Anti-Fraud Provisions of the 1933 and 1934 Securities Acts', (1997) 28 Law & Pol'y Int'l Bus 477, 491. The enactment of the Sarbanes-Oxley Act by the United States in 2002, an Act which sets forth a number of stringent corporate governance requirements, may have been

times be no less based on power than reliance on extraterritorial jurisdiction. Harmonization is not achieved nor does cooperation take place in a power-free environment. Parties to international agreements may only formally be equal.[48] In the real world, the more powerful parties will usually heavily weigh on the substantive outcome of a negotiating process. This might produce a regime that favours the interests of the powerful to the detriment of those of the weaker.[49] In the WTO for instance, conference rules provide for equal treatment of all parties, but do not apply to informal consultations.[50] In informal 'green room'-consultations, between the industrialized 'Quad-countries' often manage to build a consensus which they present as a 'take it or leave it' package to the other Member States.[51] As a general matter, richer and larger States have more access to information than poorer and smaller States. A large number of developing countries also do not have the necessary expertise to influence the negotiations and thus to ultimately enter into agreements that should be supposed to serve their interests.[52] It has therefore been argued, not unjustifiably, that current substantive international law oozes Western bias because of Western domination over the making of international law.[53]

---

informed by the view that US capital markets regulation is exceptionally good, and should be an example to follow for other nations. E Fleischman, former SEC Commissioner, quoted in 'Uncle Sam Wants You', South China Morning Post, 6 September 2002, at 1 ('It's as though they were saying that in the light of the globalisation of markets, we the Congress and the SEC have no choice but to shoulder the burden of policing the market activities of companies, investment banks and the accounting and legal professionals wherever those activities take place').

[48] Historically, however, not even this formal equality was guaranteed. While nowadays all States have the right to participate in the treaty-making process, in earlier times only the great powers were invited to international conferences, the outcome of which smaller States had to abide by. MCW Pinto, 'Democratization of International Relations and its Implications for Development and Application of International Law', in N Al-Nauimi and R Meese, eds, *International Legal Issues Arising under the United Nations Decade of International Law* (1995) 1260.

[49] Bianchi (above n 34) 82 (submitting that '[i]n order to attract investments or pushed by other policy reasons, weaker states may be forced to accept the impositions of more powerful states'); J Kaffanke, 'Nationales Wirtschaftsrecht und internationaler Sachverhalt', (1989) 27 Archiv des Völkerrechts 129, 141 ('Würde eine solche [politische] Lösung nicht gerade die Situation provozieren, dass der Stärkere den Schwächeren über den Tisch ziehen würde? Sind dann nicht ausserrechtlichen und unkontrollierbaren Einflüssen Tür und Tor geöffnet?'); Buxbaum (above n 44) 304 ('The political realities of the negotiating process lead to convergence around the policies of the more powerful states, with the result that one may question the international legitimacy of the norms adopted') (footnotes omitted).

[50] See for criticism of this method, eg WTO Watch, 'NGOs Call on Trade Ministers to Reject Closed WTO Process', <http://www.globalpolicy.org/ngos/int/wto/2002/1104reject.htm> (last visited on 31 July 2006).

[51] A breakthrough in WTO negotiations is often dependent on an initial deal brokered during quadrilateral negotiations between the United States, the European Union, Canada, and Japan. See <http://www.wto.org/english/thewto_e/whatis_e/tif_e/org3_e.htm> (last visited on 31 July 2006).

[52] More extensively, notably in the context of WTO negotiations: Wouters, De Meester and Ryngaert (above n 1).

[53] E Kwakwa, 'Regulating the International Economy: What Role for the State?' in M Byers, ed, *The Role of Law in International Politics* (2000) 227.

With respect to the economic laws that have been given extraterritorial application, the antitrust and securities laws, the risk of Western concepts being 'imposed' on poorer States is rather high. As we write, a number of developing countries do not even have or enforce laws that regulate competitive conditions or punish securities fraud. Because these States are not familiar with highly specialized business regulation, they risk swallowing whatever expert Western nations propose them. The proliferation of insider-trading prohibitions, for instance, has largely been steered by bilateral memoranda of understanding negotiated between the United States, historically the first champion of laws prohibiting insider-trading, and other (industrialized) nations that did not have such laws. These memoranda typically provided for cooperation in the enforcement of US securities laws, and provided for mechanisms for dealing with US discovery requests.[54] As an instrument of soft pressure, they cajoled the other party into inserting insider-trading prohibitions into their own laws, and thus harmonized insider-trading law largely on US terms. Proposals for 'substantivizing' other fields of economic law, eg setting up an international merger review authority, ought therefore to be viewed with suspicion, for it is not unreasonable that the small States will stand to lose.[55]

Accordingly, in terms of their results, extraterritorial jurisdiction and substantive solutions may not differ that much. Both may coax weaker States into adapting their laws in ways desired by the powerful State. In fact, extraterritorial jurisdiction and substantive solutions often work in tandem. The initial exercise of extraterritorial jurisdiction by a State may serve as a tactical prelude to later cooperation and harmonization agreements serving the interests of that State, especially in case foreign nations left the regulatory field fallow. The process of cooperation and harmonization in the field of securities law may serve to illustrate this. Because of the US emphasis on fair and open capital markets, tight US regulation of securities transactions has also extended to foreign transactions.[56] In a typical situation, after initially fully asserting its jurisdiction over foreign transactions, the United States gradually grants exemptions in order not to cause a head-on collision with foreign nations but also, shrewdly, to win over the hearts and minds of those nations for the substance of what is not exempted. Magnanimity on the part of the hegemon may persuade States with underdeveloped regulatory

---

[54] On US negotiating practice in the field of insider-trading: DC Langevoort, 'Cross-Border Insider Trading', (2000–2001) 19 Dick J Int'l L 161. The first such memorandum was signed with Switzerland after conflict had arisen over the application of US discovery laws to documents located in Switzerland in the insider-trading case of *SEC v Banca della Svizzera Italiana*, 92 FRD 111 (1981).

[55] Cf U Draetta, 'Need for Better Trans-atlantic Co-operation in the field of Merger Control', (2000) RDAI 557, 565 (stating that establishing such an authority will be impossible anyway 'because large States will fear that they will not have enough influence on this international merger control authority and small States will fear that their influence will be minimal').

[56] Cf the seminal case of *Schoenbaum v Firstbrook*, 405 F 2d 200 (2d Cir 1968) (Court applying the antifraud provisions of the US Securities Exchange Act to foreign securities transactions producing effects in the United States).

frameworks to embrace ready-made solutions provided by the United States. This may result in organic harmonization—States spontaneously adopting similar laws—or in organized harmonization—States entering into international agreements dealing with the matter. Either way, the final harmonized rules will reflect US rules and their underlying values.

In the field of corporate governance, one curiously observes the United States firstly aggressively brandishing the threat of unconditional application of the US Sarbanes-Oxley Act (2002), European corporations and the European Commission reacting furiously,[57] the US regulatory agencies accommodating foreign concerns (2002–2005), and the European Union in due course enacting its own directive on statutory audit, with its own accommodations for foreign audit firms (2006).[58] Although the substantive provisions of the US Act and the European Union do not wholly coincide, it is hard to resist the conclusion that the European Union was considerably influenced by the strengthening of the law in the United States. In sum, while the extraterritorial application of the Sarbanes-Oxley Act may initially have produced some resentment overseas, it may also have paved the way for a US-driven transatlantic 'convergence' of corporate governance standards.[59]

All this is not to say that international negotiations do, as a matter of course, give rise to an inequitable outcome. It is only to say that, if some States could not participate on an equal footing in international negotiations, because they lack capacity or expertise, or because undue economic pressure is exerted over them, the outcome of the negotiations may reflect the interests of stronger States more than those of weaker States. It should be emphasized, in all fairness, that, if substantive solutions (agreements) have been hammered out in a fair manner, they may lower transaction costs in the long run because they save litigation costs associated with the exercise of (extraterritorial) jurisdiction.

6.5 Devising a Jurisdictional Framework: Using Transnational Regulatory and Judicial Networks

It has been argued that substantivism, while having theoretical appeal, may serve, like extraterritorial jurisdiction, as a transmission belt for the interests of the powerful. In the case of cooperative solutions, this happens much more

---

[57] Letter of EU Internal Market Commissioner F Bolkestein to W Donaldson, Chairman of the SEC, 24 April 2003, available at <http://www.iasplus.com/resource/letterfbdonaldson.pdf>.

[58] Directive (EC) 2006/43 of the European Parliament and of the Council of 17 May 2006 on statutory audits of annual accounts and consolidated accounts, [2006] OJ L 157/87. On its international aspects: Chapter XI of the Directive (Articles 44–47).

[59] Against this convergence on US terms: A Schaub, 'Europe and US Must Guard Against Regulatory Clashes', (July 2004) IFLR 20, 21 (stating that '[w]hat we must absolutely avoid is the establishment of a type of first-mover regulatory advantage: that is, setting a standard and then compelling the other to match it').

implicitly than in the case of extraterritorial jurisdiction, which typically meets with stiff resistance from foreign nations. Yet once one scratches below the surface, the cooperative brilliance may fade, and substantivism may turn out to be a false friend. Kaffanke even termed it 'die schlechteste aller denkbaren Lösungen'.[60] Bereft of its illusions, States then face a choice between plague and cholera, between extraterritorial jurisdiction and international 'cooperation', between international friction and unfairness. For all the—justified—griping about unilateral extraterritorial jurisdiction, it re-emerges in the debate over just international economic regulation. It is hesitantly claimed that the exercise of extraterritorial jurisdiction may sometimes produce more equitable results than cooperative solutions.[61]

Admittedly, it has been shown how extraterritorial jurisdiction—on which substantive solutions may possibly piggyback—is as much, or even more, part of a game of power as substantivism is. A system in which the United States, and to a lesser extent the European Union, bully developing nations by applying their laws to situations arising outside their territory but purportedly producing adverse domestic effects, is surely not attractive for the downtrodden of this world. However, if one could devise a rigorous rule-based system of international jurisdiction, modulated depending on the subject matter to be regulated, to which all States have to adhere, weaker countries are more likely to go along with it. Such a system, administered by independent courts, may restrict powerful States' sphere of action and delegitimize their protest against weaker States' own jurisdictional assertions.[62]

For weaker States, stringent and elaborate rules of jurisdiction may not only serve as defences against powerful States' unwarranted assertions or as tools enabling them to actively promote their own interests by engaging themselves in extraterritorial jurisdiction. Weaker States may also use such rules to their advantage in the course of substantive processes. As Bianchi pointed out, '[t]he bargaining position of weaker states might be stronger if it is perceived as conforming with accepted principles and rules of international law'.[63] Developed jurisdictional principles may serve to pressure the powerful into drawing up an international agreement that takes the interests of the weak sufficiently into account: if the agreement were to be considered as unfair by the weak, they could leave the negotiating table and legitimately resort to exercising unilateral extraterritorial

---

[60] Kaffanke (above n 49) 140 (stating that 'die Uberlassung der rechtlichen Fragen solcher Konflikte [over extraterritorial jurisdiction] an die politischen oder diplomatischen Entscheidungsträger die schlechteste aller denkbaren Lösungen darstellt').

[61] Cf Buxbaum (above n 23) 975 ('[T]his process [of substantivism] may be criticized on foreign relations grounds in that it replaces "neutral" consideration of competing laws in the individual case with the application of law reflecting non-neutral values').

[62] Cf Kaffanke (above n 49) ('Die Lokalisierung der Entscheidung bei den Gerichten ist nachgerade die Versicherung dafür, dass die Einflussmöglichkeit von Interessengruppen so beschränkt wie möglich bleibt').

[63] Bianchi (above n 34) 82.

jurisdiction. Thus, the limits which substantivism faces could be overcome if substantivism is buttressed by a framework of international jurisdiction.

The question now is how such a framework of international jurisdiction should be developed. Clearly, while there may be some guiding principles applicable across-the-board, every field of the law ought to be subject to its own specific jurisdictional rules.[64] Antitrust regulators do indeed not face the same problems as securities regulators, let alone human rights courts. An attractive option, which confers considerable legal certainty, is the conclusion of treaties on every subject.[65] These treaties could spell out the maximal reach of a State's laws. Yet because a treaty could not possibly anticipate the variety of problems arising in the real world, because exempting foreign corporations from regulation may jeopardize the principle of equality before the law,[66] and because States may be unwilling to tie their own hands too much, such a treaty, if any could be agreed upon at all, is likely to feature a flexible 'reasonableness' or 'comity' test.[67] Comity being essentially a discretionary concept, the parties to the treaty will tend to apply the comity test in their favour,[68] and apply effects-based jurisdiction as

---

[64] eg the Restatement (Third) of US Foreign Relations Law (1987), which sets forth the general principles of jurisdiction and reasonableness in §§ 402–403, and features specific sections on tax (§§ 411–413), foreign subsidiaries (§ 414), antitrust (§ 415), securities (§ 416), foreign sovereign compulsion (§ 441), and transnational discovery (§ 442).

[65] eg Policy Statement of the International Chamber of Commerce, 'Extraterritoriality and business', 13 July 2006, Document 103-33/5 (on file with the author) ('ICC... encourages governments to explore the feasibility of an international convention on the extraterritorial application of national laws providing for means of resolving extraterritoriality disputes, where appropriate, by way of consultation, cooperation, conciliation, or arbitration'). It may be noted that an overarching convention on criminal jurisdiction, as proposed by the Harvard Research on International Law, 'Draft Convention on Jurisdiction with Respect to Crime', (1995) 29 AJIL 439 (1935), has never materialized.

[66] Exempting foreign conspiracies or mergers causing exactly the same effects in the regulating State as domestic restrictive practices may be a hard sell for a domestic constituency. In private suits, it is unlikely that enforcement authorities will be willing to cast aside imperative domestic law in an international agreement. Cf J Schwarze, 'Die extraterritoriale Anwendbarkeit des EG-Wettbewerbsrechts—vom Durchführungsprinzip zum Prinzip der qualifizierten Auswirkung', in J Schwarze, ed, *Europäisches Wettbewerbsrechts im Zeichen der Globalisierung* (2002) 59–60; AV Lowe, 'The Problems of Extraterritorial Jurisdiction: Economic Sovereignty and the Search for a Solution', (1985) 34 ICLQ 724, 729 (arguing that it is 'questionable as a matter of legal principle how far foreign policy considerations should be allowed to affect the enforcement of what are, after all, private rights being asserted in such litigation'); JR Atwood, 'Positive Comity—Is It a Positive Step?', in B Hawk, ed, *International Antitrust Law and Policy* (1993) ('It is not realistic to expect one government to prosecute its citizens solely for the benefit of another. It is no accident that this has not happened in the past, and it is unlikely to happen in the future').

[67] States may thus want to insert the malleability inherent in the custom or customary international law of jurisdiction into a treaty (jurisdiction and limits to it, if any, traditionally being governed by customary international law). On the malleability of customary international law inter alia K Wolfke, 'Some Persistent Controversies Regarding Customary International Law', (1993) 24 NYIL 1, 16.

[68] Cf MC Franker, 'Restoration: International Merger Review in the Wake of General Electric/Honeywell and the Triumphant Return of Negative Comity', (204) 36 Geo Wash Int'l L Rev 877, 901 ('[E]ven if positive comity were extended to merger review, it would achieve only the desired effect to the extent that 'both parties have similar interests in the cessation of certain

they see fit,[69] a deficit from which the current transatlantic antitrust Comity Agreements (1991/1998) suffer as well.[70] The role of international agreements in bringing more predictability to the exercise of jurisdiction should thus not be overestimated.

How to proceed then? As a matter of logic, before States start negotiations on an international agreement on jurisdiction, they should make sure that their regulators and courts are willing to rise above nationalist reflexes and exercise jurisdictional restraint if another State's sovereignty is encroached upon. It has been shown above that there is apparently not much cause for optimism given the tendency of courts and regulators to pull for the home crowd. However, in an era of 'the global village' in which economic and government actors are increasingly wired, and informal transnational government and judicial networks emerge, courts and regulators are much more connected with their foreign counterparts than they previously were;[71] a 'global administrative space' emerges.[72] Stronger contacts and better information typically result in a greater understanding of each other's legitimate concerns.[73] At the regulatory level, as aptly displayed in the field of corporate governance regulation, the positive results are undeniable: a system in which regulators mutually recognize each other's oversight mechanisms, subject to a number of safeguards, is gradually being put in place. In auditing regulation, solutions to jurisdictional conflicts were hammered out in an informal dialogue between US and European regulators, and a burdensome diplomatic procedure was avoided. This dialogue at the same time facilitated the convergence of substantive norms.[74]

In the field of antitrust law too informal dialogue has been heavily relied upon of late. Because US and European regulators work together on a daily

anticompetitive practices'); Kaffanke (above n 49) 142 ('Es ist kaum damit zu rechnen, dass in solchen Abmachungen in jeder Hinsicht konkrete und bestimmte Begriffe verwendet werden würden. Was innerhalb der jahrzehntelangen akademischen Auseinandersetzung und Erörterung nicht gelungen ist, wird nun kaum von solchen Verhandlungen geleistet werden').

[69] B Goldman, 'Les effects juridiques extra-territoriaux de la politique de la concurrence', (1972) Rev Marché Commun 612, 618–19.

[70] Kukovec (above n 10) 20 (arguing, in the context of merger control, that regulators, applying comity, are invited to weigh unquantifiable interests of such societal subgroups as consumers, competitors, and employees).

[71] On government networks in particular AM Slaughter, 'Governing the Global Economy through Government Networks', in M Byers, ed, *The Role of Law in International Politics* (2000) 177.

[72] N Krisch and B Kingsbury, 'Global Governance and Global Administrative Law in the International Legal Order', (2006) 17 EJIL 1 (defining a 'global administrative space' as 'a space in which the strict dichotomy between domestic and international levels has largely broken down, in which administrative functions are performed in often complex interplays between officials and institutions on different levels, and in which regulation may be highly effective despite its predominantly non-binding forms').

[73] Through cooperation, State sovereignty may evaporate, yet at the same time, State agencies may 'gain instrumental power over the forms of conduct subject to regulation'. Buxbaum (above n 44) 308.

[74] Schaub (above n 59) 20.

basis, there have been no major conflicts over antitrust jurisdiction since the early 1990s. At the *judicial* level, this process of mutual understanding culminated, for the time being, in the 2004 antitrust decision of the US Supreme Court in the *Empagran Vitamins* case. Influenced by a number of *amicus curiae* briefs from foreign governments (United Kingdom, Netherlands, Germany, Belgium, Canada, Japan), the Court stated that it is to be assumed that the US Congress takes 'the legitimate sovereign interests of other nations into account'[75] when assessing the reach of US law, and avoids extending this reach when this would create a 'serious risk of interference with a foreign nation's ability independently to regulate its own commercial affairs'.[76] In an important departure from the past, in *Empagran*, America's highest court thus held that it expects courts to take foreign sovereign interests adequately into account. It should be recalled that, as late as 1993, the Supreme Court still stated, in the *Hartford Fire Insurance* case, that foreign policies and laws should not be heeded by US courts when giving extraterritorial application to the antitrust laws, unless the foreign State compels conduct which US law prohibits (or vice versa)[77] (an approach which the European courts also take[78]). As a fish tends to rot from the head down, as the Russian proverb has it, courts duly restricted the comity analysis to a 'true conflict' or 'foreign sovereign compulsion' analysis in the 1990s.[79] That reasonableness has now resurfaced[80] as high up in the judicial hierarchy as the US Supreme Court testifies to a belief that courts *could* and *should* take foreign sovereign interests into account, and may limit the reach of a State's laws accordingly.

Thanks to the increased transnational contacts between governments, regulators and courts, a reciprocal and principled practice of States exercising reasonable jurisdiction may emerge. From a methodological perspective, it is important in this respect that States, before asserting jurisdiction, allow or even ask other States, including weaker States, to voice their concerns, and take them

---

[75] *F Hoffman-La Roche Ltd et al. v Empagran SA et al.*, 124 S Ct 2359, 2366 (2004).
[76] ibid 2367.
[77] *Hartford Fire Insurance Co v California*, 509 US 764 (1993).
[78] ECJ, *A Ahlstrom Osakeyhtio et al. v Commission (Wood Pulp)*, [1988] ECR 5244, § 20 ('There is not, in this case, any contradiction between the conduct required by the United States and that required by the Community since the [American] Webb Pomerene Act merely exempts the conclusion of export cartels from the application of United States anti-trust laws but does not require such cartels to be concluded'); CFI, *Gencor v Commission* [1999] ECR II-00753, § 103, citing ECJ, *Wood Pulp*, § 20 (noting 'that there was no conflict between the course of action required by the South African Government and that required by the Community, given that [...] the South African competition authorities simply concluded that the concentration agreement did not give rise to any competition policy concerns, without requiring that such an agreement be entered into').
[79] eg *United States v Nippon Paper Industries Co*, 109 F 3d 1 (1st Cir 1997) (applying the *Hartford Fire* doctrine to criminal antitrust suits).
[80] Interest-balancing was introduced in US antitrust law in the late 1970s in *Timberlane Lumber Co v Bank of America, NT & SA*, 549 F 2d 597, 605–8 (9th Cir 1976); *Mannington Mills, Inc v Congoleum Corp*, 595 F 2d 1287, 1292 (3d Cir 1979).

into account as a matter of good neighbourliness.[81] Obviously, this cooperative process may take place more smoothly on the basis of a facilitating transnational framework than on the basis of ad hoc cooperation through *amicus curiae* briefs or statements of interests. It would be useful if States were to designate official points of contact to which foreign courts could address their inquiries.

A US court, facing a problem of antitrust involving a European corporation, could then inquire with an EC office in Brussels whether the EC would have qualms about a particular jurisdictional assertion (apart from inquiring with the US executive branch whether this assertion would not raise a non-justiciable political—foreign policy—question). To that effect, the existing Comity Agreements between the United States and the European Community could be revised. Whereas for now they only provide for cooperation between antitrust regulatory agencies, they could in future also provide for information exchange between courts and regulatory agencies, or even between courts only.[82] At the global level, the International Competition Network may obviously play an important role in antitrust cooperation.[83] Regulatory cooperation within this network, which groups both developed and developing countries, could be enhanced,[84] and members could possibly open in it up for courts.

By the same token, a European court that has received a complaint alleging gross human rights violations committed in a foreign country should be able to contact the territorial State, or the national State of the foreign offender if different, for more information about the facts and the investigations underway. In the situation of gross human rights violations, bystander States could also be contacted, because for various reasons (prosecutorial capacity and expertise, cultural affinity, availability of witnesses...) these States may have a stronger prosecutorial interest and be a better adjudicatory forum. They may also have information that is useful for the prosecuting State, for instance because witnesses or co-suspects have fled to their territory. Encouragingly, in the European Union, a special network of points of contact in respect of persons responsible for genocide, crimes against humanity, and war crimes has recently been put in place on the basis of a Council decision of 2002.[85]

---

[81] In addition, courts may rely on a 'transnational community of jurists' disciplining unilateral assertions of jurisdiction. Orentlicher (above n 5) 1133–4.

[82] If courts could transnationally communicate with each other, jurisdictional deadlock stemming from parallel proceedings and reciprocal anti-suit injunctions, as arose in the infamous *Laker Airways* litigation in the 1980s in the United States and the United Kingdom, could be prevented. *Laker Airways Ltd v Sabena*, 731 F 2d 909 DC Cir (1984); *British Airways Board v Laker Airways Ltd* [1984] 3 WLR 410; [1985] AC 58.

[83] <http://www.internationalcompetitionnetwork.org>. This network was established in 2001.

[84] Policy Statement of the International Chamber of Commerce, 'Extraterritoriality and business', 13 July 2006, Document 103-33/5, recommendation nr 4 (on file with the author). So far, the network has mainly formulated policy proposals for its members (national enforcement agencies).

[85] Council Decision of 13 June 2002 setting up a European network of contact points in respect of persons responsible for genocide, crimes against humanity, and war crimes, [2002] OJ L 167/1.

It appears no wishful thinking to expect that the eventual decision of a court that has sought and/or received the opinion of other States concerned, through judicial networks, will echo other States' comments. From a public international law perspective, that decision, if it is subsequently not criticized by other States, may come to reflect customary international law in the particular field of the law where the decision is taken,[86] or at least be indicative of an emerging consensus, because it is based on consent, whether it is explicit or implicit.[87] If the same issue arises again, States may rely on that decision as constitutive of (emerging) international law—although, admittedly, fact patterns may differ considerably, and thus complicate the legal-precedential value of the decision.[88]

States might nowadays be expected to screen court decisions of which the dispositive part might cause them concern. The recent launch of a databank on international law in domestic courts may greatly facilitate their work (presumably the work of their Foreign Ministries).[89] Ideally, States should intervene when the trial is pending, so that they could still influence the outcome. A relatively brief period during which States may express their objections against the outcome may, however, be reserved. After that period, ignorance may no longer be an acceptable

---

[86] eg Meessen (above n 17) 1118–19 (arguing that the rule which the US Supreme Court set forth in *Empagran* (no jurisdiction for a State over foreign-based harm caused by a global cartel on the sole ground that inflated prices paid in that State were necessary for the cartel's success) represents a rule of instant customary international law, because six foreign governments were involved in the *Empagran* proceedings as *amici curiae* and advocated the sort of jurisdictional restraint espoused by the Supreme Court and the DC Circuit).

[87] On consent and the 'new sovereignty' in the framework of transnational regulatory litigation also Buxbaum (above n 44) 308–16.

[88] Minimalists might argue that law formed in this fashion could only bind the States involved in the initial court decision. This is, however, an overly strict view of international law formation. International law may arguably also crystallize if States do not protest against a State's jurisdictional assertion regarding a situation which, on its face, concerns only one or a few other States directly. It is submitted here that if States intend to oppose the crystallization of a norm of customary international law, they ought to object to *any* decision which might contain such a norm that might *in future* purportedly work to the detriment of their interests. This is, in fact, how we should understand the recent filing of the *amicus curiae* briefs with the US Supreme Court in the case of *Sosa v Alvarez-Machain*, 124 S Ct 2739 (2004)., a case concerning the exercise of universal tort jurisdiction under the US Alien Tort Statute over the arbitrary arrest of a Mexican by a US official in Mexico, by the European Commission, Australia, Switzerland, and the United Kingdom. The *Sosa* case did in no way directly impinge on the intervening States' sovereignty interests, but because its outcome could undeniably influence the legal position of their corporations doing business in far-flung countries where human rights are routinely trampled upon, they prospectively intervened so as to prevent a customary norm authorizing States to liberally exercise universal tort jurisdiction from arising. Brief of *amicus curiae* of the European Commission in *Sosa v Alvarez-Machain* supporting neither party, available at <http://www.sdshh.com/Alvarez/ECBriefforSosavAlvarez_Machain_v1_%5B1%5D.pdf>. Brief of the Governments of the Commonwealth of Australia, the Swiss Confederation, and the United Kingdom of Great Britain and Northern Ireland as *amici curiae* in support of the petitioner, US Supreme Court, *Sosa v Alvarez-Machain*, 23 January 2004, at p 2, available at <http://www.sdshh.com/Alvarez/Sosa%20Brief%20Final.pdf>. Also C Ryngaert, 'The European Commission's Amicus Curiae Brief in the Alvarez-Machain Case', (2004) International Law Forum, nr 6, 55.

[89] Oxford Reports on International Law in Domestic Courts, available at <http://ildc.oup.semcs.net>.

defence. Objections raised against an analogous jurisdictional assertion after the period expired should not be taken into account by the asserting State.[90]

Accordingly, a viable system of extraterritorial jurisdiction could be devised in which the legality of every single assertion is a function of the level of—reasonable—foreign protest aimed at it in a timely manner. While this system should surely take note of the glass ceiling constituted by the pervasive role of political power, low-threshold contacts among courts and regulators of different States through government networks may go a long way in circumscribing it. Power politics could not thrive in a communicative setting which considers all participants to be equal partners and fosters mutual understanding. Extraterritorial jurisdiction has its limits, but possibly less so than ill-conceived substantive solutions putting the weak at a systematic disadvantage. This is not to say that substantivism has *inherent* limits. It has not. This is only to invite negotiators, of weak and strong States alike, to ascertain whether a substantive solution is also a just solution. If States are able to find common ground without abrogating the legitimate rights of the weaker among them, a substantive solution may be preferable.[91] If they are not, a system of cooperative unilateral jurisdiction is an attractive alternative.

[90] It may be objected that some States, especially small and developing States, may lack the resources to study decisions of foreign national courts or regulators that are relevant for the law of jurisdiction. This concern should be taken seriously. If it is indeed established that absence of protest is due, not to negligence, but rather to lack of capacity, it might be argued that such States could not in any way be considered to have acquiesced in the jurisdictional assertion. As argued in section 2.2.e., however, it is not necessary for a norm of universal customary international law to come into being, that all States have actively participated in its formation, nor even that they deliberately acquiesced in it, as long as the specially affected States have done so. While customary international law is consent-based, that does not mean that the specific explicit or implicit consent of every State ought to be secured. If one were to decide otherwise, customary international law could hardly develop. This apparent injustice to small and developing States could possibly be remedied by building capacity in developing States, as a result of which they could at least identify the relevant jurisdictional assertion, persistently object to it, and even, if they could garner sufficient international support, prevent the jurisdictional assertion from gaining customary international law status. Also H Meijers, 'On International Customary International Law in the Netherlands', in IF Dekker and HG Post, eds, *On the Foundations and Sources of International Law* (2003) 92–3 (noting that customary international law could nowadays be developed quickly, and arguing that 'after *a reasonable lapse of time* has passed since the moment a state has made sufficiently clear that it is in favour of the formation of new customary law,—in the absence of objections—the acceptance of the formation of new law may be presumed') (emphasis added).

[91] The Statute of the International Criminal Court (ICC) has been hailed as one of the great creations of international law. In practice however, the ICC may put weaker, developing nations at a systematic disadvantage because they are disproportionately unable to prosecute and investigate situations in which international crimes occur. Developing nations may prefer the exercise of universal jurisdiction by single States, because they are better able to influence these States on a bilateral basis. Compare M Morris, 'High Crimes and Misconceptions: the ICC and non-Party States', (2001) 64 Law & Contemp Probs 13 (employing this as a main argument against the delegation of universal jurisdiction to an unwieldy ICC which States could hardly influence). France for instance abandoned its proceedings against Congolese officials in the *Congo Beach* case after the Republic of Congo filed a complaint with the International Court of Justice. Congo's request is available at <http://www.icj-cij.org/icjwww/idocket/icof/icoforder/icof_iapplication_20020209.pdf>. For the annulment of the proceedings in France: *Chambre d'Instruction Criminelle*, Paris, 22 November 2004, not published.

6.6 Subsidiarity

It has been shown in the previous subsection that a *reasonable* exercise of jurisdiction could spontaneously spring from a network of transnational governance and judicial cooperation. States will inform other States—and relevant private actors—that they intend to exercise jurisdiction over a particular situation. Foreign nations will comment on the proposed assertions, and the asserting States will presumably take foreign concerns into account. The question now arises whether there is a method of assessing the propriety of foreign nations' concerns. It may be well be that, even if an institutionalized cooperative framework has been put in place, different nations' jurisdictional and policy concerns may appear irreconcilable. Would the principle of jurisdictional reasonableness then require the asserting State to defer as a matter of course to the views of the protesting State? In this subsection, it will be argued that deference should not be required in every situation in which foreign nations have raised red flags. Instead, the principle of subsidiarity will be advanced as a method to solve jurisdictional problems. Under this principle, if on the part of the protesting State genuine unwillingness or inability to deal with a situation could be established, the asserting State has the right to unilaterally exercise jurisdiction over that situation in the global interest, even in the face of foreign protest. Foreign unwillingness or inability thus serves as a necessary but also sufficient precondition for a State to exercise jurisdiction.

(a) The *Schutzzweck*-based rule of reason

In Chapter 5, it has been argued that only 'enlightened self-interest' and 'voluntary self-limitation' will restrain the exercise of jurisdiction,[92] especially when the forum State is a powerful State which is not exposed to pressure by foreign States. A jurisdictional rule of reason would not be endowed with international law status, and States would be allowed to promote their interests by exercising jurisdiction as they please. This state of the law is not satisfactory, because it fails to adequately resolve normative competency conflicts.

Defeatism is, in this study's view, not a way forward. Granted, given the intricate workings of power, it is extremely difficult to identify what the international community considers, at a given moment in time, to be connections and interests that are sufficiently strong to justify the exercise of jurisdiction under international law. However, the question may be asked whether *compartmentalizing* the overarching jurisdictional rule of reason may not serve a useful purpose. Along these lines, it is proposed in this subsection to employ the German *Schutzzweck* doctrine as a method of restraining the exercise of jurisdiction, and thus reducing

[92] Meessen (above n 45) 800–1.

international conflict potential. Under this doctrine, the reach of every law is a function of the protective substantive content of that law. This implies that every law, or every legal provision, has its own particular and *reasonable* geographical scope of application, and that thus, the reach of one provision is not readily transposable to another provision.

To start with, it is noticeable that § 403 of the US Restatement (Third) makes the operation of the reasonableness factors dependent on the activity and the purpose of the regulation, and on the regulatory organ.[93] This implies that what is reasonable for one particular activity may be unreasonable for another,[94] and that the requirement of reasonableness is somewhat looser for hierarchically higher—and supposedly democratically more legitimate—State organs. In the field of criminal law, a strong justification for the extraterritorial application of US laws is ordinarily required.[95] The sliding scale of reasonableness illustrates the insight that there is no overarching concept of jurisdiction. There may be common principles, but these are applied and adapted to specific topics,[96] or as Bianchi put it: 'jurisdiction ought to be regarded as a unitary phenomenon characterized by different stages of exercise of authoritative power'.[97] While jurisdiction may depend on the particular field of the law, this need nevertheless not imply that solutions could not sometimes be transferred from one field to another.[98] Indeed, the roots of § 403 itself could be traced to the particular field of international antitrust law (although § 415 now deals specifically with antitrust jurisdiction), particularly to the writings of Brewster and the court decisions in *Timberlane* and *Mannington Mills*.

German doctrine may provide a useful clarification as to the aforementioned sliding scale of jurisdictional reasonableness. In the field of antitrust law, German courts have demanded that a jurisdictional assertion serve the *Schutz-* or *Regelungszweck*, ie, the protective or regulatory purpose, of a particular law or legal provision.[99] The specific requirement of *Schutzzweck* is in fact not alien to

---

[93] A Lowenfeld, in Panel Discussion on the Draft Restatement of the Foreign Relations Law of the United States, (1982) 76 ASIL Proc184, 193; § 403, comment d.

[94] ibid, giving the example of the regulation of different aspects of foreign flag vessels' operations, such as the requirement to take on a pilot, the requirement to produce a cargo manifest, the qualifications of the crew, the wages of the crew, and the principles of ratemaking. Also on the fact that the extent of jurisdiction is dependent on the field of regulation: FA Mann, 'The Doctrine of Jurisdiction Revisited after Twenty Years', (1984-III) 186 RCADI 9, 29; Bianchi (above 34) 76 (pointing out that 'jurisdictional issues deeply diverge from one another depending on the particular field in which they arise'); X (above n 34) 1310 (stating that 'extraterritoriality varies considerably according to the category of substantive law at issue').

[95] § 403, reporters' note 8 ('It is generally accepted by enforcement agencies of the United States government that criminal jurisdiction over activity with substantial foreign elements should be exercised more sparingly than civil jurisdiction over the same activity, and only upon strong justification. [...] Prosecution for activities committed in a foreign state has generally been limited to serious and universally condemned offenses...').

[96] FA Mann, 'The Doctrine of Jurisdiction in International Law', (1964-I) 111 RCADI 1, 52.

[97] Bianchi (above n 34) 78.

[98] Schuster (above n 8) 8.

[99] ibid 31 and 652; Kaffanke (above n 49) 137 (stating that 'die Gerichte...untersuchen...welche Interessen hinter den eigenen Regelungen stehen, und wie diese Interessen

the Restatement, as 'the character of the activity to be regulated' and 'the importance of regulation to the regulating state' feature among the balancing factors
set forth in § 403 of the Restatement.[100] Comment e to § 403 even explicitly
notes that '[t]he criteria set forth in § 403 ... are to be applied in light of the *purpose* which the law in question is designed to achieve'.[101] Under the *Schutzzweck*
doctrine, any legal rule may have its own *reasonable* scope *ratione loci*.[102] In order
to determine this scope, courts and regulators are required to ascertain the *ratio
legis* of the rule. Only if the *ratio legis* requires that foreign situations be governed
by the rule could the rule legitimately be given extraterritorial application. At
times, the legislature will itself have elaborated on the need to regulate foreign
situations if the rule is to serve its purpose. US courts and regulators are in these
situations not allowed to second-guess the legislature's appraisal.[103] However, the
legislature may well have given too wide a scope of application *ratione loci* to the
rule, and exceed by far what is actually needed to serve its protective or regulatory purpose. For purposes of reasonableness therefore, if some doubt is lingering
about the exact reach of a rule, rather than readily deferring to the legislature,
courts and regulators need to inquire into the purpose of the law, and only apply
the law extraterritorially if the purpose is served. For instance, if the purpose of
a capital market law is the protection of investors and the integrity of the capital
market, the law could only be given extraterritorial application if that application
serves that purpose, and *not* if it might serve other purposes, eg, employment or
fiscal purposes.[104] If the purpose of a secondary boycott is the isolation of a governmental regime deemed dangerous, the boycott should not be informed by the
desire to punish foreigners investing, and making profits, in the rogue State. If the
purpose of a law concerning grave breaches of international humanitarian law is
to prevent impunity, it should not be given extraterritorial (universal) application
if the purpose of that application is neo-colonialist tutelage of developing countries. As the protective or regulatory purposes of given laws are often similar in
different States, courts and regulators might be willing to consider the purposes

---

hinter den eigenen Regelungen stehen, und wie diese Interessen angesichts der Konfliktsituation
wirksam geschützt werden können'). The *Schutzzweck* doctrine has its roots in German tort law.
Under § 823 (2) of the German Civil Code (BGB), the compensation obligation 'trifft denjeni-
gen, welcher gegen ein den Schutz eines anderen bezweckendes Gesetz verstösst', ie, when a person culpably contravenes an 'enactment designed to protect someone else'. See for a discussion
in English: W Van Gerven and others, *Cases, Materials and Text on National, Supranational and
International Tort Law Scope of Protection* (1998) 272–3.
[100] § 403(2)(c) of the Restatement (Third).
[101] Emphasis added.
[102] J Stoufflet, 'La compétence extraterritoriale du droit de la concurrence de la Communauté
économique européenne', (1971) 98 JDI 487, 493 (stating that, in the field of economic law, 'les
critères [de rattachement] doivent être définis selon la finalité propre de chaque norme, alors que,
dans le procédé des conflits de lois, un ensemble de règles formant une institution donne lieu à un
rattachement unique, scientifiquement déterminé').
[103] Cf section 3.3.b on the presumption against extraterritoriality.
[104] Schuster (above n 8) 654.

of analogous laws in other States so as to ascertain the purpose of the law before them. This might, in due course, provide an impetus for the crystallization of the *Schutzzweck* doctrine as an objective doctrine of international law.[105] Even better of course would be the adoption of a multilateral Restatement, which clarifies the reach of the law in different subject matter areas, and will probably provide sufficient guidance for courts and regulators.[106]

(b) A transversal application of the subsidiarity principle

It may appear that, in accordance with the *Schutzzweck* doctrine, every single field of the law and even every single provision of every single field, have their own geographical reach, without there being any overarching principles that go substantively further than the ill-defined 'principle of jurisdictional reasonableness'. Is the international law of jurisdiction indeed to be compartmentalized, and do different substantive fields of the law, in light of their own regulatory purpose, follow their own jurisdictional dynamic of what is reasonable? One is tempted to answer this question in the affirmative. However, there seems to be a substantive dynamic at work, sometimes overtly, sometimes covertly, that is already guiding States, and should be guiding them to an ever greater extent, in almost all fields of the law studied: the dynamic of the subsidiarity principle.

Under the subsidiarity principle as understood here, a State may only exercise its jurisdiction if another State with a purportedly stronger nexus to the case fails to do so in ways that are reasonably acceptable to the would-be regulating State or to the international community at large.[107] Subsidiarity presupposes that all States have an interest in clamping down on activities that are harmful to States, and the international community. Although it is a modern concept, its roots could be traced to Grotius, who argued in his *De jure belli ac pacis* that the territorial State, ie the State with arguably the strongest nexus to a situation, is under an obligation to prosecute offences committed within its territory, and that accordingly, if it fails to live up to this obligation, other States are entitled to step in, on a subsidiary basis, so as to protect their interests:

But since established governments were formed, it has been a settled rule, to leave the offences of individuals, which affect their own community, to those states themselves, or to their rulers, to punish or pardon them at their discretion. But they have not the same

---

[105] ibid 653.

[106] Bianchi (above n 34) 91. Somewhat optimistically, Bianchi also believes that '[d]igests, scholarly works, codification by institutions of a private nature or affiliated with international organizations, already provide guidance'. ibid.

[107] In the law of federal systems or integrated international organizations, subsidiarity has a different, although not unrelated meaning. It implies that the federal entity or the international organization may only take action if and in so far as the objectives of the proposed action cannot be sufficiently achieved by the entities of the federation or the Member States and can therefore, by reason of the scale or effects of the proposed action, be better achieved by the federal entity or the international organization. See in particular Article 5, § 2 of the Treaty Establishing the European Community.

plenary authority, or discretion, respecting offences, which affect society at large, and which other independent states or their rulers have a right to punish, in the same manner, as in every country popular actions are allowed for certain misdemeanours. Much less is any state at liberty to pass over in any of his subjects crimes affecting other independent states or sovereigns. On which account any sovereign state or prince has a right to require another power to punish any of its subjects offending in the above named respect: a right essential to the dignity and security of all governments.[108]

Under this Grotian maxim, States agree beforehand, in a state of nature if one could put it this way, to grant the territorial State the primary responsibility to establish jurisdiction over activities that potentially harm the interests of other nations (ie for our purposes primarily the economic activities that have adverse effects on foreign nations' economies, such as the foreign antitrust violations and the foreign fraudulent securities transactions producing domestic effects which have been examined at length in this study), and other harmed States a secondary or subsidiary responsibility. Moreover, under another, related Grotian maxim, bystander States may assume this subsidiary responsibility also in respect of crimes, wherever committed, which qualify by virtue of their particular heinousness as violations of the laws of nature and the *jus gentium*:

It is proper also to observe that kings and those who are possessed of sovereign power have a right to exact punishment not only for injuries affecting immediately themselves or their own subjects, but for gross violations of the law of nature and of nations, done to other states and subjects.[109]

Under the subsidiarity principle, States with the strongest nexus to the case forfeit their right of protest against other States' jurisdictional assertions over that case, if the former States fail to adequately deal with it. However, if these States could advance a good reason for not dealing with the case, deference might be warranted. A good reason is a reason that is not informed by nationalistic calculation but is instead an objective reason that an (imaginary) global regulator would arguably take into account when deciding on whether or not to deal with a particular internationally relevant activity. Under the principle of subsidiarity, sovereignty becomes a relative notion. States should not blindly defer to foreign nations' sovereignty-based arguments against a jurisdictional assertion:[110] such arguments are only valid provided that they link up with the interests and values of the international community.[111] This method implies that one State's

---

[108] H Grotius, *De jure belli ac pacis*, translated by AC Campbell as *The Rights of War and Peace* (1901) lib 2, c 21, No 3.

[109] ibid l 2, c 20, No 40.

[110] Also Buxbaum (above n 44) 311 ('Because reading [*amicus curiae* briefs citing foreign relations problems] as blanket objections to all transnational regulatory litigation in U.S. courts would entirely foreclose the advantages of such litigation…a more differentiated mechanism is required').

[111] ibid 253 (stating that 'traditional jurisdictional rules unnecessarily foreclose valid arguments for marshalling the resources of national courts in order to improve the global welfare'); ibid 255

regulators and courts pass judgment on other regulatory agencies' and courts' quality and willingness to prosecute globally harmful conduct.[112] It may be anathema to a State-centred conception of international law, yet ultimately, it is a most appropriate way to enhance global welfare with minimal transaction costs.

1. Crimes against international law

The rule of reason set forth in section 403 of the Restatement is, pursuant to section 404, not applicable to the exercise of universal jurisdiction over crimes against international law. Any bystander State would be entitled to exercise universal jurisdiction solely on the basis of the heinousness of the act, without additional connecting factors being required. Unrestrained universal jurisdiction is, however, not desirable. From a criminal-political perspective, the territorial State has a stronger case for exercising primary jurisdiction: national reconciliation after gross human rights violations undoubtedly benefits from trials close to the *locus delicti*. However, drawing on the theory advanced in this study, States that fail to genuinely investigate and prosecute crimes against international law committed in their territory, or by their nationals, do ordinarily not have the right of protest against the exercise of—subsidiary—universal jurisdiction by bystander States. It may noted here that, in exceptional circumstances, the benefits of non-prosecution of such crimes (amnesty, pardons, compensation, apologies) outweigh the benefits of prosecution, in terms of long-term prospects for sustainable peace and political reconciliation. The territorial or national State may then have the right of protest against a bystander State's jurisdictional assertion, and the bystander State should defer to the former State if, after having consulted with relevant stakeholders (governments, victims groups, rebel groups, NGOs) and

(arguing that US federal courts, applying regulatory law, 'seek to apply a shared norm, in domestic courts, for the benefit of the international community'). Buxbaum advocates an expanded role for national courts in transnational regulatory litigation in her study, just as this study does. However, she restricts the application of regulatory law to transnational litigation to the situation of substantively similar laws in the relevant jurisdictions. ibid 270 (submitting that 'the primary source of [the conflict engendered by the extraterritorial application of domestic law] is differences in substance between the law applied and the law of the other country or countries involved', and that in the cases she describes as 'transnational regulatory litigation', 'the regulatory community shares the rule applied; thus, the cases do not present the situation where conduct would be permitted in a foreign jurisdiction but forbidden under U.S. law'). ibid 298–9. In this study's view, however, courts should be entitled to exercise jurisdiction over particular conduct even if a rule is not shared, provided that it is established that the conduct harms the interests of the international community. Deciding otherwise would mandate States to become safe havens from where wrongdoers could prey on foreign markets while remaining scot-free on the ground that their conduct is allowed in the territorial State.

   [112] Cf AM Slaughter, 'A Global Community of Courts', (2003) 44 Harv Int'l LJ 191 (2003) ('Over the longer term, a distinct doctrine of "judicial comity" will emerge: a set of principles designed to guide courts in giving deference to foreign courts as a matter of respect owed judges by judges, rather than in terms of the more general national interest as balanced against the foreign nation's interest. At the same time, judges are willing to judge the performance and quality of fellow judges in judicial systems that do not measure up to minimum standards of international justice').

the International Criminal Court through the proposed judicial networks, prosecuting is indeed not in the global (or regional) interest.[113]

Of all the fields of law examined in this study, it is only in the field of crimes against international law that the principle of subsidiarity has so far been explicitly relied upon as a principle of jurisdictional restraint.[114] This has notably occurred in Spain and Germany. Spanish courts, for one, have applied the principle of subsidiarity since 1998.[115] In the 2003 *Peruvian Genocide* case, the Spanish Supreme Court even tightened the principle, and only authorized Spanish courts to exercise universal jurisdiction if such was fully necessary ('principle of necessity of jurisdictional intervention').[116] Under the subsidiarity principle, Spanish authorities are precluded from exercising their jurisdiction if the territorial authorities prove able and willing to prosecute international crimes. In case of competing jurisdictional claims, the territorial or national State is deemed to enjoy jurisdictional priority.[117] Germany, for another, has

---

[113] The prosecution of those responsible for crimes against international humanitarian law committed during the conflict in northern Uganda, between the Lord's Resistance Army (LRA) and the Ugandan Government, could be a case in point. On 13 October 2005, ICC Pre-Trial Chamber II unsealed five arrest warrants against LRA leaders for crimes against Humanity and war crimes committed in Uganda since July 2002 (ICC-02/04-01/05-53-57). After long negotiations, on 22 February 2008, the Ugandan Government and the LRA reached an agreement that would end the conflict. As far as prosecution of presumed perpetrators of crimes is concerned, not all details were hammered out at the time of writing. It nevertheless appeared that, although a division of the Ugandan High Court would try the presumed perpetrators of serious crimes, some perpetrators might get away with apologizing and paying compensation to local elders. Ugandan President Museveni indeed told the press that '[w]hat we have agreed with our people is that they should face traditional justice, which is more compensatory than a retributive system', and then insisted that the ICC withdraw the arrest warrants against the LRA leaders (while it was, ironically, the Ugandan Government that had referred the situation to the ICC on 29 January 2004, ICC-20040129-44-En). Cf <http://news.bbc.co.uk/2/hi/africa/7260798.stm>, and <http://news.bbc.co.uk/2/hi/africa/7291274.stm>. Although the ICC Prosecutor refused to do so, the Ugandan situation raised interesting questions over whether prosecution is always desirable. The threat of international prosecution, by the ICC or by 'bystander' States exercising universal jurisdiction, may well deter rebels from laying down arms, and thus draw out the conflict and undermine political reconciliation.

[114] *In extenso* C Ryngaert, 'Applying the Rome Statute's Complementarity Principle: Drawing Lessons from the Prosecution of Core Crimes by States Acting under the Universality Principle', (2008) Criminal Law Forum 153.

[115] National Criminal Court, *Pinochet*, Rulings of 4 and 5 November 1998, available at <http://www.derechos.org/nizkor/arg/espana/juri.html> ('[Article 6 of the Genocide Convention] imposes subsidiarity status upon actions taken by jurisdictions different from those envisioned in the precept. Thus, the jurisdiction of a State should abstain from exercising jurisdiction regarding acts constituting a crime of genocide that are being tried by the courts of the country in which said acts were perpetrated or by an international court').

[116] Supreme Court of Spain, *Peruvian Genocide*, (2003) 42 ILM 1200. Also N Roht-Arriaza, 'Universal Jurisdiction: Steps Forward, Step Back', (2004) 17 Leiden J Int'l L 375. In the *Peruvian Genocide case*, the Supreme Court derived the principle of necessity of jurisdictional intervention from the 'nature and the finality of universal jurisdiction' ('*la propia naturaleza y finalidad de la jurisdicción universal*').

[117] Constitutional Court Spain (Second Chamber), *Guatemala Genocide case*, judgment No STC 237/2005, available at <http://www.tribunalconstitucional.es/jurisprudencia/Stc2005/STC2005-237.html>.

provided since 2002 in its Code of Criminal Procedure (§ 153 f StPO), amended
as a result of the adoption of the Code of Crimes against International Law, that
German courts will only exercise their jurisdiction over international crimes if
the directly affected State fails to do so. In both Spain and Germany, however,
application of the principle of subsidiarity may, as for now, not be seen as a hard
duty under international law.[118]

2. Common crimes

The subsidiarity principle may also apply to common crimes over which extraterritorial jurisdiction may be exercised under the accepted principles of criminal jurisdiction discussed in Chapter 4 (active personality, passive personality,
protective, and representational principle). While the asserting State may have a
stronger interest in prosecuting offenders under these principles than under the
universality principle, and while it has been argued that public international law
does not prioritize the bases of jurisdiction,[119] from a criminal policy perspective it is nevertheless arguable that the territorial State should enjoy primacy of
jurisdiction, in light of its access to evidence and of *its* public order being violated to a greater extent than a foreign State's public order. Only if the territorial
State fails to adequately prosecute the offender, should other States be allowed
to step in, relying on the above-mentioned principles. The subsidiarity principle
implies that, even if the offender is in custody of a non-territorial State, that State
should extradite him or her to the territorial State, if at least it is able and willing to prosecute the offender. In exceptional circumstances, the non-territorial
State may enjoy concurring primary jurisdiction with the territorial State, eg, in
case of an offence committed *by* a national of the former State *against* a national
of the former State (cumulative application of the active and passive personality
principle). In general however, the territorial State should be entitled to legitimately oppose *any* assertion of jurisdiction by another State over an act committed
within the territory of the former State, if at least the latter State is willing to
adequately prosecute the act concerned, or if the act is not an offence under territorial law.

---

[118] The Spanish Constitutional Court ruled in the 2005 *Guatemala Genocide* case, that subsidiarity was not required under international law, but was merely a political-criminal concept
pointing at the priority of the *locus delicti*. Also N Roht-Arriaza, comment Spanish Constitutional
Court, *Guatemala Genocide case*, (2006) 100 AJIL 213 ('Spain's Constitutional Tribunal helped
to clarify that such accommodations [deference to the home State] are neither jurisdictional nor
required—the International Criminal Court's 'unable or unwilling' requirement does not apply
to national courts'). The latter judgment reinforces the case against reasonableness as a duty *de lege
lata* under international law, a case this study made in Chapter 5.

The German federal prosecutor, for her part, is similarly not *obliged* to apply the subsidiarity
principle. § 153 (f) of the Code of Criminal Procedure merely *counsels against* prosecution of a crime
against international humanitarian law if the offence is being prosecuted before an international
court or by a State on whose territory the offence is committed or whose national was harmed by it.

[119] Cf section 4.6.

3. Economic law

In the field of economic law, the subsidiarity principle is not as straightforward a principle to apply as in the field of criminal law. Legitimate rights of protest are available on a wider scale there. Because harmful economic practices originating in one State do not violate *jus cogens*, other States that are not directly harmed by them are, in accordance with the first Grotian maxim cited above and the harm test advanced in Chapter 2, not entitled to exercise jurisdiction in the first place. Yet even States that *are*, one way or the other, harmed by these practices, do not have an absolute subsidiary right to exercise jurisdiction over them if the State with the strongest (territorial) nexus to the economic activity fails to deal with them. They should refrain from doing so when it is not in the interest of the international community. Unlike most common crimes, which are often crimes anywhere and are thus globally despicable, economic activities may be harmful to one State, but at the same time beneficial to another, and even to the international community at large.[120]

Relying on international interests is an important departure from classical jurisdictional theory, which delimits spheres of jurisdiction on the basis of State connections or interests, and solves normative competency conflicts on the basis of a formal balancing of such connections and interests. Under the principle advocated here, connections and interests are not the primary factors guiding the jurisdictional analysis. Instead, States are invited to ascertain whether regulation, or non-regulation, of a situation that has transnational economic repercussions, would be *in the global interest*. The State which has the strongest nexus to the case has the primary right to conduct the global interest analysis, yet if it does so disingenuously and replaces it with a *national* interest analysis, other States, with a somewhat weaker nexus to the case, are authorized to step in and exercise jurisdiction on a subsidiary basis.

The 'global economic interest' method is in fact a law and economics method of jurisdictional reasonableness. This method, of which Guzman is the standard-bearer, searches for rules that 'permit transactions to take place when the total impact on welfare is positive, and prevent transactions from taking place when the total impact on welfare is negative'.[121] It has mostly been applied to extraterritorial antitrust jurisdiction.

The law and economics approach makes the correct observation that States, when unilaterally regulating a particular economic transaction, only take into account their own interests, and not the interests of other States, or of the international community.[122] They are only concerned with the maximization of

---

[120] Serious economic crimes, such as antitrust conspiracies (hardcore cartels), may, however, surely be globally despicable. See as early as 1969: B Goldman, 'Les champs d'application territoriale des lois sur la concurrence', (1969-III) 128 RCADI 631, 703.

[121] Guzman (above n 34) 896.

[122] eg PC Mavroidis and DJ Neven, 'Some Reflections on Extraterritoriality in International Economic Law: A Law and Economics Analysis', *Mélanges en hommage à Michel Waelbroeck*, II

their own national welfare, and not with the maximization of global welfare. This may lead a State to permit certain anticompetitive behavior to take place on its territory, eg to condone export cartels, because so doing yields internal benefits for that State and externalizes the costs (which are passed on to another State).[123] Put differently, States often do not focus on *global* efficiency but only on the domestic distributional effects of allowing or prohibiting a particular transaction.[124]

This is not to say that a focus on distributional effects instead of on global efficiency necessarily reduces global welfare. At times, a focus on the national interest may indeed *further* global welfare, if the domestic positive effects of (non-)regulation also translate into net global positive effects, eg when a territorial State's condoning of export cartels, eg US practice under the 1918 Webb-Pomerene Act,[125] or conversely, another State's dismantling of these very cartels, yields domestic benefits that outweigh aggregate foreign harm.[126] Yet clearly, this will not happen as a matter of course. As long as a country's share of global consumption is different from its share of global production that country will 'not adopt the optimal global policy'.[127] States will indeed continue to condone or dismantle export cartels, in the former situation exercising territorial and in the latter extraterritorial jurisdiction, even if the aggregate foreign harm outweighs the domestic benefits.[128] Accordingly, granting States the power to regulate a particular transnational transaction as soon as it affects them ('effects doctrine', based on the objective territorial principle), is not an appropriate jurisdictional (or choice-of-law) method.

An unqualified effects doctrine is bound to fail if the maximization of global welfare is the ultimate goal of economic regulation. It will only lead to a *suboptimal* level of regulation.[129] This level is a level of *over*regulation, since *any* State that is adversely affected by a foreign restrictive practice will tend to assert

---

(1999) 1297, 1319 (stating that 'when government[s] rule on particular activit[i]es, they do not take into account the costs and benefits that accrue to agents outside their constituencies').

[123] AT Guzman, 'Is International Antitrust Possible?', (1998) 73 NYU L Rev 1501, 1514 ('As long as the welfare loss from anticompetitive activities is borne by foreign consumers, the optimal international antitrust policy, from a national perspective, is no policy at all'); Stoufflet (above n 102) 490 (pointing out that 'on n'imagine guère qu'[un Etat] facilite l'intégration des marchés étrangers en exerçant une contrainte sur ses propres entreprises car ses intérêts immédiats sont probablement en sens opposé'); I Seidl-Hohenveldern, 'Völkerrechtliche Grenzen bei der Anwendung des Kartellrechts', (1971) 17 AWD 53, 55–6 (speaking of a 'nationalistische Inkonsequenz').

[124] Cf Guzman (above n 34) 899.

[125] Pub L No 65-126, 40 Stat 516 (1918), codified at 15 USC §§ 16-66 (1994).

[126] For the latter situation Guzman (above n 123) 1515 ('The policy of the importing country is different from the optimal global policy because it fails to take into account the increase in profits earned by producers').

[127] ibid 1519–20.

[128] ibid 1520 (stating that 'a country that can apply its laws extraterritorially will underregulate anticompetitive behavior if it is a net exporter and overregulate such behavior if it is a net importer').

[129] Cf Guzman (above n 34) 904–5.

its jurisdiction over this practice without due regard for global regulatory efficiency.[130] As the applicable laws usually do not have the same content, concurring jurisdiction will lead to a situation in which corporations are subject to the strictest standards of every jurisdictional regime, with any more relaxed standard of one State's law being overridden by a stricter standard of another State's law.[131] From an international law perspective, such cumulative overregulation may be at odds with the principle of restricted sovereignty in a modern interdependent world.[132] From a global law and economics perspective, it results in regulatory inefficiency.

For the rule of reason set forth in § 403 of the Restatement, the law and economics approach teaches us that a sovereignty-based focus on governmental interests instead of on global regulatory efficiency is not welfare-enhancing. In most cases, courts and regulators will display a pro-forum bias. In effect, they are supposed to represent *only* the national interest. Admittedly, they may decline to exercise jurisdiction on grounds of comity, if they believe that another State has a stronger nexus to the situation. Yet in so doing, they still act in the national interest, convinced as they are that the long-term interest of the State is jeopardized by souring international relations stemming from overbroad jurisdictional assertions, and as a related argument, that restraint invites beneficial reciprocity (as in future, when the tables are turned, a foreign State might be inclined to condone harmful restrictive practices originating in the former State). They do not, however, take a bird's eye view of the matter: merely aiming at protecting short- or long-term interests of the State, they do not intervene as regulators acting in the interest of *global efficiency*.

Against the law and economics approach, it could be argued that the evaluation process under § 403 ought not to be reduced to a merely mathematical calculus. It is not so much the *number* of connections which is important, but rather the weight of the interests protected by these connections.[133] Also, a State does not have jurisdiction over a particular situation for the sole reason that this might confer more economic benefits on it than deference to another State would confer benefits on the latter State. Putting a high premium on economic efficiency risks neglecting other, non-economic considerations (eg social protection, cultural diversity,...), which are *also* protected by the principle of non-intervention.[134] By virtue of this principle, every State has the right, without interference from abroad, to build the national socio-economic order which it sees fit (provided it keeps within the boundaries of specific international norms, such as human

---

[130] Taking a law and economics perspective, Guzman has therefore condemned the Supreme Court's ruling in *Hartford Fire*. ibid 919.

[131] ibid 908.

[132] eg Schuster (above n 8) 664 and 685.

[133] ibid 686.

[134] ibid 687 (taking issue with R Deville, *Die Konkretisierung des Abwägungsgebots im internationalen Kartellrecht* (1990) 101).

rights and trade rules).[135] If emphasis is only laid on economic efficiency, Anglo-Saxon rules might easily become the standard rules in other parts of the world. Moreover, even if all States pursued economic efficiency in their regulation, an economic application of § 403 might harm the interests of smaller States, as, in absolute terms, harm to their interests will almost invariably be smaller than harm to the interests of larger States.[136] For all its suasion, the law and economics approach to jurisdiction ought therefore to be viewed with some suspicion.

Only if the application of the 'global interest approach' is limited to particular domains of the law, such as antitrust and securities regulation, and if non-economic considerations could be quantified to the same extent that economic considerations could, should it be applied by courts and regulators.

4. Antitrust law

In the field of antitrust law, according to the 'global interest' approach, cartel and merger activity ought to be condoned when this produces global economic benefits (an outcome which is more likely in the case of merger activity),[137] and to be clamped down on when it does not. The State where the cartel has been formed or where the merging corporations are located may be said to have primary jurisdiction in this respect, because, under the first Grotian maxim, it is incumbent upon that State to ensure that offences taking place or originating in their territory are adequately dealt with. Other States, on whose economies the anticompetitive effects of foreign practices are felt, are authorized to prohibit these practices on a subsidiary basis if the territorial State fails to do so, by exercising 'extraterritorial' jurisdiction. States which do not sustain substantial injuries from purportedly harmful foreign practices do not have jurisdiction, because without harm there can be no legitimate jurisdiction. The State where the anticompetitive agreement was formed or where the merging corporations are (or one of them is) located, is authorized to protest against another State's jurisdictional assertion, but, in order to be effective, these protests should not be couched in terms of a desire to create

---

[135] Seidl-Hohenveldern (above n 123) 57 ('Im Hinblick darauf aber, dass die einzelnen Staaten der Völkerrechtsgemeinschaft die durch ein bestimmtes Gesetz gesicherter Werte sehr verschieden hoch einschätzen, kann ein solcher Staat [who applies its antitrust law to foreign situations] nicht erwarten, dass die anderen Staaten die Höher-Einschätzung dergestalt nachvollziehen, dass sie infolge dieser von ihm behaupteten Höherwertigkeit ihre sorge um die Wahrung ihrer eigenen Souveränität hintanstellen würden').

[136] Schuster (above n 8) 687–8.

[137] It is, doubtless, unlikely that hard-core cartels will produce global economic effects. Buxbaum (above n 44) 300 (noting that 'a shared view emerges on the question of [the desirability of punishing] hard-core price-fixing'). Yet it has also been argued that other antitrust violations are per se internationally undesirable and should thus be internationally illegal. Draetta (above n 55) 566 (stating that 'antitrust behavior, where global in nature, should not be treated differently than other kinds of global illegal conduct (environmental crimes, drug trafficking, international corruption, insider trading, money laundering, etc.)'). For our analysis, this may imply that a State who has primary jurisdiction over restrictive business practices could not legitimately protest against other States' exercise of subsidiary jurisdiction over such practices, if it has been proved that the former State was genuinely unable and unwilling to clamp down on the practices.

a national champion in a particular industrial sector (unless the global economic benefits of the creation of such a champion outweigh the drawbacks) or a desire not to have its territorial sovereignty encroached upon by other States (for, as Lowenfeld argued, 'talk of "sovereignty" clouds, it does not illuminate').[138] It may be noted that an acceptable defence could be a State's credible offer to commence investigations and enforce competition law locally.[139]

5. Securities law

In the field of securities fraud, the State of the stock exchange on which the securities are traded ordinarily enjoys primary jurisdiction, because the impact of securities fraud is likely to be the strongest in that State, and national financial regulators monitor their own territorial financial markets more intensively than foreign markets. The States where the effects of the fraud are felt, where the conduct takes place, or whose nationals were involved in the fraud, enjoy subsidiary jurisdiction, ie, jurisdiction that only obtains if the State where the relevant stock exchange is located fails to adequately deal with the fraudulent transaction. Exceptionally, the States where the effects are felt may enjoy primary jurisdiction if they are able to make the case that the fraudulent securities transaction has stronger effects on them than on the State of the stock exchange.

If the exchange-based system to jurisdiction is applied to securities registration and corporate governance regulation, this might imply that States have primary jurisdiction to set rules for issuers, including foreign issuers, listed on a stock exchange located in their territory, and their public accounting firms, including foreign ones, since it is in the interest of investors trading securities on this exchange to have full and fair disclosure of the corporate situation of *any* issuer, whether domestic or foreign. However, foreign issuers are typically already listed on a stock exchange in their home State, and have, accordingly, already to comply with home country regulations. In this situation, in view of the nexus of both incorporation and listing, the foreign State should enjoy primary jurisdiction. The State on whose stock exchange the securities are cross-listed enjoys subsidiary jurisdiction: it should only impose burdens on foreign corporations if the foreign State is unable or unwilling to adequately regulate them. That the foreign

---

[138] Lowenfeld (above n 25) 307. In economic law, almost any jurisdictional assertion could be indeed be justified under the territorial principle, the bedrock of the sovereignty concept. PJ Kuyper, 'The European Community and the U.S. Pipeline Embargo: Comments on Comments', (1984) GYIL 72, 93. Also DW Jackson, 'Sovereignty, Transnational Constraints, and Universal Criminal Jurisdiction', in ML Volcansek and JF Stack, Jr, eds, *Courts Crossing Borders: Blurring the Lines of Sovereignty* (2005) 159 ('[Sovereignty] is a fickle world whose meanings most often have been socially constructed for instrumental purposes').

[139] Also Buxbaum (above n 44) 316 ('Having objected to U.S. litigation on the basis of conflicts with its own regulatory scheme...a foreign country might be less willing to leave the conduct unregulated. Thus, even if the claims of certain foreign purchasers were not ultimately litigated in U.S. court, their filing could potentially highlight the local enforcement of internationally shared standards of conduct and thereby improve global regulation overall').

State does not have the same regulations is not a sufficient argument for a State to apply its own laws indiscriminately. Only if the regulatory protective purpose (*Schutzzweck*) could not be met through reliance on home country regulation should it step in. At the same time, however, the State asserting its jurisdiction should ascertain whether its high level of regulation is actually justified from a global perspective, and in particular whether other, more deregulated systems could not achieve the same level of capital market integrity. Less far-reaching disclosure, internal controls, and auditor independence do, in terms of evilness, surely not measure up to such practices as fraudulent securities transactions and hard-core cartels that no State could reasonably condone. Rational States could reasonably differ over the number of reports that issuers should annually file, the number of independent directors which issuers should have, and whether and what activities beyond their core audit activities auditors should be authorized to perform. States should therefore be very circumspect in exercising subsidiary jurisdiction in the field of securities registration and corporate governance. They should only do so when a foreign corporation is blatantly underregulated in its home State. Encouragingly and rightly so, foreign corporations have in recent times been granted wide-ranging exemptions from US and EC securities and corporate governance regulations.

6. Secondary boycotts

As far as boycott legislation is concerned, every State has the primary and arguably exclusive right to decide on whether or not to impose an economic embargo against a foreign State. However, a State does not ordinarily have jurisdiction to impose a secondary boycott that requires corporations of another State to comply with the boycott laws of the former. Subsidiarity does not come into play here, because a State's decision not to impose sanctions against another State (on the grounds that that State's isolation is not desirable or that sanctions are not a useful tool to pressure it into adapting its behaviour) constitutes a legitimate decision of a State which another State is not entitled to second-guess. Only when the Security Council adopts a resolution under Chapter VII of the UN Charter may States be required to comply with a boycott regime. Secondary boycotts are acceptable only in the exceptional situation of a major security threat being posed by State X against State Y, with third States shipping goods to State X that considerably strengthen its military capabilities. This situation is likely to arise only in times of war or quasi-war,[140] and not in peacetime.

---

[140] See, eg section 5(b) of the Trading with the Enemy Act of 1917, 40 Stat 411. US Treasury Public Circular No 18, 30 March 1942, 7 Fed Reg 2503 (1 April 1942) (US Treasury including at the height of the Second World War in the category 'persons subject to the jurisdiction of the United States' set forth in the Trading with the Enemy Act of 1917 'any corporation or other entity, wherever organized or doing business, owned or controlled by [U.S.] persons').

7. Extraterritorial discovery

In the field of transnational evidence-taking, the State where the documents or witnesses are located has the primary right to decide whether these documents will be produced, or witnesses deposed, for use in a foreign proceeding. Yet, in accordance with the first Grotian maxim, they should not allow their territory to be used as a safe haven where wrongdoers could hide their materials from foreign courts and regulators. States should therefore honour other States' reasonable requests for judicial cooperation. They are authorized to reject such requests if their content reflects a particular State's idiosyncratic views on how evidence should be produced by the parties to a dispute. States could thus reject too broadly framed judicial assistance requests, such as requests for the production of materials which most States do not consider as relevant for the solution of the underlying dispute ('fishing expeditions'). If the requested State is, however, unable and unwilling to cooperate with reasonable requests by the requesting State, the latter State is entitled to exercise jurisdiction on a subsidiary basis by unilaterally ordering discovery from a person over whom it could establish personal jurisdiction.

(c) From nexus to international interests

Enlightened international lawyers have traditionally argued that jurisdictional conflicts ought to be solved by attaching a legal situation to the State with the strongest nexus to that situation.[141] They deemed it irrelevant whether the State with that nexus had a legitimate reason to apply or not to apply its laws to that situation. As soon as the nexus requirement was met, the chosen State could regulate, or not regulate, at will. Underlying this theory was the view that the international community has no interest in ensuring that the ideal level of international regulation, beneficial to the common good, is achieved, or that perpetrators of serious offences are brought to justice. In this study, the importance of the nexus factor has been recognized. However, at the same time, it has been argued that States should not be allowed to hide behind the nexus veil by allowing activities that harm the interests of other States or the international community. It has been proposed to lift that veil if the State with the strongest nexus to the case is unable or unwilling to adequately deal with an internationally or transnationally relevant situation. In the absence of a global regulator, other States that are harmed should be entitled to *subsidiarily* exercise jurisdiction in the interest of the international community.[142] Unilateral jurisdiction then in fact becomes an

---

[141] The rule of reason enshrined in section 403 of the US Restatement of Foreign Relations Law discussed in Chapter 5 was exactly aimed at doing so.

[142] Core crimes against international law may be considered to violate *erga omnes* obligations. Any State may therefore said to be harmed by such violations, and thus to have an interest in prosecuting them.

internationally cooperative exercise, with States stepping in where other States unjustifiably fail to establish their jurisdiction.[143]

Obviously, current State practice may sometimes be a far cry from these theoretical musings. Yet in several fields of the law, there is undeniably a process under way that increasingly emphasizes subsidiarity. This is clearest in the field of gross human rights violations. In Europe, prosecutors and courts tend to limit their assertions of universal criminal jurisdiction over such violations when foreign States are able and willing to investigate and prosecute. In the United States, federal courts exercising universal tort jurisdiction under the Alien Tort Statute over these violations defer to another State when that State provides an alternative and adequate forum (*forum non conveniens* analysis). Yet even in antitrust law, where hard and fast rules of jurisdiction have always proved so elusive, change is noticeable. For one, the 1998 transatlantic comity agreement on antitrust enforcement cooperation sets forth that a party may ask the other party to clamp down on a particular restrictive practice (positive comity),[144] it being understood that the one party could subsidiarily exercise its jurisdiction if the other fails to genuinely investigate and prosecute the practice. For another, there is now a lively discussion going on in the United States, in the aftermath of the US Supreme Court's decision in the 2004 *Empagran* case, relating to the question whether, from a global antitrust deterrence perspective, the United States should not have a right or duty to dismantle foreign-based hardcore cartels producing global, including US, harm, when States with a stronger nexus to the cartels do not muster the resources or willingness to do so.

Taking the insights of the last two sections together, one arrives at what may be this study's main recommendation to solve the conundrum of jurisdiction. As far as possible, States should seek and take into account comments by relevant foreign actors on their proposed jurisdictional assertions. Yet *heeding* foreign concerns should not be synonymous with *deferring* to foreign concerns. The modern law of jurisdiction may have put too heavy an emphasis on techniques of

---

[143] Unilateral jurisdiction may not only become cooperative on the basis of a customary international law subsidiarity principle, but also on the basis of treaties (eg the anti-terrorism treaties providing for universal jurisdiction under an *aut dedere aut judicare* clause). In addition, a plaintiff alleging harm sustained abroad could legitimately choose an 'extraterritorial' forum to bring his claim because of his residence in that State or his familiarity with applicable law, at least if the foreign forum could secure personal jurisdiction over the defendant. The reach of that State's laws need not undermine the protective policies underlying the territorial State's laws, because if the foreign forum were not available, the plaintiff may possibly not have brought a suit at all. This would not have furthered the regulatory interests of the territorial State. Cf GB Born, 'A Reappraisal of the Extraterritorial Reach of U.S. Law', (1992) 24 Law & Pol Int'l Bus 1, 77 (pointing out that the Supreme Court's decision in *Aramco*, which confined Title VII of the Civil Rights Act of 1964 to US territory, 'arguably detracted from the efficacy of Saudi Arabia's own prohibitions against employment discrimination, which Boureslan [the plaintiff in the case] likely could not effectively invoke once he had been forced to return to the United States').

[144] Article 6 of the Agreement Between the European Communities and the Government of the United States of America on the Application of the Positive Comity Principles in the Enforcement of their Competition Laws, [1998] OJ L 173/28; (1999) 4 CMLR 502.

jurisdictional *restraint*, and may have cast legitimate assertions of jurisdiction in a negative light. This is not to say that a return to *Lotus* is apt. It is certainly not, primarily because the *Lotus* decision was informed by considerations of State sovereignty: requiring States to restrain their jurisdictional assertions was considered to be an unwarranted assault on their sovereign prerogatives.[145]

This study recognizes the importance of sovereignty in international law, yet it advocates a jurisdictional system in which the interests of the *international community*, and not of single 'sovereign' States, become centre-stage. In the absence of an internationally centralized law enforcer, States should be entitled to exercise *subsidiary* 'extraterritorial' jurisdiction over situations which other States, which entertain a greater nexus, fail to adequately deal with. The former States should, as argued, exercise their jurisdiction with a view to furthering the interests of the international community rather to advancing their own interests. Arguably, non-affected States may be better situated than affected States to represent those global interests. Granting subsidiary jurisdiction to such (non-affected) States may be feasible as far as international crimes are concerned, as these crimes typically affect only a local community. In the field of economic law, however, where the effect of violations is often nearly global, it may difficult to find a non-affected State, let alone such a State with the wherewithal to effectively exercise its jurisdiction.

6.7 A Transatlantic Gap over Jurisdiction

This study has taken a particular interest in examining different attitudes toward jurisdiction across the Atlantic. This final chapter has so far devoted its attention to developing a new general theory of jurisdiction. Reference has been made to differences between the United States and Europe as to the exercise of jurisdiction. Yet, obviously, this study, in light of one of its main research purposes, could not do without a systematic overview of either a real or an imaginary transatlantic gap over jurisdiction. Presenting this overview is what will be attempted in this section.

It has been a starting thesis that the United States is more of a jurisdictional bully, if one can put it that way, than Europe. Throughout this study, the thesis that the United States tends to exercise jurisdiction without due regard for foreign nations' concerns, has been largely vindicated. As far as secondary boycotts and extraterritorial discovery are concerned, for instance, the European position on the issue has been merely cast in terms of opposition against aggressive US jurisdictional assertions. Yet in the other fields as well, attention has been devoted disproportionately to US practice (with the notable exception of universal criminal jurisdiction). In most fields, Europe plays second fiddle as far as engaging itself in 'extraterritorial' jurisdiction is concerned, and is often reduced to objecting to US jurisdictional assertions.

---

[145] Cf section 2.1.

The question ineluctably arises why it is that the United States has been so active in exercising jurisdiction over foreign situations, especially in the field of economic law. After all, the United States is a common law country and inherited upon gaining independence in the late eighteenth century an English legal framework which was outright hostile to geographically expanding the ambit of the law beyond a State's boundaries. It will be argued in this section that it was primarily the development of a truly international economy that caused the United States in the mid-twentieth century to shed the constraints imposed on it by its English heritage (a), a heritage which proved, at the European level, surprisingly influential regarding the 'extraterritorial' application of EC competition law until the late twentieth century (b). The scope *ratione loci* of EC competition law may nowadays be quite similar to the scope of US antitrust law. Still, the United States remains at the forefront of the expansion of the reach of economic laws, primarily because strict economic regulation is so much emphasized in the United States. The application of the 2002 US Sarbanes-Oxley corporate governance law to European issuers and their auditors may serve to illustrate this. One is tempted to believe that the United States considers its jurisdictional assertions to be justified on the ground that its underlying substantive economic laws are exceptionally good (c). US exceptionalism may also explain the US attitude toward the universal prosecution of core crimes against international law, which most European States believe is a moral imperative, but which the United States is not particularly supportive of. It will be shown how the reach of a State's universality laws is not a function of the restraint posed or latitude granted by public international law, but rather of substantive policy choices (d).

(a) Shedding common law restrictions on the exercise of economic jurisdiction in the United States

In sections 3.1 and 3.2, it has been demonstrated how the law of jurisdiction developed historically along different lines. In continental Europe, territoriality only became the main principle of jurisdictional order in the eighteenth century, although exceptions to it, mainly based on the personality principle, were, and still are, rife. In contrast, it was very early in English legal history, in the Middle Ages, that territoriality obtained an almost unassailable status as the bedrock principle of jurisdiction. Exceptions to it should not be allowed, for reasons related to English judicial organization (the jury system and the law of evidence). As of today, there are few possibilities to exercise jurisdiction over foreign situations under English law. The ambit of US criminal law is, like the ambit of English criminal law and in line with the system of US judicial organization (which is largely based on the English system), fairly modest as well. Compared to continental Europe, there are few possibilities for exercising nationality-based, protective, representative, or universal jurisdiction in the United States.

However, jurisdiction was historically almost exclusively studied in a criminal law context, and not in an economic context. The United States has precisely expanded the ambit of its *economic* laws. Admittedly, the reach of a State's civil laws was studied throughout history, but that occurred in the context of conflict of laws (private international law) rather than of jurisdiction under public international law.[146] Economic law, which is a mix of both private (civil) and public (regulatory) law, has historically not been studied at all, because it only came into being in the late nineteenth century, during the second Industrial Revolution. Because of the different challenges presented by the rapid development of the national, and later international, economy, solutions to jurisdictional questions that arose in a different time and in a different context were seen as unsatisfactory.

When, in the twentieth century, the US economy was seen as under threat from foreign business restrictive practices and foreign securities fraud, courts, often in purely private disputes, duly applied US antitrust and securities laws to foreign situations. From a legal perspective, although it required a stretch, US jurisdictional assertions were justified under the objective (or at times subjective) territorial principle. Throughout the nineteenth century, US courts had explored the jurisdictional possibilities of this principle in a criminal law context, because territoriality was the only principle under which a jurisdictional assertion could be justified.[147] In the twentieth century, it was argued that US jurisdiction over foreign antitrust violations and securities fraud that had a territorial impact (effect) in the United States could be justified under the objective territorial principle, and that US jurisdiction over US securities fraud (conduct) that caused effects abroad could be justified under the subjective territorial principle. The implicit assumption was that preying on foreign economic markets was conceptually not very different from the textbook criminal law situation of a man shooting a gun across a frontier.[148]

---

[146] See section 3.1 on the doctrine of the Italian statutists, and the comity doctrine (see also section 5.1) as proposed by Ulrik Huber, which were mainly concerned with justifying how the territorial State could give effect to another State's laws in its territory. Huber's comity doctrine was later however rediscovered as a tool of jurisdictional restraint, especially in the field of US economic law. It was argued that the asserting State should take the interests of other States into account when promoting its interests extraterritorially. See Chapter 5 (jurisdictional rule of reason).

Some twentieth century commentators stated that international law only poses limits to the reach of a State's criminal laws, but not to the reach of a State's *civil* laws. G Fitzmaurice, 'The General Principles of International Law', (1957-II) 92 RCADI 1, 218 (arguing that 'public international law does not effect any delimitation of spheres of competence in the civil sphere, and seems to leave the matter entirely to private international law—that is to say in effect to the States themselves for determination, each in accordance with its own internal law'); M Akehurst, 'Jurisdiction in International Law', (1972–1973) 46 BYIL 145, 172 ('It is hard to resist the conclusion that . . . customary international law imposes no limits on the jurisdiction of municipal courts in civil trials').

[147] Cf sections 3.4.a and b.

[148] However, see D Edward, 'The Practice of the Community Institutions in Relation to Extraterritorial Application of EEC Competition Law', in R Bieber and G Ress, eds, *The Dynamics of EC Law* (1987) 355, 356.

(b) Shedding common law restrictions on the exercise of antitrust jurisdiction in Europe

In Europe, remarkably, the evolution toward applying the objective territorial principle in international economic law, antitrust law in particular, did not occur in England (whose legal system resembles the US system). In section 3.4.a it has been shown how England stuck rigidly, until the late twentieth century, to a conduct-based, and later terminatory, approach to (criminal) jurisdiction, pursuant to which English jurisdiction only obtains when the criminal conduct takes place in England. Because the territorial economic effects of a foreign antitrust violation did not qualify as territorial conduct, effects-based antitrust jurisdiction failed to take roots in England. US effects-based assertions moreover led to fierce conflicts between the United Kingdom and the United States. What is more, because of the influence that the United Kingdom was able to wield over the formation of extraterritorial jurisdiction in EC competition matters, the English view on jurisdiction came to represent the European view, sidelining more progressive views held for instance in Germany.

In the seminal *Dyestuffs* case, a cartel case which reached the European Court of Justice (ECJ) in 1972, in which ICI, an English corporation, numbered among the defendants, the United Kingdom, at that time not yet a European Union Member State filed an *Aide Mémoire* with the European Commission, rejecting the Commission's effects-based jurisdictional assertions over ICI as incompatible with public international law.[149] The *Aide Mémoire* was instrumental in persuading the ECJ (but not the Advocate General) not to apply the effects doctrine to the *Dyestuffs* case. Instead, the Court applied the rather uncontroversial economic entity doctrine, a doctrine long known in corporate law, under which the restrictive acts of ICI's EC-based subsidiary were imputed to ICI itself. When the ambit of EC competition law came again before the ECJ in *Wood Pulp* (1988), a case in which the cartelists had no EC subsidiaries, the United Kingdom was again able to influence the decision, albeit less openly. Heeding English concerns, the ECJ, unlike the Advocate General, did not apply the effects doctrine to the case—a doctrine which was anathema to the English law of jurisdiction—but the implementation doctrine.[150] Using this doctrine,

---

[149] *Aide Mémoire* of the United Kingdom Government, 20,October 1969, on the *Dyestuffs* case, reprinted as Annex B to the *Report of the Committee on Extraterritorial Application of Restrictive Trade Legislation*, International Law Association, Report of the Fifty-Fourth Conference 184, 185–6 (1970) ('The Commission will be aware that certain claims to exercise extra-territorial jurisdiction in antitrust proceedings have given rise to serious and continuing disputes between Western European Governments (including the Governments of some EEC member-states) and the United States Government, inasmuch as these claims have been based on grounds which the Western European Governments consider to be unsupported by public international law').

[150] L Idot, Note *Wood Pulp*, (1989) Rev trim dr europ 345, 359 ('D'une prudence peut-être trop excessive, [the ECJ] a évité de prendre parti sur la «théorie des effects» que seul le gouvernement britannique persiste à combattre').

the ECJ brought the jurisdictionally relevant *conduct* inside the Community, holding that by selling directly into the Community, the cartel agreement was *implemented* inside the Community, and did not merely cause *effects* there. The implementation doctrine, while being a novelty in EC law, undeniably has its roots in England, where an English court held as early as 1876, in the case of *Regina v Keyn*, that not the locus of the effects, but the locus of the criminal act itself was decisive for purposes of jurisdiction.[151]

In practice, the reach of EC competition law nowadays hardly differs from the reach of US antitrust law. The ECJ's implementation doctrine has been considered to be almost co-terminous with the effects doctrine, and the European Commission itself relies on the effects doctrine, as it had already done as early as the *Dyestuffs* case. In the field of international merger control, effects-based jurisdiction was eventually approved of by the European Court of First Instance in the *Gencor* merger case (1999). Like the US Department of Justice, the Commission appears to apply the comity principle and thus to defer to other nations if their regulatory interests are stronger. And like the US Supreme Court in *Hartford Fire Insurance* (1993), the highest EU courts have seemingly limited the comity analysis to an analysis of foreign sovereign compulsion (deferring only when a foreign State compels a particular conduct which EC competition law prohibits, or vice versa).[152] Possibly, the initial reluctance to embrace the US-style jurisdictional notions was only partly informed by English objections, and mainly by the fact that aggressive (international) antitrust enforcement did not have priority in Europe. Nonetheless, it should not be forgotten that, since the late 1960s, the European Commission has survived all legal challenges to its claiming jurisdiction over foreign conspirators. There is no evidence that the EC has considered itself to be shackled by such presumably restrictive court doctrines as the economic entity and implementation doctrines.

(c) US exceptionalism and strict economic regulation

It has been shown that it took some time before Europe applied its competition laws to foreign situations affecting its economy. This is attributable to the lesser importance that stringent competition laws and policy may have had in Europe[153] rather than to a belief that effects-based jurisdiction was illegal under international law, or to a perception that in a world dominated by the United States, Europe could not get away with exercising such jurisdiction. This, the lack of interest in strict economic regulation or enforcement, is also apparent in the field of securities and corporate governance. The unique importance of capital market regulation in the United States may indeed go a long way in explaining why the arm of US securities laws has been much longer than the arm of European securities

---

[151] LR 2 Ex Div 63 (1876).   [152] Cf section 5.4.c.
[153] eg B Grossfeld and CP Rogers, 'A Shared Values Approach to Jurisdictional Conflicts in International Economic Law', (1983) 32 ICLQ 931.

laws.[154] Because European securities law was historically underdeveloped, there was not much of an arm that could be stretched. The prohibition of insider-trading only became a priority in the 1980s, and binding corporate governance rules are still being introduced as we write. In the United States, strict capital market regulation harks back to the Great Depression, during which the 1933 Securities Act and the 1934 Securities Exchange Act were adopted by Congress. In 1968, the antifraud provisions of these acts were for the first time given extraterritorial application by the Second Circuit (which ruled that jurisdiction obtained over foreign securities transactions that affected US investors).[155] It remains to be seen whether Europe will follow suit. Theoretically, there are fairly wide legal possibilities for exercising jurisdiction over cross-border securities misrepresentation and insider-trading,[156] yet there is hardly any European enforcement practice on the issue. In sum, in much of economic regulation, the United States could be seen as an 'early mover', and the efficiency of US economic regulation inspired—and still inspires—other States to follow suit sooner or later.[157]

---

[154] Conversely, the importance of labour legislation in continental Europe could logically inform the longer arm of European labour law. In 1980, EC Commissioner Vredeling indeed unveiled a plan pursuant to which the management of a foreign parent would have to furnish each of its EC subsidiaries with advance notice of certain decisions, in the interests of EC employees. In the mid-1980s, the plan was abandoned. In 1994, a more modest directive—the European Works Council Directive 94/95, [1994] OJ L 254/64—was adopted. However, also in the field of company law the EC planned in the early 1980s to issue rules with a certain extraterritorial effect, namely rules requiring the publication of consolidated financial statements that would reveal non-European activities. This plan prompted the proposal of a US bill which declared the disclosure of business secrets to be 'inconsistent with international law and comity'. HR 4339, 97th Cong, 1st Sess (1981), and S 1592, 97th Cong, 1st Sess (1981). Cf D Vagts, 'A Turnabout in Extraterritoriality', (1982) 76 AJIL 591.

[155] *Schoenbaum v Firstbrook*, 405 F 2d 200 (2d Cir 1968).

[156] Jurisdiction over securities misrepresentations is governed by Council Regulation (EC) 44/2001 (EEX-Regulation), because the Regulation applies to all civil and commercial matters (Article 1) and does not exclude the trade in securities from its purview. By virtue of this Regulation, the court of the EU Member State where the defendant has its domicile has jurisdiction over a securities misrepresentation (Article 2). If the defendant is not domiciled in a Member State, the jurisdiction of the courts of each Member State shall be determined by the law of that Member State (Article 4.1). If the securities misrepresentation constitutes a breach of contract, the person domiciled in a Member State may also be sued in another Member State which is the place of performance of the obligation in question (Article 5.1). If the securities misrepresentation constitutes a tort, the courts for the place where the harmful event occurred or may occur have jurisdiction (Article 5.3).

Jurisdiction over insider-trading is governed by the EC Directive on Insider-dealing and Market Manipulation of 28 January 2003, [2003] OJ L 96/16. Under Article 10 of the 2003 Directive on insider-dealing and market manipulation, 'Each Member State shall apply the prohibitions and requirements provided for in this Directive to: (a) actions carried out on its territory or abroad concerning financial instruments that are admitted to trading on a regulated market situated or operating within its territory or for which a request for admission to trading on such market has been made; (b) actions carried out on its territory concerning financial instruments that are admitted to trading on a regulated market in a Member State or for which a request for admission to trading on such market has been made'.

[157] With respect to the Sarbanes-Oxley Act: E Tafara, 'Sarbanes-Oxley: a Race to the Top', (September 2006) IFLR 12, 13 ('The U.S. was merely an early mover with respect to a series of gaps that began to appear in the protections to investors provided by various global regulatory frameworks').

Only as far as US-imposed secondary boycotts are concerned have US assertions of extraterritorial economic jurisdiction been informed by bare-knuckle power politics—with the attendant failure of such boycotts. In the field of antitrust and securities law, buttressed by the law of discovery, by contrast, the transatlantic gap over jurisdiction might be explained by different transatlantic attitudes to economic regulation rather than to the workings of power. At the international level, this translated in the United States having traditionally had little confidence in foreign regulation of situations that implicated substantial US interests, and thus applying its laws to such situations. This attitude betrays a certain US economic exceptionalism, a lingering belief that US economic regulation, perceived as tighter, is necessarily better than foreign regulation, perceived as laxer.[158] US exceptionalism was in due course often vindicated by foreign nations' adoption of economic standards similar to US standards.[159] If power had a role to play in this respect, it was mainly as 'soft power', or the global attractiveness of the US capitalist model.[160] Interestingly, because global harmonization of substantive economic law, modelled on US standards, may have been the ultimate goal of US jurisdictional assertions,[161] extraterritoriality was allowed to override objections relating to the accompanying temporary stemming of the free movement of goods and services,[162] which is the heart of capitalism, and has traditionally been cherished by US liberal internationalists as a prerequisite for the world's overall progress.

(d) The transatlantic gap over international criminal justice

US exceptionalism is not only limited to economic regulation. The United States tends to regard itself as an exceptional nation in all respects, or in John Winthrop's

---

[158] Against US antitrust exceptionalism in the field of antitrust law, eg Seidl-Hohenveldern (above n 123) 57.

[159] It has been argued that, in European competition law, this happened when the ECJ rendered its *Dyestuffs* judgment in 1973. J Ullmer Bailly, Comment on *Dyestuffs*, (1973) 14 Harv Int'l LJ 621, 630 ('The Court's articulation of the issues in terms of economic policies and its use of concepts developed under American antitrust law may well be pointing in the direction taken by the United States, which has traditionally accorded national priority to its competition policy...but there remains a definite question of how far the Court will go in its support of the toughening stance taken by the Commission in its admittedly American-influenced campaign against anticompetitive behavior in the EEC') (footnotes omitted).

[160] On soft power JS Nye Jr, *Soft Power: The Means to Success in World Politics* (2004).

[161] Dodge (above n 6) 101 (arguing that unilateral jurisdiction grants the United States the bargaining chips during multilateral negotiations).

[162] Foreign economic actors will tend to avoid commercial intercourse with the United States or US actors for fear of becoming subject to US laws. This has particularly happened in the field of securities law, where US investors are routinely excluded from foreign offerings. For a European voice fearing a hampering of trade liberalization through extraterritorial jurisdiction: J Frisinger, 'Die Anwendung des EWG-Wettbewerbsrechts auf Unternehmen mit Sitz in Drittstaaten', (1972) AWD 553, 559 (stating dass 'eine weitgehende extraterritoriale Anwendung und Durchsetzung des EWG-Wettbewerbsrechts weder mit den Grundsätzen des Völkerrechts *noch mit der sich entwickelnden Liberalisierung des Welthandels vereinbare ware*') (emphasis added).

famous words, as 'a city upon a hill'.[163] The United States is therefore unlikely to accept the extraterritorial application of other States' 'bad laws'. In the economic field, the United States has not been hindered by such 'bad laws', because the level of economic regulation abroad is lower than in the United States, and the extraterritorial application of such regulation by foreign States typically served no purpose. Outside the economic field, there are, however, 'bad laws out there' that are potentially stricter than US laws and thus pose a threat to US interests. This is notably the case with universal jurisdiction over crimes against international law, as exercised by European States since the late 1990s. Although these crimes are generally also crimes under US law, they are hardly or not amenable to universal criminal jurisdiction in the United States.

An easy explanation for US reluctance to espouse universal jurisdiction is that the common law system of criminal procedure does not lend itself to the exercise of extraterritorial jurisdiction. Yet since the United Kingdom started to exercise universal jurisdiction over torture,[164] and the United States itself has exercised universal jurisdiction over terrorist offences,[165] this argument has become less persuasive. US opposition against universal jurisdiction may now be mainly informed by foreign policy considerations, in particular the belief that exercising jurisdiction may encourage other States to bring US nationals, particularly US service members, before their own courts, and the belief that an international criminal justice may impede the chances of success of long-term political reconciliation in post-conflict societies. Because universal jurisdiction over core crimes misunderstands 'the appropriate roles of force, diplomacy, and power in the world', it has been described as 'not just bad analysis, but bad and potentially dangerous policy',[166] which the United States should vehemently oppose. The exercise of (US) power may go a long way in explaining why Belgium repealed its progressive law concerning the prosecution of these crimes in August 2003,[167] and why German prosecutors have trodden lightly when applying their Code of Crimes against International Law to US persons.[168]

---

[163] On the influence of John Winthrop, the first (Puritan) governor of Massachusetts in the seventeenth century and 'America's first great man': ES Morgan, *The Genuine Article* (2004) 5 *et seq.*

[164] Universal jurisdiction over crimes of torture is codified in section 134 of the 1988 Criminal Justice Act. It was exercised in the *Pinochet* case (*R v Bow Street Metropolitan Stipendiary Magistrate, ex p Pinochet Ugarte (No 3)* [2000] 1 AC 147) and the *Zardad* case (Central Criminal Court London, 7 April 2004, on file with the author).

[165] *United States v Rezaq*, 134 F 3d 1121 (DCC 1998); *United States v Yunis*, 924 F 2d 1086 (DC Cir 1991); *United States v Ramzi Ahmed Yousef and others*, 327 F 3d 56 (2nd Cir 2003).

[166] JR Bolton, 'The Risks and Weaknesses of the International Criminal Court from America's Perspective', (2001) 64 Law & Contemp. Probs 167, 175. Bolton's observations applied in particular to the International Criminal Court, but could be applied to international criminal justice in general, including universal jurisdiction.

[167] Act of 5 August 2003, *Moniteur belge*. At length J Wouters and C Ryngaert, 'De toepassing van de (Belgische) wet van 5 augustus 2003 betreffende ernstige schendingen van het internationaal humanitair recht', special issue Nullum Crimen, April 2007, 21 pp.

[168] cf the dismissal of the 'Abu Ghraib' complaint against (former) U.S. Secretary of Defense Donald Rumsfeld by the German federal prosecutor: decision by federal prosecutor of

In the final analysis, the transatlantic gap over universal jurisdiction may, like the gap over economic jurisdiction, be explained by substantive law and policy rather than on grounds of international law. Where the long arm of US anti-trust, securities, and discovery law is a logical outgrowth of the US emphasis laid on strict antitrust and capital markets regulation, and on maximum disclosure of evidence, the long arm of European universal jurisdiction laws is a logical outgrowth of the idea that criminal justice, even dispensed by bystander States, may be uniquely important in ensuring post-conflict reconciliation.[169] European experience with two disastrous world wars, and with the recent Balkan wars, have surely fuelled European States' conviction that basic human rights should be strictly upheld, and that European States have a historical calling to ensure that human rights standards are also enforced overseas.

As in Europe, human rights are an important aspect of how foreign policy is shaped in the United States. What is more, the United States tends to portray itself as an exceptional nation in which the pursuit of happiness is a function of human rights, democracy, and freedom. Just as it has been a US goal to spread US concepts of economic freedom, *inter alia* through extraterritorial jurisdiction, it has also long since been a stated goal of US foreign policy to promote human rights in foreign nations through a variety of sticks and carrots,[170] including the exercise of universal tort jurisdiction under the Alien Tort Statute (ATS).[171] Yet,

10 February 2005, <http://www.ccr-ny.org/v2/legal/september_11th/docs/German_Prosecutors_Decision2_10_05.pdf>, appeal decided by OLG Stuttgart, Beschl. 13 September 2005, 5 Ws 109/05, NStZ 2006, 117.

[169] European support for (international) criminal justice in post-conflict situations may have historical roots in European countries' dealings with conflicts that occurred on their own territory. Especially after the Second World War, quite some European countries were eager to prosecute those who collaborated with the German occupier. Eg for repression in Belgium L Huyse, S Dhont, P Depuydt, K Hoflack, I Vanhoren, *Onverwerkt verleden. Collaboratie en repressie in België 1942–1952* (1991). The United States, by contrast, seems not to have put a high premium on criminal justice in conflicts that took place within their territory. After the Civil War (1861–1865), for instance, traitors or war criminals were hardly prosecuted, because such would not have served politicial reconciliation, and would have hampered the ravaged country's reconstruction. Amnesties were offered to Confederate citizens by the Confiscation Act of 1862, and by the Amnesty Proclamation of December 8, 1863. After Confederate General Lee surrendered on April 9, 1865, a stipulation allowed his man and officers 'to return to their homes, not to be disturbed by United States authority so long as they observe their paroles and the laws in force where they may reside.' On May 29, 1865, the President granted amnesty to those who would take an oath of allegiance. High-ranking Confederate officers had to apply for individual pardons, but these were liberally granted. To cap it all, the Congressional Amnesty Act of May 1872 allowed Southern leaders to hold office again. Cf S Kutler, *Judicial Power and Reconstruction Politics* (1968). It remains nevertheless to be seen whether the amnesties granted during the Civil War and post-Civil War Reconstruction Era foreshadowed the United States' 21st century misgivings about international criminal justice. See email conversation with Mark Freeman, Head of Office, International Center for Transitional Justice Brussels, 3 September 2006.

[170] M Ignatieff, ed, *American Exceptionalism and Human Rights* (2005) 353. A foreign human rights policy is developed by the US State Department's Bureau on Democracy, Human Rights and Labor, which oversees the Human Rights and Democracy Fund. See <http://www.state.gov/g/drl/democ>.

[171] See Memorandum for the United States Submitted to the Court of Appeals for the Second Circuit, *Filartiga v Pena-Irala*, 630 F 2d 876 (2d Cir 1980), published in (1980) 19 ILM 585,

unlike Europe, the US political branches may put a higher premium on local justice mechanisms to deal with local human rights violations. In addition, US human rights policy is probably more Janus-faced than European policy is, with *Realpolitische* foreign policy concerns at times overriding lofty human rights goals. The recent torture memos and the Guantanamo Bay scandal are only the latest illustrations thereof. In the field of jurisdiction, the George W Bush Administration has spared no effort to discredit ATS litigation in the United States—which for reasons related to the procedural advantages of US tort law vis-à-vis European tort law sprang up there, and not in Europe[172]—on the grounds that it might jeopardize the foreign policy prerogative of the executive branch and may expose US service members to jurisdictional countermeasures.[173]

6.8 Final Concluding Remarks

Professor Meessen once stated: 'The function of scholars of international law offers less opportunity for creative thinking [compared to scholars of conflict of laws]: they may compile and analyze state practice, but they cannot replace it with their own concepts'.[174] This study, which has primarily looked at the phenomenon of jurisdiction through a (public) international law lens, has rejected that limiting claim. While the current state of the international law of jurisdiction has been described at length on the basis of State practice, a consistent *doctrine* of jurisdiction has been developed, on the basis of both State practice and rational thinking. The exercise of jurisdiction is in practice often characterized by a sheer lack of objectivity—which is not surprising as States, when *unilaterally* asserting jurisdiction, will almost variably emphasize their own interests over foreign States' interests. A doctrine that gives States almost unlimited discretion to exercise jurisdiction as they see fit—the doctrine that was seemingly coined by the Permanent Court of International Justice in the 1927 *Lotus* case—is not workable, because it justifies the exercise of concurrent jurisdiction and allows powerful States to outmanoeuvre weaker ones.

It has been shown that there are no hard and fast rules of public international law that limit States' jurisdictional assertions and confer jurisdiction on the State with the strongest nexus to a situation. Nonetheless, it has also been shown that there

---

603–604 (stating that 'a refusal to recognize a private cause of action in these circumstances might seriously damage the credibility of our nation's commitment to the protection of human rights.')

[172] C Ryngaert, 'Universal Tort Jurisdiction over Gross Human Rights Violations', (2007) NYIL 3.

[173] It has also been argued, in line with the liberal internationalist agenda of the United States mentioned *supra*, that universal jurisdiction may lead to global isolationism, as the possibility of foreign prosecutions may persuade State officials not to leave their country. Bykhovsky (above n 2) 184.

[174] Meessen (above n 45) 790.

are a number of international law principles that may serve to restrain the exercise of jurisdiction when the legitimate rights of other States would be encroached upon. The principles of non-intervention, sovereign equality, equity, proportionality, and the prohibition of abuse of law have been cited in this context. While these principles are typically used in a non-jurisdictional context, they could, given their generic nature, inform the law of jurisdiction. In Chapter 5, the use of a jurisdictional rule of reason, as set forth in § 403 of the Restatement (Third) of US Foreign Relations Law, has therefore been advocated, pursuant to which States are entitled to exercise jurisdiction only if they do so reasonably. The jurisdictional rule of reason may not be a rule *de lege lata*, for there is insufficient evidence that States, if they restrained their jurisdictional assertions, did so because *international law* obliged them to do so. Yet undeniably, a system of international jurisdiction is only viable if States balance *their* regulatory interests with the interests of *other* affected foreign nations, as if they were a global regulator who objectively assesses the merits of any one State's legal and policy interests.

Jurisdictional reasonableness has been the main focus throughout this study. In the final chapter, it has been given more 'body'. For one thing, it has been argued that reasonable jurisdiction could emerge through transnational communicative networks wiring State, international, and private actors. For another, it has been proposed that States apply their own laws only on a *subsidiary* basis. Subsidiarity serves to restrain the exercise of jurisdiction by giving the State with the strongest nexus the *primary* right to exercise jurisdiction. If the 'primary' State fails to exercise jurisdiction, even if, from a global perspective, this were desirable, the 'subsidiary' State has the right—and, it may be argued, sometimes the duty—to step in, in the interest of the global community. Such a jurisdictional system connects sovereign interests—on which the law of jurisdiction was traditionally based—with global interests, and ensures that impunity and globally harmful underregulation do not arise. Sovereignty then becomes a 'relative' concept: international law and the international interest determine when States could invoke it.[175] If, finally, States, regulators, courts, and various legal practitioners are searching for one useful jurisdictional rule of thumb in this study, it is this one: the State with the strongest nexus to a situation is entitled to exercise its jurisdiction, yet if it fails to adequately do so, another State with a weaker nexus (and in the case of violations of *jus cogens* without a nexus) may step in, provided that its exercise of jurisdiction serves the global interest.

---

[175] On the concept of relative sovereignty: H Aufricht, 'On Relative Sovereignty', parts I and II, (1944–1945) 30 Cornell LQ 137 and 318.

Index

A

Abuse of rights 36, 150–1, 177, 180, 237
Accursius 45
Admiralty 56
Akehurst, M 1, 32
Alcoa Case 62, 74, 76, 153
Alien Tort Statute (ATS) 13–4, 126, 192, 226, 234–6
Amicus curiae briefs 190, 207, 208
Antitrust law 1, 3, 9, 11, 14, 16, 18, 38–40, 62, 68, 70, 71, 74, 76, 77, 79, 82, 130, 145, 154, 163, 171–7, 187, 196, 200, 202, 206, 208, 212, 215, 219, 220, 222–3, 226, 228, 229, 233
    Antitrust Guidelines for International Operations (US Department of Justice) 176
    International Competition Network 208
    See also merger (control)
Argentré, B d' 54
Aut dedere aut judicare 52, 94, 101, 104–6, 111, 119

B

Bartolus 46–7, 90
Beale, JH 32
Beccaria 49
Bischoff, JM 177
Blocking statutes 188
    British Protection of Trading Interests Act 130
Bodin, J 48
Boycotts, secondary 1, 99–100, 130–1, 167, 187, 213, 224, 233

C

Capital markets laws, *see* securities law
Center for Constitutional Rights (US) 125
Choice of law, *see also* conflict of laws 15, 18, 20, 67, 195–6, 220
Cocceji 108
Comity 5, 13, 19, 35, 57, 64, 78, 135–42, 167–77, 170, 188, 198, 205–6, 221, 231
Competition law, *see* antitrust law
Conflict of laws, *see also* choice of law 5, 10–20, 44, 46, 54, 61, 139, 141, 167, 195–6, 229, 236
Corporate governance 203, 206, 223, 224, 228, 231
Corporate social responsibility 132
Countermeasures 148, 236

Customary international law 4, 6, 19, 26–31, 34, 36–41, 66, 82, 94, 105, 106, 109, 110, 116–8, 120, 135, 137, 142, 143, 145, 164, 166, 178–80, 192–3, 209
Cutting Case 62

D

Declaration of Independence (US) 59
Department of Justice (US) 176, 231
Diplomatic protection 35, 90, 91, 146
Discovery 79–83, 225
Dodge, W 68

E

Effects doctrine, *see also* antitrust law 62, 74, 77, 96, 154, 165, 184, 220, 230–1
Environmental law 69–70
Equity 146–8, 180, 237
Erga omnes (obligations) 107, 193
European Commission 77, 172–6, 203, 230
    Eastern Aluminium Case 173, 175
European Court of First Instance (CFI) 77, 172, 174–6, 231
    Gencor Case 172, 174–5, 231
European Court of Justice (ECJ) 39, 77, 172–6, 230–1
    Dyestuffs Case 230–1
    Wood Pulp Case 39, 172, 230
Export controls, *see* boycotts (secondary)
Extradition 50, 51, 52, 90, 102–4, 106, 122

F

Federal Trade Commission (US) 176
Forum non-conveniens 226
French Revolution 48, 169
Fruehauf Case 130

G

General principles of (international) law 178, 180–2
Genocide 102, 110, 115, 118, 208
Genuine connection 35, 145–6, 180
Grotius (de Groot, H) 52, 108, 140, 215, 219, 222, 225

H

Harmonization 200, 202
Helms-Burton Act 100
Hobbes, Th 57
Huber, U 54, 138–9, 181

I

Implementation doctrine, *see also* antitrust law 77, 172, 230–1
Insider-trading, *see also* securities law 78, 202
International Court of Justice (ICJ) 26, 30, 35, 91, 116, 145, 146, 179
  Arrest Warrant Case 30, 116
  Barcelona Traction Case 26, 91, 143, 146
  North Sea Continental Shelf Cases 147
  Nottebohm Case 35, 145
International Criminal Court (ICC) 2, 98, 119, 199, 217
International humanitarian law 2, 9, 107, 110, 116, 131, 189, 198
  Amnesty 189, 216
  Crimes against humanity 102, 110, 115, 208
  War crimes 40, 102, 110, 115, 132, 208

J

Jones v Saudi Arabia Case 39
Jurisdiction
  adjudicative/adjudicatory 10–20
  concurrent 5, 20, 22, 97, 127, 184, 193, 236
  enforcement 9, 23–25, 33, 80, 82, 144, 191
  legislative, *see* prescriptive
  personal 13
  prescriptive 9, 10–20, 24, 27, 33, 79, 80, 92, 142
  representational, *see* vicarious
  subject-matter 13–14
  universal 7, 21, 27, 38, 40, 52–3, 55, 100–25, 131, 159, 187, 189, 192, 216, 226, 228, 234
  universal, *in absentia* 114, 116, 119–25, 183
  vicarious 50, 102, 218, 228
Jus cogens 112–6, 187, 188, 219, 237

K

Kaffanke, J 177
Kovar, R 177
Kuijper, PJ 27

L

Labour law 69–70
Law and economics 219–22
Lowe, AV 177

M

Mann, FA 1
Mannington Mills Case 155, 176, 212
Matthaeus, A 45, 53, 75
Meessen, KM 18–20, 143, 176–7, 200
Merger (control) 40, 149, 164, 174–5, 177, 183, 189, 198, 231

Minimum contacts 12
Montesquieu 48
Morris/Rothmans Case 40, 164, 177, 179

N

Nationality principle, *see* personality principle
Ne (non) bis in idem 51, 52
Networks 190, 194, 206, 210, 217, 237
Non-interference, *see* non-intervention
Non-intervention, principle of 6, 29, 35, 40, 57, 80, 81, 82, 115, 121, 123, 144–5, 157, 177, 180, 188, 221, 237

O

Opinio juris 24, 34, 144, 163, 166, 167, 178, 179, 192
Ordre public 140, 167–9

P

Permanent Court of Arbitration 60
  Island of Palmas Case 28, 60
Permanent Court of International Justice (PCIJ) 4, 21–31, 58, 82, 111, 116, 140–1, 144, 236
  Legal Status of Eastern Greenland Case 29
  Lotus Case 4, 21–31, 37, 58, 66, 67, 82, 111, 116, 140–1, 144, 163, 227, 236
  Nationality Decrees in Tunis and Morocco Case 22
Permissive principles (approach to jurisdiction) 21–2, 27–31, 84, 116, 134, 144
Personality principle 7, 21, 228
  active personality principle 48, 51, 72, 88–92, 218
  passive personality principle 92–6, 218
Piracy 56, 107, 108, 109
Presumption against extraterritoriality 47, 58, 59, 63–74, 141, 162
Private international law, *see* conflict of laws
Proportionality principle 36, 148–9, 180–1, 237
Protective principle 7, 21, 72, 74, 218, 228
Protest (foreign) 24, 32–5, 37, 78, 95, 104, 106, 114–7, 132, 159, 164, 167, 188, 190, 204, 210, 211, 216, 219, 222
Pufendorf, S 50

R

Reasonableness 3, 5, 16, 19, 20, 33, 35, 36, 54, 77, 78, 84, 124, 126, 133, 134–84, 205, 211, 214–5, 237
Reciprocity 18, 29, 83, 190, 191, 192, 198, 221
Regulatory law 10–20
Responsibility to protect 152–3

Restatement (Third) of US Foreign Relations
  Law (1987) 5, 16, 35, 80, 94, 135, 141,
  144, 145, 153–63, 170–6, 179, 182, 212,
  213, 216, 237
Restraint, *see* reasonableness
Roman law 44
Rousseau 49
Rule of reason, *see* reasonableness

S
Sarbanes-Oxley Act 72, 161, 203, 228
Savigny 170
Schuster 143, 177
Securities and Exchange Commission 161
Securities law, *see also* corporate governance 1,
  3, 10, 11, 14, 16, 68, 70, 77, 78, 83, 187,
  191, 196, 202, 213, 215, 224, 229, 231,
  233
Security Council (UN) 224
Self-defence 97
Self-regulation 183, 189
Sharon Case 125
Slaughter, AM 182
Sovereignty 2, 5, 6, 18, 24, 25, 28, 44, 46,
  48, 54, 57, 61, 80, 81, 89, 93, 96, 97,
  105, 112, 114, 120, 140–1, 144, 186,
  194, 195, 206, 221, 227
Sovereign equality 6, 23, 29, 61, 115, 188,
  190, 237
Soviet Pipeline Regulations 130
State responsibility 98
Statute of limitations 122
Story J 54, 61, 139
Subsidiarity (principle) 186–7, 194, 214–27,
  237
Supreme Court (US) 41, 60, 61, 62, 63, 64,
  66, 72, 89, 137, 139, 145, 153, 163, 166,
  174, 179, 207, 226, 231
  American Banana Case 62
  Antelope Case (The) 61
  Appolon Case (The) 61

Aramco Case 63, 64, 69
Bowman Case 72–3
Charming Betsy Case 66–7, 162
Empagran Case 145, 166, 179, 207,
  226
Erie v Tompkins Case 41
Foley Bros v Filardo Case 64, 69, 162
Hartford Fire Insurance Case 66, 137, 163,
  164, 166, 173–4, 207, 231
Hilton v Guyot Case 137
Ogden v Saunders Case 139
Rose v Himely Case 60
Schooner Exchange v McFaddon Case 60

T
Territorial principle 42–84
  Subjective territorial principle 76, 77, 78,
    229
  Objective territorial principle 30, 76, 78,
    96, 229
Terrorism 94, 96, 101, 104, 105, 107, 234
Timberlane Case 176, 212
Tort (law) 15, 38, 39, 126–7, 188, 192, 226,
  234–6
Torture 39, 87–8, 94, 102, 106, 110, 117–8,
  234
Treaty (law) 4, 36, 134, 205

U
Universality principle, *see* jurisdiction,
  universal

V
Voet, P 47, 108, 139

W
Weintraub R 68
Wharton, F 61
Wolff, C 50
World Trade Organization (WTO) 100, 131,
  148, 196, 201